History of the Internet:
A Chronology, 1843 to the Present

History of the Internet:
A Chronology,
1843 to the Present

Christos J. P. Moschovitis

Hilary Poole

Tami Schuyler

Theresa M. Senft

ABC-CLIO

Santa Barbara, California
Denver, Colorado
Oxford, England

Executive Editor:	Valerie Tomaselli
Senior Editor:	Hilary Poole
Design and Layout:	Annemarie Redmond
Copyediting:	Kim Kazemi, Elizabeth H. Oakes
Factchecking:	Kim Kazemi, Elizabeth H. Oakes
Proofreading:	Amy Kaiman
Index:	AEIOU, Inc.

Library of Congress Cataloging-in-Publication Data
History of the Internet : a chronology, 1843 to the present / Christos
    J. P. Moschovitis . . . [et al.].
        p. cm.
    Includes bibliographical references and index.
    Summary: A chronology of telecommunications from Babbage's
earliest theories of a "Difference Engine" to the impact of the
Internet in 1998 to future trends.
    ISBN 1-57607-118-9 (alk. paper)
    1. Internet (Computer network) 2. Telecommunication—History.
[1. Internet (Computer network) 2. Telecommunication—History.]
I. Moschovitis, Christos J. P.
TK5105.875.I57H58   1999
004.67'8'09—dc21   99–13275
                                                          CIP

ISBN 1-57607-118-9 (hc)

ABC-CLIO, Inc.
130 Cremona Drive, P.O. Box 1911
Santa Barbara, California 93116-1911

This book is printed on acid-free paper ∞.

Manufactured in the United States of America

Table of Contents

Preface

Writings about the Internet tend to focus, quite reasonably, on computing. But the big picture is, well, bigger—and far more spectacular. It's certainly true that the Internet is an evolution in the computer science field. But it also marks a development in telecommunications and mass media. And as any NASDAQ watcher knows, the Net is big business. The Internet is a unique creature, sharing some attributes with print publishing, others with telephones and mail, still more with television—and in other respects it is unlike any system that has preceded it.

Many texts have focused on the technological side of the Internet or, even more commonly, the commercial side. This book will try to steer a somewhat different course, weaving together—à la Lady Byron's Jaquard loom—the many strands that make up the history of the Internet: technological, military, educational, corporate, and civilian. The cast of characters is as varied as the Internet itself—captains of industry and alienated 15-year-old boys, engineers and philosophers, law officers and law breakers, and, for good measure, the occasional mad genius.

The first seven chapters of this book trace the evolution of the Internet in chronological entries. Each entry describes a key event in Net history, including background information and an assessment of the event's place in the big picture. The final chapter introduces a few of the issues and innovations that will likely shape the Internet's future. Alongside the chronology, special features and sidebars highlight historical, biographical, cultural, and ethical aspects of the story. These recurring features cover such topics as insider stories from the hacker culture; the development of the Internet as a medium of mass communication; highlights of philosophical and scholarly thought on the digital revolution; and the relationship of the Internet to broader events in society and politics.

We would like to acknowledge the invaluable assistance of members of Echo's Computer Conference, who graciously read and fact-checked portions of this material. In addition, crucial information was provided throughout by Steve Barber, Jim Baumbach, Christopher Belanger, Thomas S. Benjamin, Grant Bremer, Alex Burgos, Josh Chu, Greg Costikyan, Pete Curtner, Corrin Eckert, Lenny Foner, Philip Galanter, Mike Godwin, Jason Anthony Guy, Andrew Herman, Eric Hochman, Joe

Hobaica, Stacy Horn, George Hunka, Tom Igoe, Steve Jones, Lisa Kamm, Nancy Kaplan, Art Kleiner, Kevin Kroos, Danny Lieberman, Mia Lipner, J. Henry H. Lowengard, Angus MacDonald, Scott Mason, Nathan J. Mehl, Morgan Noel, Jim Patrick, Ben Rosengart, Greg Sewell, Jesse Sheidlower, Thomas Swiss, Hadley Taylor, Jack Taylor, Michelle Tepper, David Tezlaff, C.D. Thomas, Cindy Tittle-Moore, Paul Wallich, Stefan Wray, Toni Wuersch, and Cathy Young. Naturally, we assume responsibility for any errors.

The Prehistory
of the Internet

Most histories of the Internet begin with the creation of the ARPAnet, the computer network sponsored by the United States military that spawned what we know now as the Internet. Since the ARPAnet marks the first time that a number of computers in different locales were connected together in order to exchange data and messages, this is certainly a logical place to start. But taking the long view, one can see that the Internet is not only a computer science phenomenon, but also an evolution of the telecommunications field, the media, and the economy.

Viewed in this light, a history of the Internet is a history of more than computer networking. It is a history of a fundamental sea change in communications, commerce, manufacturing, labor, and media that is unprecedented since the 1800s. So it is perhaps not surprising that although computer networking is only fifty years old, we can find its conceptual building blocks in the Industrial Revolution of the 19th century.

From the Industrial Revolution to the Information Age

During the Industrial Revolution, the social and economic landscape of European nations and the United States underwent profound transformations. Traditional agrarian economies gave way to machine- and manufacturing-centered societies in

1

the nineteenth century, and the pace of commerce and industry accelerated dramatically. The development of the steam engine, the completion of a continental railroad, the invention of the telegraph, and the application of electricity were among the technological advances that made travel and communication possible across distances that hitherto had been difficult or impossible to bridge. The concept of a mass popular culture also began to emerge in the nineteenth century, as people became accustomed to the rapid delivery of goods and information and the ability to communicate and travel more easily across long distances.

What one sees increasing in the 1800s is the application of scientific knowledge to serve industrial processes—developing consumer goods, as well as the machinery needed to produce those goods, with increasing efficiency and speed. The growing volume of goods and the increasing speed with which they were brought to consumers depended on the completion of extensive communication and transportation networks. Similarly, the Information Revolution we're experiencing today has emerged from the application of sophisticated concepts in the computer sciences to serve business and communications industries.

By the early twentieth century the United States was one of the world's most successful industrialized nations. Its further progress and dominance in the world economy was bolstered in large part by Henry Ford's introduction of the Model T and his use of moving assembly lines in his Detroit auto plants. The automobile gave Americans a previously unknown degree of personal mobility. Ford's mass production techniques also dramatically transformed the U.S. workforce. Beginning in the Industrial Revolution, skilled craftsmen began to be replaced by machines in many industries. With the automobile propelling much of the economic growth of the early twentieth century, this trend continued to increase. Mass production also reduced manufacturing costs and allowed automakers to sell cars at prices that large numbers of Americans could afford.

The computer has played just as influential a role in the second half of this century as the automobile did in the first—only this time the mobility is of a virtual sort. And like the automotive industry, which was established by individual entrepreneurs who turned their ideas into corporations, the computer industry was spurred on by business machine companies, such as Remington Rand, Burroughs Adding Machine, National Cash Register, and last, but certainly not least, International Business Machines (IBM).

Computers have also had a dramatic impact on the workforce, again replacing low-skilled workers with machines. They, too, have transformed production and distribution processes. The ease with which documents, files, and even software programs, can be duplicated on one computer and sent off to another has made it possible for virtually anyone with a computer and a modem to become a mass producer. For example, in the 1980s John McAfee wrote an antivirus software and began giving it away on bulletin board services. It cost him only the time it took to write the program—manufacturing costs were nonexistent because the distribution channel was the network itself. The Internet has inspired a new business model—utilized not only by McAfee but also Netscape and many others—in which products are free; it's the updates that will cost you.

Early Computing Machines

The first step down the path of what would become the information superhighway was taken in 1833, when Charles Babbage developed his Difference Engine. Babbage, an English mathematician, created the machine to expedite the calculation of astronomical tables. In 1840 he refined his Difference Engine and proposed a design for the Analytical Engine. A much more powerful machine than the Difference Engine, the Analytical Engine was to be powered by a steam engine. Babbage touted it as being capable of performing any mathematical calculation.

An essential feature of Babbage's design concept was the use of punch cards. With these cards, a person could "program" the machine, telling it what calculation, or series of calculations, was to be performed. Babbage's machine was never constructed because the British government withdrew its funding for the project, but nonetheless it is considered a precursor to the modern computer. Indeed, in 1991 the British Science Museum constructed and tested Babbage's Analytical Engine and found that the machine could calculate polynomial equations to the seventh power with an accuracy extending to thirty digits. Pretty impressive.

The most lasting imprint of Babbage's model—in terms of the development of computers—was the concept of programming. This concept was plainly laid out in *Sketch of the Analytical Engine*, a treatise written in 1843 by Ada Byron, the countess of Lovelace. In her work, Lovelace gave high praise to the Analytical Engine and the scientific principles underlying it. She likened Babbage's computing machine to the Jacquard loom, which relied on punch cards to create intricate weaving patterns. It's not surprising that Lovelace, writing as the Industrial Revolution was sweeping across Europe, would compare the Analytical Engine to a machine then being put to practical commercial use.

Like Babbage's computing machine, the developments underlying the computers and networking of today begin with arcane scientific concepts. Many of those design concepts never get off the drafting board. It takes an Ada Byron to proselytize for a new technology and convince a government or some well-heeled patron that the design has a practical and profitable commercial application. The Internet, too, depended on such visionaries for its development—be it scientists like J.C.R. Licklider who imagined a universal computer network as early as the 1960s, or entrepreneur Larry Brilliant, who envisioned and then funded a bulletin board system called the WELL, just to see what would happen.

Another landmark in early computing machines was Herman Hollerith's development of his Hollerith Tabulating System in 1890. Hollerith created his machine in response to a contest sponsored by the U.S. Bureau of the Census. The bureau was in search of a device that would help it conduct the national census. The United States was experiencing wave upon wave of immigration and the government knew that the census would prove a daunting task for its traditional counting methods. Hollerith, a German immigrant who was a statistician for the Census Bureau, created a machine that won the contest. His machine used an electric current to detect holes in punch cards inserted into the machine. The machine reduced both the time and the costs involved in conducting the census. The government used the machine again for the 1900 census.

The Hollerith machine is also significant because it became the foundation for the firm that launched the computer industry. With the success of his machine, Hollerith established the Tabulating Machine Co. in 1896. Fifteen years later his company merged with two others to create the Computing-Tabulating-Recording Co., or CTR. CTR changed its name to IBM in 1924. That IBM, or Big Blue as it's often called, was a titan in the computer industry needs no explaining—for more than fifty years IBM was *the* computer company. But Big Blue unwisely decided to ignore computer networking until it was too late; in the 1990s, their dominance is a thing of the past. Later in the book we'll see Microsoft very nearly make the same mistake. As the saying goes, the computer industry is like a steam roller—you roll with it or it rolls over you.

What Hath God Wrought

In addition to the many advances made in computing technology, the late 1800s and early 1900s brought remarkable achievements in communications. The telegraph, the telephone, and radio were all developed within a span of sixty years.

Each of these communications technologies unleashed profound changes on society, just as the Internet has today.

People first experienced the novelty of direct communication over long distances with the development of the telegraph. Samuel Morse sent the first message by electric telegraph in the United States in 1844. Morse's development of the telegraph grew out of conversations he had with Thomas Jackson, a scientist he had met on a voyage home from Europe. These conversations piqued Morse's interest in electricity and its possible application for use in communications. Morse gave up his pursuit of an art career and devoted himself to the development of what became the telegraph. He convinced the U.S. Congress to pay for the construction of a telegraph cable that stretched from Baltimore, Maryland to Washington, D.C. Morse's dramatic first message, "What hath God wrought!" proved prophetic. The rapid communication made possible by the telegraph transformed American life. A decade after Morse delivered his first message, thousands of miles of telegraph lines were connecting communities across the United States.

In addition to transforming communications, the telegraph proved helpful in transportation and commerce. Rail conductors were able to wire messages for help or report delays to engineers at other stops along their routes. Businessmen were able to accelerate the sale and purchase of goods by communicating with suppliers and retailers through telegraph messages.

The funding for the telegraph also highlights another crucial component required for bringing new technologies to the public—money. While the U.S. government was certainly interested in the development of the telegraph, it was primarily the British who funded the transatlantic cable, which was finally completed in 1866. The United States was unable to divert its attention or scant resources away from the Civil War.

Morse's message was delivered in Morse code, a staccato string of dot- and dash-length electrical pulses. It's interesting to note that Morse code parallels the "on/off" nature of binary code—a series of zeroes and ones—used in modern computers.

Just as Morse's electric telegraph thrilled the public by carrying their words along a wire, electronic mail has become one of the most popular attributes of the Internet. While Morse delivered a message that indicated his awareness of the historical importance of his new technology, the inventor of e-mail, Ray Tomlinson, can't quite recall what he typed when he sent the first e-mail message in 1971. Tomlinson has said it was some sort of test message between two computers that were sitting right next to each other in his lab at Bolt, Beranek and Newman (BBN), which the Defense Department had contracted to build the ARPAnet.

Tomlinson's test might not have traveled the distance or carried the weighty words of Morse's message, but his e-mail technology has proven to be a vital springboard in launching the popular use of the Internet.

Communication was truly revolutionized in 1876, when Alexander Graham Bell received a patent for the telephone. With this new medium, two-way, immediate communication over long distances was possible for the first time. The telephone changed the way people conducted business, relayed important information, and, as the technology became more affordable, socialized with one another. As teenagers once aggravated their parents by spending hours talking on the telephone, today they can fulfill the same urges on the Internet—in chat rooms and on the Web. Much to the dismay of long-distance service providers, the Internet is also making inroads into the telephone market with equipment that allows computer users to make telephone calls over the Internet. In 1998 the technology was not yet widespread, but it's expected to become a popular attribute of the Net.

The advent of another communications medium was one of the inaugural events of the twentieth century: radio. Guglielmo Marconi sent the first successful transatlantic radio transmission in 1901. Marconi, an Italian physicist, had invented a system that used electric waves to relay Morse code messages in 1896, but the device generated little enthusiasm. People were not convinced that Marconi's device could be put to any practical use. But his successful transmission in 1901 of a message to Newfoundland from England garnered praise from around the world, and in 1909 Marconi received the Nobel Prize for Physics for his work.

The event launched the beginning of a new era in communications. As is often the case with new technologies, radio was supported by and exploited for military interests. It found practical use in ship navigation during World War I. However, radio presented new problems for the government. It was surprisingly vulnerable to manipulation: during World War I, amateur radio "hams" intentionally interfered with military signals in attempts to confuse messages to U.S. naval vessels. Hacking, in other words, is much older than the Internet.

The U.S. government passed the Radio Act of 1927 to regulate the new medium, allocating wavelengths on the electromagnetic spectrum and licensing stations that could broadcast over those wavelengths. The Radio Act has since evolved into the sweeping telecommunications legislation that now regulates communication on the Internet.

In Chapter One many of the essential ingredients that have led to computer networking and the Internet begin to emerge. The invention of early computing machines, the beginnings of mass media, and an ability, through mass production, to keep pace with the appetites of a voracious consumer society are all critical points in the evolution of the Internet.

1843 SKETCH OF THE ANALYTICAL ENGINE DETAILS THE FUNDAMENTALS OF COMPUTER PROGRAMMING

English mathematician Ada Lovelace writes Sketch of the Analytical Engine, *a poetic and technically thorough account of Charles Babbage's design for a programmable automatic computing machine. The treatise publicizes Babbage's ideas, which nevertheless are not realized within his lifetime. However, more than a century later, his work influences the engineering of the first programmable computers.*

In 1833 Babbage had designed and built a small-scale prototype of the Difference Engine, an automatic machine capable of simple calculations and intended for the production of mathematical and astronomical tables. He then conceived of a more powerful, versatile machine—which he called the Analytical Engine—that would be able to perform any calculation.

In 1840 Babbage presents his design for the Analytical Engine at a seminar in Italy, where he meets Italian mathematician Luigi Menabrea and commissions him to write a technical description of the engine. Babbage then encourages Ada Lovelace to translate Menabrea's account. She extends herself far beyond a translation, quadrupling the original manuscript's length with her own additions and interpretations. Lovelace writes of the similarities between the engine and the Jacquard loom, an automatic weaving machine capable of turning out varieties of pattern in cloth, noting "the Analytical Engine weaves algebraic patterns just as the Jacquard loom weaves flowers and leaves."

Babbage's design for the Analytical Engine involved punched cards (as did the Jacquard loom) that enabled a person to instruct the machine to perform any mathematical computation. This idea was a precursor to the modern computer program. But by 1842 Babbage lost both the government's confidence and its financial support. This destined the Analytical Engine to remain a project on paper.

In the 1850s Swedish printers Georg and Edvard Scheutz read of the Difference Engine and build a simplified version of it. They enter their fully operational but error-prone machine in the Paris Exposition of 1855 and win a gold medal.

In 1886 Babbage's son Henry donates a scrap of the Difference Engine prototype to Harvard University, where it will later come to the attention of Howard Aiken, a twentieth-century computer pioneer.

1844   Samuel Morse Transmits Telegraph Message from Washington to Baltimore

On May 24 Samuel Morse inaugurates the first electric-telegraph line in the United States with the message "What hath God wrought!" Covering 60 kilometers from Washington, D.C. to Baltimore, Maryland, the underground telegraph line ushers in the modern era of mass communication.

Morse's telegraph transmission is the culmination of several decades of electromagnetic discovery. Back in 1820 Danish physicist Hans Christian Oersted had demonstrated that an electric current generates a magnetic field, defining for the first time the relationship between electricity and magnetism. Subsequent investigation of electromagnetism yielded technological applications, such as the galvanometer (1822) and the electromagnet (1825). These instruments led to the first electric telegraph, completed in 1833 by Carl Gauss and W. E. Weber at the University of Göttingen, Germany.

Relying on self-taught principles, Morse had constructed an electric telegraph in 1837. It employed a single wire, which relayed signals more quickly than the multiple wires used in European telegraph lines.

The Washington-Baltimore telegraph is also a single-wire model and demonstrates to the international community the superiority of this design. The 1844 message is transmitted in Morse code, a system in which letters are represented

---

NEW MEDIA

"New media" today means the Internet: Web-casting, home-page building, and global chats. But every media was new to somebody sometime. Here are some "new media" highlights prior to the Net.

1833: Newspapers mass marketed.

1838: Photography becomes popular.

1844: First telegraph message transmitted.

1876: Telephone invented.

1891: Early motion picture camera invented.

1901: First radio signal sent across the Atlantic.

1907: Theory of television developed in Russia.

1914: First transcontinental telephone call.

1927: First "talking" motion pictures.

1939: Television's public debut at World's Fair.

1950: Color television broadcasts begin.

by combinations of dots and dashes. Single-wire lines and Morse code become the international standards of telegraphic engineering and signaling.

During the next several decades telegraph lines are installed in Europe, North America, and the European colonies, and in 1866 a submarine telegraph cable is laid across the Atlantic Ocean. Telegraphs transmit messages many millions of times faster than do horses and ships, allowing people to send and receive long-distance messages with an unfamiliar and intriguing immediacy. As this immediacy becomes increasingly commonplace, more sophisticated forms of mass communication emerge.

1854 George Boole's An Investigation of the Laws of Thought Is Published

Self-taught British mathematician George Boole's pioneering treatment of logic appears under the full title An Investigation of the Laws of Thought on which are Founded the Mathematical Theories of Logic and Probabilities. *The work introduces a system of symbolic logic that becomes the foundation of modern digital computing.*

Boole's first foray into mathematical theories of logic had resulted in a hurriedly written book, *Mathematical Analysis of Logic,* published in 1847. In it, he represented classes of objects by single symbols (such as x and y) and used the symbols to relate the classes through algebraic equations. The application of algebra to classes of objects, rather than to numerical values, was a simple but novel idea. With this idea Boole had succeeded at grounding logic, the study of the formal principles of reasoning, firmly within mathematics—an achievement dreamt of for centuries by philosophers.

In the 1850s Boole realizes that his first book begs extension and begins to compose *An Investigation of the Laws of Thought.* His intention is to establish a rigorous science of logic based on mathematics and to extract from it some truths about the nature of the human mind. More fully developing the principles of his algebra of classes, he applies symbols and algebra to logical statements as well.

Boole's algebra of classes, known as Boolean algebra, is defined today as the study of calculations performed on variables (unknowns) that can have only two values, 1 and 0. It is the basis for certain common programming functions, such as connecting two or more queries with *and,*

BOOLEAN LOGIC

George Boole's algebra provided part of the foundation for high-level programming. But the rest of us can use the same principles to make the most of Web-powered search engines. Boolean logic uses three types of "logical operators": AND, OR, and NOT. To focus and coordinate online searches, use "AND logic." For instance, the construction

Internet AND communities AND teenagers

tells the search engine to retrieve all documents with the words "Internet," "communities," and "teenagers" in any order, anywhere in the document. "AND logic" tends to turn up lots of material. To narrow the results, try combining "NOT logic" with the search.

Internet AND communities AND teenagers NOT games

will retrieve all documents with the words "Internet," "communities," and "teenagers" but will omit documents with the word "games" (thereby narrowing the field of online teen communities by a great number). If you aren't getting precisely the answers you'd hoped for, expand your search using "OR logic." For instance:

Internet OR online AND communities OR clubs AND teenagers NOT games

This will search for documents that have the word "Internet" (or the word "online") plus the word "communities" (or the word "clubs") plus the word "teenagers." It will omit any of documents with the word "games."

---

or, or *not*. Boolean algebra is crucial to the development of twentieth-century computer programming.

1866 AN EFFECTIVE TRANSATLANTIC CABLE IS ESTABLISHED

On July 27 four British ships arrive at Newfoundland, Canada, completing the laying of a telegraphic cable across the Atlantic Ocean. The cable, which remains operable for nearly a century, marks the beginning of global communication.

The cable-laying project succeeds where three previous attempts had failed. The dream of a telegraphic link between North America and Europe had emerged after cable was laid across rivers, harbors, and the Irish Sea in the 1840s and 1850s. An enthusiastic American entrepreneur, Cyrus Field, initiated the effort by laying a New York-to-Newfoundland cable in 1855. During the next eleven years, Field directed the three doomed attempts to establish a transatlantic telegraph, displaying undaunted perseverance in the face of obstacles such as public disappointment, withdrawal of government funding, and technological shortcomings.

The 1866 attempt follows immediately on the heels of the third attempt, which had collapsed when the cable snapped only 900 kilometers from the Newfoundland destination. Speculating that the next attempt is likely to succeed, British corporations and private investors fund the final venture.

The cable's core consists of twenty-seven interwoven copper wires surrounded by an insulating layer of gutta-percha (a rubberlike substance), with an outer sheath of woven iron strands encasing the core. Trailed from a steamer (accompanied by three other ships), the cable runs from Valentia Bay, Ireland, to St. John's, Newfoundland, a distance of approximately 4,000 kilometers.

British Queen Victoria and United States President Andrew Johnson exchange messages via the new cable. In Britain grand celebrations are launched, but Americans are not immediately excited by the cable's operation because their attention has been focused on the Civil War.

Other submarine cables begin to proliferate around the world upon completion of the transatlantic line, allowing rapid global communication for the first time and altering society in numerous profound ways. Telegraphs establish an international network for commerce, political exchanges, and the dissemination of news, and bureaucratic systems emerge to deal with an overload of information. Modern propaganda techniques are developed to reach a public increasingly eager for information. Long-distance telegraph communication connects local communities to the larger world, foreshadowing a coming era when individuals will be similarly wired to a global web of information exchange.

1876 ALEXANDER GRAHAM BELL INVENTS THE TELEPHONE

On March 7 Alexander Graham Bell receives a patent for the telephone from the United States Patent Office. This convenient electrical-sound apparatus revolutionizes communications and everyday life.

Bell had been trained in speech therapy for deaf people and was teaching vocal physiology at Boston University. In 1873 the families of two of Bell's deaf students generously offered to fund his technological pursuits. He and his assistant Thomas Watson began investigating telegraph technology, searching for a way to transmit speech via electricity.

WHERE'S THE BODY?

These days, it's common to speak about close friends from the Internet, whom we've never actually met in the flesh. But today's sense of "virtual reality" is as old as communications itself. Ironically, many of our most cherished communications inventions have come by way of studying the lives and needs of people with disabilities, for whom the world is always, in some sense, "virtual."

For instance, the first typewriter was invented for a blind nobleman who wanted to be able to write as well as his sighted neighbors. A long-time researcher of the deaf, Alexander Graham Bell, perfected the "phonautograph"—a device that translated sound into mechanical motions that deaf students could visualize. This device paved the way for the later invention of the telephone. And there are still teeth marks on the phonographs in the workshop of Thomas Edison, where the deaf inventor used to "listen" to his "talking machine" play recordings.

While inspired by the needs of people with disabilities, these writing, listening, and talking machines now play a crucial role in what we think of as the "virtuality" of our Internet experience. For example, typing on a keyboard allows us to speak and listen without sound, in online locations we call "chat rooms." State-of-the-art text-reader computer programs allow Net surfers with visual impairments to "see" what's being said online— by hearing it read aloud by their computer.

Turn-of-the-century Americans were as exhilarated and suspicious about their virtual technologies as we are about ours today. When Edison played "Mary Had a Little Lamb" from his phonograph, his assistants checked the room thoroughly, convinced he was pulling off a hoax. Bell had simlar experiences with the introduction of his telephone. As people grow more familiar with the technologies of their day, suspicions wane and enthusiasm grows. After all, what's not to like? In one sense, virtuality promises a kind of immortality for our physical bodies. Edison recognized this potential; he once described the phonograph as a technology that "speaks with your voice and utters your words, centuries after you have crumbled into dust."

Others worry that technologies that mimic our bodies will eventually become better at being human than we are. Internet lore is full of stories of very smart folks who still mistake "bots" (computer programs roaming chat rooms and MOOs) for actual people and even fall in love with them. When pressed, these people insist that the bot seemed more human (and had better social skills) than most of the people on the Net.

Even this isn't new. Most communications enthusiasts through history have preferred the virtual to the fleshly. Legend has it that Edison himself turned down an operation that would have improved his hearing. He explained that "being deaf has saved me from having to listen to a lot of small talk."

Imagining the Net

Bell's telephone operated by translating vocal sounds into a fluctuating electric current, which passed through a wire and was converted back into vocal sounds by a receiver at the other end of the wire. The fluctuating electric current was similar to the vibrations that vocal sounds produce in air.

Three days after Bell's invention is patented, he sends the first telephone message: "Mr. Watson, come here; I want you." Watson hears the request through the receiver in an adjoining room.

The telephone is widely celebrated after its introduction to the public at the 1876 Centennial Exposition in Philadelphia, Pennsylvania. Telephone networks soon link major cities within North America and Europe and are built in many other locations within the decade. Suddenly people are able to talk directly to each other across long distances without having to leave home or work. The telephone vastly increases public reliance on instantaneous communication, and the amount of information exchange swells.

1890 THE U.S. BUREAU OF THE CENSUS USES THE HOLLERITH ELECTRIC TABULATING SYSTEM

On July 1 two thousand clerks begin processing the 1890 U.S. census, assisted by engineer Herman Hollerith's mechanized tabulating system. This event—the most extensive information-processing effort ever undertaken—launches the creation of the office-machine and paves the way for the founding of IBM (International Business Machines).

Illustration of a man operating Hollerith's Tabulating Machine, which was used to calculate the 1890 Census (CORBIS/Bettmann).

Working at the Bureau of the Census during the long, tedious, manual processing of the 1880 census, Hollerith recognized the need for mechanization. He developed the idea of recording each person's information (age, sex, and ethnicity) as a pattern of punched holes on a card. An electromechanical machine, of his design, could tabulate the information from the card automatically.

In 1888 Hollerith's system is chosen for the 1890 census tabulation. On August 16, 1890, the system yields a total population of 62,622,250—a disappointingly low figure, according to a public that had been led to expect at least 75,000,000. The media paint a disparaging picture of Hollerith's machines, but his confidence never wavers.

The tabulation continues, with one hundred machines operated by eighty clerks who can each process about one thousand cards an hour. Two and a half years later, the census processing is complete. Hollerith's system shaves more than four years off the previous census processing and saves the government an estimated $5 million.

The Hollerith Electric Tabulating System is used again in the 1900 census, but by 1905 Hollerith's interests have gravitated toward commercial ventures. He tailors his machines for processing information in business settings, and by 1911 he runs a prosperous punched-card office-machine company. That year, his health failing, Hollerith sells the business to a holding company, which in 1924 becomes the enormously successful IBM.

1919 The Flip-Flop Electronic Switch is Invented

Also called the Eccles-Jordan switch after its inventors, the flip-flop electronic switch first appears in 1919.

The switch is a two-circuit digital device with two stable states. It remains in one state, in which one circuit is conducting and the other is off, until it receives the designated trigger and switches to the other state, in which the second circuit is conducting and the first is off.

Throughout the 1930s the flip-flop is used primarily as a counting device in instruments that detect high-speed events, such as the decay of radioactive materials. As electronics technology matures during the 1940s and 1950s, the flip-flop serves as both a counter and a switch. It becomes an invaluable part of machines that operate in binary, a numeric system represented by the digits 0 and 1.

1936 Alan Turing Establishes the Theoretical Principles of Digital Computing

British mathematician Alan Turing's paper, "On Computable Numbers," is published. In it Turing demonstrates that there are problems to which no mechanically computable solution exists by detailing the design of a theoretical digital computer.

ALAN TURING

According to biographer Andrew Hodges, Alan Turing was at times "eccentric, solitary, gloomy, vivacious," and acquaintances speak endearingly of his unconventional and amusing habits. Turing also crossed conventional boundaries in his scientific endeavors, introducing new ways of thinking about scientific problems.

Born on June 23, 1912, in London, England, Turing developed an active interest in science during early childhood. At age eight he was performing chemistry experiments in a basement laboratory and impressing his teachers with remarkable mathematical capabilities.

Turing attended King's College, Cambridge University, and Princeton University, receiving a Ph.D. in mathematics from the latter. Some of his most innovative and rigorous work appeared in the influential paper, "On Computable Numbers," published in 1936. With it he established the theoretical foundations of digital, stored-program computing.

During World War II, Turing put his skills to use for the government, cracking the German Enigma code and assisting in the production of Colossus, the first operational electronic computer.

Anecdotes from the war years illustrate Turing's colorful personality. At one point he became convinced that Germany was about to invade England, and taking precautions, he exchanged his money for bricks of silver and buried them in the woods. He was never able to find the treasure after the war. Riding a bicycle everywhere, even in the pouring rain, he often wore a gas mask to control raging bouts of hay fever. He appeared indifferent to what others thought.

Turing was also a competitive long-distance runner; he often surprised his colleagues by running to meetings and arriving before those who took public transport. He would have been a contender for the 1948 Olympics, but a serious injury prevented him from competing.

After the war, he turned his attention to artificial intelligence, formulating criteria for judging whether a machine can be considered intelligent. He asserted that if someone poses the same questions to a machine and a human being and cannot distinguish the machine's answers from the human's, then the machine is defined as intelligent. This scenario is now known as the Turing test and appears in modern discussions of artificial intelligence.

Turing was openly gay at a time when such a lifestyle was not only frowned upon but also illegal. In 1952 he was convicted of indecency for participating in homosexual activities and was ordered to take the hormone estrogen, intended to neutralize his sex drive. Although exasperated by the effects of the drug and angry at the injustice, Turing continued his work. He studied the chemical and mathematical basis for the formation of asymmetrical patterns in biology.

However unaffected Turing may have appeared outwardly, his end indicates he became tragically unhappy. He was found dead on June 7, 1954, at his home in Manchester. A partly eaten apple dipped in cyanide, a lethal poison, led authorities to conclude he had killed himself.

HACKERS, HAMS, AND THE RADIO ACT

Ask the average person to tell you about the "early days of hacking," and you'll probably hear a story about computers that takes place around 1980. But hackers operate within more media than just the Internet; the term encompasses everyone from computer-code writers to phone "phreaks" to satellite jammers. Loosely, hackers are any "unofficial personnel" who muck around with regulated communications technologies.

Considered this way, it's easy to see the earliest operators of amateur radio as the first hackers and the Radio Act of 1927 as the granddaddy of anti-hack legislation. The Radio Act, which originally sought to "maintain U.S. control over all interstate and foreign radio transmission" evolved into the Communications Act of 1934. This Act is updated on a regular basis and continues to regulate telecommunications innovations of today.

Before it became a one-way broadcast medium, "the wireless" was a place where people who built their own radios talked to one another. (Some would say that before the advent of the World Wide Web, the same was true of the Internet.) Early ham radio operators were a colorful bunch of folks: some entertainers (hence the term, "ham"), others techno-geeks, all pioneers of virtual community. Radio pioneers shared a belief in the power of the new technology to change the world for the better. Long before it was bandied on the Net, the slogan "information wants to be free" belonged to the hams.

As early as 1912, so many amateur radio operators were broadcasting that military signals were being interrupted. Frustrated with the increased traffic, the government decided to issue licenses to only those radio operators who could demonstrate superior equipment and power. Unfortunately, this relegated the airwaves primarily to corporations and the government. Hams were squeezed out of broadcasting space (or "bandwidth") on the radio dial and limited to only a few frequencies. By and large, ham operators complied with government wishes. However, there were exceptions. According to legend, many a bogus message was sent to World War I Navy ships for the amusement of "pirate" operators angered by the fact that they had been forbidden to use the airwaves.

On the Net, government regulation (at least in terms of bandwidth) is not the problem it is in radio, and some people are using digital radio technologies to host their own radio stations online. Will the fact that everyone can have his or her own Net radio station mean the end of radio as we know it? It's possible, but certainly not likely—at least not until computers come standard in every car.

From the Hacker File

Turing's paper had originated with a subject introduced by prominent German mathematician David Hilbert in 1928. Hilbert believed that all mathematical problems could be solved and imagined that an automatic machine might be able to compute such solutions.

Venturing that Hilbert was incorrect, Turing approaches the issue by describing a theoretical computing machine, now known as a Turing machine. The machine mechanically scans a tape that is punched with coded instructions consisting of digital sequences of 1s and 0s. The instructions, or algorithms (step-by-step procedures for solving a problem), for particular computations have been programmed by a person. The values of a given problem are also recorded on the tape. As the machine computes, it delivers the outcomes in sequences of 1s and 0s. Thus the machine handles information digitally throughout the computation process, without human intervention.

In Turing's theoretical scenario, a problem is solvable only if his machine is capable of computing a solution to it. Turing demonstrates that some mathematical and logical problems cannot be solved by an algorithm. For example, there exists no algorithm capable of computing certain real numbers (the set of all rational and irrational numbers).

"On Computable Numbers" introduces the basic concepts of digital computing, upon which modern computer science is based. The paper cements Turing's importance in the computer science field.

1938　Konrad Zuse Builds the Z1 and Z2, Electromechanical Binary Computers

Konrad Zuse of Germany completes his first two electromechanical, universal computing machines, designated the Z1 and Z2. The computers operate in binary (a system in which numbers are represented by sequences of 1s and 0s) and have stored-program capability.

Zuse had approached automatic computing from the viewpoint of a civil engineering student in 1934, recognizing the potential value of a machine that would deal quickly with the tedious algebraic calculations he and his peers could spend months performing.

In 1936 Zuse began to construct the Z1, a computing machine with faster, more extensive calculating abilities than the existing limited-function desk calculators. He decided on a binary system because it allowed greater calculating speed than the traditional decimal system.

To express the binary digits, the Z1 contains numerous mechanical gates opened and closed by sliding plates. This design replaces and simplifies the gears and axles of desk calculators. Powered by electricity, the plates read calculating instructions from strips of film punched with binary

REPORTS OF MY DEATH HAVE BEEN GREATLY EXAGGERATED

Do you believe everything on the news? In 1938 Orson Welles and his Mercury Theater dramatized the sci-fi classic *War of the Worlds* on the radio. They learned a painful lesson about the power of media.

Welles, who had originally feared the story of an invasion from Mars was "too old-fashioned for modern consumption," decided to make things "more realistic." He scripted the story as a series of late-breaking news reports, with reporters interrupting a program of dance music to give updates on a Martian attack on a New Jersey town. Although there were four announcements stating that the broadcast was fictional, listeners began to panic. Thousands of calls flooded police switchboards around the country, and scores of people were treated for shock and hysteria. One man encountered his wife attempting to drink a bottle of cyanide, yelling, "I'd rather die like this than like that!"

Partial blame for the *War of the Worlds* panic lay with the nature of radio itself. Through the early 1920s amateur radio was a type of two-way communication where people could, and often did, cross-broadcast and contradict one another's news. By the 1930s "commercial radio"—one-way entertainment and news broadcasting—had become the standard. In the mid-thirties, three out of four American homes had radios, but there were no clear guidelines regarding radio's responsibilities to the public.

As for Welles, he was reported to have been "stunned" by the reaction, and mused that he perhaps misunderstood "the special nature of radio, which is often heard in fragments." Today, we know Welles' observations also apply to other media. In 1996 hundreds in Madrid panicked about a televised "breaking report" on space aliens attacking New York; it turned out to be a commercial for the film *Independence Day*.

The Internet faces many of the same credibility problems. Not long ago Congress expressed its sympathies to the family of the late Bob Hope, who was very much alive at the time. Newspapers often write obituaries in advance and keep them on file; unfortunately Hope's was "filed" on the Web and spotted by an overeager Congressional aide. Even more disturbing was reporter Pierre Salinger's recent theory that a downed TWA airplane was actually shot by spies. When pressed for further facts, Salinger admitted that he "read about it on the Internet."

The evolution of the Internet, and our growing dependence on it as a news source, makes it ripe for all types of misunderstandings and hoaxes, from phony "virus warnings" to more dangerous pranks. Fortunately the Net, like earliest radio, is still a two-way medium. Before forwarding one of those cautionary messages about an online virus, check out a reliable source like the virus hoax web page at http://www.europe.datafellows.com/news/hoax.htm.

It's too bad the Mercury Theater didn't have a Martian hoax web page. They could have saved themselves a lot of grief.

Media History

codes. The Z1 functions moderately well but has trouble routing electrical signals from one location within the machine to another.

To solve this problem in the Z2, Zuse installs an electromagnetic relay system that replaces the mechanical plates of the first machine. Electromagnetic relays, used for telephone exchanges, are quick-operating switches turned on and off by an electric current. Zuse finds that relays serve as an excellent mechanism for expressing binary numbers.

The Z2 is still not an impressively functional machine, but it demonstrates the potential of Zuse's ideas and convinces the German Experimental Aerodynamics Institute to fund Zuse's subsequent computing project in 1941. The Z3 turns out to be the first fully functional general-purpose programmable computer. Unfortunately, Zuse's electromechanical designs do not influence the concurrent development of computers in England and the United States, where the seeds of a superior technology—electronics—are already germinating.

1939 John Atanasoff Completes Prototype of Electronic Binary Computer

John Atanasoff, professor of mathematics and physics at Iowa State College (now University), builds an electronic binary computer that represents the first application of electronics to automatic calculation. Although the machine is never fully operable, Atanasoff's ideas are important to the design of modern electronic computers.

As a physicist, Atanasoff had long been familiar with the difficulty of solving extensive systems of linear equations. In the 1930s he had begun investigating the use of electronics to construct a device that would be faster and more efficient at solving linear equations than the existing electromechanical calculators. Electromechanical machines are powered by electricity, but they are capable only of simple, repetitive tasks. Electronic devices, on the other hand, are more versatile because they use electricity itself to influence the flow of electric currents. Electronic devices can change their behavior instantly in response to incoming information.

By the 1930s electronics—in the form of vacuum tubes—had been introduced to radio and telephone technology as a means of amplifying electrical signals. The vacuum tube was also capable of acting as a switch for routing electrical pulses through a circuit. Calculating devices required such switches, but the early vacuum tube's reliability in that capacity was questionable, and thus calculating devices of the 1930s used electromechanical switches (also called relays) to route signals.

In the winter of 1937, Atanasoff devises the architecture of his computer; he and his associate Clifford Berry complete a prototype of the machine in 1939. It operates electronically, uses binary numbers, and includes regenerating condensers (now known as capacitors) for memory, all of which become fundamental elements of the modern electronic computer.

In 1941 physicist John Mauchly, who is involved in the military's computing research, visits Atanasoff and learns about the Atanasoff-Berry Computer (ABC). It is a subject of controversy whether Mauchly later applies any of that information to the development of the first fully operational electronic computer, Electronic Numerical Integrator and Computer (ENIAC).

The ABC never runs without error, and Atanasoff is obliged to abandon the project in 1942 when inducted into war-related work. But in 1973 he wins a court case that concludes he is the official inventor of the electronic computer.

1943 Colossus—an Entirely Electronic Deciphering Device—Is Operational

Designed by the Department of Communications of the British Foreign Office, the first fully operational electronic deciphering device, named Colossus, is built. It helps establish the superiority of electronics.

World War II is the driving force behind the invention of Colossus. From the outset of the war, the Germans had used an electromechanical machine called Enigma to codify and exchange secret messages among military stations. From a Polish immigrant, the British had obtained enough details about the Enigma to intercept German messages and crack many of their codes using their own electromechanical machines called Bombes.

In the early 1940s the British decide to build a more powerful device for cryptoanalysis. The project is top secret, and many of its details remain undisclosed to this day. The first machine is completed in 1943, and ten more—each improving upon the previous—are in operation by the end of the war. All are called Colossus.

Each Colossus contains hundreds of vacuum tubes as switches, operates in binary, and reads incoming data off punched tape. As single-purpose machines designed to decipher Enigma codes, they successfully compare messages with known codes, find a match, and print the results. Performing all logical functions electronically, the Colossi are the first entirely electronic computing devices in the world. They operate at much higher speeds than the Bombes and aid the Allies enormously in defeating Germany.

The Collossi are not used beyond the late 1940s because they are practical only for code breaking. However, those engineers involved in their design and construction have gained experience with electronic circuits, and some later apply this knowledge to the development of multiple-purpose electronic computers.

1944 HOWARD AIKEN AND IBM PRESENT THE MARK I AT HARVARD UNIVERSITY

The Harvard Mark I, or the IBM Sequence Controlled Calculator, is introduced to the public with a dedication ceremony at Harvard University. The machine—a fully automatic, multiple-purpose, electromechanical calculator—jump-starts IBM's transformation into a computing giant.

In 1936 Howard Aiken, the Harvard University graduate student who formulates the original blueprint for the Mark I, had gotten stuck trying to solve a set of nonlinear differential equations for his dissertation on vacuum-tube physics. Inspired by his knowledge of Charles Babbage's Difference Engine, Aiken proposes to the physics department a plan for building a large-scale automatic calculator that could solve these equations. Finding little enthusiasm there, Aiken eventually

Howard Aiken poses with his "giant calculator," the Mark I, at Harvard University on August 4, 1944 (CORBIS/Bettmann).

obtains financial and technological backing from IBM, then making punch-card electromechanical office machines.

Aiken lays out the computational requirements for his envisioned calculator, and top-ranking IBM engineers polish the plans and complete the machine in 1943. Powered by a five-horsepower electric motor, the Mark I measures two feet by fifty-one feet, weighs five tons, and contains hundreds of miles of wiring. Its computation speed is actually quite slow compared to other automatic computers being developed simultaneously, because it is not electronic.

The dedication ceremony at Harvard University creates a media frenzy. The huge machine, encased in glass and stainless steel, captures the public's attention and demands a close look by scientists and engineers—many of whom hope to test out their own problems on it. Perhaps the most significant aspect of the dedication is Aiken's conspicuous failure to acknowledge IBM's role in the creation of the Mark I during his speech. Thomas Watson, IBM's president, is furious and left feeling resentful, which later motivates him to produce something far superior to the Mark I: electronic computers.

Although intended for use as a general-purpose calculating device, the Mark I ends up being used exclusively for producing mathematical tables for the Navy. It is valuable, nonetheless, as a training ground for other computer pioneers, such as Grace Murray Hopper.

1945 John von Neumann's Report on EDVAC Describes Stored-Program Computing

On June 30, mathematician John von Neumann writes "A First Draft of a Report on the EDVAC," which establishes the logical and technological architecture of the stored-program computer. The report becomes the theoretical foundation of modern computer design.

Ideas for EDVAC (Electronic Discrete Variable Automatic Computer) had grown out of plans for another computer, ENIAC (Electronic Numerical Integrator and Computer). ENIAC had originated in the minds of John Presper Eckert and John Mauchly at the Moore School of Electrical Engineering, University of Pennsylvania. Plans for building ENIAC got underway in 1943 and came to the attention of von Neumann, a renowned mathematical genius, the following summer.

THE COMPUTER IN YOUR HEAD

Thanks to John von Neumann, we now think of our computers as having brains. Thanks to modern neurology, we know that in some ways, human brains actually do resemble computers: both can function electrically, process input and output, and store instructions (in the brain, these are called "memories").

Yet for all their surface similarities, computers and brains actually function very differently. In an average computer, every part has a different job: the processor can't act like the memory and vice versa. Although they can work many times faster than human brains, almost all computers operate serially—processing one piece of information at a time—so they struggle with tasks the human brain handles with ease: recognizing one voice in a crowded room of talkers; having a "gut reaction"; imagining new solutions to problems.

In his book *The Computer and the Brain,* von Neumann theorized that the brain's "parallel architecture" allows it to process information all at once, rather than in one-at-a-time bits the way a computer does. Electrical, biological, and chemical information moves indiscreetly among neurons, so there are no rigid divisions of labor between things like reasoning and remembering—we can easily do both simultaneously. Von Neumann predicted that in order to build more creative, "brain-like" computers, scientists would have to develop workable parallel computer architectures. These days, most artificial intelligence and biotechnology researchers tend to agree.

After enjoying a brief flash of interest in the 1980s, parallel architecture development has been exiled out of industry and into universities. Most corporations have chosen to focus on making faster serial processors, rather than gamble on the unknown elements of parallel research. Nevertheless, pioneers like Danny Hillis continue the exploration. Hillis hands out vials full of DNA, encoded with his name and address, as "calling cards" to remind people that the future of computing may well belong to parallel architecture.

While parallel computer architecture languishes, parallel processing—hundreds or even thousands of serial computers working on the same project simultaneously—is becoming an everyday occurrence. The rise of the Internet has vastly increased the potential for ordinary people to parallel process: when you post a question on a bulletin board, that question goes out to thousands of individual subscribers. Businesses use parallel processing, or "neural nets," to do stock forecasting, fingerprint recognition, and business research.

Be aware, however, that terms like "neural nets" can be misleading; a thousand serial computers working together still can't match the complex architecture of a single human brain. Artificial intelligence expert Marvin Minsky points out that although computers can use parallel processing to perform "genius" tasks like code-breaking, they still struggle with simple things—motor skills, aesthetic awareness, and emotions—that human brains can manage from birth.

Thought of this way, the combined computation power of the entire Internet still seems paltry compared to the neurological miracle of a single infant, unconsciously navigating her crib in the dark.

Imagining the Net

Von Neumann is greatly intrigued by Eckert and Mauchly's project and joins their effort as a consultant. The group recognizes that ENIAC, as designed, has three major shortcomings: its storage capacity is too small, it contains too many vacuum tubes, and it requires inconvenient and laborious reprogramming to undertake a new task. While ENIAC is under construction, the researchers design a new computer—EDVAC—that overcomes ENIAC's limitations.

EDVAC's logical design embodies the concept of stored programming, an idea born of the collaboration among Eckert, Mauchly, and von Neumann. The idea is that the computer's storage device will hold both the instructions of the program and the input data upon which it carries out the instructions. This extends the amount of memory available and also indirectly solves ENIAC's other problems, reducing the tube count and eliminating reprogramming.

Von Neumann compiles the designs for EDVAC in his report. In it, he employs biological metaphors to describe the computer's design, establishing computing terms such as "memory," input and output "organs," and "gates" (analogous to neural gates in the brain).

Although unpublished, the EDVAC report is eventually distributed internationally within the nascent computing community, which prevents Eckert and Mauchly from pursuing a patent on stored-program computers. EDVAC is finally built in 1952 and operates for ten years. The basics of modern computer technology are modeled after its design.

1945 Vannevar Bush Proposes Memex, an Information Machine

The July issue of Atlantic Monthly *features "As We May Think," an article by Vannevar Bush detailing a theoretical desk-like machine that holds a whole library of information on microfilm. This instrument, which he dubs "memex," is a vision of the future: electronically stored information accessed through a personal computer.*

Bush had entered the computer science field in the 1930s and become one of the chief designers of early mechanical and electromechanical machines for mathematical computation. A respected expert in information management and technological innovation, he authored several influential articles on those topics prior to "As We May Think." During

World War II he held posts as presidential science advisor and head of the government's Office of Scientific Research and Development.

Bush's memex idea is a reaction to the information explosion of the early 1900s. Similarly the eighteenth century's Age of Enlightenment had yielded a vast store of knowledge, and the first encyclopedias had been produced to organize that knowledge into an accessible and empowering form. Accumulation of knowledge and information accelerated throughout the nineteenth century such that specialization was already common in the first few decades of the twentieth century. It was the rare individual who could keep up with the progress in more than one field of learning.

Bush had formulated his idea for memex several years before the war. But it is not until 1945 that circumstances permit the publication of "As We May Think." Following its publication in the *Atlantic Monthly*, the article reappears in *Life* and thereby reaches a broader audience. Memex, as envisioned by Bush, is a desk that contains large amounts of information compressed onto microfilm. The memex user sits at the desk, swiftly accessing information by operating a board of levers and buttons. The desired information appears on translucent screens propped on the desktop. Bush imagines that the rapidly advancing technology of computers will be involved in the realization of memex or a similar information system, making him one of few who sees computers as having applications beyond mathematical computation.

Memex is Bush's envisioned means of harnessing the information explosion and enabling people to share resources at the tap of a few buttons. His article inspires several attempts to build a memex machine during the next two decades, but microfilm technology is neither sophisticated nor cheap enough to allow any success.

Bush's work remains important in the 1960s, influencing J. C. R. Licklider, Ted Nelson, and Doug Engelbart, three important figures in the development of computer networking and hypertext systems.

1946 ENIAC IS UNVEILED AT THE UNIVERSITY OF PENNSYLVANIA

On February 16, the University of Pennsylvania's Moore School of Electrical Engineering inaugurates ENIAC, an electronic computer many times more complex than any previous, at the University of Pennsylvania. The event leads to the Moore School Lectures, at which the stored-program concept of computing is introduced.

FAIRHOPE PUBLIC LIBRARY

The plans for ENIAC, formulated primarily by Eckert and Mauchly (University of Pennsylvania scientists), had begun in 1943. The $400,000 construction cost was funded by the Ballistics Research Laboratory (BRL).

ENIAC runs its first trials in November 1945. Built into a basement room at the university, its superstructure covers 650 square feet and sports 300 neon lights. It contains 10,000 vacuum tubes that produce 150 kilowatts of heat at full power, requiring the installation of two twenty-horsepower fans to keep the unit cool. As widely reported by the media, everything about ENIAC is large, except the time it takes to compute. Capable of 5,000 operations per second, it is a thousand times faster than the Harvard Mark I, an electromechanical computer that had captured the spotlight two years prior. Eckert and Mauchly are known to boast that ENIAC can calculate the trajectory, or path, of a speeding object faster than the object can fly.

The excitement cast by the unveiling brings numerous requests from the scientific community for more information about electronic computing. Eager to transmit technological knowledge, the university organizes an invitation-only series of lectures at the Moore School. Taking place that summer, the lectures explain ENIAC and more importantly reveal the design of EDVAC, a stored-program computer. Several dozen young scientists walk away with the framework of future computing scribbled in their notebooks.

1947 GRACE MURRAY HOPPER DISCOVERS COMPUTER BUG IN HARVARD MARK II

Grace Murray Hopper finds that a moth has caused a relay failure in the Harvard Mark II, an electromechanical computer. The event popularizes the term "bug" for computer program malfunctions.

In 1944 Hopper, a mathematician and a lieutenant in the United States Navy, had been assigned to the government's computer project at Harvard University. There she programmed Howard Aiken's Mark I and Mark II computers.

One day in the summer of 1947, the Mark II is suddenly producing faulty results. Hopper unmasks the mystery when she discovers that a moth had gotten stuck in one of the machine's electrical relays, disrupting the smooth routing of signals. She removes the dead insect and tapes it into the logbook, with the words "First actual case of a bug being found."

Biography

GRACE MURRAY HOPPER

Grace Murray Hopper, a woman among the many men on the frontier of early computing, was an enthusiastic mathematician and pioneering programmer who firmly held the notion that the untried is not necessarily impossible. By the time she retired as the oldest member of the Navy, Hopper had contributed several decades of expertise and inspiration to the advancement of computer science.

Hopper was born Grace Brewster Murray on December 9, 1906, in New York City. At age seven she undertook her first technological project, exploring the mechanical processes of an alarm clock. She took one apart, and then disassembled another in order to determine how the first should be reassembled; to reassemble the second, she took apart another, and so forth through seven clocks. Her well-to-do family encouraged her curiosity.

Hopper studied mathematics at Vassar College and received a Ph.D. from Yale University in 1934. She married a childhood friend, Vincent Foster Hopper, in 1930; they had no children and divorced in 1945. Until World War II she taught mathematics at Vassar, steadily climbing in professorial rank.

Hopper was to climb the ranks in another institution, the Navy, starting at age 37— unusually late to begin a military career. Assigned to work under Howard Aiken as a programmer for the Harvard Mark I and II computers, she was a dedicated and tireless engineer. One morning upon finding her at the end of an all-night session, Aiken asked what she had been doing all that time. She replied, "Chaperoning these two damned computers!"

After the war she applied her programming knowledge to business computing, temporarily working in the civilian sector. John Mauchly and John Presper Eckert recruited her in 1949 to lead the programming team for the UNIVAC, a stored-program computer that was to set trends within the industry. In 1952 Hopper invented the compiler, a piece of software that translates a programmer's instructions (written in symbolic logic) into an operational program in binary, the computer's language. The compiler was a much-needed solution to the many errors that inevitably occurred when programs were manually transcribed into binary digit by digit. She continued to formulate software, playing key a role in the creation of Flow-Matic and COBOL, business-machine languages.

In 1967 the Navy recalled Hopper to serve as a computer programmer and educator. Two years later she was honored as the Data Processing Management Association's first computer science "Man of the Year." She remained with the Navy until 1986 and died six years later, leaving a legacy of computing solutions and a cast of young people trained to undertake difficult tasks innovatively and without trepidation.

While this has been mythologized as the moment when the term "bug" was coined, the expression actually dates back to the time of Thomas Edison. Hopper and her colleagues refer to machine failures as "bugs," and to the procedure of fixing the failures as "debugging." Today, a bug is commonly defined as an error in programming, although it can still also apply to hardware.

Netspeak

WOMEN: THE FIRST COMPUTERS

Today the word "computer" means silicon chips nestled in gray boxes. But before it was a machine, a computer was a person—specifically, a woman. During World War II the development of the artillery gun demanded calculations for the firing tables. In the United States, these tables were made by one hundred women equipped with electric calculators at the Moore School in Pennsylvania, each of whom had the official job title, Computer.

When research began on the ENIAC, six women from the original group of Computers were enlisted to staff the world's most powerful electronic calculator. The ENIAC eventually took on the name "computer," and the six women—Kathleen McNulty, Frances Bilas, Betty Jean Jennings, Elizabeth Snyder, Ruth Lichterman, and Marlyn Wescoff—went on to became computer science pioneers. Elizabeth Holberton (her married name) went on to give renowned programmer Grace Murray Hopper the idea for the compiler and was also involved in the development of COBOL in 1960.

The "ENIAC 6" are relatively well documented, but other early women computers are difficult to trace, perhaps because much of their work was classified as top secret. For instance, we are only now beginning to learn about the British "Wrens" (Women's Royal Naval Service) and the American WAVES (Women Accepted for Volunteer Emergency Service). Working on opposite sides of the Atlantic, these women were the primary users of electromechanical machines called Bombes, which decoded messages intercepted from enemy signals during World War II.

1947 TRANSISTOR IS INVENTED

Three scientists at Bell Telephone Laboratories devise the transistor, an electronic switching mechanism and amplifier that makes the vacuum tube obsolete. The transistor and its descendants allow electronic equipment to become much more compact and energy efficient as well as less expensive.

In the 1930s Bell Labs had begun to focus on improving telephone technology, and in the 1940s electronics technology in general. A replacement was sought for vacuum tubes, which were bulky, fragile, and energy intensive. In 1945 engineer John Bardeen joined Walter Brattain and William Shockley at Bell Labs in their effort to apply semiconductors to electronics. Semiconductors, such as silicon, are materials whose conductivity can be readily controlled and manipulated with electricity.

The team has a breakthrough in 1947: Bardeen and Brattain successfully translate Shockley's design for a transistor into a working physical model. The first transistor, called the point-contact transistor, is primitive but promising. Standing ten centimeters high, it contains a semiconducting crystal of germanium, which serves as the amplifier, connected to three wire probes. A current entering through one probe is amplified when it passes through the crystal and out through another probe.

A few years later Shockley invents the junction transistor, which is more reliable and efficient and thus more commercially viable. The early transistor makes its way into radios and telephone exchanges. In 1953 transistors are first used in a computer, and after 1958 technological improvements make transistor-run computers (such as IBM's 7000 series) much faster and more powerful. In the 1960s the transistor is miniaturized into a tiny pattern etched onto a slice of silicon—the integrated circuit, which in turn evolves into the microprocessor, the heart of the modern computer.

1948 FIRST STORED-PROGRAM COMPUTER IS OPERATIONAL IN MANCHESTER, ENGLAND

On June 21 the "Manchester Baby Machine" computes its first result, establishing that the practical feasibility of stored-program computing matches its theoretical promise.

During World War II, the British had gained significant experience with computers, which they used to decipher German codes. In fact, the first fully operational electronic computer, Colossus, was completed in England in 1943. After the war, Manchester University hires Max Newman, one of the Colossus engineers. Newman is familiar with stored-program computing, the details of which had been outlined in the EDVAC report by John von Neumann in 1945. Entranced by the promise of this new concept, Newman secures funding to build an EDVAC-type computer. He and radar engineer F. C. Williams construct a small, simple stored-program computer, the Small Scale Experimental Machine (SSEM), nicknamed the "Baby." It works as intended and, according to Williams, "nothing was ever the same again."

From this small-scale machine came the Manchester Mark I, which is completed in April 1949. The Manchester Mark I is used at the university, but it is improved upon and replaced two years later by the Ferranti Mark I, the world's first computer to be offered on the commercial market. The first Ferranti Mark I is available in February 1951.

1948 "A Mathematical Theory of Communication," by Claude Shannon, Formulates the Link Between Communications and Computers

Claude Shannon, an electrical engineer at Bell Telephone Laboratories, writes "A Mathematical Theory of Communication," in which he outlines theories on transferring information efficiently through "noisy" channels. The paper introduces the term "bit" for a unit of information.

Since the beginning of World War II Shannon had worked at Bell Labs, where he was encouraged to steer his studies of communications in any direction he pleased. The electronic transmission of messages, in its infancy, was among his primary concerns. Electronic transmission was sometimes obscured by encryption, or distorted by noise inherent to the transmission medium. Believing that mathematics would yield a way to improve transmission, he sought to quantify the content of communications.

Shannon reveals the results of his pondering in "A Mathematical Theory of Communication." In it he proposes a fundamental unit of information, called a "bit," which provides a mathematical basis for information and allows him to analyze mathematically the electronic flow of communications. This analysis yields several theorems describing ways to encode messages such that information can be exchanged reliably with a minimum of noise, distortion, and error.

Shannon's theorems influence the design of electronic circuits, computers, and communications systems.

1951 UNIVAC is Delivered to the U.S. Bureau of the Census

On March 30 Remington Rand delivers the UNIversal Automatic Computer (UNIVAC), a stored-program computer tailored for data processing, to the U.S. Bureau of the Census. Designed by John Presper Eckert and John Mauchly, UNIVAC marks the beginning of commercial computing.

Plans for UNIVAC had taken shape immediately following the breakup of the Moore School group that designed ENIAC and EDVAC. In 1946 John von Neumann and several devotees returned to Princeton University, while Mauchly and Eckert formed their own company with the intention of marketing stored-program computers.

Computing up to that point had been focused primarily on mathematical calculation for scientific and military purposes. At the end of World War II, computer engineers began to look toward designing computers for data processing and other business applications.

In 1946 Mauchly and Eckert had secured a contract with the Bureau of the Census to produce their first data-processing computer. Over the next four years, they designed and built UNIVAC—but the story is not that straightforward. Having drastically underestimated the financial scale of their endeavor (which ends up being about $1 million), they found themselves on the edge of bankruptcy more than once. They pulled through with funds from investors and advance payments on orders, but in 1950, again desperate, their only hope was to sell the company to the first bidder, Remington Rand. All plans for UNIVAC remained in operation.

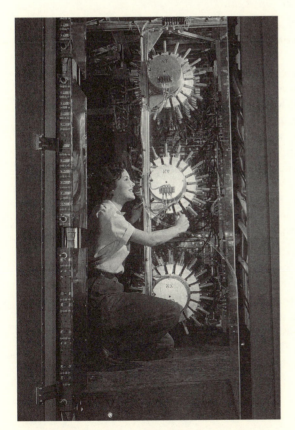

UNIVAC technician Joyce Cade at a U.S. Bureau of the Census installation in Maryland in October 1955 (CORBIS/Bettmann).

Working arduously in the scorching Philadelphia heat, Mauchly, Eckert, and their staff of nearly 150 employees completed UNIVAC early in 1951. After crucial software developments—spearheaded by Grace Murray Hopper—were in place, UNIVAC performed seventeen consecutive hours of fault-free computing as a trial run. The machine was then delivered to the census agency.

In 1952 Remington Rand pulls off a tremendous publicity stunt: it uses UNIVAC to predict the outcome of the presidential election. Mauchly devises a program that can use voting patterns from the 1944 and 1948 elections to compute the 1952 result based on early election night returns from numerous key states. CBS television films the event at the Philadelphia UNIVAC building, and by 8:30 p.m. the machine shows Eisenhower beating Stevenson by a landslide. UNIVAC's prediction turns out to be accurate to within four electoral votes, which causes a sensation. The spectacle introduces computers to the public and makes UNIVAC a household name.

ATTACK OF THE KILLER MAINFRAME

When Walter Cronkite politely asked a gray box, "UNIVAC, what do you predict the election results to be?" millions of television viewers saw how easily computers could be confused with human beings. Things haven't changed much since then. If you want to see just how confused Americans are about the differences between themselves and their computers, take a trip to the movies.

In many classic sci-fi movies, computers fit neatly into good guy/bad guy dichotomies. There are films like *Forbidden Planet* (1956), *2001* (1969), and *Colossus: The Forbin Project* (1969), where supercomputers out-think their creators, gaining human motivations like greed, insecurity, and pride. But for every bad computer, there are heroes like Robby the Robot (*Invisible Boy*, 1957) and C3PO/R2D2 (*Star Wars*, 1977).

In recent years the terrain has changed: the gray box of the supercomputer was exchanged for the gray matter of the human brain. *Blade Runner* (1982), *Terminator* (1984), and *Robocop* (1987) feature computer's newest bodies: androids (computers that look human) and cyborgs (humans with technological

components). In the 1990s, films like *Lawnmower Man* (1992) and *Gattaca* (1997) juxtapose disabled human protagonists and bioengineered, computerized humans against one another in order to ask, "Which of these bodies is more significant?"

Our modern dependence on computers becomes the worry for the newest sci-fi genres: hacker and Internet films. In a sense, hacker films like *War Games* (1983) and *Johnny Mnemonic* (1995) are nostalgia movies, in that they still portray computer life as full of good guys and bad guys. Internet films like *The Net* (1995) are more complex. Although there was a "bad hacker" in *The Net*, the story draws most of its power from our collective fear of faceless, computerized bureaucracy; *The Net* suggests that computers now have the ability to entirely erase a human identity.

The history of sci-fi films shows that in less than fifty years, we have gone from asking our computers, "What do you predict?" to "Do you think I exist?" For answers, you might check out the University of Pennsylvania's excellent Web site devoted to computers in the movies, at http://128.174.194.59/cybercinema/.

Beyond the Net

From *Sputnik* to the ARPAnet

There is a rich irony, for anyone who cares to look, in the fact that the Cold War was both backdrop and motivation for the Internet. What is now an anarchic zone of commerce and free speech was at first a tightly controlled investment in national defense.

Inspired by the Cold War and changed forever by the counterculture, the birth of networking required major advances in computer technology, the participation of many universities and small businesses, and a diverse cast of characters including Cold War hawks, resourceful graduate students, and the Orson Welles of Software.

A Sputnik Cocktail (Two Parts Stolichnaya and One Part Sour Grapes)

The late 1950s and 1960s were a time of prosperity in the United States, but also of intense social upheaval. In 1957 the Soviet Union's launch of *Sputnik* stunned the United States. How did this happen? How could it be that Soviet scientists knew enough to send a satellite into orbit? How soon, and in what ways, would the Soviets' advanced space-exploration knowledge be applied to military endeavors? And why had the United States not accomplished a similar feat? A crisis of confidence and a rapid reassessment of priorities followed. The United States did not know why it had fallen behind, but it was determined to regain the ground it had lost and to overtake the Soviets in scientific know-how. The space race had begun.

Scientific research was more than just academic: advances in science were a matter of national defense, and ultimately, national pride. All manner of legislation was soon couched in the terminology of international competition. In 1958 Congress created the National Defense Education Act, a government-subsidized student loan program promoted as essential for the training of tomorrow's scientists. The designation of scientific advances as a top priority led to dramatic increases in government funding for scientific research: it nearly tripled over the course of five years, climbing from $5 billion in 1959 to $13 billion in 1964.

The vigorous new national commitment to science also led President Dwight Eisenhower to create the Advanced Research Projects Agency (ARPA) in 1958 as part of the Defense Department. ARPA was presented to the public as an agency with a mission—the bolstering of national defense. But it also gave Eisenhower, a passionate believer in scientific exploration, an opportunity to use government funds to carry out open-ended research. ARPA and its projects easily won congressional approval in an atmosphere charged with fears that the United States lagged behind its Cold War competitor. The new agency's exploratory mandate attracted many of the nation's most talented and ambitious scientists.

However, ARPA was not an only child for long. Shortly after ARPA's creation came the National Aeronautics and Space Administration (NASA), a sexier younger sibling who stole all of ARPA's thunder and most of its budget. With responsibility for space exploration removed from ARPA's mandate and given over to NASA, ARPA scientists had to turn toward other areas of experimental research. Under the visionary leadership of J. C. R. Licklider, ARPA soon began exploring the possibilities of computers and information processing. How could they help humans to be more productive? In addition to conducting its own extensive research on the feasibility of connecting computers across long distances, ARPA also funded independent efforts to establish networks. One such effort came to fruition in 1965, when Larry Roberts, a Boston-area computer scientist who would later head the agency, connected his computer via phone line with one in California. The connection proved that faraway computers could indeed exchange messages with one another.

As it turned out, it was a very real need to share scarce computer resources, rather than any grand theoretical scheme, that ultimately spurred the creation of ARPAnet. A frustrated ARPA manager, Bob Taylor, was exasperated at the sorry state of his own computers and weary of persistent requests for additional machines. He gave instructions for the agency to connect its computers with those of other computer scientists across the country. The ultimate result was ARPAnet, the first multicomputer network, consisting of an initial four research sites in late 1969. Twenty more would join within the next two years.

It is worth noting that ARPAnet was not, as is often repeated, created as part of some Cold War doomsday scenario. It is true that Paul Baran, a computer scientist at the military think tank RAND Corporation, had convinced government officials that the United States needed to establish a distributed communications system that could withstand a nuclear attack. In 1962 Baran presented a paper outlining the concept of a so-called distributed network. Unlike traditional networks, in which information traveled over one pathway to get to its destination, a distributed network would allow information to be sent over many different possible routes. This concept, also known as redundant routing, is a key element in the Internet.

Although Baran's work was extremely influential on the ARPAnet founders, his imagined network never came to fruition. Nevertheless, the nuclear war legend has been tenacious. That the ARPAnet was really created by scientists who wanted to exchange information had been all but forgotten by the time it was up and running.

Breakthrough Technology

The period stretching from the late 1950s to 1970 saw the computer itself change rapidly. In 1957 Seymour Cray and William Norris cofounded Control Data Corporation (CDC) with the intent of producing a new breed of supercomputer—a machine capable of performing a high volume of calculations at very high speeds. The supercomputers of the 1960s were indeed the fastest and most powerful yet, and they were hugely successful. They continued to improve in speed and memory capacity as the decade progressed, and the more powerful they became, the more problems they could solve, and the more researchers became interested in using them. This cyclical phenomenon—the more technology can do, the more it is needed to do—drives the evolution of computers in general, and networking in particular, to this day.

During the same period that the CDC was making computers much more powerful, technology was also developing that would make them much smaller. In 1959 two patents were filed for the integrated circuit, later to be known as the microchip. Up until then, the transistor had been the best technology available for wiring electronic equipment. The microchip made it possible to create much smaller versions of all kinds of electronics, including computers. But microchips also vastly increased computers power, measured in the number of calculations performed in a second. The first commercial chip could do sixty thousand; today's microchips can do more than five million—and what the chips did for processors and computer architecture, they did for networking as well.

The 1960s also saw the development of something we take for granted in the age of networks, "real-time" computing—systems that respond to input and integrate it with existing data immediately. Efforts to develop real-time systems for defense purposes were underway at Massachusetts Institute of Technology (MIT) and IBM in the 1950s. But the private sector did not seem to be clamoring for the technology. It was not until the skies were crowded with commercial airlines that real-time computing found its first nonmilitary use. Since the reservations process required constant updating, real-time systems were ideal for airlines. The first real-time reservations system, called SABRE, was completed by IBM for American Airlines in 1964. Its hardware was clunky by modern standards, but real-time systems were a revelation and were soon adopted throughout the business world. SABRE, which is still in wide use, was one of the first applications to be deployed across a wide area network—in that sense, one might think of it as the earliest Internet application.

As if all this weren't enough, the late 1950s to 1960s era also saw the birth of the most vital Internet tool after the computer: the modulator-demodulator, popularly known as the modem. Built by communications engineers at Bell Labs in 1958, the modem made it possible to use existing phone lines, which were analog, to transfer computer information, which is digital, to connect computers in different locations. While the original 300 baud modem seems impossibly slow compared to the 56,000 baud modems of today, it was the transport mechanism that allowed the Internet to exist. And soon enough, 56K modems will join the 300s—as fellow fossils.

Unfortunately, the rapid advances in computer hardware were not matched by forward movement in software. A defining event served as a wake-up call to the industry—the ill-fated debut of IBM's ambitious and error-ridden OS/360 operating system in 1967. Software code writers convened in Garmisch, Germany, the following year to address the problem. A consensus emerged that programmers were trying to do too much—they were creating programs that were all-encompassing but terribly complex, and therefore doomed to fail. A better approach, it was agreed, would be for individual developers to concentrate on discrete aspects of a program that could then be fitted together. Software developers began to call themselves engineers. The Garmisch conference was a milestone, marking the emergence of software as a rigorous discipline that took itself seriously.

Visionaries

Even a cursory look at the writings of Joseph C. R. "Lick" Licklider makes it clear: Licklider, a psychologist and a computer scientist, conceived the essential vision for the Internet. He had written extensively on the future of computers and on the human-computer relationship in the 1950s. Soon after he joined ARPA as director of its information technology division in 1962, he directed its staff to explore questions that were not strictly defense-related, and in fact, quite far afield.

Licklider instructed ARPA scientists to research time-sharing, a system that would allow several users to access one computer through individual stations. Although a small-scale time sharing system (allowing thirty users simultaneous access) had been funded by ARPA and was operational at MIT in the early 1960s, Licklider had commissioned and implemented a much larger system, one that let three hundred people log on, by 1965. The new time-sharing system, with hardware by General Electric and software by Bell Labs, soon became a computer industry standard.

Of equal if not greater importance was Licklider's move to forge professional ties with people at computer science departments at universities and research centers across the nation. In 1963 Licklider penned a now-famous memo addressed to these colleagues, whom he referred to as "the Intergalactic Computer Network." He proposed the creation of what would become the Internet: a network that would link people together across geographical distances and allow them to communicate through their computers. At the time, Licklider's vision exceeded his hardware, but wheels were already in motion to change that.

Another major idea put forward in the 1960s would be critical to the way the Internet works. Computer enthusiast and antiestablishment thinker Ted Nelson, the self-described "Orson Welles of software," suggested that information stored on computers—documents that were normally accessed in sequential order—could be accessed *nonsequentially*. That could be accomplished, he theorized, through connections between documents called hyperlinks. Nelson argued that a system of texts that were linked together would give the user more control and make for more practical use of information. Hyperlinks and hypertext would soon form the basis of operating systems such as Microsoft Windows and later the World Wide Web. Nelson and his fellow "computer liberators" helped bring computing to the general public—they opened the doors to the library, metaphorically speaking, that others had built.

Nelson would go on to become a sainted leader to some and a comical figure to others—in 1995 Gary Wolf of *Wired* called Nelson's Xanadu project "the longest-running vaporware project in the history of computing." As digital gurus go, many prefer Canadian scholar Marshall McLuhan. With the publication of his *Understanding Media* (1964), McLuhan raised a cautionary flag that electronic forms of media were not neutral and would inevitably have effects on humans. He warned that the spread of a new kind of media on a mass scale would transform society's way of thinking.

In particular, McLuhan was fascinated by the differences between what he called "hot" and "cool" media. Hot media engage the senses but provide limited interactivity. Radio, because it enters directly through the ear, is a hot media. Cool media allow more sensual distance and increased interactivity. Print is cooler than radio because of the sensual distance. But because it keeps the distance and also encourages interactive channel surfing, television is cooler than print. Television was, during McLuhan's time, the ultimate "cool" medium. He warned politicians to save in-depth debate for a "hot" media like radio or print, and focus television campaigns on visually arresting symbols which would stop the viewer from changing the dial.

Of course, this was before the Internet, which McLuhan acolytes argue is the coolest of all. Today, new media enterprises carry on McLuhan's observations with hot terms like "hits" and "splash page" (the first page to catch a viewer's eye) versus cool "click throughs" (the number of times a surfer actually clicks an icon, rather than scanning it). McLuhan's ideas about the effects of media on communities also continue to add fuel to current debates about the Internet. Is the Internet a medium that will bring people together in virtual communities and open up new avenues of connection and intimacy between strangers? Or will it only isolate, drawing people into their homes and away from connection, community, and contact with their fellow humans?

These dilemmas were mere embryos in this 1957–1969 period, but not for long. Since ARPAnet's original links were to computer science departments at universities, the government-sponsored network was soon to be in the hands of the nation's students. Little did Congress know that it was funding the backbone of a system that would link the nation's young people, facilitating communication among hotbeds of social unrest in the midst of anti-Vietnam War protests—that a system designed as a strategic military tool would ultimately help hippies to find each other. In the late 1960s, computer networking begins its escape from the hermetic confines of military-sponsored computer labs and into the hands of visionary young scientists eager to stretch the limits of this new technology.

1957 SOVIET LAUNCH OF *SPUTNIK* KICKS OFF THE SPACE RACE

On October 4 the Union of Soviet Socialist Republics (USSR) launches the first human-made Earth satellite, Sputnik, *into orbit. To many Americans, the* Sputnik *launch indicates that the United States has allowed its scientific and military technology to lag perilously behind. The event causes hysteria in some circles and kindles a technological revolution.*

In 1952 the International Council of Scientific Unions had dubbed the period July 1, 1957, to December 31, 1958, the International Geophysical Year (IGY). The council's members resolved to launch Earth satellites during the IGY to map the planet's surface. In 1955, the U.S. government chose a contractor to build a satellite that was to be called *Vanguard*, but *Sputnik* threw a wrench in these plans.

Sputnik hurtles into orbit in 1957, its presence marked by a rocket booster that is visible from the ground. The satellite, a metallic object the size and shape of a beach ball, weighs 184 pounds. It remains in orbit around Earth for three months and then plummets back, burning up upon reentry into the atmosphere. Its sequel, *Sputnik II*, is launched November 3, 1957. This second satellite is the size of a small car, weighs one thousand pounds, and carries a live dog aboard for measuring biological data (no arrangements are made to return the dog safely to Earth, which makes a poor impression in the United States).

A crisis erupts in the United States in the weeks following the launch of the satellites. The Soviets' success suggests that they might be capable of launching intercontinental ballistic missiles and that they are ahead of the United States in cutting-edge technology. The *Sputnik* satellites jump-start the space race between the two countries.

U.S. President Eisenhower responds with tremendous, unprecedented support for the development of space and other technologies. The *Vanguard* project is scrapped, making way for the more ambitious satellite *Explorer I*, launched on January 31, 1958. It carries scientific instruments, initiating the age of extraterrestrial exploration.

The *Sputnik* crisis also yields the Advanced Research Projects Agency (ARPA), which gives rise to ARPAnet, the predecessor of the Internet. Other results include the National Aeronautics and Space Administration (NASA) and general progress in many fields of science made possible by a drastic increase in government funding for scientific research: from $5 billion in 1959 to $13 billion in 1964.

WHATEVER BECAME OF THE MILITARY-INDUSTRIAL COMPLEX?

In his presidential farewell speech in 1960, Eisenhower warned the nation that "we must guard against the acquisition of unwarranted influence, whether sought or unsought, by the military-industrial complex"—his name for the sprawling connections between the military, universities, and American industry.

One aspect of this unwarranted influence that troubled Eisenhower was the sacrifice of pure scientific research. Pure science—not specifically related to defense—was being compromised in industry and at universities by the "cash cow" lure of American military contracts. In Eisenhower's words, "Today...partly because of the huge costs involved, a government contract becomes virtually a substitute for intellectual curiosity."

With the sense of a good businessman, the president used ARPA to consolidate military spending and encourage pure research. Eisenhower stressed to the public that ARPA was created in the interest of national defense. But many historians assert that Eisenhower himself was never as concerned about "missile gaps" as the public was, primarily because the president had access to classified spy plane footage that showed precisely what the Russians were stockpiling.

Similarly while ARPAnet, ARPA's most famous program, won its funding thanks to Cold War panic, fear of Russia may not have been the real motivator. Paul Baran, a computer communications specialist at the RAND Corporation (the premier military think tank of the time), had been talking for years about building a decentralized information system to withstand nuclear attack; ARPAnet was proposed to do just this. It's not at all clear, however, whether scientists running ARPA were particularly interested in fulfilling Baran's vision. What they really wanted to do was trade scientific knowledge, and RAND's nuclear war scenarios provided the perfect rationale for military funding of a digital communications system.

Funds for scientific research continued to flow throughout the Cold War, but in the late 1980s the situation changed dramatically. By 1989 the Berlin Wall had come down and the collapse of the Soviet Unions was imminent, leading to a general downsizing of military spending more appropriate to peacetime politics. Aerospace companies, once fiercely competitive for military moneys, were now forced into unholy alliances with their competitors. Old "winner takes all" contract rules of the past were made more equitable, as companies struggled to keep profit margins high enough to continue doing business.

In short, observes *Scientific American* contributing editor Paul Wallich, "the military-industrial complex still continues to exist, but it's less, well, complex." Some critics have warned that as military contractors like General Electric and Westinghouse switch their capital from military to entertainment investments (buying television networks NBC and ABC, respectively), we may be in more danger from a "media-industrial complex" than from a military one.

Nevertheless, the military-industrial complex is far from over. In spite of a 40 percent reduction in military manpower since the 1950s, critics charge that there has yet to be even a 15 percent reduction in overall military spending enacted through Congress. And while the Internet may well have outgrown its military parentage, other popular computer applications (digital imaging, video technologies, and virtual reality) mewl in their infancy, swaddled in the thick funding of the Pentagon.

Beyond the Net

1957 SEYMOUR CRAY COFOUNDS CONTROL DATA CORPORATION

Computing engineers Seymour Cray and William Norris establish Control Data Corporation (CDC) to build supercomputers—large-scale machines with high processing speeds—for scientific calculation. Thought by some observers to be a risky and costly endeavor, CDC becomes an enormous success.

Cray and Norris had worked for Sperry Rand (previously Remington Rand), producing successors to UNIVAC (UNIversal Automatic Computer), the first successful electronic computer built for data processing. Designing logic, circuits, and software for UNIVAC-like machines, Cray developed an interest in pushing the limits of the computing frontier. When his desire to increase computing power began to conflict with Sperry Rand's main goal of increasing computer sales, he decided to form a new company.

With Norris and several other UNIVAC engineers, Cray organizes CDC in Minneapolis, Minnesota, and begins to design computers capable of high-volume, high-speed, very accurate arithmetic. The team hopes to sell its machines to a few select customers who perform large amounts of scientific computation, such as the government's Department of Defense, aircraft companies, and universities.

CDC's first computer, the model 1604, is completed in 1958 despite troubling cash shortages. Designed mostly by Cray and containing some of the cheapest electronic equipment to be found in Minneapolis, the CDC 1604 is among the most powerful supercomputers of the time but less expensive than other firms' models. Cray tops himself in 1964 with the CDC 6600; the fastest, most powerful computer yet developed. It makes CDC into an industry leader.

Cray forms yet another new company in 1972, Cray Research, Inc. The CRAY-1 supercomputer, released in 1976, is the breathtaking result of more than a decade of Cray's methodical, reclusive design efforts. Far more powerful than any of its contemporaries, it performs 240 million calculations per second. Cray's machines are the precursors of modern supercomputers, which are prized for mathematical modeling of such complex systems as air and water flow, nuclear technology, global economics, airline traffic, and weather patterns.

1958 RESEARCHERS AT BELL TELEPHONE LABORATORIES DEVELOP THE MODEM

Working at Bell Telephone Laboratories, communications engineers build the first modem, a device that converts data from the computer format (digital) to the telephone-line format (analog) and back again. Modems make computer networks possible, and advances in telecommunications and computer technology continually improve the modem during the next four decades.

The motivation for the development of modems was the need for communicating over "long haul networks," such as between computers located in different buildings, cities, or even countries. The obvious choice was to attempt to connect these systems by using the existing telephone network.

In 1950 government authorities wanted to speed up the transmission of remotely gathered radar data to processing centers. In a few years Bell Labs provided equipment, compatible with teletypewriters, that operated at 1,600 bits per second. But by then digital computers were on the rise, and a new type of modem was going to be required to convert digital computer data into analog signals for transmission on telephone lines. (Digital information is represented in discrete units, whereas analog information is represented along a smooth continuum; digital and analog clocks provide a useful example of the difference between the two formats.)

The DATAPHONE, the first commercial modem, designed by Bell Labs (Image courtesy of The Computer Museum History Center).

By 1958 researchers at Bell Labs have developed a device that can convert data between digital and analog format. The device is called a modem (short for modulator-demodulator), or a data terminal or data set. A commercial service is offered based on this equipment, which transmits at only 1,000 bits per second. As research continues during the 1960s, modems that transmit as swiftly as 250 kilobits per second are introduced. In the late 1960s AT&T develops the completely digital DATAPHONE system, which requires new transmission cables that can carry digital information.

In the 1970s the technology of integrated circuits (electronic devices that contain numerous transistors etched onto the surface of a silicon chip) allows the construction of modems with considerably enhanced speed and performance. These advances in hardware and software ultimately paved the way to the much faster current modems employing data compression and highly advanced error detection and correction algorithms.

1958   THE ADVANCED RESEARCH PROJECTS AGENCY BEGINS OPERATION

The Advanced Research Projects Agency (ARPA) is organized as a response to the Sputnik *crisis of the previous year. ARPA researchers, who are given free reign to develop advanced technology with long-term potential, eventually devise a computer network that predates the Internet.*

Late in 1957 the Soviets had launched the first two human-made satellites (*Sputnik I* and *II*), setting the stage for a space race with the United States. U.S. President Dwight Eisenhower assured the panic-stricken public that he was committed to overshadowing the Soviets' accomplishments by throwing massive support into science and technology. By the end of 1957 he envisions ARPA, whose roots had already been taking shape prior to *Sputnik.*

A vociferous supporter of science, Eisenhower works closely with his recently sworn-in secretary of defense Neil McElroy and presidential science advisor James R. Killian Jr. to get ARPA rolling. Congress approves a start-up fund of $520 million and a planned annual budget of $2 billion. Roy Johnson, a vice president at General Electric, is chosen as ARPA's first director; he supervises a staff of seventy who evaluate research proposals from individual contractors.

At its inception ARPA has control over all space and missile programs, and at first nearly all the agency's efforts are thrown into the development of space-related military technology. But by late summer 1958, the National Aeronautics and Space Administration (NASA) has been formed and all space research moves to the new organization. ARPA is left with relatively few funds.

Johnson resigns as ARPA's director, leaving his staff with a recommendation to make a complete overhaul of the agency's goals. Quickly ARPA is sculpted into a general-purpose research and development engine with the aim of pursuing advanced, far-reaching, and even high-risk scientific projects. In the following years ARPA attracts some of the most highly respected and hardest-charging researchers from around the country.

Within a few years ARPA researchers become happily entangled in the computer revolution and formulate the basic architecture of modern computer networks and communications.

1959 Texas Instruments and Fairchild Semiconductor Introduce the Integrated Circuit

Two independent patents for the integrated circuit, now commonly known as the microchip, are filed with the U.S. Patent Office. The integrated circuit, a tiny device in which all elements of an electronic circuit are etched onto a single slice of semiconducting material (usually silicon), makes it possible to create miniaturized electronic equipment.

In 1948 Bell Telephone Laboratories had introduced the transistor, an electronic switching and amplifying mechanism that replaced the bulky vacuum tube. Transistors became so widely implemented that engineers were devising electronic equipment containing numerous transistors interconnected by a complex array of wiring. This began to cause roadblocks in the design and assembly of electronics, and by the mid-1950s many research institutions were actively seeking a solution.

Two inventors independently come up with the idea for an integrated circuit at about the same time: Robert Noyce of Fairchild Semiconductor, and Jack Kilby of Texas Instruments. In the summer of 1958 Kilby outlines the basic design of a "monolithic circuit" (from the Greek monolithos, meaning single stone), a circuit contained entirely on one piece of silicon. In September he demonstrates a crude prototype (made of germanium rather than silicon) and follows up with continued improvements. Texas Instruments files its patent for the integrated circuit on February 6, 1959. Meanwhile, Noyce is gearing up to solve the "tyranny of numbers," as the transistor-interconnection problem has been dubbed. On July 30 he submits (in the name of Fairchild Semiconductor) his integrated-circuit design for patent consideration.

Due to its greater specificity, Noyce's patent is accepted in 1961, before Kilby's. Nevertheless, the two engineers share the title co-inventor of the integrated circuit or microchip.

NASA is the microchip's first major champion, purchasing one million devices by 1969 for the *Apollo* lunar flight program. In 1964 the first commercially available microchip appears in a hearing aid. These early microchips measure less than one-quarter of one square inch and carry the equivalent of ten transistor circuits; by 1969, one thousand circuits are embedded on a single chip; and modern microchips now carry thousands of circuits. Microchips revolutionize computing by transforming room-sized machines into individual computers that sit on desks across the world. The microchip is one of the crucial elements in computer history, allowing miniaturization and making possible the intimate human-machine interaction that characterizes modern computing.

1962 PAUL BARAN'S PAPER OUTLINES PACKET SWITCHING

Computer engineer Paul Baran writes a paper, "On Distributed Communication Networks," describing what later becomes known as packet switching, in which digital data are sent over a distributed network in small units and reassembled into a whole message at the receiving end. Packet switching will be an integral part of the ARPAnet a few years later.

Baran had approached the packet-switching idea out of concern for national security. In 1959 he had begun working for RAND Corporation, an agency set up after World War II to shelter United States' defense-related research. One of RAND's major endeavors was strengthening national communications systems, a crucial element of any defensive action that might be taken against a theoretical nuclear attack. Baran joined these efforts, which were driven by the mounting tensions of the Cold War. Baran was convinced that communications systems—particularly those controlling strategic weapons—were extremely vulnerable and would not survive even a mild disruption, let alone a nuclear attack. In 1960 he began formulating ideas for a system that could continue to function effectively even after some of its sub-components were destroyed. After two years of work on the problem, he writes "On Distributed Communication Networks," a document containing two creative, farsighted ideas.

THE FIRST WAR GAME: SPACEWAR, 1962

As politicians raged over the Cuban Missile Crisis, Steve Russell wrote Spacewar, the first official computer game, in 1962. "We had this brand new PDP-1 [computer]," the Massachusetts Institute of Technology (MIT) student recalled in *Rolling Stone*. "Here was this display that could do all sorts of good things! . . .We decided that probably you could make a two-dimensional maneuvering sort of thing, and decided that naturally the obvious thing to do was spaceships."

Primitive by today's standards, Spacewar, which used text characters to rotate rocket ships and fire torpedoes, was an immediate hit. Within weeks of its introduction, versions of the game (which was never copyrighted) were being played around the country. Digital Equipment, the company that provided MIT with the computer in the first place, was delighted by the hack; they began using Spacewar to demonstrate the capabilities of the PDP-1 and included it free with every installed system. Later, Spacewar enthusiasts at MIT devised the first gaming joystick, which helped players to better control the ships.

Spacewar garnered rabid fans; chief among them was Nolan Bushnell, who later founded Atari in order to "play Spacewar at home." The game was most certainly one of the earliest programs ported across the ARPAnet. According to computer scientist Alan Kay, "Spacewar blossoms spontaneously wherever there is a graphics display connected to a computer."

The computer game industry began by simulating the struggles of the Cold War. Today experts claim that soldiers trained on video games have faster reflexes than their non-gaming counterparts. War games like the specially developed Marine Doom are required training in many parts of the military. It all began with the first war game—Spacewar—which you can check out at: http://lcs.www.media.mit.edu/groups/el /projects/spacewar/.

From the Hacker File

Baran's first idea proposes modifying the general structure of existing communications networks. Instead of the common decentralized network (used by the telephone system), in which several interconnected main centers are linked to nearby locations, Baran envisions a distributed network. A distributed network looks more like a net, with each point, or location, connected only to its immediate neighbors. Messages have multiple pathways by which to reach their destinations.

His second idea concerns the method by which messages are sent through the distributed network. He concludes that the most efficient way is to chop up the original message and send it in small portions, each one able to travel by a different route. The whole message is then reassembled at its destination. The traditional method of sending messages in streams of data is inefficient because the data travel in bursts linked by pauses—empty, wasted time that ties up the line. Baran's proposal allows lines to remain relatively free and to carry numerous brief blocks of messages simultaneously.

Baran's theory is so unconventional that it fails to gain the support of any communications giants, such as AT&T, that could promote and institute it. By 1965 Baran resigns himself to focusing on other projects.

Coincidentally, in England physicist Donald Davies independently develops the chopped-up message idea at about the time Baran abandons it. Davies calls the method "packet switching," a name that sticks. Packet switching takes the stage two years later when Larry Roberts adopts it for ARPA's nascent computer networking program.

1963 ASCII CHARACTER REPRESENTATION IS STANDARDIZED

The American National Standards Institute (ANSI) renders the ASCII character table as the standard character representation system for the computer industry. ASCII stands for American Standard Codes for Information Interchange.

A keyboard displays the characters (numbers, letters, punctuation marks, symbols, etc.) that make up the language people use to communicate. But internally, computers use the binary system, in which numbers are represented by sequences of ones and zeros, to store, process, and exchange information. Computers need to translate all information into binary numbers, and ASCII is one way to accomplish this task. ASCII designates a particular binary number to each character. Each time a key on the keyboard is pressed, the corresponding ASCII number is transmitted to the computer.

The ASCII character table contains several coding schemes: decimal, hexadecimal, octal, and binary. Since computers work by translating everything into binary code, a programmer only needs the character representation ("A") and its binary equivalent ("1000001"). Early programmers, however, finding it hard to memorize and work with the binary system, used octal (base eight), and hexadecimal (base sixteen, also referred to as "hex") notation.

ASCII, one of the first standards in the computer industry, allows for the quick and efficient data translation and exchange between computer components and different computer systems.

1963 Joseph C. R. Licklider Pens Visionary Memo to "Members and Affiliates of the Intergalactic Computer Network"

J. C. R. Licklider, head of ARPA's command and control division, asserts in a memo to his coworkers and contractors that the time is ripe for developing an integrated computer network. His vision shifts the research focus of the command and control division from defense-related computing to time-sharing systems, computer graphics, and computer languages.

Licklider's background was in psychology. While working at MIT's Acoustics Laboratory in the 1950s, he became at first interested in, and then passionately preoccupied by, computing and its future. In a paper titled "Man-Computer Symbiosis," he offered the unorthodox view that computers would become much more than just calculating tools. They would augment the powers of the human intellect, he wrote, by performing the tedious, complex tasks associated with advanced research. This would provide the researcher with more information, more accurate results, and more time to make informed, intelligent decisions. Licklider's enthusiasm infected his students and colleagues and established his reputation as a computer scientist.

In 1962 Licklider accepted the job of directing a newly formed and loosely defined division at ARPA that soon adopted the name Information Processing Techniques Office (IPTO). Essentially shaping IPTO's goal to fit his vision of computing's future, Licklider mandated research into time-sharing computers. The time-sharing system took full and efficient advantage of the computer's capabilities by allowing numerous people (on separate terminals) to use a single computer simultaneously. The time-sharing idea had been introduced at MIT in the late 1950s to circumvent the bottleneck of students and researchers waiting to use the few available computers. It fit perfectly with Licklider's commitment to exploring human-machine interaction.

To see his research projects carried out, Licklider forms alliances with computer scientists at the most advanced academic computer centers across the country: MIT, Stanford University, the University of Utah, Carnegie Mellon University, and the University of California at Berkeley and Los Angeles. He calls this group of researchers and scientists the "Intergalactic Computer Network." In 1963 he sends all "Members and Affiliates" of this network a memorandum outlining an idea for an

J. C. R. LICKLIDER

As a psychologist, Joseph Carl Robnett Licklider (or "Lick") was unique among pioneers in the computer revolution. He insisted on the importance of the human factor in computing, and he advocated research into the interaction between humans and computers. Before the advent of personal computers, he viewed computers as an extension of the human being, and his radical notions were crucial stepping stones toward modern interactive computing.

Licklider was born in 1915 in St. Louis, Missouri. His technological interests began with an early and impassioned fondness for model airplanes. He studied physics, chemistry, the fine arts, and psychology at Washington University, earning undergraduate degrees in psychology, mathematics, and physics. For his Ph.D. in psychology, he studied the puzzle of how animals' brains determine the distance and direction of sounds.

Licklider continued to perform research in physiological psychology and in the 1940s became a professor at Harvard University, where he was admired by students and respected by fellow faculty. He remained at the forefront of technology research with a move to MIT in the late 1940s. Recruited to head a new human-engineering group at Lincoln Lab, MIT's air-defense laboratory, he worked extensively with computers for the first time.

Licklider believed that technological progress had the power to save humanity. He spoke of computers as the key to this progress, of "home computer consoles" connected in a network that linked people to information and knowledge. In 1960 he published the essay "Man-Computer Symbiosis," in which he discussed his idea that computers would eventually help people make decisions. Computers and human brains, he imagined, would exist in tight partnerships, yielding more efficient data processing and creative work than either humans or computers could perform alone.

During his two years as head of ARPA's information technology division (1962-1964), Licklider made some indispensable contributions. He was responsible for planting the seeds of a revolutionary idea, that of connecting computers at remote sites into a vast network. Licklider died in 1990, after the ARPANet had transformed into an Internet with millions of users worldwide.

interactive network linking people together via computer. He envisions geographical barriers falling, as researchers share information and like-minded people communicate, all at the push of a few buttons. The seeds of the Internet are sown.

1964 IBM's SABRE, THE FIRST COMPUTERIZED AIRLINE RESERVATIONS SYSTEM, IS IMPLEMENTED

The SABRE project, developed by IBM in association with American Airlines, comes into full operation, revolutionizing airline reservations. It represents the largest real-time computing task ever undertaken in the civilian sector and highlights the superiority of real-time systems for the future of computing.

In the 1940s, airline reservation centers were hectic, noisy enterprises where scores of clerks processed hundreds of phone calls per day and handled all data manually. The absence of automation was due to the nature of existing computer technology—batch processing, which was ill-suited to the needs of airline reservations. Batch-processing computers (at that time, electromechanical machines) operated by sorting hundreds of transactions into a batch before processing. This method was more efficient than processing each transaction individually because it enabled the computer to perform preparatory tasks for a given transaction type only once for a batch of numerous transactions. However, batch processing was not appropriate for airline reservations, as each transaction (making or canceling a reservation) required immediate processing in order for the whole system to remain current and effective. Airline reservations were to become automated with the introduction of real-time computer systems, those that respond to input within seconds (or faster)—that is, within "real time."

SABRE's history began with MIT's Project Whirlwind, an enormous, ambitious plan to build a real-time flight simulator for training pilots during World War II. Whirlwind, an eight-year, $8-million project, gave rise to the SAGE (Semi-Automatic Ground Environment) air-defense network, an $8-billion product of Cold War tension. The SAGE project involved several industrial contractors, but the largest participant was IBM, which thereby gained extensive experience in real-time technology and became a leader in the subsequent commercial application of real-time systems. Whirlwind and SAGE, both military efforts, were the first significant real-time computing endeavors.

By 1953 American Airlines was faced with a crisis situation: air traffic had increased, scheduling had become more complex, competition and demand had forced ticket prices down, and new jet airplanes— costing several million dollars—had been introduced. In 1945 American had installed an electromechanical reservation system, Reservisor, but it was far too slow and limited to accommodate increased reservation activity. American's executives turned to IBM in 1957 to help them plan a real-time reservation system. A team of researchers from the two companies was formed to select the specifications of the mainframe and terminal computers, the communication lines, and the system architecture. In 1960 the name SABRE was chosen for the project—reportedly from an advertisement for the Buick LeSabre automobile—and an acronym was concocted: Semi-

Beyond the Net

MATTERS OF LIFE AND DEATH

In 1963 Licklider predicted computers might one day process information so accurately, humans would rely on them to make crucial decisions. Late that same year, Americans shocked by the assassination of their president turned to the most accurate technology available at that time—film—just as Licklider envisioned they would one day turn to computers.

On November 11, 1963, President John F. Kennedy was shot to death by an unknown gunman, in full view of network television cameras. The mystery and confusion following the assassination demanded the visual coverage only television could provide, and some have called this "the day TV grew up." Television completed its passage from entertainment oddity of the 1939 World's Fair to America's main source of news coverage. Nevertheless, it was Abraham Zapruder—an ordinary man with a home movie camera—who wound up capturing the most accurate view of the crime. Because of its position, Zapruder's camera saw more of what happened to the president than did the television crews or panicked witnesses. To this day, the Zapruder film remains "the most-debated 5.6 seconds in movie history."

Anyone who has watched a photo finish in sports can understand why we have come to think of film as a reliable indicator of truth. Cameras access information faster than the human eye, and film can be replayed as many times as needed for comprehension. Today, investigators use computers to "watch" film footage for them, searching for significant patterns indistinguishable to the unaided eye. It is now unthinkable to present a controversial piece of video in a trial without first subjecting it to a battery of computerized analyses; so in one sense, Licklider's prophecy of computer-aided decision-making has become a reality.

But it took the Internet to bring the Licklider's dream to the public. Because they are relatively cheap and easily moved from server to server, Net sites often serve as forums to challenge official media coverage of controversial events. For instance, the Zapruder film—once classified material—has been readily viewable in MPEG format to anyone who knows where to look on the Net. Likewise, if you do searches using the words "Zapatista" or "Free Tibet," you'll eventually stumble onto information deemed "classified" by the governments of Mexico and China.

It's hard to know what Licklider would think about a time when teenagers with good Net connections might know more about the world than technophobic politicians. He would probably be delighted, providing that the teenagers in question have the sophistication to think critically about what they see. As Licklider, a psychologist, was well aware, we can use our computers to process information, but only the human mind can decide what is true and what is false.

Automatic Business Research Environment. The system was also referred to as Saber, a word connoting sharpness and accuracy.

Costing $30 million, SABRE is fully implemented in 1964. At its heart are two IBM 7090 mainframe computers connected to a storage unit capable of holding 800 million characters. The mainframe is linked to the individual terminals of 1,100 travel agents in fifty cities across the country. Able to process ten million reservations per year, the system also successfully handles the company's internal planning, reporting, scheduling, and management of flights, crew, and maintenance.

In response to SABRE, other leading airlines institute similar real-time reservation systems throughout the 1960s. Over the next few decades, real-time computer systems make their way into other industries such as banking, retailing, and the stock market.

1965 LARRY ROBERTS CONNECTS COMPUTERS IN MASSACHUSETTS AND CALIFORNIA VIA A DEDICATED PHONE LINE

Larry Roberts, a young computer scientist at Lincoln Laboratory in Boston, creates the first long-distance computer connection, a rudimentary telephone-line link between his computer and one in Santa Monica, California. The event demonstrates the feasibility of connecting distant computers and breaks a path toward computer networking.

After receiving his Ph.D. from MIT in 1963, Roberts had begun working at MIT's Lincoln Laboratory, writing computer operating systems and learning the design of computers inside and out. Much of his work there was funded by ARPA. In 1964 he attended a national computing conference, where he became enthralled by the prospect of building computer networks after listening to the inspiring words of J. C. R. Licklider.

In 1965 psychologist Tom Marill proposes that ARPA fund a long-distance computer connection between Lincoln Laboratory's TX-2 computer and System Development Corporation's Q-32 in Santa Monica. ARPA agrees and Lincoln appoints Roberts as the project supervisor. The link, which is realized over a four-wire Western Union telephone line, allows the machines to send messages to each other. The device that connects the computers to the phone line operates extremely slowly and is not terribly reliable. However the experiment offers hope, proving that such a connection is possible.

In 1966 ARPA recruits a reluctant Roberts to head its computer networking program. Roberts is concerned that his new job will entail undesirable bureaucratic responsibilities, but instead he becomes one of the chief designers and advocates of the ARPAnet, the first multiple-computer network.

1965 ARPA Conducts a Study on Networks of Time-Sharing Computers

A time-sharing computer system called Multics (Multiplexed Information and Computing Service) is launched by ARPA to stretch the limits of time-sharing and interactive computing. The program illustrates the strength of the time-sharing concept.

When J. C. R. Licklider had taken over the computer division at ARPA in 1962, he immediately designated time-sharing systems as a research priority. The largest time-sharing system that ARPA funded at this time was MIT's Project MAC (Multiple Access Computer), which consisted of an IBM mainframe hosting 160 terminals, funded by a $3-million grant. MAC allowed thirty users to log on at the same time; they could do calculations, write and run programs, and prepare documents using a primitive method of word processing.

By 1965 MAC is successful but overloaded, leading ARPA to finance Multics, a more extensive time-sharing system. MIT computer scientists decide to commission a new mainframe computer from General Electric instead of IBM, because they feel that IBM's machines are ill-suited for time-sharing and its administrators reluctant to adopt the appropriate technology. General Electric designs the model 645 computer, which supports one thousand terminals and allows three hundred simultaneous log-ons. Bell Telephone Laboratory prepares the software, and Multics is completed at a cost of $7 million. Subsequently, IBM and many other computer manufacturers introduce time-sharing computers.

1965 Ted Nelson Coins the Terms Hypertext and Hyperlink

Ted Nelson, self-appointed "computer liberator," introduces the terms hypertext and hyperlink to refer to the structure of a (theoretical) computerized information system through which a user navigates nonsequentially.

In the early 1960s amateur computer enthusiasts had increased in numbers across the United States and Europe. A group whose members called themselves "computer liberators" was organized around the desire to bring computing power to the ordinary person at a reasonable cost. Computer liberators were afraid that if the government and large corporations retained exclusive control over computing technology, the computer's extraordinary potential for serving all of humankind would be lost to bureaucratic regulation and censorship. By the mid-1960s, Nelson, a technologically educated, antiestablishment figure, had become an outspoken advocate of computer liberation.

Nelson also develops a revolutionary vision of the future of computers. Among his ideas is Xanadu, an information library contained on a computerized system, not unlike the famous memex concept developed by Vannevar Bush in 1945. Nelson's system is organized in a novel fashion. It consists of hypertext, in which users are allowed access to documents in a nonsequential manner, and hyperlinks, the weblike connections among the documents. Non-sequential retrieval of information (as opposed to the sequential organization of a book that is intended to be read page by page in a numbered order), asserts Nelson, makes the system highly efficient and facilitates the user's access to its contents.

Hypertext later becomes the standard structure of many personal computer software systems, and it is also integral to the architecture of the World Wide Web in the 1990s.

1966 BOB TAYLOR'S THREE COMPUTERS INSPIRE PLANS FOR THE ARPANET

Bob Taylor, head of computing programs at ARPA, starts the ball rolling for the creation of a national computer network. His goal is to provide scientific researchers with a convenient, inexpensive, and quick way to share resources across geographical distances.

Taylor had joined ARPA the previous year as deputy to Ivan Sutherland, the head of IPTO, the agency's computing division. Taylor shared the view of his boss's predecessor, J. C. R. Licklider, that computing's potential lay in increasing the sophistication of the interaction between humans and computers.

Early in 1966 Taylor is promoted to head of IPTO, where he inherits a room filled with the hardware of three computer terminals. The computers are three different makes, connected by telephone lines to mainframes operating in three different remote locations. To use each one Taylor has to remember a distinct set of commands, and he becomes frustrated with such a tedious procedure.

Imagining the Net

"THE MEDIUM IS THE MESSAGE"

Embarrassingly, when Canadians were asked in a recent survey, "Who said, 'The medium is the message'?" a large number responded "Bill Gates." In truth, credit for "the medium is the message" and another hot Internet slogan, "the global village," goes to Marshall McLuhan (1911-1980), a former professor at the University of Toronto. With the publication of *Understanding Media* (1964), McLuhan secured his position as, according to *Wired* magazine, "the patron saint of the Internet."

McLuhan argued that the form any communication takes—its medium—is identical to its meaning, or "message." On the Net, for instance, we constantly compare media and get different messages. When two people who've been typing to one another all day agree to exchange GIFs in order to see who they've been "talking" to, they are comparing media. If they like what they see, they may agree to "go voice" and speak over the phone. While the content of what is being said online or over the phone may remain the same, meanings shift with the technologies used. An image means something different than a text description; hearing someone's voice means something different than reading their words online.

McLuhan's work was visionary for its time. Prior to 1964, there was no Internet, and "comparative media" was nonexistent as an academic discipline. When McLuhan came to fame, print was the only thing deemed worthy of intellectual attention. There were no multimedia presentations in classrooms. Suggesting that a culture could be studied through its television commercials and pop songs was unthinkable.

McLuhan used his extensive training in the history of literature to make the case that "media" has existed forever: speech is a form of media, he was fond of saying, as is writing. Moreover, when the printing press was invented, critics of the seventeenth century were afraid of the same things people fear about "couch potato culture" today: that the new media of the day would cause too much time wasting, isolation from society, and a tenuous grasp on the truth.

But McLuhan was by no means a technophile; nowhere is this more clear than in his 1967 book *The Medium is the Massage* (his pun on "message.") These days, the term "global village" is associated with a kind of utopian vision of mass communication, but when McLuhan came up with the phrase in 1967 he wasn't so optimistic. He wrote, "Whether it is bombs being dropped upon Baghdad or Italy being defeated in a World Cup, many people around the world can share the same moment," but he also worried that the world, suffering from a type of "information overload," might collapse in on itself. If the advent of print moved man away from oral traditions, he warned, electronic media may well be moving us back toward our "tribal" beginnings—with their attendant dangers of nonlinear thought, panic, and irrationality. In other words, that which moves us technologically forward may well move us ethically backward.

McLuhan's theories were controversial in the 1960s and remain so today. It's not even clear whether he believed what he wrote; he was famous for responding to criticism with, "You don't like those ideas? I've got others." Yet his soundbites live on, as does his virtual persona. Though McLuhan died in 1980, he "co-authored" a book in 1989 (*The Global Village*) and was *Wired's* first e-mail interview in 1996.

Taylor's "terminal problem," as he dubs it, is a small-scale version of a more dire situation. At various IPTO-funded research projects at corporations and universities across the country, researchers are requesting increased funding for more extensive computer resources. As computers are neither cheap nor small, Taylor turns to networking, which has been at the top of IPTO's to-do list since its inception. He decides to go forward with a plan for creating a network of electronic links among the computers at the various research centers. Armed with a $1-million budget, he hires Larry Roberts to supervise the project, and three years later the ARPAnet is born.

1967   The Hypertext Editing System Is Formulated

Andries van Dam of Brown University develops the first operational hypertext system. It serves as an early model for subsequent hypertext programming endeavors.

Van Dam, a specialist in graphics, joined Brown University in 1965 as an instructor of computer science. With funding from IBM, he began a collaboration with students and Ted Nelson, an outspoken computer-liberation activist, to create the latter's dream of a hypertext system.

In 1967 van Dam's team completes the Hypertext Editing System (HES), a simple, unsophisticated program that allows nonsequential access to the various sections of a document. Students and professors affiliated with the university find uses for HES but quickly identify its many weak elements. IBM sells the program to the Houston Manned Spacecraft Center, where NASA uses it during the Apollo space program.

Van Dam goes on to develop more successful hypertext systems, such as FRESS (File Retrieval and Editing System) and the Electronic Document system, which are widely used in the 1970s in teaching and research. The systems' highlights include innovative aids to navigating documents, such as bidirectional reference links, keyworded links, and color graphics. Van Dam's work on hypertext systems introduces revolutionary elements that become standardized methods of interactive programming.

1967   Simula, the First Object-Oriented Computer Language, Is Written

Kristen Nygaard and Ole-Johan Dahl of the Norwegian Computing Center in Oslo formulate Simula, the first object-oriented programming language.

Netspeak

YOU SAY "HACKER," I SAY "CRACKER"

Net historian Steven Levy traces the earliest official use of the term "computer hacker" to the Tech Model Railroad Club (TMRC) at the MIT. Founded in the 1940s, the TMRC became a hacker haven in the 1960s, when Digital Equipment Corporation donated a minicomputer called the PDP-1. Although it was intended for academic research, the computer was quickly commandeered by the club to help run their model railroad station, complete with a (then revolutionary) digital clock.

The New Hacker's Dictionary (which evolved from a TMRC dictionary) calls a hacker "a person who enjoys exploring the details of programmable systems and how to stretch their capabilities." Steven Levy differentiates today's destructive hackers from the original computer pioneers with the word, "crackers." Some people dispute the hacker/cracker distinc-

tion, arguing that the line between "fun" and destruction is often a fuzzy one. Is there really that much difference, they ask, between MIT students who hacked administration systems simply because they were told not to and today's kids who break passwords to play pranks?

To people like Levy, the answer is an unequivocal "yes." Levy insists that old-time hackers never intentionally damaged the computers or systems with which they tampered. As TMRC puts it, "We resent the misapplication of the word [hacker] to mean the committing of illegal acts. People who do those things are better described by expressions such as 'thieves,' 'password crackers' or 'computer vandals.'"

Wherever you stand on the subject, you can keep current on all the latest hacker/cracker terminology by reading the hacker's bible, called the Jargon File, which is located at: http://earthspace.net/jargon/.

Object-oriented programming allows the user to assign specific procedures to sets of objects.

Simula is designed for simulating and analyzing the flow of traffic. The objects, or "data types," in a traffic scenario are the traveling vehicles such as cars, buses, and trucks. The "procedures" involved in traffic flow are the vehicles' responses to things like red lights, obstructions in the road, merging cars, and ambulance sirens. Simula assigns specific procedures to each data type, corresponding to the distinct ways that each vehicle responds to common elements of traffic. Given certain input (number of vehicles, percentages of each type of vehicle, locations of red lights and obstructions, etc.), the program can simulate the flow of traffic through a specified area.

Simula itself is never widely implemented, but it introduces terms and concepts that help shape the methodology of object-oriented programming. Object orientation becomes a common tool for graphic design, mathematical manipulation, and the creation of reusable software components tailored to a user's specific needs.

1967   THE SYMPOSIUM ON OPERATING PRINCIPLES FEATURES PACKET SWITCHING AND DESIGN FOR THE ARPANET

In October computer scientists gather in Gatlinburg, Tennessee, for the Symposium on Operating Principles, at which packet switching is described and the first plan for the ARPAnet is unveiled. The meeting adds crucial finishing touches to the proposed architecture of the ARPAnet.

When Larry Roberts joined ARPA in 1966, he began working on ARPA director Bob Taylor's vision of a computer network linking the leading computer science centers in the nation. Taylor and Roberts agreed that speed and reliability were to be important elements of the network, but they had not determined how to map it out or what type of lines to use. In early 1967 Taylor called a meeting of ARPA's university researchers at Ann Arbor, Michigan, to discuss the unresolved issues of network design. His and Roberts' leading proposal designated a portion of each center's computing power for routing and receiving messages within the network, an idea that proved unpopular. The meeting revealed that most of the researchers were unenthusiastic and in some cases hostile to the very idea of a network.

Despite the disappointments at Ann Arbor, Taylor and Roberts continued full speed ahead with their plans. Building on an idea put forth by Wesley Clark, a computer scientist at Washington University in St. Louis, Roberts devised a system of intermediate computers, or nodes, which he called Interface Message Processors (IMPs). The IMPs interconnected the network, sent and received data, scanned for errors, routed messages, and checked that messages arrived at their destinations. Roberts sent a memorandum outlining the new idea, and by that time the researchers had warmed up to the network idea, especially since the IMPs would allow them to keep all their computing power out of networking tasks.

In October, the Association of Computing Machinery sponsors the Symposium on Operating Principles in Tennessee, and again the leading computer scientists from across the country convene to discuss their progress. Roberts details a well-sculpted version of the ARPAnet plan, representing the first official public announcement of the network. More significantly, Roger Scantlebury, a member of a team headed by Donald Davies (the British engineer who coined the term "packet switching"), presents the design for a packet-switching network. This is the first Roberts and Taylor have heard of packet switching, a concept that appears to be a promising recipe for transmitting data through the ARPAnet.

Scantlebury also introduces the ARPA team to Paul Baran's packet-switching work, and in 1968 Baran becomes a consultant to ARPAnet's construction crew. Roberts completes the preliminary design for the ARPAnet—incorporating packet-switching technology—and begins planning the network.

1968   GARMISCH CONFERENCE ADDRESSES THE SOFTWARE CRISIS

In October computer scientists from around the world gather in Garmisch, Germany, to discuss an escalating problem: software developers are unable to keep pace with advances in computer hardware. The conference marks the birth of software development as a rigorous engineering discipline.

In the 1950s, as stored-program computers (those whose memories held both programming instructions and input data) entered the market, the art of programming had begun to take shape. The first major programming languages for scientific applications were FORTRAN and COBOL, and their dominance helped standardize software development. By the end of the decade, many computer manufacturers were writing software for business applications and including it with the purchase of a computer.

From 1960 to 1965 a crisis began to unfold in the computer-science community. Progress in computer hardware exploded, increasing the memory size and speed of the most advanced computers by a factor of ten. Meanwhile the technology behind software development remained stagnant. The underlying problem was the great complexity of large programs.

The spark that ignited the software crisis was the utter failure of IBM's operating system OS/360, the most ambitious programming endeavor to date. (An operating system [OS] is the software package that comes installed in a computer and enables a user to create and run programs.) In 1967 OS/360 entered the market, one year late and chock-full of errors. Designed to take advantage of the most powerful hardware available, the system was huge, involving more than a million lines of code written by hundreds of programmers working at full tilt for more than four years. OS/360 was the disastrous result of an untried methodology.

Similar frustrations crop up as other software developers attempt to produce large programs and operating systems. In 1968 the situation is reaching crisis proportions when the Garmisch conference is called to order, with hundreds of software designers at attention. Naming the meeting

Don't Trust Anyone Over Thirty

Like the teenagers who left their suburban homes, seeking out new paths as hippies, activists, and anarchists, computer networking in the 1960s went through an adolescent rebellion of its own. Originally a spawn of the establishment, the ARPAnet was turned over to universities, where it was forever transformed by the counterculture.

By 1969 ARPAnet host computers (called IMPs) had been set up at universities across the country. Professors barely had enough time to prepare for the arrival of their computers, never mind try to connect them to computers at other schools. Since the "grown-ups" were busy, the job of figuring out how to get computers across the country to speak to one another was left to graduate students.

That summer sixty-eight graduate students calling themselves the Network Working Group met to discuss networking protocols. Their first discussions were documented and titled "Requests for Comments" (RFCs). By deciding to call the documents "Requests for Comments" rather than "guidelines" or "memoranda," the students broke down the command and control that typified most computing circles of the time. In the book *Where Wizards Stay Up Late*, authors Katie Hafner and Matthew Lyon observe that the group's open, nonhierarchical style allowed people to feel that the ARPAnet was going to be "a kind of open club, that all were invited to join."

Net historian Steven Levy notes that the "hacker ethic" includes tenets such as "information wants to be free," "mistrust authority," and "hackers should not be judged based on degrees, age, race or position"—ideas that have roots in the sixties counterculture, particularly in the Free Speech movement at the University of California at Berkeley. On the Internet, the hacker ethic began with the Network Working Group, and the Net remains a place where protocols are discussed and debated in open forums among equals, rather than handed down from "on high."

The Internet's hippie inheritance is more than just philosophical, as evidenced by *The Whole Earth Catalog*, published in San Francisco in 1968. Once described as "the Sears catalog for the New Age," *The Whole Earth Catalog* featured products and advice for the counterculture lifestyle. In 1985 the makers of the catalog started their own Internet community, the Whole Earth 'Lectronic Link (WELL). Later on the catalog would spawn the magazine *Mondo 2000*, which in turn begat *Wired*. As this genealogy suggests, although most computer projects in the 1960s were sponsored by the military, the pioneers of the Internet were strongly influenced by the youth movement of the time.

Today some people argue that the Net has become so commodified that it has outgrown its military-turned-hippie beginnings. Nevertheless, no matter what the future holds, there will always remain certain elements of the Internet—online community-building, social activism, preteen computer wizards—that are reminders of 1968, the year young people changed America.

"Software Engineering," the organizers and attendees initiate the transformation of software development into an engineering discipline.

Following rough guidelines laid out at the conference, the next few years witness the establishment of theoretical foundations and practical methods for software design. One of the more influential ideas is "structured design methodology," in which first the overall program architecture is delineated, from which point the programmer's attention is focused solely and narrowly on the program's smallest details. This scheme frees the programmer from the distractions of the broader picture and yields fewer errors in programming code.

Software engineering evolves into a highly specialized field. By the early 1970s the standard practice of computer manufacturers is to sell packages of software separately from hardware, which helps to cover the skyrocketing costs of software development.

1969   THE ARPANET IS BORN

The preliminary connections of the ARPAnet, the first multiple-site computer network, are created successfully in December. The ARPAnet, intended to link research centers across the country, provides the foundation for advanced networking and breaks a path toward the Internet.

By 1968 Larry Roberts, the ARPAnet's original architect, had devised an outline of the network. It would rely on machines he had dubbed IMPs (Interface Message Processors), which would connect the individual sites, route messages, scan for errors, and confirm the arrival of messages at their destinations. In July 1968 Roberts sent a request for proposals to build the IMPs to more than one hundred computer companies. In December, surprising many contenders, he announced the decision to award the IMP contract to Bolt, Beranek and Newman (BBN), a small firm in Cambridge, Massachusetts.

For the next year BBN researchers, directed by Frank Heart, commit themselves to designing the IMPs. Enlisting the talents of the most promising computer scientists inside and outside the company, BBN works around the clock to deliver the first IMP by the Labor Day 1969 deadline.

BBN and ARPA request the assistance of computer scientists at the four initial sites to be connected: the University of California at Los Angeles, the University of California at Santa Barbara, the University of Utah, and

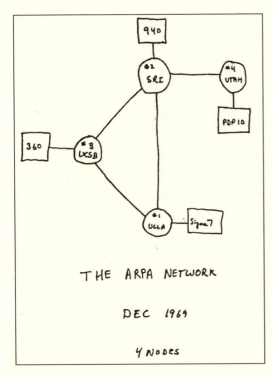

THE ARPA NETWORK

DEC 1969

4 NODES

A sketch of the original ARPAnet structure as outlined by Larry Roberts and his team: the first four nodes were the University of California-Santa Barbara and UCLA, SRI International, and the University of Utah (Image courtesy of The Computer Museum History Center).

Stanford Research Institute. The request elicits an overwhelming response, and numerous researchers—mostly graduate students filled with curiosity and enthusiasm—undertake to prepare their host computers for connection to the IMPs. The participation of so many graduate students shapes the anarchic culture of the ARPAnet and of networking communities in general.

Many are ultimately involved in ARPAnet design and completion, including Will Crowther, Dave Walden, Severo Ornstein, Bob Kahn, Vint Cerf, Steve Crocker, Ben Barker, and Truett Thach. Finding themselves on the cutting edge of computer technology, they develop new protocols, write software, connect wires, and unknowingly start the network revolution.

Two days before Labor Day, the first IMP, all nine hundred pounds encased in gray steel, arrives in Los Angeles. Right on schedule, the second reaches Stanford on October 1, and the third and fourth are installed by early December. Linked by dedicated telephone lines, the IMPS allow users to log on to remote computers and run their programs. The ARPAnet's four-node preliminary trial is a success.

A quickly formulated system for logging on to remote sites, Telnet, is implemented at the last minute. It is replaced by a glitch-free program, Network Control Protocol (NCP), in 1971. By spring of that year, nineteen other sites across the country have joined the ARPAnet. The following year, the network makes its public debut at the International Conference on Computer Communications in Washington D.C., and the idea for a much more expansive network sprouts roots all over the country.

What Does a Network Do?

The ARPAnet proved that computer networking was possible: more and more government and university computers were being linked together each year. But the civilian population had largely been left out of the loop. Most people were unaware that computer networks even existed. During the period covered in Chapter Three, regular people begin to have access to computer networks and to realize that they can do all sorts of things—in particular, communicate with each other in extraordinary new ways.

This chapter tells the story of vital technologies and events that all made the Internet what it is—the birth of the PC, the debut of e-mail, and the first virtual communities. In addition, several prominent individuals—crucial players in the Internet's development—will make their appearance. Bob Metcalfe, who invented Ethernet (a networking protocol), enters as a grad student and exits as the successful founder of 3Com. Vint Cerf, a professor at Stanford, will organize and chair an international working group to create a global network of networks. Together, Cerf and Bob Kahn will write a landmark paper that describes "an internet"—a network that will allow different types of computer networks to communicate through a transmission control protocol (TCP). Finally, an ambitious young software entrepreneur will found Microsoft and start a feud before the chapter is out.

Burn the Mother Down

The 1970s was the decade of disco, drugs, and women's lib. It was also a decade of high inflation and high unemployment—the first indication that the seemingly unperturbable prosperity of the 1950s and 1960s was turning sour. But without a doubt, two traumatic events shaped the nation the most profoundly—Vietnam and Watergate.

The Vietnam War, which the United States joined in 1965, did not officially end until May 1975, when Saigon fell. The war left fifty-six thousand U.S. soldiers dead and the nation profoundly disillusioned. For the first time, a large proportion of the populace had keenly opposed a war effort, opening up a painful national rift between patriots and peace lovers.

Watergate began with the break-in at Democratic National Committee headquarters at the Watergate Hotel in June 1972 and did not end until Nixon's resignation in August 1974. John Doar, who headed the House's impeachment investigation, summed up what had happened: "What [Nixon] decided should be done... required deliberate, contrived, continued, and continuing deception of the American people."

Nixon had broken laws and lied to cover them up, and he had used the Justice Department, CIA, FBI, and Secret Service to help him do it. It was surely not the first time a president had engaged in shady behavior, but it was the first time the dark side of an administration—the explicit details and sprawling extent of its unlawful activities—had been laid bare. It seemed that Americans lost an innocence they would never regain. It was replaced by a skepticism, and in some cases a permanent distrust, of all things governmental.

It was inevitable that some of the rampant antiwar and antigovernment sentiment of the 1970s would be funneled into aggression at computer networks, since they were mostly government-run at the time. Hacking, or breaking into computers, came into its own during this period, as did its kissing cousin, "phreaking," or breaking into telephone lines. Phreaking in particular was intimately connected to Vietnam, Watergate, and defiance of the System: in fact, Abbie Hoffman and the Yippies disseminated a how-to guide for stealing phone service as a form of war protest. The outlaw spirit continues today, as hackers register their contempt for the government and the commercialization of the Net by sabotaging government and corporate Web sites.

Three Networks Are Connected

In the 1970s three kinds of networks were forming simultaneously that would eventually be connected, although no one knew it at the time—networks that linked computers through radio connections such as ALOHAnet, established in Hawaii; SATnet, which used satellites to connect computers in the United States with several sites in Europe, and the growing ARPAnet.

Kahn, who oversaw Satnet's development in the early 1970s, soon became interested in connecting it to the other existing networks. Vint Cerf had been fixated on creating an international network of networks since 1971, and the two had already begun collaborating. But the three networks had different modes of transmission. ARPAnet, which by the mid-1970s had dozens of host computers, sent data over telephone lines, SATnet used satellites, and radio networks used radio waves.

A way had to be found for the three systems to communicate, and that way was the transmission control protocol (TCP), first described in a paper by Cerf and Kahn. In July 1977 the first message was successfully sent across the three networks using the TCP protocol. For some Net historians, this feat of connectivity marks the Internet's birth. In truth, the event may be too dryly technical to be selected as the Internet's true birthday: after all, television was invented in the earliest part of the twentieth century, but it is rightly viewed as a late-century phenomenon. The Internet as we know it is far more than a feat of engineering.

But still, every revolution—political, social, or technological—has to start somewhere. Cerf, Kahn, and their cohorts proved in 1977 that the theoretical idea of a network of computers could become a physical reality. From this point on, innovation would pile upon innovation, going from snowball to avalanche in a few short years.

Getting Ahead of Ourselves

When first J. C. R. Licklider, and later Cerf and Kahn, dreamed of creating an international network of networks—an Internet—nobody could have foreseen the extent to which the PC would affect it. People were trying to create the Internet long before the PC's arrival in the mid- to late-1970s, but the PC would open up a whole new array of possibilities.

Similarly, Bob Metcalfe's 1973 invention of Ethernet, the network design that allows computers to talk to each other over a local area network (LAN), also predated the wide use of the PC. Metcalfe had studied the architecture of ARPAnet and ALOHAnet and had brought ideas about both together in a design he called the Ethernet, after *ether*, a nineteenth century term for a theoretical substance that was believed to transmit electromagnetic waves. Metcalfe's Ethernet was realized when he was a researcher at Xerox PARC (Palo Alto Research Center) in California—then the unofficial world headquarters for computer research. Ethernet was actually developed to speed up the time it took to print from PC to laser printer, and it succeeded. The first Ethernet implementation sent data at three megabits per second, cutting printing time from fifteen minutes to an amazing twelve seconds.

LANs were revolutionary, and a major improvement on the technology they would replace—time sharing systems—because they allowed more than one person *at one location* to access the same files and printers. They were perfect for offices and universities. Again, it was for applications as yet unseen that an invention would be most useful. In an interview with *The Straits Times*, Metcalfe remarked, "The ironic thing was, I built Ethernet at a time when there weren't more than a hundred personal computers around the world, and most of them were at the Xerox laboratory."

The Ethernet standard now connects more than 100 million computers in networks across the world, but its commercial success was far from assured at the outset. Selling computer users on Ethernet was a bit of a job, Metcalfe explained in an interview with *The Herring* magazine; he had to convince people "one, that LANs were a good idea; two, they should be standard; and three, the standard should be Ethernet." In 1979, he started 3Com, now a telecommunications giant, to develop Ethernet-compatible products.

The Birth of the PC

The PC has unquestionably made the Internet what it is today, fundamentally shaping the medium and what it is used for. The PC has allowed people to go online at home, at work, or from the beach—given a laptop and a satellite connection. Says Tim Berners-Lee, the creator of the World Wide Web, "When you actually look at the spread of the Web...it needed ubiquitous computing, which means personal computers."

The debut of the Altair 8800, the first microcomputer, in 1975, sparked the PC revolution. Ed Roberts, the founder of Model Instrumentation Telemetry Systems (MITS), wanted to create a computer that individuals could afford, but he had no idea if people would want such a product. Intel Corporation was making microchips at the time but had no intention of building small computers around them. Roberts bought Intel's chips and made them the heart of the Altair 8800—a huge business risk that paid off when the company was overwhelmed with orders.

To actually do anything, the Altair needed software, and that is where young Bill Gates and Paul Allen came in. They wrote a programming system for the Altair in BASIC, an accessible language developed by programmers at Dartmouth College in the 1960s. They soon founded Microsoft and set to work on programs to interpret BASIC for more new PCs. The huge success of the MS-DOS and Windows operating systems—and domination of the world software market— were still in the future.

One cannot mention Gates' entry into the software world without learning about the debate he initiated in the 1970s, sometimes called the software flap. Gates' central argument was as follows: It is wrong to share software with your fellow computer users that someone else (such as Gates) could have sold them. Underlying that argument was the simple premise that there is money to be made from good ideas, as long as they are kept a secret. Gates throws the issue on the table when he becomes outraged that an Altair user has stolen and distributed the BASIC interpreter that Gates is supposed to be paid royalties for. Rallying to Gates' battle cry, business interests quickly form a consensus that software represents intellectual property—and potential revenues—that should clearly be protected.

Prior to the incident, researchers at computer science departments were unaccustomed to the notion that solutions to problems should be fiercely protected and sold. Most computer hobbyists were happy to share information amongst themselves and accept peer recognition as payment for their contributions. Many continue to be—indeed the "open software movement" of the late 1990s is entirely based on this philosophy. The philosophical conflict symbolized by the software flap remains unresolved today, as proponents of open-source software argue that, as a hacker motto puts it, "information should be free." Open-source fans point to the success of the Linux operating system, where many of its millions of users log on to help each other solve technical problems.

Unix, E-Mail, and Virtual Communities

Linux is a child of Unix, an operating system created by programmers at Bell Labs in 1969-70. They also developed a new programming language, called "C," that made Unix portable—able to run on different kinds of machines. By late in the decade the Unix to Unix Copy Protocol (UUCP) had been developed—a communications transfer protocol for the system. UUCP was the first answer to the question of how operating systems would talk to one another. Unix, rewritten in C, became hugely popular by mid-1980s, allowing many more people access to computers.

In 1973 at the University of Illinois, PLATO Notes, a program devised to facilitate the reporting of problems with the computer system, allowed users to read "posted" messages and to post their own. The program was soon expanded to set aside "conferences" for specific interests and hobbies, and the first chat rooms were born. The first Computerized Bulletin Board System (CBBS) would be open to the public in Chicago in 1979. In setting up the system, hobbyists Ward Christensen and Randy Suess accomplished a major feat—developing the first electronic posting network for civilians that was *not* a time-sharing system. Gradually, BBSs began to spring up all across the country.

Finally, this chapter will also tell the story of the first e-mail programs. In 1971, Ray Tomlinson wrote two programs that allowed ARPAnet users to exchange messages. The message programs immediately became the network's most popular feature. E-mail remains, without a doubt, the most popular feature of online services. Indeed, it is the main reason many people subscribe to them and is often singled out as the "killer app" of the Internet—although the World Wide Web may be giving e-mail a run for its money as the primary function of the Net.

Potential Problems Emerge

Yet another facet of computer networks became apparent in the 1970s—potential misuse by government entities. To a 1990s reader conditioned by conspiracy theorists and *The X-Files*, the idea that a government-run computer network could be used for surveillance purposes hardly raises an eyebrow. But in Watergate- and Vietnam-weary 1975, when a rumor circulated that Army officials had used the ARPAnet to store files on politically active individuals, the public was naturally up in arms. The incident made the public aware of the ARPAnet for the first time, and taught the government to keep a close eye on its network.

Not long after that first outbreak of electronic paranoia, the first encryption pro-grams were developed—programs that scramble digital information so that it can only be read by its intended recipient—to address online privacy concerns. As the Internet has exploded in the 1990s, fears of online privacy violation have only inten-sified. Recent concerns have focused on the security of electronic commerce and the issue of "cookies," files placed on surfers' hard drives that allow site operators to track their comings and goings on the Web. Encryption software is now standard for sites featuring online banking and commerce, as firms must guarantee that their cus-tomers' personal data and credit card information will not fall into the wrong hands.

The 1970s not only offered a glimpse of what computer networks could do for us, but what kinds of problems and conflicts they could engender. In the early days of BBSs and chat rooms, who would have believed that people would one day meet their future spouses online? On a more sinister note, few participants in the first online communi-ties could have imagined that virtual communities could also be dangerous, as people could shield their true identities and forge seemingly genuine ties with lonely strangers.

Similarly, who could have predicted how reliant people would become, both in their personal lives and in business communications, on e-mail? On the other hand, in the excitement over the first e-mail programs, who could have seen that in twenty years, direct marketers would be filling people's in-boxes with annoying or X-rated spam on a daily basis, and that lawmakers would be debating whether to legislate against it? In 1977, when that first message was successfully routed through three different types of computer networks, who could have seen the extent to which both international commerce and crime would flourish in such a new, vast, and largely unregulated medium? In Chapter Three, only the very tips of those icebergs will slide into view.

1970 ALOHAnet Is Created by Norman Abramson

Computer scientist Norman Abramson designs ALOHAnet, a network of radio links that allows the exchange of data among computers located on four Hawaiian islands. The ALOHAnet later becomes important in the formula-tion of cross-network connections, which in turn lead to the early Internet.

In 1969 networking enthusiast Robert Taylor was head of the Information Processing Techniques Office (IPTO) at ARPA. ARPA had just funded the formation of ARPAnet, the first multiple-site computer network, which sent data via telephone lines. Taylor decided to also fund a computer network that sends messages through radio connections, to test whether this method is feasible.

WHEN NEW HIGHWAYS ARE OLD

Many cyberspace enthusiasts believe that the term "information superhighway" was coined by Vice President Al Gore in the 1990s to describe the growth of the Internet. The metaphor has actually existed since 1970, when an article by Ralph Lee Smith in *The Nation* outlined the revolutionary potential of the new media of the day—cable television.

Like the Internet, cable didn't start as a revolutionary tool. Cable TV was born in 1948, when television store owner John Walson decided to improve his unsatisfactory reception. He put an antenna on top of a large utility pole, installed it on the top of a nearby mountain, and ran the signal to his shop using coaxial cable. By the 1960s enterprising cable television owners had started to use microwave technology rather than antennas, which not only improved reception but brought programming in from far-away cities. Pressured by local television stations who feared the competition, the Federal Communications Commission (FCC) decided to restrict the ability of cable companies to sell television programming to distant areas.

Political progressives disagreed with the government's decision to back television stations over the infant cable industry. At the time, technology was being developed to make cable a two-way communication device (two-way cable has largely been abandoned), and activists saw revolutionary potential in the medium. Enthusiasts wrote that cable would one day deliver everything from interactive education to home shopping to virtual democracy. In his influential article, "The Wired Nation," Smith argued, "In the 1960s the nation provided large federal subsidies for a new interstate highway system . . . . In the 1970s it should make a similar national commitment for an electronic highway system, to facilitate the exchange of information and ideas."

In 1972 the development of useable satellites expanded the potential for nationwide broadcasts by eliminating earthbound signal blocks. That year the government—themselves interested in pursuing satellite communications—began lifting the restrictions on cable. Soon Time Inc. launched Home Box Office, the first station to broadcast via satellite. Fearing that large corporations would take over the cable television industry, users petitioned the government to assign non-commercial space for cable broadcasting, and the public access show was born.

The 1984 Cable Act effectively deregulated the industry; from 1984 to 1992 cable companies spent more than $15 billion wiring the country—the largest private construction initiative since World War II. Today approximately seven out of every ten homes in the United States opt for cable television. The Telecommunications Reform Act of 1996 allowed cable and telephone companies to combine to enter the information services markets. Now cable companies have their sights set on the Internet.

Cable companies are adept at marketing the idea of techno-revolution on the Internet, but observers maintain that it remains to be seen whether cable will help or hurt the quality of the Net. Just as commercial broadcasts crowd out public access shows on cable, personal home pages on the Web must now compete with mega-sites like Time-Warner's Pathfinder (http://www.pathfinder.com). As Mark Surman of Canada's Information Highway Working Group (IHWG) puts it, even though the wired enthusiasts of the electronic highway dreamt of a cabled utopia, all they got was "a whole lot more television."

In 1970 he recruits Abramson at the University of Hawaii to oversee the design of the network. Naming the network ALOHAnet, Abramson sets up a system of small radios that transmit on the same frequency. Each of the seven radios is linked to a host computer and sends data at random intervals. When message traffic is heavy, transmissions collide and the radio terminals try to send their messages again later.

Larry Roberts, who succeeds Taylor as head of IPTO later in the year, is intrigued by the radio network. He and associate Bob Kahn develop an idea for a mobile computer network, with small computers transported to desired sites by vehicle. The idea is for the small mobile computers to communicate with a larger central host terminal located at a radio station. The army expresses interest in such a network, and several packet-radio networks, as they are called, are installed during the 1970s.

The packet-radio projects send Kahn's thoughts whirling. As the distance between radio terminals is limited, he envisions a satellite-based network that would be capable of transmitting messages nearly anywhere on Earth's surface. Over the next several years he organizes a small packet-satellite network, called SATnet, with links from the United States to several European sites.

The development of packet-radio networks and SATnet leads Kahn to think about the possibility of connecting all networks into a global network of networks.

The ALOHAnet also influences Bob Metcalfe, a graduate student enrolled at Harvard University. In 1972 he is searching for a topic to round out his Ph.D. thesis. His original proposal, a study of the ARPAnet, had been rejected on the grounds that it contained insufficient theory. He learns of the ALOHAnet, studies Abramson's papers, and submits a complex analysis and restructuring of the network; his dissertation is accepted the following year.

1970 UNIX OPERATING SYSTEM IS DEVELOPED AT BELL LABS

The Unix operating system, designed by Ken Thompson and Dennis M. Ritchie at Bell Telephone Laboratory, spreads throughout the global computing community. New versions of Unix appear as the original is altered and improved at various sites. The simple, functional design of Unix makes it immensely popular; by 1985 it is running on nearly 300,000 computers.

In 1965 programmers at Bell Labs had written the software for Multics, an ARPA-sponsored time-sharing computer system. Time-sharing services, which allowed numerous people at different terminals to use a single mainframe computer simultaneously, was a common answer to the growing demand for computing time in the 1960s. Multics became a model for the development of other time-sharing systems. However, by 1969 time sharing was beginning to fall by the wayside as advanced hardware became less costly, allowing more users direct access to computing power.

The Multics project is canceled in 1969. Ritchie and Thompson, who had worked on Multics, immediately begin cooking up something to replace their lost venture. Guessing at future trends, they set out to design a small, clean operating system that they call Unix (an operating system is the main program that controls a computer and allows access to the computer's power and resources). Working with a limited, primitive computer from Digital Equipment Corporation, the PDP-7, they complete a working Unix system in early 1970. A valuable feature of this original design is a program called "pipes," which enables complex programs to be built from simpler ones.

Ritchie and Thompson receive funding for a more powerful computer on which to continue developing their operating system. After Ritchie invents a new programming language called "C," he and Thompson rewrite Unix in the new language, which enables Unix to be imported onto any computer system.

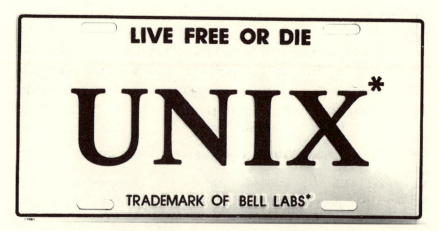

The Unix operating system has a devoted following among programmers, as suggested by this novelty license plate (Image courtesy of The Computer Museum History Center).

Unix finds its niche in the early 1970s, as time sharing and large mainframe computers decrease in popularity. Frustrated with inefficient software and competition for access to mainframes, universities order multiple smaller computers for use by their individual departments. The simplicity of Unix makes it a good fit for these computers.

By 1977 Unix is spreading from universities to corporations and government agencies. Its popularity skyrockets. Programmers at the University of California at Berkeley develop the original Unix into a more powerful version that is widely adopted on the West Coast. In 1979 Unix and its communications transfer protocol, Unix to Unix Copy Protocol (UUCP), are instrumental in the evolution of Usenet, one of the earliest and most influential non-ARPAnet newsgroup networks.

1971 RAY TOMLINSON WRITES EARLY E-MAIL PROGRAMS SNDMSG, CPYNET, AND READMAIL

Ray Tomlinson, a computer engineer at Bolt, Beranek and Newman (BBN)— the company that designed and built the ARPAnet—composes two programs to facilitate the exchange of electronic messages among ARPAnet users. He introduces the @ symbol, which becomes the standard way of separating the user and the user's server in electronic-mail addresses.

ARPAnet was not designed with the intention of providing personal communication among users. However, electronic mail (or e-mail, as it comes to be known) became the most commonly used feature of the network in its early years. Pre-ARPAnet time-sharing systems, in which numerous terminals scattered over one site are linked to one host computer, had offered e-mail-like systems. But those systems provided little advantage over regular office or campus mail.

The first e-mail exchange between two separate machines is accomplished by Tomlinson at BBN in 1971. He had written a program called CPYNET (pronounced "copynet") for transferring files between computers. Tacking on programs for sending and receiving messages, SNDMSG ("send message") and READMAIL, he transfers mail from one computer to another.

In July 1972 the final specifications of ARPAnet's protocol, or recipe, for enabling participating hosts to communicate with each other is being completed. A recommendation is made and adopted to include Tomlinson's e-mail programs in the protocol. In ensuing years many other e-mail programs are designed and favored by various ARPAnet groups, and together they form the foundation of modern e-mail systems.

While writing his programs Tomlinson had decided on a formula for electronic addresses. A user's address would consist of a personal "name," followed by the @ symbol, followed by the identification of the user's host machine. Despite some opposition, the formula sticks. Soon the @ symbol is a standard of Internet-based e-mail.

1972 THE ARPANET HAS ITS PUBLIC DEBUT AT THE INTERNATIONAL CONFERENCE ON COMPUTER COMMUNICATIONS

In October 1972 the International Conference on Computer Communications (ICCC) convenes at the Washington, D.C., Hilton. The ARPAnet is presented to a wide computer science community for the first time, via dozens of terminals displaying interactive programs that can be accessed through the network. Most visitors are surprised, excited, and even awed by the capabilities of the new technology.

By the end of 1971 the ARPAnet had grown to include about two dozen sites, but its use was still limited to those within the small networking branch of the computer science community. Its capabilities had not been expanded to accommodate scientists performing research in other computer fields, such as graphics, robotics, and artificial intelligence. ARPAnet aficionados wanted others to get involved.

A second motivation for staging a public demonstration of the ARPAnet was the desire to speed up attempts to solidify the network's various unfinished programs and tools. Larry Roberts, now head of IPTO and thus the ARPAnet's supervisor, decided the ARPAnet community needed a little shove to get things in optimal working order.

In 1971 the ICCC had already been planned and Roberts was a member of the meeting's program committee. He concluded that the ICCC's single exhibit would be an extensive, live demonstration of the ARPAnet, and he asked Bob Kahn to supervise this huge endeavor. Kahn, who had been involved in getting the ARPAnet up and running, worked for Bolt, Beranek and Newman (BBN) and was acquainted with most people in the ARPAnet community. He recruited several computer scientists from across the country to help him, and for the next nine months they planned the conference.

From the Hacker File

A High Price for a Free Call

In June 1972 *Ramparts*, a radical magazine in California, was closed down by police at the request of the telephone company. Mistakenly believing they were covered by the First Amendment, *Ramparts* published designs for a "blue box." A blue box is a device able to mimic a 2600 hertz tone, allowing the user to access long-distance lines for free. Blue-box building has been a time-honored hacker pastime, done by such computer luminaries as Stewart Nelson (an early MIT hackers) and Steve Wozniak, cofounder of Apple.

Blue boxing was hardly the earliest form of phone hacking, otherwise known as "phreaking." In *The Hacker Crackdown*, author Bruce Sterling points out that the practice is as old as Alexander Graham Bell himself—the earliest telephone operators were teenage boys, who were later replaced by women because the boys routinely played pranks with incoming calls.

The debate about whether phreaking deserves to be considered a serious crime has a long history. Sterling puts it this way: "If you're not damaging the phone system, and you're not using up any tangible resource, and if nobody finds out what you did, then what real harm have you done? What exactly have you 'stolen,' anyway?" Phone companies have always felt differently, of course, viewing their maintenance of the nation's phone lines to be a public trust.

During the 1970s, the public trust was precisely what was coming under critique. When a federal tax was placed on phone service during the Vietnam War, the Yippies—members of the Youth International Party—advocated stealing phone service as a legitimate way to protest the war. *Party Line,* the phreaking newsletter founded by Yippies Abbie Hoffman and "Al Bell," inspired a later group known as TAP (Technical Assistance Program). By the time "Tom Edison" took over the TAP newsletter, its 1400 readers had shifted their interests according to changes in the phone industry: instead of building blue boxes, they were learning how to hack computerized telex switches.

When Edison's computer was stolen and his house was set on fire in 1983, the TAP newsletter died out. But by this time, underground BBSs (bulletin board systems) devoted to phreaking were flourishing, and "philes" (files detailing tricks of the phreaking trade) were available to anyone with a modem and a password.

Because today's telephone networks are increasingly digital—consisting of components like cellular routes, voice mail systems, and satellite linkups—it's hard to tell the difference between a computer hacker and a phreaker. But while hackers are primarily stereotyped as American teenage males, phreakers run the gamut of gender, age, and nationality. This may explain the fact that while hackers have their champions, there have been no texts examining the history of phreaking to date. Furthermore, because exploring phone companies' computers is a federal offense, the most stringently prosecuted hacking crimes today are phone system hacks. The message is clear: if you hack a phone company, you go to jail.

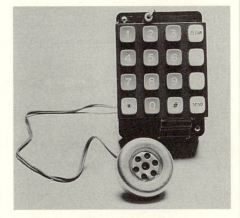

Steve Wozniak made and sold Blue Boxes like this one in the dormitories of University of California-Berkeley (Image courtesy of The Computer Museum History Center).

A few days before the ICCC was to open, computer vendors and university representatives began to arrive in Washington to set up their equipment. The Hilton site became a madhouse of frantic computer technicians wildly connecting and disconnecting wires, testing programs, and troubleshooting problems. AT&T installed two fifty-kilobit lines to power the demonstration. The evening before opening day, as adrenaline pumped through anxious participants, a faulty link capable of crashing the whole system is fixed just minutes before a group of government officials arrive for a preview tour.

When the ICCC opens the following day, more than one thousand visitors are greeted with copies of the conference guide, written by graduate student Bob Metcalfe. It describes nineteen ARPAnet experiences that await them on the conference floor. Forty terminals offer exhibits such as chess games, geography quizzes, and air-traffic control simulations. Visitors can program a robotic turtle, access news stories and remote databases, and perform interactive graphics. Among the most popular exhibits are conversation programs, in which the user can "talk" to a computer-simulated persona such as a psychiatrist. In some conversation programs, the computer responds to the user's input in a surprisingly humanlike manner.

The conference lasts two and a half days, and the system crashes only once. The visitors—computer executives, telecommunications technicians, and engineers—leave convinced that networking technology is not only viable but also holds great potential. The ICCC gets the word out: computer networks are the new frontier of electronic communications.

At the conference, network enthusiasts in the United States, England, and France form the International Network Working Group (INWG), chaired by Vint Cerf (who becomes an assistant professor of computer science at Stanford University the following month). The group's goal is to pursue the dream of creating an international network of networks.

1973 ONLINE COMMUNITY EVOLVES ON THE PLATO TIME-SHARING SYSTEM

At the University of Illinois (Urbana-Champaign campus), a program called Notes is added to the PLATO time-sharing system, paving the way for the development of an accidental—and perhaps the original—virtual community.

A result of professor Don Bitzer's successful attempt to bring computers into education, PLATO had been active since the early 1960s. It was a time-sharing system in which one mainframe computer supported simultaneous use by numerous people at different terminals. Bitzer had founded the Computer-based Education Research Laboratory (CERL), whose members created and maintained the PLATO system. From its inception through the early 1970s, PLATO was used mainly as a teaching and learning tool for students and instructors at the university.

In 1973 PLATO employee David R. Woolley devises a program to enable users to post public reports of problems on the system. His creation is called PLATO Notes. It displays a file of original reports, followed by their responses connected in sequence, so users can follow the thread of an online conversation. Woolley also broadens the program to encompass not only general system bug messages but also notes with help for new users and system announcements.

PLATO Notes appears just after CERL has installed a more powerful mainframe that increases the system's capacity from a single classroom of terminals to several hundred users. The message program is immensely popular, and within a year it begins to evolve. First a conferencing system in which several users can chat online is added; then a simple personal electronic-mail program called Personal Notes is introduced. In 1975 Woolley and colleague Kim Mast unite the various Notes programs, establishing new features such as the abilities to view a public note and copy it to another file, forward it to someone else, and respond to the author with a personal message. The following year a group conferencing program yields public conferencing files set aside for people's extracurricular activities: hobbies, religion, sports, music, science fiction, and so on. These files are similar to the microcomputer-based electronic Bulletin Board Systems (BBSs) that will flourish a decade later.

In the mid 1970s PLATO software is commercialized and PLATO time-sharing systems open in other parts of the country. In 1985 more than one hundred interlinked PLATO systems are operating worldwide. However, by the late 1980s most of these systems have been run out of business by the availability of microcomputers and the popularity of BBSs.

But PLATO leaves a legacy. Many BBSs feature concepts that originated in PLATO, and various educational and business programs designed in the 1980s, such as Lotus Notes, are modeled after PLATO software.

1973 Bob Metcalfe Outlines Ethernet Specifications in Doctoral Dissertation

In a Ph.D. thesis submitted to Harvard University, Bob Metcalfe lays the theoretical foundation for a new networking protocol that he calls Ethernet. It represents the architecture of a local area network, or LAN, which comes to serve as the standard intranetworking system at universities, businesses, and other organizations.

Metcalfe had earned undergraduate degrees in electrical engineering and management from MIT and then enrolled in a Harvard graduate program. He disliked the "old money" atmosphere and worked on his thesis research at MIT, although he remained matriculated at Harvard. His thesis was a technical examination of the government-funded ARPAnet, a computer network which had grown to include several dozen host sites. Metcalfe's thesis was rejected because it contained too much engineering and not enough theory. Having already taken a post at Xerox Corporation in Palo Alto, California, he stayed there and began to revise the dissertation. Investigating the ALOHAnet, a radio-based computer network established in Hawaii, he found several errors in the original blueprints. His subsequent analysis of the ALOHAnet provides the theory his thesis was lacking, and the reworked paper is accepted.

Metcalfe molds the ideas he presents in his thesis into the design of a new network, which he calls Ethernet after "ether," the fictional medium through which nineteenth-century physicists imagined light traveled. Ethernet systems are networks that link computers, through hardwiring, within a single location such as an office or a school.

Metcalfe borrows a transmission protocol from the ALOHAnet for the Ethernet. Messages to be transmitted wait for a pause in the activity on the line and then transmit. If two messages are sent at the same time, they "collide," and both stop transmitting, wait a random number of microseconds, and retransmit.

The first Ethernet system, built at Xerox in May 1973, operates at three million bits per second (Mbps). In 1980 Xerox begins marketing Ethernet systems running at ten Mbps. They become the standard LANs worldwide until the mid-1990s, when one hundred Mbps becomes commercially viable. LANs allow more than one person in the same location to access the same files and printers from different terminals or personal

ROBERT METCALFE

Recipient of numerous scientific awards and honors, Bob Metcalfe is among the most respected thinkers in the high-technology field. His magazine column, in which he rallies for progress and change in the networking world, has a weekly readership of more than 600,000. He and his family live on a farm in Maine, where they raise rare breeds of farm livestock and educate thousands of visitors each year about the importance of agricultural biodiversity.

Metcalfe was born in 1946 in Brooklyn, New York. By age ten, he knew he wanted to go to MIT and become an electrical engineer, and his parents, who had never attended college, were committed to helping him realize this dream. Enrolling at MIT in 1964, he left five years later with the desired diploma in hand. He subsequently earned a Ph.D. in computer science from Harvard University.

In 1973 while working at Xerox Palo Alto Research Center (PARC), Metcalfe invented Ethernet, a local area network (LAN) system for connecting computers located within the same building or campus.

In 1979 Metcalfe founded 3Com Corporation ("3Com" stands for computers, communications, and compatibility) in Santa Clara, California. His purpose was to promote networking—Ethernet in particular—as an important tool in the emerging information age. Due in part to his superior management and marketing skills, Ethernet became the most widely used LAN, and 3Com became a Fortune 500 company.

After leaving 3Com in 1990 Metcalfe began to publicly voice his concerns about problems in the computing and networking industries by writing, giving speeches, and advocating change. In 1993 he became vice president of technology at the International Data Group (IDG) and wrote about a wide range of information-technology issues in a weekly column ("From the Ether") for IDG's *InfoWorld Magazine.*

In late 1995 he launched a debate by declaring in his *InfoWorld* column that the Internet would collapse in 1996 due to technical shortcomings, financial stresses, lack of standards, and the dominating forces of the telecommunications monopolies. Several Internet service providers (ISPs) did undergo serious crashes in 1995 and 1996, but the lapses in service were largely downplayed, forgiven, and forgotten. Metcalfe good-naturedly—and literally—ate his words. Before a large audience at the Sixth International World Wide Web Conference in April 1997, he blended and then consumed his column. Nonetheless, Metcalfe continues to argue that major networking changes, particularly financial ones, need to be instituted to save the Internet.

computers; they become commonplace in businesses and universities by the late 1980s.

1974 TELEnet, the First Public Packet-Switching Service, Is Established

Bolt, Beranek and Newman (BBN), the company that designed and built the ARPAnet, spins off a daughter company, called TELEnet, to provide commercial data-packet service.

The proposal for TELEnet emerges after the announcement that control of the ARPAnet will be turned over to a nongovernment entity. BBN decides to start a subsidiary company that will be able to take over the ARPAnet. It asks Larry Roberts to run the company, which is called TELEnet.

In essence, TELEnet is the civilian twin of ARPAnet. It links people in seven cities through their computers and marks the first attempt at bringing networking to consumers.

1974 Paper Outlining Network Intercommunication, by Vint Cerf and Bob Kahn, Is Published

In May a paper by Vint Cerf and Bob Kahn entitled "A Protocol for Packet Network Intercommunication" is published in the Institute of Electrical and Electronic Engineers' Transactions on Communications, *an engineering journal. The revolutionary paper describes the architecture of a system, which they call an internet, that will enable disparate networks to communicate with each other. The authors introduce datagrams and transmission control protocol (TCP).*

Since 1972 Kahn and Cerf had both been thinking about issues related to creating an international network of networks. They had been close colleagues since 1970, and it seemed natural to come together to confront a new problem; they began their collaboration in 1973. They wanted to connect radio-packet networks, satellite networks, and the ARPAnet into an extensive international network. Several radio-packet networks, a concept originating at the University of Hawaii in 1970, had been established in the United States. There was also a satellite network linking computers in Britain, France, Germany, Italy, Norway, and the United States. The ARPAnet was growing by one new site a month.

The main difficulty facing Kahn and Cerf was figuring out how to enable the computers of each network, which were designed to function differently, to communicate with each other without causing glitches in the flow of data. They determined that they needed a special computer to sit between the distinct networks and serve as a routing machine, or gateway, for the exchange of messages. This would be much easier than actually altering the small networks themselves. Gateways would have to be recognized by the networks as normal host sites, rather than as something unfamiliar, and would therefore need to speak two languages to two different networks simultaneously.

Beyond the Net

SURVEILLANCE NATION

On a hot night in August 1974 Americans everywhere watched President Richard M. Nixon resign from office. Private conversations on the "Nixon tapes" proved he had obstructed justice during investigations of the 1972 burglary and wiretapping of rival Democratic Party Headquarters in the Watergate Hotel.

Those who watched the Watergate hearings on television learned that technology cuts both ways. Certainly it was true that Nixon had arranged (with the help of the FBI) to bug the phones of his opposition and had recorded conversations of people in the Oval Office without their consent. But the president's personal audiotapes were also his own undoing; once subpoenaed by the government, Nixon found his own privacy violated—albeit in the name of justice.

Thanks to digital media, today's surveillance takes more complex forms than mere wiretapping. Both the *London Telegraph* and the *Village Voice* recently reported that an international consortium headed by the U.S. National Security Agency routinely taps satellite and underground communications. The tapping operation—codenamed "Echelon"—scans incoming e-mails, international phone calls, and faxes, storing them for later examination by authorities in the consortium. Using a "dictionary" program not unlike a Web search engine, Echelon can be used to search for security-related words like "bombing." Unfortunately, Echelon has also been used to target organizations like Amnesty International and Greenpeace.

You needn't be a conspiracy theorist to be concerned about digital surveillance. Today many students and business employees are shocked to find that if they are using a university or corporate Internet account, their e-mail isn't theirs at all. Likewise, advertisers have discovered that by using "cookies"—small files placed by Web sites into the permanent memory of your browser—they can successfully gather information about the habits of Net users visiting programmed sites. Although every browser has an option to disable the cookie programs, most users are unaware their movements are being tracked and do nothing to stop the process.

Networks are the boon and the bane of the information age. On one hand, many people can access information that was once only available to a few. On the other, it seems as though our every move is being recorded on some network, somewhere. As science writer Paul Wallich says, "It used to be only people in your vicinity could eavesdrop. Now everywhere is your vicinity." To learn more about how to protect your privacy online, check out http://www.privacy.org/. And if you want to read Woodward and Bernstein's *Washington Post* articles that prompted the Watergate investigation, they can be found at: http://www.washingtonpost.com/wp-srv/national/longterm/watergate/.

The transmission of messages for this international network was also a formidable design project. Although the three small networks were similar in that they all sent messages in little packets, they each used different packet sizes and different transmission rates. Cerf and Kahn realized they would have to formulate a new protocol for internetworking. The small networks would still maintain their own internal architectures and transmission programs, but they would have to be set up so they could use the internetworking protocols to exchange messages with other networks.

Cerf, who had become an assistant professor at Stanford University in 1972, worked with his graduate students on the design of the international network. Kahn, working for DARPA (ARPA had been renamed the Defense Advanced Research Projects Agency), was helped by his colleagues. They were also assisted by Louis Pouzin and his coworkers, who had developed a network called Cyclades in France. In September 1973 Cerf and Kahn wrote a preliminary paper and presented it at a meeting of the International Network Working Group (INWG), of which Cerf was director. The meeting generated new ideas, and they refined and completed the paper by the end of the year.

The paper, widely read upon publication in 1974, lays out the architecture of an international network. It describes gateways, which sit between networks to send and receive "datagrams." Datagrams, similar to envelopes, enclose messages and display destination addresses that are recognized by gateways. Datagrams can carry packets of various sizes. The messages within datagrams are called transmission control protocol (TCP) messages. TCP is the standard program, shared by each network, for loading and unloading datagrams; it is the only element of the international network that must be uniform among the small networks, and it is the crucial element that makes global networking possible.

The following year, Stanford graduate student Yogen Dalal squashes the bugs present in the first version of TCP. The protocol is smoothed through three more sets of specifications, and in 1977 it is successfully implemented.

1975   The MITS Altair 8800, the First Personal Computer, Is Released

The Altair 8800, a personal computer made by Model Instrumentation Telemetry Systems (MITS), debuts in the January edition of Popular Electronics. Computer hobbyists around the country immediately flood MITS with orders for the Altair 8800, and the personal computer revolution unfolds.

Ed Roberts had founded MITS in the early 1970s to build products for electronic hobbyists. He produced light flashers for model rocket ships, temperature sensors, digital clocks, and finally digital calculators. But by 1974, unable to compete with giants like Texas Instruments, MITS was $365,000 in debt.

But Roberts had a new idea. He had become intrigued by computers and was frustrated by the difficulty of accessing them. He dreamed of building a computer affordable to the average person, and he knew that Intel, of Silicon Valley, California, was making microprocessor chips that could serve as the heart of a small computer. He made a deal with Intel to buy its newest chip, the 8080, for $75 apiece—despite the fact that Intel authorities had first quoted him $350 a chip.

Intel had no intention of using its microchip to build small computers, seeing no market for such things. But Roberts and his colleague Bill Yates were full of hopeful enthusiasm and went to work designing the nuts, bolts, and memory of a microcomputer to surround the 8080. (Microcomputers, of which a few had already been built for use in businesses, are computers powered by a single microprocessor.)

The Altair 8800, as featured in the January 1975 issue of Popular Electronics (Image courtesy of The Computer Museum History Center).

Roberts arranged to have Les Solomon, the technical editor at *Popular Electronics,* publish an article about MITS' computer-in-progress. The computer had not even been named. One night, the story goes, Solomon asked his daughter to suggest a name for the machine, and she came up with "Altair," after a planet featured on an episode of the television show *Star Trek.*

The January 1975 *Popular Electronics* hits the stands with the MITS Altair 8800 displayed prominently on the front cover. The article announces that readers can send a check for $397, and the Altair 8800 will be sent to them in pieces for home assembly. This is exactly what computer hobbyists have been waiting for; indeed, the fact that they have to build the computer themselves is viewed as a bonus by most.

At MITS headquarters in Albuquerque, New Mexico—where there are only a handful of employees left—the phone rings off the hook with orders. The mail brings more, day after day. Hundreds of thousands of dollars' worth of the orders for the Altair 8800 and related additional equipment (some of which had been advertised but not yet designed) arrives at MITS within weeks, and Roberts and his crew are flabbergasted.

Over the next few months, MITS employees scramble to satisfy their eager customers. When the hobbyists receive their packages and assemble their parts, they have before them the first personal computer, a blue box with switches, levers, and blinking lights. There is no monitor, no keyboard, no disk drive, and in fact no way of putting information in or taking information out of the machine. It has 256 bytes (a byte contains 8 bits, the individual units of electronic information) of memory, which drastically limits its programming potential. The computer can't really do anything useful. But the majority of new owners are nonetheless excited just to have an electronic computer to tinker with in their homes, even if it doesn't work much of the time.

In response to the popularity and technological shortcomings of the Altair 8800, dozens of enthusiasts start their own companies to build and sell additional equipment for the computer, such as memory boards, audio-cassette recorders, and teletype terminals. Similarly, in the realm of software, several people develop programs specifically for the Altair 8800.

1975 Bill Gates and Paul Allen Develop the Altair 8800 Programming System and Found Microsoft

Software whizzes Bill Gates and Paul Allen write a programming system for the MITS Altair 8800 in the language BASIC. After their Altair collaboration, they found Microsoft, which becomes the world's leading software manufacturer.

John Kemeny and Thomas Kurtz had developed BASIC (Beginner's All-Purpose Symbolic Instruction Code) in 1964 at Dartmouth College. It was a high-level computer language that could be used readily by nonexperts. Kemeny and Kurtz allowed BASIC to be freely distributed and used by anyone. Eventually widely used to introduce students to

Netspeak

MAY THE EGOBOO BE WITH YOU

It is only fitting that the first personal computer had a *Star Trek*-inspired name. The early days of personal computing were certainly like something out of science fiction. Legend has it that Altair enthusiasts were getting divorced at alarming rates due to their "mad scientist" lust for the blinking boxes in their basements. But it went deeper than that.

When the Altair was released, people began to meet and trade information in groups like the Homebrew Computer Club. Before they evolved from happy hackers to big businesses, personal computing groups resembled nothing so much as science fiction (SF) fan communities—where professionals and hobbyists have long met with mutual respect.

Outcast from "legitimate" literature lovers, SF fans have long enjoyed a strong sense of community. With roots as far back as the 1920s, SF fan groups were some of the first "virtual commmunities." Then, SF readers corresponded to one another through the letter columns of pulp magazines like *Amazing Stories*. By the 1930s SF "fanzines"—magazines written by fans—began, inspiring groups to meet face to face at regularly scheduled conventions around the world. In the early days of the ARPAnet, scientists moved fan-dom into the digital age, and the first nonmilitary mailing list, SF-LOVERS, was born. The list was and remains wildly popular, so much so that it has outlived its ARPAnet origins and continues on the Net with many of its original members.

A love of SF was certainly behind the design of the earliest shoot-em-up computer video games. Spacewar was patterned after Doc Smith's *Lensman* series. Many computer enthusiasts were also motivated by the fantasy genre. J. R. R. Tolkien's elf-based series *The Lord of the Rings* inspired "elven" fonts on early Stanford lab printers. Adventure (one of the earliest nonwar games ported on the ARPAnet) included a Tolkienesque setting where the user could recover treasures. Computing historian Steven Levy contends that Adventure was a metaphor for computer programming itself: "The deep recesses you explored in the Adventure World were akin to the basic, most obscure levels of the machine that you'd be travelling in when you hacked in assembly code."

The key to understanding the dedication of both hackers and SF fans is "egoboo"—slang for the ego boost that comes when other fans take notice of you, complimenting your insights. Today, thanks to the broadcast potential of the Net, egoboo is more of a social force than ever. Confounding cynics who think that volunteerism is an outdated notion, programmer Eric Raymond argues that the "rush of egoboo" is actually responsible for today's free software movement. He cites the success of the Linux operating system, an Internet-wide volunteer movement where people happily contribute their remarkable ideas for no payment, save mention of their name among other software fans.

Considering that they predate—and will likely outlive—personal computers, SF communities must be doing something right. Though the glory days of home computing may have passed, the SF meritocracy still serves as a model for virtual communities on the Internet. To learn where it all began online, check out the SF-Lovers home page at http://sflovers.rutgers.edu/.

Bill Gates

Biography

William Henry Gates III, popularly known as Bill Gates, is cofounder, chairman, and chief executive officer of Microsoft Corporation, the world's leading developer of computer software. Both lauded as a savvy entrepreneur and defiled as a greedy monopolist, Gates has become a household name, known for his wealth, his nerdy appearance, and his utter domination of the software market.

Gates was born in Seattle, Washington, on October 28, 1955. Growing up in a well-to-do and socially prominent family, he had opportunities to explore both technology and business at a young age. As a teenager he exercised an already shrewd business sense, earning substantial pocket money programming computers for local businesses: at age twelve, he and friend Paul Allen earned $4200 writing a scheduling program for the uppercrust Lakeside School. Just four years later, he and Allen founded a company, Traf-o-Data, to process traffic data for the state government. Subsequently entering Harvard University to study law, he dropped out after two years to return to programming.

With Allen, Gates wrote the BASIC interpreter for the first personal microcomputer, the Altair 8800, in 1974, just before leaving Harvard. The following year Gates and Allen founded Microsoft Corporation to write software for the personal computer industry. A success from the beginning, the company's big break came in 1980, when Gates released MS-DOS (Microsoft Disk Operating System), the operating system for IBM's first personal computer (the PC).

Whatever criticisms may be leveled at Gates, his extraordinary vision and competitive drive are undeniable. As author Robert Cringley points out, "Gates was vowing to put 'a computer on every desk and in every home running Microsoft Software,' when there were fewer than a hundred microcomputers in the world." In 1985 the first version of Windows, Microsoft's graphical-user interface (GUI) operating system, was released, and when Microsoft stock was put on the public market the following year, Gates became a billionaire. By the early 1990s the majority of the world's computers were running Microsoft operating systems.

In the late 1990s Microsoft came under heavy government scrutiny for possible infringement of anti-trust laws, when other software companies alleged that Microsoft had been pursuing a number of illegal tactics aimed at crushing all competition for its Internet Explorer web browser. In July 1998 Gates appointed colleague Steve Ballmer as the new president of Microsoft. Gates remains Chairman and CEO, but he plans to let Ballmer run the day-to-day operations of the company while he focuses on product development and future directions for Microsoft.

programming, BASIC convinced educators that computers could be a valuable learning tool for everyone, not just engineers and computer scientists. BASIC was easy to program with and made computers more accessible to more people. It was the perfect vehicle to help launch microcomputers into homes.

MITS founder Ed Roberts introduced the first personal microcomputer, the Altair 8800, in January 1975. It consisted of a bunch of functioning electronic parts, but to actually perform it needed software—preferably written in BASIC, to reach the largest number of people. Soon after the release of the Altair 8800, Roberts received a phone call from two young computer experts, Bill Gates, a law student at Harvard University, and his friend Paul Allen, a systems programmer at Honeywell in Boston. They were eager to write a BASIC interpreter, or programming system, for the Altair 8800. Roberts told them that others were also attempting to write one and that he would purchase the first one to reach his desk.

Gates and Allen feverishly set about devising a compact, bug-free BASIC system. Allen flies to Albuquerque to deliver the result, which he loads onto a barely functioning Altair 8800 at MITS. To the onlookers' delight, the software works. It will eventually allow users of the Altair 8800 to write small programs that utilize their computers' capabilities.

In the spring of 1975 Gates and Allen found Micro-Soft (later dropping the hyphen) and find themselves in demand for creating BASIC interpreters to run on several emerging microcomputers. Within a few months they net several hundred thousand dollars.

The spread of easy-to-use BASIC and the hunger for home computers create a revolution in computing: the personal computer, which puts the power of computing at the individual's fingertips.

1975   THE PUBLIC LEARNS OF THE ARPANET

A rumor, suggesting that army intelligence officers had used the ARPAnet to relocate files concerning the whereabouts and behavior of political activists, leads to a public fit and a Senate investigation. The related news stories alert citizens to the existence of the network.

Previously, knowledge of the ARPAnet had been limited to scientists and students at the host sites and others involved in the computer science community. The majority of people in the United States were unaware that it existed, probably because it was not accessible to them. However, the network was expanding rapidly, and its users were taking advantage more and more of the resource-sharing opportunities that had driven its development. Computer users at universities and other research institutions were sharing electronic resources by logging into hosts at distant sites.

Meanwhile, during the 1960s, political unrest in the United States was growing. The government was paying attention and had instructed the army to gather information about the precise locations of police stations, hospitals, and government buildings in handfuls of cities. The army was also alleged to have kept files on political troublemakers.

In 1972 news of these clandestine activities reached the public. Under pressure from an outraged populace, the army succumbed to the demand that all files on individuals be destroyed. In 1975, however, reporters unleash a rumor suggesting that army officers had used the ARPAnet to shuffle the files into hiding instead of getting rid of them. The story makes big news, and people who had not known about the ARPAnet—the majority of the public—are clued in.

The ensuing government investigation determines, by analysis of old printouts of ARPAnet transactions, that the network had not, in fact, been used as a getaway vehicle for the files. But authorities at the Defense Communications Agency (DCA) become keenly aware that their network is now in the public eye and that they should monitor how the network is used (the DCA had replaced DARPA as ARPAnet manager).

1975 A Letter by Bill Gates Initiates the "Software Flap"

Agitated that his BASIC program has been copied and distributed by an anonymous Altair user, Bill Gates writes a letter decrying "software piracy," thus launching the now famous "software flap."

In writing BASIC for the Altair, Gates and his partner Paul Allen had made a deal with Ed Roberts to be paid royalties from each sale of their BASIC software package. Roberts agreed with them that software represents work, and that it should be paid for just like hardware. However, computer hobbyists—the majority of MITS' customers—had long been freely sharing software among themselves and believed that computer resources should be available to everyone. In addition, many of them were frustrated that they sent MITS hundreds of dollars only to wait impatiently for the promised equipment and software to arrive. Many felt that the $150 price tag of the Altair BASIC system was way too high in the first place.

Netspeak

THE FREE SOFTWARE MOVEMENT

From the "software flap" to today, Bill Gates has had his critics. Gates' precedent-setting agreement with Ed Roberts eventually allowed thousands of software authors to claim their code as sellable property—and grow rich as a result. On the other hand, Microsoft and its ilk helped usher in an era of digital property rights, and they have been criticized in some quarters for benefiting software producers at the expense of consumers.

In his defense, Gates did not begin the practice called "closed source code," a way of locking out competitors from hacking into software to see what makes it work. Closed source code has long been standard among mainframe computer companies. But mainframe software manufacturers never targeted neophyte users, nor did they claim to sell "user-friendly" programs. Some industry observers are troubled that although it costs many times more to support their customers than it does to develop programs, most software companies still consider themselves manufacturers, rather than personal computing service providers.

In an interview with *Salon*'s Andrew Leonard, programmer Eric Raymond argues that instead of fighting to keep trade secrets, software companies should reconceptualize their code as having a life span of sorts: closed in the early years, but open once market saturation is reached. Raymond is part of a movement—called the "free software" or "open source" movement—that advocates the production and use of software with open source code, readily available for anyone who wants to adapt the software.

"The first thing to realize about free software," Leonard explains, "is that it's not actually free." Microsoft's Explorer browser is given to users gratis, but it's not free software because the source code is closed. As famed MIT hacker and open-source guru Richard Stallman is fond of saying, "think of free software as in freedom of speech, rather than free beer."

Business conservatives have long fought free software, maintaining that while proprietary code may be buggy, at least there is someone to sue when it fails. Ironically, free software advocates have never been interested in how much a company charges (or doesn't charge) for open code software. Today companies like Red Hat and Caldera are licensing the free software Linux—a Unix-like operating system—to companies like Intel and Southwestern Bell. These blue-chip companies happily pay for free software because it is bundled with support, troubleshooting, and the Red Hat name to sue if something goes wrong. Ordinary users don't have to pay—they can download Linux for free, install it themselves, and find all the support they need by going to http://www.linux.org/.

Even so, the Microsoft empire is in no immediate danger from free software. While Linux has approximately seven million users, Microsoft has 300 million for its Windows operating system. As Tim O'Reilly of Web publisher O'Reilly & Associates explained in a recent *New York Times* article, "In the first round, open-source software will not beat Microsoft at its own game. What it is doing is changing the nature of the game."

So when the opportunity arises, the BASIC system written by Gates and Allen is stolen by an unidentified person, copied onto paper tape, and distributed among a growing network of Altair-8800 owners and owners-to-be. Gates, passionately upset, writes an open letter criticizing software piracy, which appears in several hobbyist newsletters. It causes a controversy that becomes known as the "software flap." The controversy does not halt piracy, but nor does piracy hamper Gates' career.

The software flap reveals a profound difference of opinion within the computer science community as to what the field is really all about—the open sharing of information among users or a proprietary business venture. The controversy will never be resolved and indeed will only intensify with the advent of the Internet.

1977 THE INTERNET'S THREE DISTINCT NETWORKS EXCHANGE FIRST MESSAGE

In July a TCP message makes a trip through a packet-radio host, a satellite network host, and an ARPAnet host without losing a single unit of information. The transmission demonstrates the feasibility of TCP-based networking.

TCP was the tool that enabled distinct networks to communicate with each other. The details of TCP systems presented by Bob Kahn and Vinton Cerf in a 1974 paper had been continually improved upon since then. TCP messages, enclosed in datagrams, were to travel via gateways that served as the border controls between networks.

In the July 1977 implementation of a TCP system, the message originates in San Francisco. It is sent from a mobile unit—a computer in a van traveling down a freeway—via radio link to an ARPAnet site at BBN (Bolt, Beranek and Newman), and over the Atlantic Ocean via satellite link to Norway. The message continues through radio and ground networks to University College, London, back across the ocean via satellite to the ARPAnet, and finally to the University of Southern California's Information Sciences Institute in Marina del Rey. Between each site the message is routed by a gateway computer. Funded by the Department of Defense, the experiment is intended to simulate a mobile battlefield unit sending and receiving messages from across the Atlantic. The message travels 94,000 miles and arrives completely intact.

In 1978 an idea put forth by engineers from Xerox Corporation causes a TCP enhancement: Internet Protocol (IP), a separate program that handles the routing of individual messages. The TCP portion is now responsible only for the construction and unloading of datagrams. Together, the protocols become known as TCP/IP and represent the standard system used in most large networks. The creation of TCP/IP yields less expensive, more efficient gateways and ultimately allows the Internet to expand.

1977 THE RSA ENCRYPTION SYSTEM IS PROPOSED BY RIVEST, SHAMIR, AND ADLEMAN

RSA, a public-key encryption method, is invented by Ron Rivest, Adi Shamir, and Leonard Adleman. One of the first public-key cryptographic systems, RSA is highly effective and becomes a commonly used encryption tool in the computing world.

Cryptography, loosely defined as any method of keeping communication private, had probably been around for as long as language itself. Cryptography generally involves encrypting a message or piece of information with a secret code, called a key, and sending the encryption to another party. The recipient decrypts the message back into an understandable form, with the aid of a secret key. The study of cryptography is called cryptology, from the Greek *kryptos logos*, or "hidden word."

With the emergence of electronic communications, cryptography had come to encompass not only the communication of secret messages but also the authentication of documentation. For example the secret code, or PIN number, we use to identify ourselves to a bank machine is an authenticating form of cryptography. Digital signatures and time stamps, electronic banking, and pay-per-view television all use cryptographic techniques to confirm authenticity.

Traditionally, cryptography was based on secret-key systems, in which the sender and receiver of information both hold the same encryption key. Such systems are also called symmetric or private-key cryptography. The main disadvantage of secret-key systems is that the two parties involved have to communicate the secret key to each other somehow, and if they are not in the same location, they have to send the key over the phone, through the mail, or via a courier, etc. None of these methods is completely trustworthy; all carry the potential of an unwanted party becoming privy to the key.

In 1975, cryptographers Whitfield Diffie and Martin Hellman introduced public-key systems of encryption. These are based on advanced mathematical techniques whereby messages are encoded with a key that anyone can access—a public key—and decrypted by the recipient with a key that only the recipient knows. There is a mathematical relationship between the private key and the public key, but the sender does not know the relationship. It does not matter if someone intercepts the message, because only the intended recipient has the secret key.

The advantage of public-key encryption is that the two parties exchanging information never have to send secret codes to each other, so it is more convenient and safe than secret-key encryption. The public key is published for any potential sender to use. Public-key encryption was intended to supplement, not to replace, secret-key encryption, and its most common utility is as a means of securely communicating a secret key from one party to another. A disadvantage of public-key encryption is that it takes longer than secret-key systems to encrypt and decrypt.

In 1977 Rivest, Shamir, and Adleman devise a public-key encryption system that is named RSA after the first letters of their last names. RSA employs calculations among very large prime numbers. (A prime is a number that is evenly divisible by only itself and 1. For example, 5, 7, 11, and 13 are small prime numbers.) Virtually impossible to break, RSA encryption is lauded as an innovative, fail-safe creation.

In 1982 RSA's inventors found RSA Data Security, Inc. to market their product, and by the 1990s they have sold more than 300 million copies of RSA encryption tools. RSA encryption technology is embedded into widely used computer products distributed by firms such as Microsoft, Netscape, Intuit, IBM, Intel, and Sun Systems. RSA becomes a standard within the security and cryptography fields, which become increasingly important as electronic systems for banking and business spread.

1978 The First Computer Bulletin Board System, CBBS, Goes Online

Ward Christensen and Randy Suess develop the Computerized Bulletin Board System (CBBS) in Chicago. Opened to the public the following year, it is the first electronic message-posting network.

Christensen, a physicist by education and a mainframe programmer by profession, was an electronics hobbyist in his spare time. By the late 1970s he had become expert at programming computers to transfer files from one machine to another via modems and telephone lines.

Christensen and Suess lived in Chicago, where winters bring below-freezing temperatures and piles of snow, and in January 1978 there was plenty of indoor time for programming and fiddling with digital equipment. The idea had been building for awhile, and that winter they decided to devise a simple computer communication system. Christensen developed the software and Suess assembled the hardware.

On February 16, 1978, their system is complete; they name it the Computerized Bulletin Board System (CBBS). When it finally goes online to the public in 1979, Christensen manages the system under the title "system operator" (soon shortened to "sysop"). CBBS operates like a virtual thumb-tack bulletin board. Participants can post messages to a public "board," and others can read and respond to those messages, creating an ongoing virtual discussion.

In November 1978 Christensen and Suess publish an article in *Byte* magazine, describing CBBS and outlining the technology for devising virtual bulletin boards. The article drums up interest in CBBS and gives others the opportunity to build their own systems.

Since the ARPAnet is still restricted to defense-funded institutions, CBBS is the first civilian experiment in creating virtual community (apart from time-sharing systems). In 1979 most individuals who own computers and modems—or have access to and knowledge of computing hardware—are computer hobbyists and scientists. So at first, most topics on CBBS hover within the realm of computers and electronic communication, but eventually the talk broadens.

CBBS kindles a revolution in electronic communication. Virtual bulletin boards begin popping up around the country; they are given the generic name BBS, for bulletin board system. Some cover a range of topics, and others are intended for highly specific discussions. By the early 1990s most BBSs are connected to the Internet, and a whole new virtual world is introduced to BBS members, who had previously roamed within the limited parameters of one system (or in some cases several interconnected systems).

In the mid-1990s membership to BBSs begins to decrease, as the graphics-oriented World Wide Web bursts on the scene and grabs computer users' attention.

Because It's There

By 1979 the Defense Department's ARPAnet has been up and running for a decade and more than one hundred sites have access to it. Networking is clearly a driving force in computer research at this time, as academics have a growing desire to link their computers and share information quickly with their colleagues at other universities. Outside of the academic world, people are largely unaware of the amazing strides being made in computer science technology. This changes, and fast, during the first half of the eighties, thanks to two companies—a giant called Big Blue and an upstart called Apple.

In retrospect, it makes sense that this period ushered in the era of Silicon Valley start-ups and twenty-four-year-old millionaires—after all, it was the eighties, when greed was good. Once computers and computer networking got into bed with capitalism, the future was assured: out of the ivory towers of academia and into the boardrooms and living rooms of America.

It's Morning in America . . .

As the idealism that had accompanied the political activism of the late 1960s and early 1970s faded, the United States was blanketed with a vague communal malaise. Amidst this social retrenchment among Americans in the late 1970s and early 1980s, activists faced a serious backlash from political moderates and conservatives. The civil rights movement was unable to retain its earlier prominence on the national agenda, and feminists were increasingly blamed for the breakdown of the American family. Major cities were struggling with high poverty and crime as businesses and middle-class families fled urban centers. On top of this, a weak economy, the energy crisis of the mid-1970s, and the taking of fifty-two American hostages in Iran in 1979 instilled a new sense of vulnerability in Americans. The public had become increasingly dubious of the government's ability to deal with the problems facing everyday people.

In 1980 Ronald Reagan was elected president in a landslide victory over incumbent Democrat Jimmy Carter, demonstrating a resurgence of political conservatism on a massive scale. Lamenting the decline in American values, Reagan pledged to launch an era of national renewal. In this increasingly conservative climate, computer-literate folk in the liberal and radical communities began to exploit computer networks as a new means for maintaining their activism. Hundreds of moderated political discussion groups surfaced on Usenet during this era.

During this period the Reagan administration launched far-reaching government deregulation initiatives aimed at fostering growth in business enterprises and therefore spreading economic wealth throughout society. In what came to be called "trickle-down" economics, Reagan sought to revitalize American industry by reducing tax burdens and governmental red tape that he saw as an impediment to aggressive economic competition and growth.

Against this backdrop of laissez-faire economic policies, new software innovations and companies sprang up and were widely adopted for business use. Spreadsheet applications were designed specifically with financial analysis in mind, and the applications were created to run on microcomputers (i.e., PCs). And as the creation of the ARPAnet was inspired by a simple need to connect one enormous computer to another, so corporate necessity was the mother of invention that would facilitate networking desktop PCs.

. . . and IBM Gets a Wake-up Call

The company that should have, by all logic, led the way towards an era of PC networking was resistant to the very idea. In 1980 IBM was the dominant player in computer hardware for the business world. But the company's principal product line, a series of mainframe computers, came face to face with some stiff competition from an unexpected source: this new and seemingly irrelevant piece of equipment called the microcomputer. Small start-up ventures producing microcomputers were generating enormous interest in the press and public. Microcomputers from Apple, Commodore, and Radio Shack were becoming a flies in the ear of Big Blue. IBM had the cash, the prestige, and the reputation to maintain its dominance as the main supplier to the business community; however, it was on the verge of finding itself without a competing product.

IBM recognized this as a serious threat. It also recognized that it could not build its own microcomputer in time to seize this emerging market niche. Smartly cobbling together components from various companies—a sixteen-bit chip from Intel and an operating system from a young start-up company from Washington state called Microsoft—IBM introduced its IBM personal computer in 1981.

IBM's decision to use standardized components was one of necessity rather than desire; up until that moment in IBM's history all hardware and software designed and deployed by Big Blue were proprietary to IBM. This strategy of building proprietary systems reinforced IBM's near-monopoly position in the computing universe: if you wanted to compute, you bought an IBM mainframe; if you wanted software, you bought IBM; if you needed spare parts and supplies, you bought IBM. However, IBM couldn't follow the same strategy for the PC if they wanted to get it to market on time.

Once IBM went heart-and-soul into the microcomputing business, Wall Street and the business world eagerly and passionately embraced the technology. The old adage "Nobody ever got fired for buying IBM" came into play, making IBM the number-one source of personal computers in the business world. At the same time IBM's revolutionary but necessary choice of using standardized, "off-the-shelf" components to build their PCs made IBM develop the first open-architecture personal computer. This allowed other manufacturers to come to market with compatible PCs; Compaq, for instance, was the first manufacturer to do so. IBM tried to reverse the strategy a few years later, with its introduction of microchannel architecture, a proprietary input/output standard for designing add-on components for the PC. The strategy had very limited success.

While IBM managed to inadvertently fuel the PC wave, its position as undisputed market leader was changing. Failing to anticipate the huge number of PCs that had become fixtures in homes, offices, and schools, and misguidedly attempting to protect its mainframe business, IBM chose not to enter the PC-networking game. Into the networking vacuum left by IBM stepped a number of visionary software engineers who created networking technologies and established high-tech companies that became among the fastest-growing companies in U.S. history. These were the companies to watch. They, not Big Blue, were the future.

Bob Metcalfe, who had developed Ethernet in 1973, was one of the key players who provided the software needed to network PCs. In 1979 Metcalfe founded 3Com Corporation and set out to convince corporate America that its PCs should be linked together via his Ethernet in local area networks, or LANs. He was persuasive. By the late 1990s more than 100 million computers worldwide were networked on Ethernet.

Beginning in the mid-1980s more firms surfaced that specialized in particular technologies that facilitated PC networking. The concept of the client-server structure emerged at this time. "Clients" were the PCs and "servers" were the larger computers that fed data and software applications to individual PCs. In 1985 Novell introduced its Netware 2.0, which set the standard for network operating systems. Cisco, launched by a married couple at Stanford University, developed a new technology to link computer networks together more efficiently.

Business and technology were now in a truly interdependent relationship. Not just businesses but entire markets could be crippled if computers failed. Similarly, the development of new technologies depended on a particularly ambitious breed of businessperson—the venture capitalist (VC). One of the most famous—or notorious, depending on one's perspective—VC firms was the Silicon Valley-based Sequoia Capital. In the 1970s and 1980s Sequoia funded Atari, Apple Computer, 3Com, and Cisco Systems, among many others. More recently, Sequoia has invested in a large number of Internet-focused companies, including eToys, PlanetRx, and the wildly successful Yahoo! Web site.

Because It's There!

Despite the ever-increasing popularity of networking amongst computer scientists, only sites performing military research were officially allowed to connect to the ARPAnet. Even for those sites, network access was expensive and strictly limited. The ARPAnet's program manager, Vint Cerf, established the Internet Configuration Control Board (ICCB) in 1979 in an effort to monitor the network's architectural growth. It became increasingly evident that the network was not accommodating the needs of researchers and students, who were all clamoring for greater network access.

Graduate students continued to lead the way in Internet expansion. In 1979 graduate computer science students Tom Truscott, Jim Ellis, and Steve Bellovin set up a connection between computers at Duke University and the University of North Carolina (UNC), thus creating Usenet. Initially intended as a vehicle for researchers to share information, Usenet quickly evolved into an enormously popular network. With Usenet we see the emergence of newsgroups, in which people share ideas and information on specific topics by "talking" to one another through their computers. The anarchic—sometimes to the point of brutality—atmosphere of Usenet reflects the frontier spirit of its users. By the end of the 1990s Usenet has been besieged by "newbies" (newcomers) and spam attacks (massive junk mail postings), but for many Netizens it remains the true heart and soul of the Internet.

As more and more civilians acquired computers in the early 1980s, networks and bulletin board systems (BBSs) proliferated. In 1981 the City University of New York and Yale University in New Haven, Connecticut, followed the lead of Duke and UNC, connecting their computers via BITnet, which originally stood for "Because It's There Network." BITnet served universities that didn't have access to the ARPAnet. Also that year, the Computer Science NETwork (CSNET) was built by universities, the RAND Corp., and Bolt, Beranek and Newman (BBN). In 1983 computer programmer Tom Jennings launched FidoNet, a bulletin board system dedicated to free speech.

Posting to a BBS was only one way to use a network. Other adventurous souls preferred to exploit the technology by adopting alternative identities in electronic role-playing games known as MUDs, or Multiuser Dungeons. The first MUD was inaugurated in 1979 at England's Essex University. Inspired by the work of British fantasy writer, J. R. R. Tolkien, MUDs created elaborate fictional worlds, accessible by multiple users. In his 1937 work, *The Hobbit*, and in his *Lord of the Rings* trilogy of the mid-1950s, Tolkien created a fantastic world, known as Middle Earth. MUDs drew a great deal of imagery from Tolkien's realm. Because this technology allowed visual anonymity, it was extraordinarily liberating for many.

The proliferation of networks that occurred in the early 1980s presented a new quandary for network users: how to shepherd a message from one computer network to another. To solve this dilemma, the transmission control protocol (TCP) and Internet protocol (IP) are developed in 1982. The Internet was "officially" born the following year. It was defined as any network that uses TCP/IP.

From PARC to Living Room

By all historical accounts, no single place and no one group of scientists proved more influential to the evolution of modern computing than those working at the Xerox Palo Alto Research Center (Xerox PARC) in the early eighties. Not only was Ethernet created there by Metcalfe, but the first notion of the graphical user interface (GUI—pronounced "gooey") was born there as well. With GUI, a user can simply point her mouse and click on the icon she wants to activate. This was a major departure from earlier PCs, which required users to type in long strings of commands.

Xerox management did not know what to do with this "renegade" group at Palo Alto. Steve Jobs, on the other hand, took one look and saw the future. With a dramatic 1984 television commercial, Apple debuted the Macintosh, a PC that relied heavily on PARC-born concepts. As the first affordable PC featuring windows and icons, Macs allowed users to intuitively manipulate the software on their computers; the Macintosh introduced the notion of "user friendliness" to PC design.

The relationship between "man" and "machine" has never been the same since. Countless mice, trackballs, pens, and tablets have been rolled, clicked, dragged, and poked as users do everything from writing a letter to navigating the World Wide Web. The GUI redefined the relationship between humans and computers. It is this more "friendly" relationship that fosters the widespread use of PCs amongst the civilian population and paves the way for the "information revolution" of the 1990s.

1979 FIRST MULTI-USER DUNGEON (MUD) IS FUNCTIONAL

Students Roy Trubshaw and Richard Bartle develop the first MUD (known as Multiuser Dungeon, Multiuser Dimension, and Multiuser Domain) at Essex University in England. MUDs are electronic role-playing games, each located on a host computer and accessed by multiple users who interact within the game through virtual characters. MUDs create communities in which participants have visual anonymity.

Role-playing games were nothing new in social history. Children and adults alike had long assumed altered identities, for play, in the theater, in psychotherapy, and so forth. In 1978 TSR Games published the *Advanced*

Dungeons and Dragons Players Handbook, by Gary Gygax. Dungeons and Dragons (D&D) was a popular, complex adventure role-playing game that groups of people played together in the same room. Some aspects of D&D would appear in MUDs, but by most accounts D&D was not an inspiration for the creation of the first MUD.

Earlier, in 1937, J. R. R. Tolkien had published *The Lord of the Rings,* telling the story of several fictional characters' adventures and exploits in an intricate fantasy world. Tolkien's creation was commonly referred to as a starting point for MUD development.

In spring 1979 Trubshaw writes the first MUD, using the MACRO-10 machine code for the Digital Equipment Corporation's Programmed Data Processor (PDP)-10. (Trubshaw's first version is not the first multiuser game played on computers; earlier ones include ADVENT and ZORK.) This first MUD allows more than one player to move and converse within a simple web of locations.

That winter and the following year Trubshaw and Bartle drastically improve the design and increase the complexity of the MUD program through versions two and three. Players, entering the game as made-up characters, can now navigate through a virtual landscape and interact using a selection of objects and commands.

MUDs contain no graphics. The game is played through text only, which enhances individual imagination and fantasy. In the early 1980s players access the game through terminals, which consist of a monitor and a keyboard hooked up to a large mainframe (usually at a university). Because players participate behind the veil of a virtual character, their real-life identity can remain unknown to the other players. Such visual anonymity creates, particularly for the shy or antisocial individual, a remarkable new avenue for interaction and adventure.

In the beginning most MUD players are students at Essex University. But even as early as 1980, the university has a link to the ARPAnet in the United States, and external players begin to access MUDs through remote logins and across transatlantic connections. As MUDs gain in popularity, role-playing enthusiasts across the world obtain MUD programming technology and create their own MUDs. By the 1990s MUDs can be accessed through the Internet, and most players do so from the comfort of their own home computers, rather than borrowing late-night time from their schools' mainframes.

1979   Usenet Is Created by Graduate Students at Duke University and the University of North Carolina

Usenet, a multidisciplinary computer network of news and discussion groups, is formed on two campuses in North Carolina. Providing a unique forum to gather information and exchange ideas, Usenet grows from its origin as an underground activity among graduate students into a vast international phenomenon. Its popularity influences the government to consider connecting the ARPAnet (the Defense Department's large computer network) to smaller, independently established networks.

The ARPAnet, which had begun operation in 1969, had grown to include more than one hundred sites by 1979. Most sites were university computer science departments, and the ARPAnet provided them with abundant shared resources and electronic mail services. Faculty and students at non-connected universities felt at a disadvantage; they wanted access to ARPAnet opportunities too. But the ARPAnet was officially available only to sites conducting defense-related research (also, connecting to the ARPAnet and maintaining the link were extremely expensive), and most institutions were left out in the cold.

Graduate computer science students Tom Truscott, at Duke University, and Jim Ellis and Steve Bellovin, at the University of North Carolina, decide to connect their departments' computers (via phone lines) to communicate more efficiently with each other. They use Unix, an operating system developed at AT&T's Bell Laboratories in 1969, and UUCP (Unix-to-Unix Copy Protocol), a communications protocol designed to transfer data between Unix computers. Welcoming other sites into their network, which they call Usenet, they create a number of discussion groups on various topics in which all users can participate by posting and responding to messages. Usenet is also called the "poor man's ARPAnet," reflecting its relatively low cost.

In the early 1980s Usenet connections to Europe and Australia are established, and people who will never have a chance to meet face to face can "talk" to each other, exchange information, and freely state their opinions

Netspeak

In Cyberspace, No One Can Hear Your Sarcasm

One of the downsides of free speech in cyberspace is the flame war. In 1979 flaming (online fighting) was at an all-time high on MsgGroup, one of the ARPAnet's mailing lists. Frustrated by miscommunication online and by loss of emotional nuance in cyberspace, list user Kevin MacKenzie proposed a way to fight back. Using an idea he found in *Reader's Digest*, MacKenzie proposed that if someone meant sarcasm in a post, he use an accompanying symbol to indicate as much. The first "emoticon"—an ASCII symbol representing a facial expression—was born.

Emoticons have long been controversial. Purists argue that "real Netizens" don't use symbols; one's words should be self-explanatory. Populists reply that for new people joining the Net, emoticons help online discourse more than they hurt it. Much less controversial than emoticons are acronyms, which convey similar information, but in a shorthand text style. Wherever you come down on the Great Debate, here are some of the more popular emoticons and acronyms for your delectation.

EMOTICONS

:-)	smiling
:-(	frowning
;-(	crying
;-)	winking
:-0	yelling
:-/	skeptical
:-\	undecided

ACRONYMS

<G>	grinning
LOL	laughing out loud
ROFL	rolling on the floor laughing
TIC	tongue in cheek
IMHO	in my humble opinion
IMNSHO	in my not so humble opinion
FWIW	for what it's worth
YMMV	your mileage may vary
OIC	oh, I see
HTH	hope this helps
BFN	bye for now

in an uncensored space. Usenet is eventually incorporated into the ARPAnet's successor, the Internet.

Discussions on Usenet eventually cover a wide range of subjects. Different discussions, called "newsgroups," are organized along a loosely based thematic hierarchy. Newsgroups in the "sci" hierarchy are devoted to scientific topics, "rec" groups are devoted to recreational topics, "soc" groups are devoted to discussions of social issues, and so on. There are academic news groups, in which students exchange ideas relating to their field of study, but more popular are the forums of serious debate, earnest advice, and light-hearted banter about hobbies, business, science, politics, recreation, social issues, car maintenance, and many other topics. By 1991 Usenet hosts more than 35,000 nodes and generates close to 10 million words of discussion daily.

1979 DARPA ESTABLISHES THE INTERNET CONFIGURATION CONTROL BOARD

The Defense Advanced Research Projects Agency (formerly the Advanced Research Projects Agency), or DARPA, founds the Internet Configuration Control Board (ICCB) to assist with Internet standardization procedures and technical difficulties.

By 1979 DARPA had established connections between the ARPAnet and several radio-based and satellite-based networks, creating what some users were beginning to call the Internet (after "Internet Protocol," the program that was responsible for routing messages through the network). The network's expansion meant an increasing number of hosts and users, a situation that begged coordination and standardization.

Vint Cerf, DARPA's Internet program manager, recognizes the need for an organized body to field technical questions and oversee the network's architectural evolution. He forms the ICCB to fulfill these roles. In association with the ICCB, he also establishes the International Cooperation Board (ICB) to coordinate satellite-network research with European sites, and the Internet Research Group (IRG) for the formal exchange of network-related information. The introduction of these groups smoothes the growth of the Internet by providing a strong internal structure of support for network participants.

In 1983 the Internet connects four thousand host computers, and its continuing rapid growth requires a restructuring of the ICCB. Barry Leiner, who replaces Cerf as the Internet program manager at DARPA, disbands the ICCB and creates the Internet Activities Board (IAB). Ten task forces, each of which is responsible for one particular part of the underlying network technology, are to report to the IAB.

By 1985 the Internet Engineering Task Force (IETF), one of the IAB's ten subgroups, is overloaded with work. Its chair, Phill Gross, creates further substructure, breaking the IETF into smaller, more specialized working groups. As the Internet expands, the IAB's organization remains flexible, changing as the network's needs change and facilitating the adoption of standards and solutions.

1981 BITnet Is Started Between City University of New York and Yale University

BITnet, or Because It's Time Network, begins operation. BITnet grows to include hundreds of research and educational institutions and evolves into an extensive electronic communication network reserved for education-related e-mail, file exchange, and mailing lists.

The origins of BITnet are similar to those of Usenet, formed two years earlier. Because the ARPAnet was restricted to institutions performing defense-related research, most university students and instructors were without network opportunities. Such advantageous resources had become important to the success of academic programs and the receipt of grant funds; some students were even beginning to consider ARPAnet connection as a criterion for school choice.

With membership to ARPAnet impossible and creation of a whole new network financially unfeasible for educational institutions, networking was in the hands of ambitious, resourceful students and faculty at individual schools.

In 1981 BITnet is set up by the computer science department at the City University of New York (CUNY), and its first link is to Yale University in New Haven, Connecticut. At first BITnet stands for "Because It's *There* Network," in reference to the NJE communications protocol that is freely available on the IBM (International Business Machines) computers at CUNY. Programmers hardwire the universities' mainframes via modems and leased telephone lines, and users access the link from terminals.

The original BITnet users report great success with their project, and soon other universities want to join. The network grows, link by link, to include more than three thousand nodes (institution-sites) worldwide by the late 1990s. Academics share resources, exchange e-mail, and create mailing lists covering a variety of subjects.

BITnet's architecture is a store-and-forward design. A message travels from node to node along a predetermined path to its destination node. At each node along the path, the message is stored until it has successfully arrived at the next node. If that next node is overloaded or has crashed, the message continues to be stored rather than deleted.

VIVE LE CYBERSPACE!

Long before cyberspace was part of the average American's life, Europeans were experimenting with telephone-based information systems called videotext. As early as 1981—a decade before the World Wide Web—the French were working and playing on the world's first mass-market online information service: Minitel.

It began in the 1970s, when the French government declared its state of telecommunications a national crisis. In *Virtual Communities,* Howard Rheingold states that as late as 1968, only 60 percent of French homes had telephones—"nearly a third-world state of telecommunications." The French government decided that it was not enough to merely upgrade existing phone systems. Instead, they launched a national phone information system called Telematique—combining the words *telecommunications* and *informatique.* Throughout France, volunteers received terminals, complete with a small screen, a keyboard, and a phone jack. The

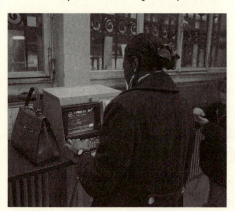

A woman uses the Minitel system in a Paris post office (AP Photo/Remy de la Mauviniere).

public nicknamed the system Minitel, after the terminals.

To fund Minitel, the government eliminated paper phone directories, listing the information on the teletex service instead. The system began with basic information: directory listings, weather reports, bank statements, and stock exchange information. Later, "smart cards"—credit card-sized cards with embedded computer chips—allowed consumers to use Minitel to order train tickets and pay some bills online. But like ARPAnet, what people really liked to do on Minitel was talk, which they could do through a messaging system not unlike Internet Relay Chat. Among the many types of chat lines, the sex-chat services called *messageries roses* ("pink messages") remain the most popular—and the most controversial. Conservatives have campaigned against *messageries roses,* denouncing them as "electronic urinals."

Minitel enthusiasts have long resisted getting connected to the Internet, suspicious of what they view as an American cultural invasion—only two percent of French homes currently have Web access. But times are changing. Recently, French Telecom and IBM announced a joint venture to provide an open-platform, Net-surfable version of Minitel called "Britany," available as early as 1999. There are plans to market Britany to countries where computer costs make widespread Internet use unlikely. For more about the system that still thrives in France, check out http://minitel.co.uk/premiere.htm. *Vive le Minitel!*

Beyond the Net

The brunt of BITnet's cost is covered by IBM for the first several years. In 1989 the Corporation for Research and Educational Networking (CREN) takes over BITnet management, and the network is thereafter funded by membership dues collected from each participating institution.

1981 DESIGN OF TED NELSON'S XANADU, A CENTRALIZED HYPERTEXT DATABASE, IS COMPLETED

Ted Nelson writes Literary Machines, *in which he outlines the architecture of a universal network server for Xanadu, his theoretical computer system for interactive electronic publishing. Xanadu is organized in hypertext, or non-sequential documentation. Hypertext is adopted by the creators of the World Wide Web in the 1990s.*

In 1965 Nelson had coined the terms "hypertext" and "hyperlink," giving language to his new concept of "sideways," nonsequential connections among blocks of information. Hypertext refers to the information that is organized in such a fashion, and hyperlinks are the connections between the blocks of information. Nelson envisioned a global library of information organized as hypertext.

Nelson's ideas took on new dimensions throughout the 1970s. He and several devotees imagined a global multimedia system, with an extensive hypertextual organization, for electronic publishing of literary and artistic work. Readers would be able to access all files and create their own links among files. There would be a simple royalty system to redeem authors when a user made a copy of a file. This system was intended to provide an open publishing forum relatively free of copyright restrictions. Nelson dubbed the system Xanadu, from Samuel Taylor Coleridge's 1816 poem *Kubla Khan,* in which Xanadu is a place of unending magic and pleasure. Aside from representing a useful resource of information, Xanadu was to offer a means of storing today's work safely for future generations.

Nelson's team of programmers and visionaries, who by 1979 is working on the officially named Project Xanadu, includes Roger Gregory, Mark Miller, Stuart Greene, Roland King, and Eric Hill. In 1981 they complete the preliminary design of the networking server that will be required to host Xanadu, and Nelson makes the design public in *Literary Machines.* Various members of the original team form the

Ted Nelson

Biography

Theodor Holm Nelson, inventor of hypertext, computer-liberation activist, and author of several books, has made a name for himself as an eccentric computer scientist. Both ridiculed for working on a huge unfinished project for more than thirty years and admired for his singular devotion, he has long dreamed of creating Xanadu, a worldwide publishing network more complex, extensive, and accessible than the World Wide Web (WWW).

Nelson was born in 1937 in Chicago. When he was six his director father (Ralph Nelson) and actress mother (Celeste Holm) transplanted the family to New York City. As a boy Ted loved to write, read, and watch movies. Extensive writing and rewriting, he has said, made him aware of the intricacies of arranging ideas into coherent structures of thought. He was frustrated mostly by having to express thoughts in a sequential manner, paragraph by paragraph, page by numbered page. Why, he wondered, wasn't there a way to represent ideas in a spatial—rather than linear—manner? These ruminations were the seeds of hypertext.

Nelson received an undergraduate degree in philosophy from Swarthmore College and enrolled in a graduate sociology program at Harvard University. There he began to work with computers and attempted (unsuccessfully) to devise a word processing program before any such thing existed. He also began to formulate hypertext, the nonsequential organization of information involving sideways links (the use of links on the WWW is a modern example of hypertext). In the 1970s his hypertext ideas blossomed into Xanadu, and he began to develop software with a number of computer programmers.

Concerned that computers would forever remain only in the hands of government officials and big businesses, Nelson launched a crusade to transfer computing power to the masses through the introduction of affordable, accessible computers. In 1974 he wrote *Computer Lib* (eration) to disseminate his views. The tome made him a hero among electronics enthusiasts who dreamt of owning a personal computer someday.

Most of Nelson's public and professional life since the early 1980s has centered around the Xanadu project. He is currently a visiting professor of environmental information at Keio University in Japan and a visiting professor of multimedia at the University of Southampton in England.

Xanadu Operating Company (XOC) in 1983, with the aim of constructing the Xanadu database.

After several years of disappointing setbacks, XOC is taken over by a company called Autodesk, which gives ample funding to the Xanadu project. Development continues, but Xanadu never reaches a marketable stage due to the difficult programming required to complete the system. Autodesk, mired in financial straits, dumps XOC in 1992 after spending an estimated $5 million on Xanadu.

During the following years Nelson introduces Xanadu to Japan and Australia, where ambitious believers continue to work on the project. Some programming activity also continues in the United States.

When the World Wide Web (WWW) makes its debut in 1991, it introduces hypertext organization to the world. Although the creators of Xanadu maintain that the WWW is inspired by Xanadu, most discussions of WWW history do not mention this connection.

1982 THE EXTERNAL GATEWAY PROTOCOL IS ESTABLISHED AS THE STANDARD CROSS-NETWORK ROUTING PROTOCOL

ARPAnet administrators adopt the External Gateway Protocol (EGP) as the standard protocol for the exchange of information at gateways between networks. EGP governs the operation of routing tables, which are responsible for directing the traffic of data smoothly through gateways.

As more and more independent networks established links to the ARPAnet, it became important for all gateways between networks to use the same protocol to route messages toward their destinations. In the absence of a standard, messages might get lost or systems might crash due to having to perform multiple translations.

EGP is developed and instituted as the standard routing protocol. It ensures that each packet of information, as it passes through a gateway, proceeds along the best available route to reach its destination. A more advanced gateway protocol, the Border Gateway Protocol, is introduced in the 1990s (although it does not entirely replace EGP).

1983 INTERNET IS DEFINED OFFICIALLY AS NETWORKS USING TCP/IP

On January 1 the ARPAnet—and every network attached to the ARPAnet—officially adopts the TCP/IP networking protocol, developed in the 1970s by pioneering network engineers Vint Cerf and Bob Kahn. From then on, all networks that use TCP/IP are collectively known as the Internet. The standardization of TCP/IP allows the number of Internet sites and users to grow exponentially.

When the ARPAnet had begun operating in 1969, its programmers had instituted an early version of Network Control Protocol (NCP). TCP

(Transfer Control Protocol), outlined in a 1974 paper by Kahn and Cerf, was introduced in 1977 for cross-network connections, and it slowly began to replace NCP within the original ARPAnet. TCP was faster, easier to use, and less expensive to implement than NCP. In 1978 IP (Internet Protocol) is added to TCP and takes over the routing of messages.

As other networks (radio, satellite, local area networks, Usenet, BITnet, etc.) established connections to the ARPAnet in the late 1970s and 1980s, experts realized that the adoption of a single networking protocol would be an important step toward maintaining order within this growing community. They chose TCP/IP. TCP/IP provides a technological bridge for small networks to connect to the Internet much more readily than before. The links branch in every direction, hugely increasing the number of people connected within a single, broad system of information and communication.

As 1983 dawns, every site within or connected to the ARPAnet is supposed to switch to TCP/IP. Some sites are given a grace period of a few months, but by the spring any system that has not converted is bumped off the network. Although the event plays out with few problems for most networkers, buttons circulate that boast "I survived the TCP/IP transition." The networking community has already begun to call the ARPAnet and affiliated networks the "Internet," and in 1983 this evolution in language is made official.

The Internet's exploding frontiers create the need for order and subdivision. The government's Defense Communications Agency, which has authority over the network, splits it into MILNET, for military-related sites, and the regular Internet, for other sites.

1983 A Name Server Is Invented, Enabling Translation of IP Numbers into Names

The first name server allows Internet locations to have electronic addresses that consist of words instead of numbers.

Computers on the Internet communicate with each other using sequences of numbers, so prior to the invention of name servers, network addresses were designated as sequences of IP (Internet Protocol) numbers, such as 205.62.131.127. Sending mail to a user at a particular location or logging on remotely to use the location's resources required entering a list of numbers.

From the Hacker File

WILL THE INTERNET SAVE THE VIDEO GAME STAR?

Wacca wacca wacca. Ask anyone in Generation X to name that tune, and the answer comes easily: it's the theme from the video arcade game, Pac-Man. In *Joystick Nation* author J. C. Herz reports that video games grossed six billion dollars in 1981—more money than the U.S. movie industry and Nevada gambling combined.

Although digital superstars like Pac-Man (and later on, Nintendo's Mario Brothers) were famous enough to inspire television shows and movies, their creators went virtually unknown. Legend has it that Namco Chairman and CEO Masaya Nakamura made millions from Pac-Man, but only gave its designer $3,500. This all changed when some upstart programmers began game companies of their own (such as Activision and Electronic Art) where programmers were both paid large salaries and promoted by name as part of the company's marketing strategy. As historian Steven Levy puts it, game authors were the "third generation of hackers, idiot savants of the microprocessor, kids who didn't know a flow chart from Shinola, yet could use a keyboard like a palette."

Not everyone was happy about the video game revolution. Most school administrators saw arcades as havens for delinquency. In language almost identical to critiques of the Internet, conservatives argued that video games "smacked of moral turpitude," exposing children to sex and violence.

Soon, the wildly successful industry grew greedy and lazy. Believing that people would play anything, they produced a series of unoriginal and unexciting games.

Gamers got bored, and sales dropped. In 1982 Atari (then owned by Warner Communications) announced a stunning $500 million loss the preceding quarter. In 1983 Warner froze all research and development on video games, a move that forced a generation of savants of the microprocessor into filling out time sheets. By the time video games made their comeback in 1986, Nintendo and Sega had spent millions to make their code virtually unbreakable, making the game hacker an endangered species.

Today, mall arcades that survived the crash of 1983 have been "Fisher-Priced," their environments made more suitable for daycare than delinquency. Video games exist side by side with distinctly nondigital games, appealing to a more family-oriented crowd. In the words of Herz, "Video killed the radio star, but Skee-ball killed the video arcade."

But all is not lost. There is one place you can go to exercise your inner juvenile offender: the Internet. If you want to play video games online, head to networked environments like TEN (http://www.ten.net) and white-knuckle with strangers. You may not be able to see your opponents in cyberspace, but as Herz says, "You know they're lurking around the next Hexen corridor waiting to blow you into a bloody pulp." If you want to hack video games online, visit related mailing lists and newsgroups, where reverse-engineering conversations abound. And if you long for the glory days of arcades, you can play Pac-Man online at http://www.davesclassics.com/.

The name server introduced in 1983 can translate IP numbers into words, and words into IP numbers. Acting as an interpreter between the language of computers and the language of users, it allows addresses to have more convenient and descriptive names. This makes the Internet seem more friendly and accessible.

This first name server, consisting of a single file called a host table, is operated by Stanford Research Institute's Network Information Center.

1983 FIDONET GOES ONLINE

Tom Jennings introduces FidoNet, a computer bulletin board system (BBS) committed to free speech. FidoNet is influential not only in spreading the popularity of BBSs, but also in bringing computers and networking into elementary and secondary schools.

In the fall of 1983 Jennings had just moved from Boston to San Francisco to take a new position as a computer programmer for a small software firm. Having some vacation time before the new job was to start, he decided to write the software for a new BBS.

In December 1983 Jennings' BBS is operational. He names it FidoNet, after a computer from a past workplace that colleagues had dubbed "Fido." Within a year he has given or sold the FidoNet program to people around the country so they can start new local nodes of the system. Jennings wants FidoNet to be run by its participants; he wants them to determine the content and rules, or lack thereof. He gives free reign to his sysops (system operators), the people who manage the nodes of a BBS and their members. The FidoNet sysops, in turn, run things loosely by keeping in mind the philosophy, "Thou shalt not offend; thou shalt not be easily offended."

By 1985 Jennings has instituted "National Fido Hour," a period in the middle of the night when all FidoNet nodes are closed to users. During this time each node sends and receives pre-addressed messages to other FidoNet nodes, so that FidoNet users all over the country are connected without having to make personal long-distance phone calls. The sysops at each node choose either to pay for Fido Hour phone bills or to charge their members a small fee. FidoNet thus constitutes one of the earliest wide area public computer networks. It foreshadows a time ten years

Imagining the Net

VIRTUAL HIPPIES: THERE GOES THE NEIGHBORHOOD

Those who take a utopian view of the Internet often forget that online communities are made up of real people who don't always behave as well as you'd like them to. One of the first hard lessons in the realities of online community-building came in 1982, when a small San Diego-based bulletin board named CommuniTree was forced to close shop.

CommuniTree began in 1978 as an experiment in free speech. The board used a treelike structure, which encouraged posting on multiple topics, rather than the one-topic-at-a-time organization of most early BBSs. Each topic on CommuniTree was analogous to a tree branch, flourishing or dying based on user interest. There was no censorship or moderation whatsoever, and deleting material from the board was nearly impossible.

CommuniTree was emblematic of the spirit of "virtual hippiedom" that pervaded the online world of the 1980s. Offline, the hippies were a phenomenon of the 1960s, synonymous with the peace movement, communes, and "free love." As the Vietnam War wound down, so did hippiedom: by the 1980s hippies were scarce. But as real-world hippiedom was in decline, personal computing was taking up its cause. *Wired*'s executive editor, Kevin Kelly, told *The New York Times Magazine*: "The reason why the hippies and people like myself got interested in [networks] is that they are model worlds, small universes.... We get to ask the great questions of all time: What is life? What is human? What is civilization?"

Theorist Sandy Stone argues that the similarities between authentic hippies and computer programmers really only ran surface deep: the grubby attire and financially precarious lifestyle were often a "thin cover over graduate-level degrees and awesome technical proficiencies." CommuniTree's motto (from a remark by Stewart Brand) suggests the way many virtual hippies viewed their mission: "We are as Gods, so we might as well get good at it."

What CommuniTree's Gods hadn't counted on was the introduction of the first barbarian hordes of cyberspace—kids. In 1982 Apple Computer began a campaign to bring computers into American classrooms. Armed with modems, kids dialed onto BBSs but were largely uninspired by the intellectual and spiritual "grand experiments" they found there. Instead, the (mostly) boys posted obscenities and scatological messages—virtual graffiti. CommuniTree was especially vulnerable, as the board's owners were reluctant to erase or even moderate posts, regardless of content.

After being continually bombarded with graffiti hits, CommuniTree suffered a fatal disk crash and closed for business. Stone argues that the death of CommuniTree imparted hard lessons for virtual hippies, "about what was and what was not possible in an unstructured and unprotected conference environment." They had hoped to create new societies online, but virtual hippies discovered that in order to survive, online conferencing software would have to include mechanisms for surveillance and control. As Stone puts it, many online systems begun by virtual hippies ended up using ARPA's "benevolent despot approach" to system administration.

later when people all over the world communicate via computer networks and electronic mail.

By 1986 there are about one thousand FidoNet nodes, and five years later there are ten times that number. The system is connected to the Internet in 1991.

FidoNet opens many of its users' eyes to the potential benefits of online communication in other areas, such as education. Teachers push for telephone lines and computers in their classrooms so their students can participate in FidoNet conferences that are tailored for elementary and secondary schools. It takes a few years, but slowly some classrooms are outfitted with the necessary equipment.

1984 Apple Macintosh Debuts, Featuring a Graphical User Interface

Computer manufacturer Apple introduces the Macintosh, the first personal computer to feature a graphical user interface (GUI). GUI, a system of operating a computer by manipulating windows, menus, and icons with a mouse, is much easier to use than the traditional system requiring precise text input. The Macintosh revolutionizes the way people interact with their computers.

By 1981 many people had personal computers sitting on their desks at work and at home. The first widely available personal computers, the Apple II and the Commodore PET, had entered the market in 1977. They were followed by Tandy's TRS-80 later the same year. And in 1981 IBM (International Business Machines, Inc.) launched its Personal Computer (PC), which became an industry standard within a few years as smaller companies made compatible machines.

These early personal computers were a challenge for users who were not computer experts by trade or hobby. The interaction between user and computer occurred via "command line interface," in which the user had to type explicit instructions that the computer could recognize. If one letter was incorrect, the user had to retype the entire line of instructions. There was no standard interface for different applications, such as word processors and spreadsheets; each application had its own screen layout and set of conventions that users had to learn.

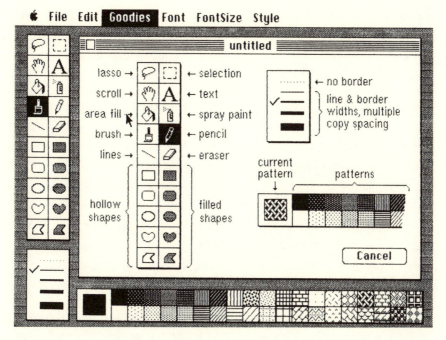

The Macintosh revolutionized personal computers with its Graphical User Interface, or GUI (Image courtesy of The Computer Museum History Center).

But the origins of GUI (pronounced "gooey") were more complicated than the need for a more user-friendly interface for personal computers. Back in 1963 the Stanford Research Institute (one of the first four nodes on the ARPAnet) had established the Human Factors Research Center (HFRC) for the study of human-computer interaction. There, Doug Engelbart had invented the mouse in 1965. He had also led a team of researchers who devised crude programming for a system of integrated text and graphics. Although computer technology of the 1960s was too limited to build such a system, the ideas generated at HFRC influenced the development of GUI.

The first company to build a computer featuring a GUI was Xerox Corporation. Concerned about competition from Japanese photo-copier manufacturers and fearful of losing business to a "paperless office" of the future, Xerox created the Xerox Palo Alto Research Center (PARC). Scientists at Xerox PARC, led by Bob Taylor of ARPA fame, spearheaded the company's effort to branch out into new technologies. Familiar with the research performed at HFRC in the 1960s, the Xerox PARC development team set to work devising a desktop workstation featuring a composite of text and graphics. The result, the Xerox Star, was marketed in 1981 amidst great fanfare. It had a mouse, icons, folders, and documents. The Xerox Star was a commercial failure because of its high price tag, but it offered a vision of the future.

Many Xerox PARC scientists felt strongly that their own company was lacking enthusiasm for experimental work: Xerox executives were paying researchers to create the future, but when they saw it, they weren't interested. *Someone* was interested, however: Apple CEO Steve Jobs. In 1979 Xerox had invested venture capital in Apple Computer, and Jobs had visited Xerox while the Star workstation was under development. He took home a brainful of ideas about GUI and brought Apple engineers to Xerox PARC to see it. Apple's first attempt at marketing a GUI-based personal computer, the Lisa, went nowhere for the same reason that the Star had failed: too expensive. But the second try, the Macintosh, hit the target.

As head of the Macintosh's original development team, Apple employee Jef Raskin named the computer after his favorite apple. Jobs took over soon thereafter and spearheaded most of the effort that yielded the finished product. The main problem was to maintain the performance of the Lisa but make it run on cheaper hardware and a much smaller memory. Creativity and the ability to write tight machine code characterized the team that participated in the Macintosh project.

In 1983 Apple begins to devise marketing schemes to differentiate its emerging product from its competitors—various low-cost personal computers without GUI. On January 22, 1984, a television advertisement for the Macintosh is broadcast during the Super Bowl. Apple follows up the commercial with $15 million worth of publicity. The Macintosh sells well (for $2,500) initially, mostly to computer enthusiasts, but the hype is unable to sustain sales. Apple executives relaunch the computer as a business machine, but its small memory is not well suited for business applications. Eventually the Macintosh finds its niche: publishing, media, and education, and during the late 1980s and early 1990s more advanced versions of the original are a resounding success in those arenas.

The Macintosh's immediate impact is to make GUI an industry standard, quickly adopted by other operating systems such as Windows. GUI introduces a completely new relationship between human and computer, one that makes computers more "friendly" and accessible. GUI enables nonexperts

Media History

YOU SAY YOU WANT A REVOLUTION? COMPUTERS MEET MADISON AVENUE

The 1984 Super Bowl wasn't all that exciting—the Los Angeles Raiders beat the Washington Redskins, as predicted. Perhaps that's why the most shocking thing that happened that day was the content of a sixty-second television spot for the Apple Macintosh. "We needed a movement," recalls Director of Marketing Mike Murray. "The movement was Macintosh, the democratization of technology. After all, who was IBM? Big Brother."

The ad began with a room full of shaven-headed workers glued to a video screen, watching Big Brother. Suddenly, a woman in bright-colored running clothes ran into the room and hurled a sledgehammer into the screen. The screen exploded. A voice was heard: "On January twenty-fourth, Apple Computer will introduce Macintosh. And you'll see why 1984 won't be like 1984."

Few personal-computer commercials have been able to capture the excitement of the original 1984 ad, but this certainly isn't for lack of trying—think Gateway's "cow boxes" or Intel's Homer Simpson campaign. Apple now uses the catch phrase, "Think different," to market their newest computer—the iMac—as "A Computer for the Rest of Us." As *Mac World*'s Andrew Gore points out, "Just as the [new Volkswagen] Beetle harkens back to its flower-powered ancestor, the iMac capitalizes on nostalgia for the all-in-one 'classic' Mac of 1984."

In an ironic twist, advertisers are now finding *themselves* plunged into the computing age, via the Internet. For years, advertisers lacked enthusiasm about the Net. They complained that Net advertising was too small and plain and that Web banners garnered meager "click rates" from viewers. But the times are changing. An Internet Advertising Bureau study recently reported that when viewers saw even a single ad banner, there was a "positive impact on intent to purchase." A similar study from NetRatings, a Web market research firm, declared that banner advertising campaigns increase a company's brand-name recognition, regardless of whether viewers click through or not.

What's more, the sheer number of people going online (current estimates at twenty to fifty-two million; future estimates as high as two hundred million) have forced advertising agencies to take note of the Net. As Forrester Research reports, 46 percent of Fortune 500 executives already believe the Internet will have "a huge or significant" impact on their sales over the next three years. Where sales possibilities go, advertising follows.

Web advertising is expected to increase from $312 million in 1995 to $5 billion by 2000, according to Jupiter Communications. With this much money being thrown at the Web, ad agencies are beginning to form "new media" divisions and make themselves familiar with interactive technologies like Shockwave and Java. While ad expenditures for the Web are still extremely small compared to other media types, the rate of increase is expected to accelerate. Madison Avenue brought the concept of revolution to personal computing. Perhaps it's only right, then, that the Internet may revolutionize advertising.

to use computers more freely; even children can operate a point-and-click GUI system. GUI revolutionizes computer graphics and introduces graphical methods of organizing files and documents. And when the Internet and World Wide Web emerge in the 1980s and 1990s, GUI is the standard that allows them to be adopted so easily by the public.

1984 DOMAIN NAME SYSTEM IS INSTALLED, ENABLING EASIER CROSS-NETWORK ACCESS

Internet software designer Paul Mockapetris authors RFC 882, which outlines the Domain Name System (DNS), a broad network of name servers. Its open structure allows more efficient cross-network access and unlimited network growth.

The Internet's rapid growth had recently been causing havoc and begetting changes throughout the network. The DNS originated as a solution to network overgrowth. The problem had begun with the limitations of the original name server (a program that translated IP numbers into word-based host names) invented the previous year. As more and more sites added their addresses to the name server, it became unmanageable. In 1982 Jon Postel and Zaw-Sing Su broadly outlined the DNS in RFC (Request for Comment) 819. Mockapetris expands and details the system further in 1983's RFC 882.

The DNS makes it possible for numerous name servers to coexist, accommodating the exploding number of Internet sites. The DNS consists of software that enables communication between name servers. When network users attempt to connect to an Internet address, their computer sends a request to the nearest name server, which searches for the IP number for that address. If it can not find the number, it asks another name server, and so on until the correct IP number is found and the message is delivered or the site is called up. The first name server stores the IP number for a set amount of time, so that the user (or other users) can access the site more quickly on the next attempt.

The DNS is what is known as a distributed database; it encompasses all the name servers around the planet, but there is no single organization or site that stores all the information on all the name servers. Distributed databases can typically handle vast growth without encountering problems related to size.

Beyond the Net

CYBORGS IN OUR MIDST

Cyberpunk popularized the concept of the cyborg—a body part organic, part inorganic—to a generation of readers. But cyborgs are not merely the stuff of science fiction. Molly, the *Neuromancer* heroine with the retinal implants, is certainly a cyborg. But so is Stephen Hawking, the real-life disabled hero of modern physics, who has reconceptualized the universe from the confines of his wheelchair.

In her influential 1994 essay, "A Cyborg Manifesto," feminist thinker Donna Haraway argues that the natural body—if it ever existed to begin with—is a thing of the past. People's bodies, she explains, are inescapably linked to technology. We eat food that has been grown with the help of agricultural technologies. We receive advanced technological medical treatments. Our interaction with the world, also, is enmeshed with technology: we communicate via telephones and computers; we compete in athletics with the help of high-tech equipment and diets. Haraway, who declared, "I'd rather be a cyborg than a goddess," argues that we should embrace the blurring of the distinction between organism and machine because it offers the opportunity to reformulate social relations.

Haraway argues that in traditional western culture, the concept of what is "natural" has played a crucial role in the exploitation of the underclass. The predominant belief for hundreds of years was, for example, that women were "naturally" fit only for motherhood, which created a cultural situation in which women were largely in a position of servitude to men. Haraway rejects the idea that "natural" means something inherently better than "artificial" or "technological." She posits that if we think of ourselves as both organism and machine, if we let the distinction between "natural" and "technological" disintegrate, then we can rebuild our social relations and our identities.

"A Cyborg Manifesto" is widely read among academics and is a standard text in many undergraduate courses. Although Haraway does not use the term herself, her manifesto is credited as one of the inspirations for the cyberfeminism movement that emerged in the 1990s. Cyberfeminists embrace Haraway's vision of people as cyborgs and her view that this vision offers the opportunity to reconstruct ourselves and our society in nontraditional ways.

1984 WILLIAM GIBSON'S BOOK NEUROMANCER INTRODUCES THE TERM "CYBERSPACE"

The science-fiction novel Neuromancer, *by William Gibson, is published. It introduces the term "cyberspace," which comes to refer to the virtual realm of electronic communication, interaction, community, and information storage.* Neuromancer *is widely read and influences popular images of the future potential—both exciting and dangerous—of the cyberspace age.*

Neuromancer describes the adventure of two cyberspace-savvy individuals in a futuristic world, a world in which advanced computer technology and cyberspace play crucial roles in people's lives. As the story unfolds, it introduces variations on a central theme: the connections between the human body and technology. In the book these connections are both physical, as illustrated by "cyborgs" (entities that are part human and part machine), and virtual, as demonstrated by the act of "jacking" one's mind into cyberspace.

In *Neuromancer*, Gibson neither praises nor denounces the advancing pervasiveness of technology in human culture. Rather, the book explores futuristic possible directions for technology and demands readers' attention to the positive and negative aspects involved. As such, it is widely read and written about in interdisciplinary college courses that investigate the interaction between individuals, society, and advanced technology.

As one of the first science-fiction books to address issues surrounding the potential capabilities of computer technology and networks, *Neuromancer* quickly earns cult status. It is soon recognized as one of the earliest and most influential novels in an emerging genre called cyberpunk, a branch of science fiction that explores the impact of cybertechnology on society. Throughout the 1980s cyberpunk authors produce a library of futuristic tales; literary critics respond with an expansive collection of magazine articles and scholarly essays about the cyberpunk movement.

The Wild
Frontier

In the late eighties, more and more regular people get online—through BBSs, online services, and other virtual communities—and are exposed to the wonders of being connected. At the same time, however, the sinister potential of networks becomes more apparent, as a string of events demonstrates that interconnectedness can be both dangerous and costly. While the Internet begins to be used as a tool for political organization and the federal government funds a new and faster backbone to carry Internet traffic, computer crime hits the front page. Chapter Five explores the problem of balancing the desire for openness, shared resources, and the free flow of ideas with the need to keep valuable data private within secured systems.

Throughout the 1980s supplying the corporate world with PCs and networking services becomes a bigger and bigger business. In addition, the home computer market begins to open up as more people become interested in computers. The Commodore 64, the Tandy, and lesser known PCs debut, and home use increases. Virtual communities bloom and grow, many of them patterned after the San Francisco Bay Area's successful Whole Earth 'Lectronic Link (the WELL). One prominent member of the WELL, John Perry Barlow—writer, lyricist, Wyoming rancher, and respected alderman of cyberspace—will have an enlightening run-in with the FBI.

A Kinder, Gentler Network?

What can be said of the political climate in the second half of the 1980s? It was good for business. The Reagan administration's small government, probusiness policies made sworn enemies of consumer, environmental, and civil liberties groups. With Reagan's decisive reelection over Democratic challenger Walter Mondale in 1984, Americans sent the message that they wanted more of what the early 1980s had brought them, including more of the same laissez-faire government and upper-bracket tax breaks that had increased many people's wealth.

In his second term Reagan would finally soften his stance on the 'evil empire,' signing a landmark treaty with the Soviet Union to reduce stockpiles of the weapons the nation had gone into unprecedented debt to purchase. And just in time, too: the Berlin Wall was about to come crashing down. By the end of the decade despite the Iran-Contra scandal, which had muted the Reagan's administration's political success, Americans had elected George Bush, Reagan's faithful Vice President, to lead the country on.

By the end of the eighties it had become abundantly clear that software, networking tools, and other Net-based technologies could be profitable, and that companies, once they got off the ground and went public, would feel little or no loyalty to their founders. Start-ups funded with maxed-out creditcards became major Wall Street players, often leaving their founders in the dust. By 1990 Sandy Lehner and Len Bosack, the founders of Cisco Systems—which found phenomenal success in selling network routers—had been fired, Bob Metcalfe had been forced out of 3Com, and Steve Jobs had been ousted from Apple.

Cowboys on an Electronic Frontier

In 1983 the film *War Games* spoke to the public's new fears about the dangers of computer networks, as well as their old fears of a nuclear Armageddon. To recap, a high school student unwittingly taps into an air force computer and nearly starts a nuclear war. The movie may have seemed far-fetched, but subsequent events proved that it was not entirely wide of its mark.

In 1986 astronomer and computer expert Cliff Stoll noticed that an unauthorized user was gaining access to confidential files at the Lawrence Berkeley Laboratory in California. He tracked the trespasser. It turned out to be a spy who had hacked his way through to sensitive military information and was selling it to the KGB. The hacker had gotten dirt on the Strategic Defense Initiative (better known as 'Star Wars'), U.S. space shuttle flights, intelligence satellites, and semiconductor designs.

In 1989 Stoll's detective work led to the apprehension of three West Germans, and his book, *The Cuckoo's Egg*, became a bestseller.

That same year Kevin Mitnick became the first hacker to become a household name when he was convicted of stealing software from Digital Equipment Corp. Mitnick had graduated from surreptitiously improving his friends' high school grades (and not by tutoring) as a teen to stealing software and long-distance telephone codes as a young adult. He would go on to more sublime exploits, deleting his own criminal record from police and court systems. If there were any programmers and systems administrators who weren't concerned about network security by the time Mitnick's exploits hit the papers, you can bet they became so.

And so the late 1980s ushered in a new era of law enforcement: computer crimebusting. The Mitnick conviction caused law enforcement officials, from local police departments to the FBI, to initiate a "hacker crackdown." Unfortunately, many of those doing the busting were less than equal to the task. In more than one instance, adrenaline-filled agents found themselves in the embarrassing position of breaking down doors only to find that they were not really sure whether they had caught someone red-handed or not, because they really didn't know what they were looking for.

The Secret Service organized Operation Sun Devil in response to concerns that hackers were becoming a serious financial drain on U.S. corporations—a perceived threat to the nation's economy that had to be dealt with harshly and decisively. The hackdown, if you will, got underway in the first half of 1990. Feds seized computers, disks, phones, and other equipment under even the vaguest suspicion that computer fraud had been committed.

Several suspected hackers were arrested. One, known as Acid Phreak, was accused of crashing AT&T's computer system and causing $1 billion in damage, but he was never charged with anything. Another accused hacker was charged with publicizing a confidential document; the case was dropped when it became clear that the document could be obtained legally. To a few prescient members of the growing cyberspace community, the events of early 1990 were a wake-up call. They brought to light not only the fact that those accused of computer crime were seeing their constitutional rights abridged, but that law enforcement personnel knew shockingly little about how computer networks worked and what would constitute crime if it *was* being committed.

There has always been a fine line between granting law enforcement authorities the legitimate powers they need to stop crime and ensuring that suspects' constitutional rights are upheld. The emerging world of the Internet was no different, except it seemed that constitutional abuses were being taken very lightly indeed. It was at this point that John Perry Barlow and Mitch Kapor (who had founded Lotus 1-2-3 in the early 1980s) grasped the magnitude of what was at stake.

The Internet was the first new frontier the United States had seen in over one hundred years. Like all frontiers, it would have its outlaws, its law-abiding citizens, its prudish schoolmarms, its claim stakers and stealers, its bounty hunters, and its sheriffs. But this was new territory. And if the people who settled it first were going to have anything to say about the way it was governed, they were going to have to get together and have a town meetin' or two. The Electronic Frontier Foundation (EFF), a group that works to protect civil liberties on the Internet, was born. Cyberspace had gotten its own lobby.

The EFF organized to provide legal defense for people whose rights were being trampled in the crackdowns—some of them hackers—and to establish a voice for the citizens of cyberspace in the formation of laws that would ultimately govern it. EFF got its seed money from Kapor and Steve Wozniak, Apple's cofounder. It continues to work to protect freedom of speech and privacy rights on the Internet, among other issues.

The Changing Face of the Establishment

The 'hackdown' and the birth of the EFF signaled a fundamental change in the federal government's relationship to its baby, the Net. The government goes from being the Internet's proud parent—its funder, nurturer, and cheerleader—to its disciplinarian and cop.

Why the change in relationship? In the 1980s most businesses were interested in networking for their own purposes, but they were generally not so hip to the potential of the Internet. Businesses certainly had valuable proprietary information stored on computer networks, however, making network security a major issue. The government's computer crimebusting frenzy was a response to the cries of corporate America, as well as the increased concerns of national security agencies.

By the mid-1980s the line between establishment and antiestablishment had shifted somewhat, although not as far as it would shift in the 1990s. In his 1990 history of the founding of the EFF, Barlow remarked: "It appeared possible that one side effect of current government practices might be the elimination of the next generation of computer entrepreneurs and digital designers." In other words, if corporate bigwigs and cops weren't careful (or weren't *watched* carefully), they might put tomorrow's best and brightest behind bars.

In the 1980s corporate America wanted to be defended against those dangerous kids who sought to wreak havoc and steal stuff; companies needed the Feds to protect them from the young, computer-savvy set. But the corporate world also needed to *become* computer-savvy, and it could only do that by employing the computer savvy. In the late-1990s that change has been fully effected. The companies that lead the astronomical growth in the stock market and have pull in Washington are information technology firms are such as Intel, Microsoft, Netscape, and Sun Microsystems.

One of the first inklings of the establishment changeover was seen when Kapor cofounded the EFF in 1990. Kapor was a key figure because he represented corporate success and could thus command a respectful Wall Street audience. The media didn't quite know how to react to the news of Kapor's role in the EFF, but the general consensus was that he had sided with hackers against the government. Although Kapor had left Lotus in 1986, he had ample experience in protecting impressive profits (Lotus had earned $53 million in its first year). Because of that, he could not be dismissed as a radical, hacker-friendly scofflaw. Kapor's presence in the EFF helped some, especially the liberty-loving business interests, begin to understand that unless hackers' rights were protected, nobody's rights would be.

By the late 1980s a leitmotif had emerged that replays with more maddening frequency in the 1990s—the government's ability to create legislation to govern cyberspace lags woefully behind the actual pace of new technology. In a footrace, the law would not only be well behind the technology pack, the pack would have lapped it.

To this day we see the federal government being called in to settle cyberdisputes. And to this day the government—in the form of the Justice Department, Federal Trade Commission, and the Judiciary—is severely limited by a lack of expertise about all things cybertechnical. In 1997, in the Justice Department's antitrust suit against Microsoft, Judge Thomas Penfield Jackson of U.S. District Court in Washington, D.C. felt the need to call in Lawrence Lessig, a Harvard professor, as a "special master," admitting that the court lacked the know-how to make an informed ruling in the case.

The Growth of Online Communities

In 1986 the National Science Foundation laid down the hard wiring for a new computer network to expand the ARPAnet, now commonly referred to as the Internet. NSFnet allowed researchers who were *not* working on defense-related projects to get connected. Independent networks such as BITnet had been established between non-ARPAnet universities in the early 1980s, but NSFnet facilitated a much more widespread network. And smaller, formerly independent networks began linking up to the Internet, thanks to new routing technology made possible by the NSF.

In the late 1980s most of the Internet's estimated sixty-thousand members were still affiliated with military installations, universities, or corporations. But the decade witnessed the creation and explosive growth of many civilian and nonhobbyist networks—networks other than the ARPAnet and NSFnet. Perhaps the biggest sign that computers weren't just for nerds anymore was that people began going online to do more than talk about their computers. BBSs cropped up around the country, and free public online access debuted in the form of the Cleveland Free-Net in 1986.

The Cleveland Free-Net was of major significance because it represented the first time that *anybody*, regardless of income, education, or affiliation, could access the Internet. A computer and modem were all that were required. And the network's character was entirely determined by its users, who maintained it. The Cleveland Free-Net served as a model for more freenets across the nation.

People began freenets with the philosophy that people needed to *own* computer networks, not just use them. The WELL was special in that regard and became a model for online community building. The WELL's membership grew quickly and would link to the Internet in 1992. The late 1980s also saw the creation of America Online. It began as Quantum Computer Services, a BBS that utilized a graphical user interface (GUI). Founder Steve Case insisted that the company reach out to the nongeek population—mainstream consumers. AOL would begin offering Internet access in the early 1990s, and the rest is history.

The end of the 1980s also saw an explosive expansion of Internet hosts. In 1987 there were roughly 10,000 such hosts; by the end of the decade, there were more than 100,000. The Internet's scope was also becoming increasingly international. By 1989 Australia, New Zealand, Germany, Israel, Italy, Japan, Mexico, the Netherlands, Puerto Rico, and the United Kingdom had established connections to NSFnet.

An Ending and a Beginning: the ARPAnet and the Web

As the 1990s began, another groundbreaking event in the evolution of the Internet took place: the development of the World Wide Web. In the freewheeling 1960s Ted Nelson had invented hypertext, a way to navigate between documents in a nonsequential order. In the late 1980s Tim Berners-Lee, working at the European Laboratory for Particle Physics (CERN) in Geneva, was looking for a way to distribute information across different kinds of computers and operating systems.

Using a NeXT workstation (the product of Steve Jobs' latest computer company), Berners-Lee was inspired by the computer's operating system, which utilized object-oriented programming (OOP). OOP had been around since the late 1970s but had not often been utilized as a production or programming tool. He used it to create a hypertext system to link, store, and retrieve information. In 1991 Berners-Lee and a team at CERN introduced the building blocks of what would become the Web: HTTP (Hypertext Transfer Protocol), HTML (Hypertext Markup Language), and URL (Universal Resource Locator). Berners-Lee and colleague Robert Cailliau called the system the World Wide Web.

In 1992 those concepts debuted on the Internet, and programmers everywhere went to work to refine the system. Of course, once there was a system of documents linked by hypertext, people needed a way to navigate through them and actually find things. The first browsers would soon follow, as would search engines.

While something big was beginning in Geneva, something was coming to an end in the United States. In 1990 ARPAnet was finally decommissioned and its hosts retired. The nodes that had launched a thousand packets (many millions, actually) had finally outlived their usefulness. The future of the Internet, the future dreamt of by Berners-Lee and his team, will evolve and flourish in the much-faster NSFnet backbone.

1985 THE WHOLE EARTH 'LECTRONIC LINK GOES ONLINE

Larry Brilliant and Stewart Brand establish the Whole Earth 'Lectronic Link (WELL), which quietly transforms into one of the most influential virtual communities in the age of computer networks. Despite slow growth, bouts of rocky leadership, and chronic financial instability, the WELL is viewed as a model for building online communities because of its unique, sophisticated (virtual) ambiance.

The WELL had originated as an idea of Larry Brilliant, who owned Network Technologies International, a company that sold computer-conferencing systems. Convinced that computer networking would be the wave of the near future, he approached Stewart Brand, visionary risk-taker extraordinaire. Brand had founded *The Whole Earth Catalog* and *Whole Earth Review*, publications aimed at providing people with alternative, progressive tools for reshaping approaches to issues such as the environment, politics, and education.

Brilliant wanted to offer a group of people the means to communicate via computer, just to see what would happen, and he thought an interesting crowd of curious and articulate computer users might be found among Brand's *Whole Earth* readership.

Brilliant made a proposal to Brand in fall 1984: Brilliant would provide the capital, Brand would provide the people, and they would each own half of the new enterprise. Brand agreed and began to spin ideas. The notion was not totally new; there were dozens of bulletin-board systems (BBSs) springing up all over the country, systems that offered a members-only forum for public postings and private correspondence. But Brand wanted the WELL to have some distinct differences, including the absence of anonymity. This would be obtained by encouraging face-to-face contact among members (at, for example, WELL parties) and by requiring that members be identifiable online by their real names and e-mail addresses. Brand's view was that this would force individuals to be responsible for what they wrote.

In March 1985 the WELL goes online. For the first few weeks, members of the *Whole Earth* community are its only users, but over the following months a few hundred outsiders join via word-of-mouth. Located in Sausalito, California, the WELL's office holds the system's VAX computer, six modems, and six phone lines. The hardware is slow, and the software—a program called PicoSpan—is a text-only, user-unfriendly conferencing tool.

The WELL is organized into a number of conferences, each with its own subject. The conferences cover general categories of interest (for example, religion, law, and gardening), and within them there are more specific topics—at which members post messages and respond to others' postings. The threads of conversation are saved indefinitely; as a general rule, members cannot go back and erase what they have written. As planned, members' names are linked to their postings, and the phrase "You own your own words" becomes the WELL's credo. Conversation on the WELL tends to be more articulate and intellectual than the scrawls found on other BBSs, drawing an educated, sophisticated membership consisting largely of writers, artists, reporters, teachers, activists, and programmers. Most early WELL members feel that the network they belong to is indeed a true community, where people meet, argue, form friendships, and rally together to support someone in need.

The WELL has more than five thousand members by 1991 and the following year hooks up to the Internet. Despite growing membership, the network is continually limited by financial roadblocks until 1993 when Bruce Katz, wealthy inventor of Rockport shoes, acquires half of the com-

THESE BOOTS ARE MADE FOR ECHO

The success of the WELL inspired the creation of many other virtual communities. One of them, the New York-based Echo, was founded by WELL member Stacy Horn in 1990. Echo is noteworthy not only because it has survived the onslaught of big services like America Online, but also because its users are forty percent female—a remarkable achievement in male-dominated cyberspace. Here Horn answers questions about the making of a virtual community.

Q: What was your first virtual community? What got you hooked?

The WELL. Kathleen Creighton got me hooked. Someone on the WELL said something along the lines of "You suck," and I probably came back with the always snappy, "Oh yeah? Well, you suck," then Kathleen e-mailed me and said, "Will you just ignore that person already? They're an idiot." Virtual chemistry. I had made my first online friend.

Q: What caused you to branch out from the WELL and start Echo?

Their humor was very different than mine, there were almost no women, and few people from NYC. It made me homesick.

Journalists wrote that I started Echo to provide a safe place for women on the Net. This was not the reason at all. I wanted to get more women on Echo to make Echo better. And safety is not an effective lure. Come to Echo, we're safe. That would be like hanging out a sign that said: BORING.

Q: How did you secure the money to begin Echo?

I used the severance pay I got from my employer. I tried to raise capital but I couldn't convince *anyone* that the Internet was going to be hot. I think this makes me the worst salesperson that has ever lived, *ever*.

Q: How do you go about recruiting women?

The most effective thing I did to get more women online was also the most controversial. I made sure that half the [conference] hosts on Echo were women. Cyber-affirmative action. The Echoids cried: Quotas! Tokenism! But I suspected that it mattered less how differently men and women communicate. What mattered was that there were so few of us. If we were a force, our style would be incorporated into the discourse of cyberspace.

Q: If a financial "angel" were to show up with $100 million to improve Echo, what sorts of things would you do?

First I'd tell them to keep most of it. Then I'd put in a new interface, upgrade the equipment, have a lot more face-to-face events, finally do some real marketing. Then I'd buy a nice new outfit with cute little black boots.

pany and pours some money into it. He buys the other half the following year, moves the headquarters into new offices, and upgrades the hardware.

By the late 1990s WELL membership reaches ten thousand. Often appearing in the media, it develops a reputation as the prime example of how to build a virtual community. However, the ingredients for the WELL's success (in terms of fostering community) remain elusive and are probably the unique result of having been started at the right time, in the right place, with the right mix of people.

STEVE JOBS

Steven Paul Jobs, cofounder of Apple Computer, is known for ample amounts of both eccentric behavior and entrepreneurial success. Colleagues' stories have sketched a public portrait of Jobs as demanding and egotistical, yet charming and inspirational. Consistent with such contradictions, observers note, was his transformation from a meditative youth to one of the most driven, influential business people in the revolution of personal computing.

Jobs was born in 1955 and raised by adoptive parents in the heart of what was to become California's Silicon Valley. As a teenager he was swept up by the infectious enthusiasm of electronics hobbyists. Already brimming with self-confidence at age thirteen, he phoned multimillionaire William Hewlett (cofounder of electronics company Hewlett-Packard) to ask for some equipment he needed for a school project. Hewlett not only provided the requested materials, but also offered Jobs an after-school job.

Around 1971 Jobs met Stephen Wozniak, a fellow hobbyist five years his senior, and the two built and sold "blue boxes." These gadgets, which enabled users to make free long-distance telephone calls, were not illegal to make and sell—however, using a blue box was indeed a crime.

Jobs enrolled at Reed College, in Portland, Oregon, but dropped out after one semester.

After working at Atari for a few months in 1974, he set off for India on a spiritual quest and studied transcendental meditation, a meditation technique popular in the 1970s.

In 1975 Jobs and Wozniak joined the Homebrew Computer Club, a gathering of electronics hobbyists, and learned about microprocessor technology. Wozniak, the superior engineer of the two, built a crude computer around the Mostek 6502 microchip and called it the "Apple." Jobs foresaw the potential of personal computing and convinced Wozniak that they could market the creation. They assembled the early Apples, which consisted basically of naked circuit boards, in Jobs' parents' garage and sold about two hundred of them.

Following this legendary beginning, Jobs and Wozniak launched the Apple Computer company. Its subsequent success was due to Jobs' dedicated evangelism and intuitive marketing sense. He rustled up sufficient capital, an experienced president, and a public relations account at a time when the personal computer had not yet entered public consciousness. Under Jobs' direction, Apple grew into a computer-manufacturing giant.

Leaving Apple in 1985 Jobs founded NeXT, Inc. It is here that Jobs made his major contribution to the Internet, as the hardware and software created by NeXT would ultimately change the Net forever, when Tim Berners-Lee uses it to create the World Wide Web.

1985 STEVE JOBS RESIGNS FROM APPLE AND FORMS NeXT, INC.

Steve Jobs, cofounder of Apple Computer, leaves Apple and establishes a new company called NeXT, to build educational computer hardware. Later focusing on software instead, NeXT does pioneering work in the field of object-oriented programming.

Steve Jobs had begun to lose his authority at Apple in 1984, shortly after the release of the Macintosh. The Macintosh—first conceived of by engineer Jef Raskin and pushed through to completion by Jobs—was reasonably successful, but as the year rolled on Apple executives believed Jobs was no longer contributing valuable work to the company, and they eventually stopped assigning him new projects. A power struggle between himself and CEO John Sculley led Jobs to leave the company and, in a rage, sell all his Apple stock in September 1985.

Earlier that month Jobs had been inspired by a conversation with Nobel-winning biochemist Paul Berg. After Berg had described some of his research, Jobs asked him whether he had ever considered using a computer to simulate his experiments. Berg said that universities generally didn't have computers and software that could perform such things. Jobs decided he would put his energy toward developing computers for the higher-education market.

After quitting his Apple post Jobs pours money into his new venture, NeXT. He wants to develop a desk mainframe—a whole workstation for researchers and students to have on their desks. A few universities and individuals invest in Jobs' company, enabling him to proceed with

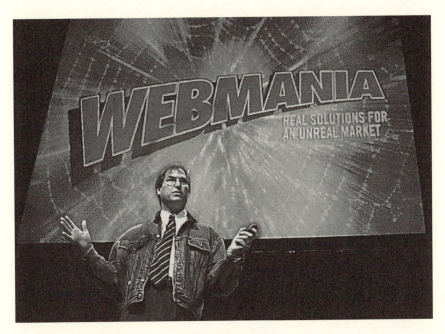

Steve Jobs, CEO of NeXT, Inc., at the 1996 Webmania conference in San Francisco (AP / Wide World Photos).

Smaller, Better, Faster, More!

In 1985 the Intel Corporation plastered California with billboards as part of an ad campaign for their new 386 chip. On each board was the number "286" with a red slash across the middle. Industry insider Larry Magid recalls, "The first time I saw one . . . I figured it was the work of an aggressive Intel hater." It later dawned on Magid that Intel "wasn't just trying to convince us to buy machines with 386 CPUs, it was telling the world that the 286 was now dead." Intel was, in Magid's words, "committing infanticide."

Intel Corporation had released the world's first commercial microprocessor (microchip) for public consumption in 1971. The first microchip was as powerful as the original thirty-ton ENIAC machine, and it opened the door to a new kind of computer user: the hobbyist, whose relationship with her machine is personal, rather than businesslike. The design of Intel's improved second chip inspired the 1974 invention of the first home computer, the Altair. From then on, hobbyists eagerly awaited the arrival of the next chips.

The 1985 ad campaign touted the release of the 80386, a 32-bit processor which could run powerful operating systems like Unix. For enthusiasts, this was a godsend: now individuals could afford to own machines comparable in power and storage capacity to minicomputers and ultimately more capable of connecting to the Internet. But the technology took some time to catch on with the general public. Intel set its sights on the average home user by coordinating the release of the 386 chip with Microsoft's "kinder, gentler" operating system, Windows, which also debuted in 1985. As Magid points out, it was the Windows tie-in that forced Intel to kill off their baby, the 286—machines with 286 chips would run just fine, but they couldn't run Windows.

In his article "We've Gotta Have It," Magid argues that Intel has a history of aggressive marketing, all the way up to the current campaign behind their Pentium II. Today there remain a huge number of 386 and 486 machines connected to the Internet. Yet Intel pushes consumers ever forward. As Intel is now a full-fledged monopoly, owning ninety percent of the semiconductor market, Magid wonders if we should trust them to tell us when our computers are obsolete.

On the Internet, debates rage about just how much computer firepower is enough to have a successful cyberspace experience. Netizens like Magid have begun to question whether networking needs are stimulating the need for faster processors or if the need for speed is being created by the very people who sell it.

research and manufacturing, and in 1989 NeXT introduces its first workstations. The machines are slow, offer few software applications, and are more expensive than comparable hardware that buyers already know and respect. Only about fifty thousand NeXT machines are built between 1989 and 1993, when Jobs turns the company's attention solely to software.

Jobs tries, with little success, to sell the NeXT operating system, called NeXTSTEP, for operation on other manufacturers' computers. Despite its limited value as an operating system, NeXTSTEP gives programmers and users experience with object-oriented programming (OOP). OOP had been developed in the 1960s, but early versions were extremely slow; its usefulness accelerated in the 1980s with more advanced hardware and languages.

OOP consists of software that includes both the code (instructions) and the data (the information upon which the computer operates the code). In traditional programming, code and data are kept separate, and the code can be reprogrammed only by an expert programmer; if an amateur tries to change the code to make the computer do something different, a small error could put the brakes on the whole program. OOP enables programmers to create software from OOP building blocks (called "objects"), which already contain both code and information. Programmers can create large programs by adding and removing objects (the objects themselves cannot be altered). OOP is useful particularly for graphic design, mathematical manipulation, and simulation programs. It also proves vital to the development and evolution of software for the World Wide Web (WWW) in the 1990s.

1985 LUCASFILM'S HABITAT, AN ONLINE GAME-PLAYING ENVIRONMENT, IS CREATED

Chip Morningstar and F. Randall Farmer design the software and architecture of an online multiple-user game world called Habitat. Funded by Lucasfilm Games and Quantum Computer Services, Inc., it is available commercially in the United States in 1985 under the name Club Caribe (later changed to Habitat).

At Habitat's core is a central system which runs its game programs and can support thousands of participants at a time. Participants log in via telephone lines from their home computers and interact with other players in a simulated world. But unlike the MUDs (Multiuser Dungeons) of the early 1980s, Habitat incorporates graphics as well as text. The game runs only on Commodore 64 computers.

By 1990 Habitat is no longer operating in the United States, but it is flourishing in Japan (with a Japanese-language interface). Fujitsu, the new proprietor of Habitat, markets the game to run on its online service, called NiftyServe.

The original popularity of Habitat in the United States and its continuing popularity in Japan make it an object of study for social scientists interested in how online game environments are created and evolve. In 1990 Morningstar and Farmer write a paper entitled "The Lessons of Lucasfilm's Habitat," in which they outline their insights. They discuss issues such as multiple users, object-oriented programming, and data communications standards, and they conclude that the interaction among players is a more important element than the interface technology used to implement the game. Finally, they warn, it is impossible to determine the structure and evolution of the game; the task of planning the details of the system should be left to the users themselves.

1986 The National Science Foundation Network Is Created

The United States National Science Foundation (NSF) establishes NSFnet, providing a high-speed backbone to extend and improve the ARPAnet. NSFnet allows universities and research institutions that are not funded by the defense department to gain access to Internet resources.

The ARPAnet, the first wide-area computer network, had been launched in 1969. The four original host sites grew into hundreds during the 1970s as computer scientists—followed by researchers and students from every field—scrambled to get their institutions connected. Because the ARPAnet was open only to hosts that received funding for defense-related research, several nonfunded universities established independent networks in the early 1980s. As government authorities began to grasp the importance of being able to connect to the ARPAnet—which was by then referred to as the Internet—they considered enhancing and restructuring the network to include a broader membership.

In 1986, NSFnet is created, with an original backbone of five supercomputer centers in New Jersey, Pennsylvania, Illinois, New York, and two locations in California. Funding and technical support for NSFnet arrives not only from NSF but also from the National Aeronautics and Space Administration and the Department of Energy. The new network operates at 56K bps (bits per second); within a few years MCI develops lines running at 1.5M bps.

The creation of NSFnet leads to an explosion of new Internet sites, primarily universities. In 1987 there are more than 10,000 hosts, and in 1989 the number exceeds 100,000.

1986 The Cleveland Free-Net Is Established, Offering the World's First Free Public Internet Access

On July 16 the Cleveland Free-Net is opened, paving the way for public networking within the local nonacademic community. It provides the world's

*first public Internet access that is free of charge and serves as a model for
many other cost-free public networks.*

The origins of the Cleveland Free-Net trace back to 1984, when physician
Tom Grundner set up a computerized information dispensary at Case
Western Reserve University's Department of Family Medicine in
Cleveland, Ohio. People from the local community were encouraged to
connect, via modem and telephone line, to a computer bulletin board
where they could post health-related questions or read the answers to
other visitors' queries. The experiment was so successful that Grundner
received financial backing from several Cleveland telecommunications
companies and hospitals to expand the project.

In 1986 the resulting system, dubbed the Cleveland Free-Net, goes online
with the support of the state governor and city mayor. Operated by the
Society for Public Access Computing (SoPAC), the Free-Net draws more
than seven thousand users from the Cleveland area and receives more than
five hundred calls per day. It offers electronic-mail services, discussion
forums, interactive chat sessions, and general local information organized
within a system of menus. Anyone can dial in to the system for free, from
a home, office, or library, as long as a computer and modem are available.

The developers of the Free-Net do not institute any central regulation
beyond providing the original software to run the system (a text-based program called FreePort). Rather, users volunteer their time to shape and maintain the network, fostering the development of a community ambiance
online. The Free-Net is among the first public computer networks to offer
features for children and free advertising for local small businesses.

In 1989 the Free-Net's computers are replaced with faster, more powerful
hardware to accommodate a swelling membership. SoPAC is dissolved
and the National Public Telecomputing Network (NPTN) is formed to
run the system. In addition to maintaining the Cleveland network, NPTN
helps develop similar network services in other cities. Free-Nets modeled
on Cleveland's system pop up across Ohio, in neighboring states, and
finally across the country.

As of 1995 the Cleveland Free-Net boasts 160,000 registered users. In subsequent years, as the immense growth of the World Wide Web (WWW)
refocuses many people's online attention, the Free-Net loses some membership. However, its original popularity and value to the local community—

as well as its importance as a pioneer among free public networks—continue to be recognized within the Internet community.

1988 INTERNET WORM IS UNLEASHED, DISABLING SIX THOUSAND HOST COMPUTERS

On November 2, Robert T. Morris, a twenty-three-year-old Cornell University computer science graduate student, releases a worm onto the Internet. The worm, a self-replicating program, spreads rapidly across the country, overloading host computers and jamming networks. The incident draws attention to long-ignored weaknesses in the network.

Computer worms are distinct from computer viruses. Viruses insert themselves into programs and begin running only when the infected program itself is running. The majority of viruses are not capable of running or replicating independently. Worms, on the other hand, run by themselves and multiply unaided, spreading from computer to computer within a network, without assistance from users.

The first computer worms were designed in the 1980s to facilitate the efficient use of networks. Some early worm programs traveled through networks to post announcements; others performed complex tasks at night while the computers were not needed for other work. The destructive power of worms was demonstrated when one of these nighttime "vampire" worms malfunctioned at Xerox Corporation, crashing computers throughout the company. Worm research dropped off, and news about worms was scarce until Morris's Internet worm appeared in 1988.

On the evening of November 2, 1988, Morris is sitting in front of a computer at Cornell University, in Ithaca, New York, logged on to a computer at the Massachusetts Institute of Technology (MIT). Both computers are attached to the Internet. Morris takes advantage of a loophole in an e-mail program called SendMail to unleash the worm. The loophole allows the worm to spread quickly from its source to other Internet-connected computers. The illicit program also includes provisions that enable it to easily infect any Sun Microsystems machine or Digital Equipment VAX machine. Morris later claims that he intended his program to be harmless; he simply wanted to show that a program could travel through the Internet, copy itself from computer to computer, and remain unnoticed. But bugs in the program make it replicate with such frequency that an hour after its introduction, it has shut down entire subnetworks at universities, military installations, and corporations. The worm does not damage or destroy any of the programs, data, or hardware on the computers it infects. It just consumes the computers' power, causing more than six thousand Internet host machines—10 percent of the total—to crash. Later, the direct and indirect costs of the Internet worm invasion are said to have reached nearly $100 million.

The infection blazes through the Internet quickly, but by the following morning, systems administrators are aware of the problem and have made progress toward calming the chaos. Unhooked from the network, they are battling the worm and altering their SendMail programs to thwart new copies of the invader. The worm itself contains some bugs that allow it to be hunted down and tamed, within days, by teams at the University of California at Berkeley, MIT, and Purdue University. Morris is apprehended and charged with violating the Computer Fraud and Abuse Act. His sentence, handed down in 1990, includes three years of probation, four hundred hours of community service, and $10,000 in fines.

While some observers within the computer science community advocate severe punishment for crimes like Morris', others note that his stunt, while costly, reveals numerous holes in network operations that need to be patched up to ensure improved security. The Internet worm receives significant media attention, appearing on the front covers of several newspapers for more than a week. Although the Internet has long been a household name in some circles, for many others the news stories provide a first glimpse into the world of the network.

1989 THE CUCKOO'S EGG, BY CLIFF STOLL, TELLS TRUE TALE OF GERMAN HACKER INFILTRATING U.S. FACILITIES

Cliff Stoll's The Cuckoo's Egg *is published and remains on* The New York Times *bestseller list for more than four months. In it Stoll tells the story of his yearlong virtual pursuit of a German computer spy.*

Stoll, an astronomer working as systems manager for the computer division of Lawrence Berkeley Laboratories (LBL) in Berkeley, California, had detected a seventy-five-cent discrepancy in his accounting programs in the fall of 1986. An authorized user, it appeared, was logging onto LBL's system using a stolen account and granting himself the powers of a systems manager. The hacker, as Stoll referred to the visitor, was a talented programmer who watched his back and left few traces of his activities.

The Bill Gates of Africa

In 1989 mathematician Philip Emeagwali shocked the supercomputer industry by performing the world's fastest computation—3.1 billion calculations per second—using the power of Internet. The results, as computer scientist Marsha Lakes put it, were "phenomenal . . . three times faster than a supercomputer."

How did Emeagwali beat supercomputing at its own game? First, he started with a parallel processing device (see Chapter One: the Computer in Your Head) called a Connection Machine. Then he linked the Connection Machine to 65,000 separate computers on the Net. As he explained to *New African,* "Just picture the conventional supercomputer, costing $30 million each, as eight oxen pulling a cart and the Connection Machine as about 65,000 chickens pulling the same cart. The old thinking is that the oxen will do a better job, but if the chickens coordinate their efforts, they'll do a better job than the oxen."

Born Igbo in Yorubaland, Nigeria, Emeagwali had to drop out of high school at age fourteen because his father could no longer afford the fees. He taught himself college-level mathematics, physics, chemistry, and English at the local public library. At seventeen, Emeagwali won a scholarship to Oregon State University in the United States. He has since earned four advanced degrees: a doctorate in scientific computing and three separate masters degrees in marine engineering, civil engineering, and applied mathematics.

During the late 1980s, the U.S. government listed "petroleum reservoir simulation" among the twenty "grand challenges" to scientists in America. Back then, supercomputer simulations were locating oil reserves with only 10 percent accuracy. Harnessing the power of parallel computing, Emeagwali was able to effectively simulate petroleum reserves—and change oil exploration history. His 1989 breakthrough won him the prestigious Gordon Bell Prize, known as the "Nobel Prize of computing."

Emeagwali has been dubbed "Africa's Bill Gates" by the media. Amused but not seduced by the comparison, Emeagwali tells *New African,* "I like to work on problems that are important to society because you get satisfaction. Research is hard work, so you might as well work on important research." As Britain's One World News Service reports, Emeagwali's celebrity is not without its costs: "His work has brought him recognition but also a lot of hate and racism from white supremacists." Emeagwali's answer to racism has always been to keep on working. In 1996, he patented the Hyperball computer, which he promises will one day be able to predict the world's weather a century in advance.

As an outspoken advocate of African presence on the Net, Emeagwali advocates AFRICA ONE, a plan to bring fiber optics technology to forty-one points on Africa's coastlines. As a resident of the United States, he also sees himself as a role model for African Americans, noting, "I want my son to be inspired by the fact that I was a high school dropout and ex-refugee who overcame racism and made scientific contributions that benefited mankind."

Despite his fourteen-hour workdays, Emeagwali still spends time tending his Web site at http://emeagwali.com. And unlike Bill Gates, Emeagwali even encourages e-mail at philip@emeagwali.com.

However, Stoll was able to create an undetectable program that allowed him to monitor the hacker's every move.

For nearly a year Stoll carried a beeper that alerted him every time the hacker logged onto the LBL system. He watched the uninvited guest search LBL's files and then use the stolen account to access computer systems—especially sensitive military systems—all over the United States. As the chase transformed from a curiosity to a criminal investigation, Stoll made contacts with authorities at the Federal Bureau of Investigation (FBI), the Central Intelligence Agency (CIA), and various other government organizations.

In 1989 Stoll publishes an account of his experience pursuing the hacker, who turned out to be a German computer whiz who was selling information to Soviet intelligence officers. The book, *The Cuckoo's Egg*, is a detailed, personal story and draws a large audience of readers.

During his dedicated effort to track down the hacker, Stoll had begun to believe that computer break-ins damage the feeling of communal trust that characterize—and are essential to the maintenance of—shared computer networks. His passion is evident in *The Cuckoo's Egg*, and the lessons he learned are spelled out for readers to consider. In particular, the book makes public several major security weaknesses in widely used systems. But more generally, it brings to light a theme that will become increasingly important in the coming years: the problem of balancing the desire to have open, shared computer resources and the need to protect them from ill-intentioned, unauthorized hackers.

1989 HACKER KEVIN MITNICK IS CONVICTED OF COMPUTER FRAUD

After several inconsequential run-ins with the police during the 1980s, Kevin Mitnick is arrested in 1989 for breaking into Digital Equipment Corporation's computer systems and stealing software. He is convicted and sentenced to one year in prison. As his escapades continue, Mitnick becomes the first high-profile computer hacker.

Computer hacking had not originally signified something illegal or morally questionable. It had meant, simply, computer programming. "A good hack" was a clever or skilled creation of computer code. Hackers of the 1970s and 1980s were the first computer enthusiasts, academics, and engineers. As the

Internet grew during the 1980s, it became possible for computer-savvy outsiders to gain entrance, via the network, to confidential material stored within institutions' computer systems. In the mainstream media the term "hacking" eventually came to refer to such illegitimate actions.

Born in 1964, Kevin Mitnick had grown up in a Los Angeles suburb. He first tested his hacking skills by altering friends' grades on their high school's computer system in the late 1970s. In 1981 he broke into a system at the North American Air Defense in Colorado, an event which got him into minor trouble with legal authorities. Mitnick initiated computer break-ins and stole software and confidential information throughout the 1980s. Caught several times, he avoided conviction as an adult and underwent observation by the juvenile justice system while serving probationary punishment.

By 1989 Mitnick has been collaborating with a hacker named DiCicco. Agents from the Federal Bureau of Investigation (FBI) investigate and suspect the two are compromising computer security at Digital Equipment Corporation and stealing long-distance telephone codes from MCI. Having gathered sufficient evidence, the FBI apprehends Mitnick and DiCicco in Los Angeles.

DiCicco pleads guilty to one felony and is sentenced to five years' probation for testifying against Mitnick. Mitnick's attorneys argue that Mitnick is addicted to hacking—similarly to the way people can be addicted to behavior such as gambling. Psychological profiles taken of Mitnick throughout his young-adult life support this notion. Mitnick, found guilty, is sentenced to one year at a minimum-security prison in Lompoc, California. He is also required to attend rehabilitation sessions.

Mitnick's story launches a frenzy of police activity aimed at putting a sharp stop to illegal hacking. It also makes computer security a primary concern of programmers around the country.

Upon release Mitnick continues to serve probation. Soon, signs of the hacker's behavior return: his probation officer's phone is disconnected, his judge's credit record is altered, and computer records of his arrest and conviction disappear from the system. Going into hiding in 1992, he is not arrested until 1995, when he is dealt much harsher treatment to serve as an example to other would-be hackers.

From the Hacker File

THE REVOLUTION WILL BE DIGITIZED

It began as a peaceful gathering in Beijing, but as weeks passed, student protesters in Tiananmen Square swelled to a million in number. For a while Communist leaders did nothing, but they worried about the planned arrival of Mikhail Gorbachev and the impact his presence might have on the students requesting economic and social reforms. Finally, on June 3, 1989, military units from the countryside moved to disperse the crowds, killing hundreds (possibly thousands) of protesters and jailing thousands more.

Notoriously naive about the power of media, the Chinese government hadn't counted on the fact that so many members of the native and foreign press would be on hand to cover the first Sino-Soviet summit in thirty years. But the students knew full well the media would be there. In addition to traditional media outlets, savvy protesters exploited burgeoning technologies: Tiananmen was dubbed by many commentators a "revolution by fax," as the students used faxes and e-mails to spread their message to the outside world.

Today, the Net is changing the way we protest. Efforts like the Free Tibet Web pages and the Burma List create "virtual citizenship," helping to protect dissidents from censorship by local authorities. And "hacktivists" like Electronic Disturbance Theatre and the Free Kevin Mitnick movement encourage media manipulation for political struggles. Linking a worldwide community of dissent, the Net is making clear the slogan, popularized by Mexican revolutionaries the Zapatistas, "the revolution will be digitized."

Hacktivists advocate both old-style political actions and new aggressive tactics like "flooding" (bombarding an opponent's Web site with multiple hits and crashing its server) as acts of civil disobedience. As Net theorist Stefan Wray points out, hacktivism is effective "if we define effectiveness as being able to manipulate the media sphere." Like those who question the ability of computer hackers to alter "technopolies" like Intel and Microsoft, Wray endorses hacktivism as a political practice—he calls flooding "conceptual art"—but wonders just how useful media manipulation is as a tool for social change.

Almost a decade after Tiananmen, China hasn't changed much. But while the Chinese government might like to forget the spring of 1989, the Net remembers. As *The New York Times* reported, the day after China's human rights agency announced its 1998 Web site, the site was hacked and a message was inserted: "China's people have no rights at all, never mind human rights. How can the United States trade millions and millions of dollars with them and give them most-favored trade status when they know what is happening?"

If you have an urge to be "part of the solution," you can learn more about online activism by checking out Protest Net at http://www.protest.net. To learn about hacktivism, see Electronic Disturbance Theatre's site at http://www.thing.net/~rdom/ecd/ecd.html.

1989 QUANTUM COMPUTER SERVICES IS REBORN AS AMERICA ONLINE

The Internet bulletin board system Quantum Computer Services acquires a new name, America Online (AOL), and focuses on recruiting a diverse, broad-based subscribership. From 1989 to 1998, AOL grows from its roots as an insignificant start-up with barely one hundred thousand members, to an industry leader with more than fourteen million members.

The founder of Quantum, Steve Case, claims he was born with entrepreneurial blood. His childhood venture, a lemonade stand, was profitable, as were four companies he founded while attending Williams College in Massachusetts. Graduating with a degree in business, he worked for Proctor and Gamble and Pizza Hut, gaining valuable experience in the corporate world.

In 1982 Case bought a Kaypro personal computer, hoping to participate in the early world of online bulletin board systems (BBSs). He had a tough and costly time getting the equipment—computer, modem, software, cable—to work together, but when the system was rolling, he was thrilled to be able to reach out via computer from his home in Wichita, Kansas. His frustration with the difficulty of setting up his connection and his excitement to communicate with others outside his local community were experiences that likely influenced his ease-of-use focus when he founded his own BBS a few years later.

Case moved to Virginia in 1983 to work for Control Video, a company planning to send Atari video games to customers' computers via modems and telephone lines. The company failed, but Case picked up the pieces and started Quantum Computer

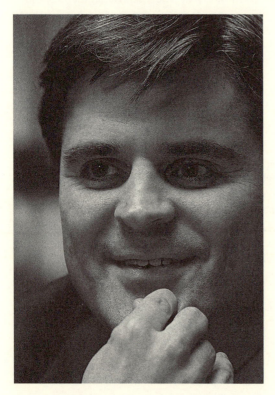

Steve Case, president of America Online (AP / Wide World Photos).

Services, a BBS for users of Commodore 64 computers. In 1985, Quantum began offering a graphical user interface (GUI) BBS for PCs and soon expanded GUI services to Apple and Tandy computers. Implementing vigorous marketing schemes, Quantum was attempting to catch up and compete with existing online services and BBSs, such as CompuServe, the Source, Genie, Viewtron, and Prodigy. Quantum, with a few thousand subscribers, had a long way to go; Prodigy, a joint venture of IBM and Sears, already boasted more than a million members.

In 1989 Case gives Quantum a face lift, renaming it America Online, and continues to recruit members by appealing to a technically inexperienced, mainstream audience. AOL expands its services to offer general Internet access in the early 1990s and grows quickly, gathering four million members by 1994. Through some troubling times in 1995 and 1996—service bottlenecks and crashes, dissatisfied customers and lawsuits—AOL emerges scathed but still strong. With a single 1997 deal, AOL takes over CompuServe (and its 2.6 million members) and WorldCom, a telephone company with hundreds of miles of high-capacity line. And in 1998 AOL announces plans to swallow Netscape Corporation, makers of World Wide Web tools and software. AOL promises to be a dominant player in the next phase of online multimedia technology.

1990   OPERATION SUN DEVIL ENTERS SEARCH-AND-SEIZURE MODE

From January to May an organization of government agents, law officers, and security personnel unleashes the publicly visible arm of Operation Sun Devil, a nationwide crackdown on computer hackers. Searching under unsigned warrants, the group seizes equipment and data from a handful of hackers accused of computer fraud. The event unleashes a wave of controversy and demonstrates the importance of developing a legal architecture to deal with computer and networking technologies.

By the late 1980s computer systems were heavily used and networks were widely connected, making it possible for skilled outsiders to gain access to electronically stored confidential material. Numerous such outsiders, computer enthusiasts with vast amounts of experience, had begun to form a computer underground community. Its members, who harbored a general distrust of convention and authority, broke into the computer systems of corporations and other organizations. Most of these hackers performed these acts out of curiosity, meant no harm, and neither destroyed nor stole any data. But a few were more prone to altering records, making free long-distance telephone calls, and committing credit card fraud.

The U.S. government became concerned about financial losses due to electronic break-ins, and it established Operation Sun Devil in 1988 to investigate hackers, whom authorities perceived as a threat to business and government. The Secret Service, a department of the U.S. Treasury, was charged with the operation because the criminal issues were thought to be mostly financial. Sun Devil agents recruited the assistance of police departments and security personnel from institutions at particular risk of undergoing security breeches.

In 1990 the investigations culminate in a flurry of arrests as agents arrive, weapons drawn, at the homes and businesses of suspected criminal hackers across the country. One hundred-fifty agents confiscate forty-two computers, twenty-three thousand disks, and various equipment such as telephones, answering machines, books, and notes. Hackers who go by the names of Phiber Optik, Acid Phreak, Scorpion, Knight Lightning, and the Prophet, as well as the real-name figures Steve Jackson and Craig Neidorf, are arrested by Sun Devil agents.

Phiber Optik and Acid Phreak are well-known members of a hacker group called the Legion of Doom, a primary target of Operation Sun Devil. Acid Phreak is accused of causing the whole AT&T system to crash, resulting in close to a billion dollars of damage. He is, however, never actually charged with any crime.

Craig Neidorf is accused of publishing, in an online newsletter, a Bell South document that had been electronically stolen by a fellow hacker. While Neidorf faces trial, the prosecution is informed that the supposedly stolen and confidential document is, in fact, legally available from Bell South. Charges against Neidorf are dropped. Steve Jackson, whose computer-game company headquarters were ransacked during the Sun Devil raids, later files a lawsuit against the Secret Service for the financial damages he incurred. The judge awards him $50,000 in lost profits and deems the seizure of his equipment unlawful.

Operation Sun Devil brings together concerned members of the computing community, and they rally for better public understanding of computers and new legislation adapted to the unique characteristics of cyberspace. Several prominent figures do this under the newly formed group Electronic Frontier Foundation.

1990 ARPANET IS DECOMMISSIONED

The Advanced Research Projects Agency (ARPA) decommissions the ARPAnet, replacing its antiquated lines and nodes with the faster NSFnet backbone.

ARPAnet, established in 1969, had been the first multisite computer network. Originally intended as a resource for the computer science community, ARPAnet had grown into a widely shared system as the number of nodes and users continuously increased. In 1986 the National Science Foundation (NSF) had implemented NSFnet, a faster network, to allow more connections to the ARPAnet (or Internet as it was by then popularly known).

In 1990 authorities at ARPA and the NSF decide it is time to relieve the ARPAnet's original nodes of their heavy message load. All information on the Internet is thereafter routed through the NSF backbone. Interconnections between smaller networks and the Internet, facilitated by NSF-funded routing technology, broadens Internet use. Network growth climbs to more than 10 percent per month.

1990 THE ELECTRONIC FRONTIER FOUNDATION IS FOUNDED TO PROTECT THE CIVIL LIBERTIES OF INTERNET USERS

Mitchell Kapor and John Perry Barlow establish the Electronic Frontier Foundation (EFF) to fund legal efforts related to government crackdowns and to educate the public about issues relating to cyberspace. They are motivated by the unlawful conduct of the Secret Service toward hackers and the lack of a legal structure applicable to cyberspace.

The events leading to the formation of the EFF had started in 1989, when Barlow—a writer, rancher, politician, and computer enthusiast—had been introduced to members of the Legion of Doom, an underground computer-hacker group. *Harper's* magazine, interested in running a story about infamous teenage hackers with names like Acid Phreak and Phiber Optik, sponsored an online meeting between two fronts: the older, academic computing establishment and the younger, hacker, antiauthoritarian establishment. The meeting took the form of a private conference on the WELL, a virtual community of online discussion. Barlow was among the "established" computer users offered entry to the conference. Through WELL interactions, Barlow became friendly with several hackers, and they invited him to a private yearly gathering called the Hacker's Conference.

MITCHELL KAPOR

In the past Mitchell Kapor has been a transcendental meditator, software developer, entrepreneur, and teacher. He continues to be an investor, advisor, writer, and Buddhist. Most well known for the founding of Lotus Development Corporation and the Electronic Frontier Foundation, Kapor has visions that extend beyond the material realm of spreadsheets and litigation. He thinks computer technology—cyberspace in particular—has the potential to lead people out of a material-obsessed culture and toward a liberation of the human spirit.

Mitchell Kapor was born in 1950 in Brooklyn, New York, and grew up on Long Island. Starting college in the late 1960s, he experimented with drugs but quit after a series of distressing experiences. Afflicted with acid flashbacks, he sought relief in transcendental meditation (TM), a popular nonreligious technique from India. For Kapor, TM lived up to its promise of offering deep relaxation, curbing stress, and promoting health, creativity, and happiness. His flashbacks subsided. After being involved for seven years and becoming a TM instructor, he left in 1976 when the TM program adopted an approach at odds with his beliefs.

In 1971 Kapor had received a bachelor's degree from Yale College in cybernetics, a combination of psychology, linguistics, and computer science. In 1978 he received a master's degree in counseling psychology from Beacon College and practiced mental health counseling near Boston. Then he bought an Apple II computer, an event

that shifted his focus to software development. Quickly gaining expertise in this new field, Kapor took a job at Personal Software Inc. in California and designed companion programs to VisiCalc, one of the first electronic spreadsheet programs.

In 1982 Kapor founded Lotus Development and introduced Lotus 1-2-3, a technically sophisticated spreadsheet package. In its first year Lotus earned $53 million, and in the second year it tripled this revenue. Kapor left Lotus in 1986 and pursued teaching and administrative endeavors. By 1990 Kapor had become involved, personally and politically, in national discussions of law, society, and cyberspace. That year, he and John Perry Barlow founded the Electronic Frontier Foundation (EFF), a nonprofit civil liberties organization.

An interview in the summer 1994 issue of *Tricycle: The Buddhist Review* touched on Kapor's opinions about the potential dangers and virtues of cyberspace. He warned that society must not allow participation in cyberspace to become a mind-deadening, addictive activity akin to watching too much TV. He also claimed that to erase or ignore the distinction between physical reality and virtual reality—which he viewed as a possible side effect of being engulfed in electronic media—would be a tragic mistake. However, he suggested that people can shape the evolution of cyberspace and use it to relieve suffering and enact social justice. He described his hope that cyberspace would become one of the tools the public can use to dislodge a social system embedded in centralized authoritarian control and to redistribute power among individuals and small groups.

Biography

At about the same time, the Federal Bureau of Investigation (FBI) was beginning to get nervous about computer fraud committed by youngsters. Authorities were focusing on the Legion of Doom, an easy target because its members—skilled hackers—were adopting visible and threatening personae. FBI agents acquired a list of Hacker's Conference invitees, identified Barlow's name, and visited his Wyoming home to question him. According to Barlow, the FBI was greatly misinformed about many aspects of computing, the Internet, and several key figures of the computing world.

Through the winter and spring of 1990, Barlow read about Operation Sun Devil, a series of government raids on suspected criminal hackers, in which agents seized equipment and subsequently arrested several people, with very little evidence to back their actions. Barlow became worried about the computing ignorance of the FBI, which he had witnessed in person, and the misguided fear of other government authorities that had been apparent in Operation Sun Devil.

In May 1990 Barlow is joined in his concern by Mitchell Kapor, cofounder of Lotus Development Corporation. Kapor, also, had participated in Harper's private WELL conference, was on the Hacker's Conference roster, had been investigated by the FBI, and had watched Operation Sun Devil unfold. Barlow and Kapor meet to discuss their view that the situation is heading toward a catastrophe of misunderstanding, distrust, and unjust legal actions. The two decide to establish an organization to uphold civil liberties in cyberspace; they call it the Electronic Frontier Foundation (EFF).

According to EFF's mission statement, "The Electronic Frontier Foundation has been established to help civilize the electronic frontier; to make it truly useful and beneficial not just to a technical elite, but to everyone; and to do this in a way which is in keeping with our society's highest traditions of the free and open flow of information and communication." The statement outlines the main objectives of the EFF: to support legal efforts aimed at upholding freedom of speech in computing and telecommunications realms; to increase public awareness of issues related to technology and law; and to assist policy-makers in the development of new approaches to computer technologies.

Kapor puts forward $200,000 for EFF's initial fund; the amount is doubled by the contribution of Steve Wozniak, a cofounder of Apple

BATTLE OF THE NETWORKED STARS

In 1990, six months after Cisco Systems went public, the founders of the world's biggest networking system were dismissed by their investors. *Nerds 2.0.1* author Stephen Segaller writes, "Sandy Lehner and Len Bosack were no longer working at the company they founded on their credit cards." Thus ended corporate networking's first strange decade.

It began in 1981 when IBM legitimized the personal computer for use in American offices. Hoping to protect their mainframe business, IBM chose not to network their PCs, and a market vacuum was created for vendors willing to hook desktop machines together. The first person to take up the challenge was Bob Metcalfe, of Ethernet fame. Metcalfe had already developed a "mini-Internet" at Xerox PARC. In 1982 his company, 3Com, sold Ethernet cards for PC networks at $1,000 each. In 1983 the Novell Corporation answered the need for "traffic cop" software for PC-based LANs (local area networks) connected through 3Com's Ethernet cards. Novell's contribution, called Netware, dominated offices around the United States throughout the 1980s.

Meanwhile in Redmond, Washington, Bill Gates tried unsuccessfully to make a dent in the corporate networking market. First, Microsoft failed with LAN Manager for OS/2 (Gates was committed to IBM and OS/2, its follow-up to DOS.) Microsoft proposed to 3Com that they team up on LAN Manager; the hope was that a Gates/Metcalfe partnership would bring down then-giant Novell. Instead, OS/2 failed so badly it resulted in an $80 million loss for 3Com. In 1990 Metcalfe (like Apple's Steve Jobs before him, and the Cisco founders after him) was forced to resign from the company he created.

Cisco Systems' 1984 contribution to networking—the router—was an old technology renewed. According to founder Bosack, routers were not much more than updated Interface Message Processors (IMPs), the devices originally used to connect hosts on the ARPAnet. But Cisco made routers cheaply and well, and by 1990 founders Bosack and Lehner were ready to take their company public. Sick of working twelve-hour days, they joined forces with venture capitalists Sequoia Capital, and "signed agreements no lawyer would have let us sign." Six months later Cisco was a goldmine, but it no longer belonged to its creators.

Noting that Cisco (like 3Com) has grown more profitable since firing its founders, Segaller muses that he can't tell if the Cisco story is "a fairy tale or a cautionary tale. In reality, it is both." Bosack and Lehner sold their stock in Cisco as soon as they left. No one can say for sure whether taking the money and running was a good business decision or a bad one, but Segaller points out that "[t]he pain of not having a $10 billion fortune can be compensated by having $100 million to your name." But one thing is sure. With more than sixty million people currently working in networked offices, IBM's 1981 decision to let other people have what could have been their monopoly has to rank among the worst business decisions ever.

Beyond the Net

Computer. The highest profile case that EFF supports is that of Steve Jackson, whose computer-game company had been ransacked by the Secret Service during Operation Sun Devil. Jackson sues the Secret Service and wins $50,000 in lost profits in 1993, representing a major victory for EFF and hackers in general.

EFF's education program begins with another conference on the WELL, this time involving the defendants and prosecutors in cases related to Sun Devil, as well as various criminologists and cryptographers. They discuss law in cyberspace. In 1992 EFF opens a national office in Cambridge, Massachusetts, and a lobbying office in Washington, D.C., as members hold press conferences and publish newsletters. Due to conflict between the two branches, the Cambridge office is closed in 1993 so that the foundation can concentrate on legal efforts. EFF spearheads the struggle to fit digital media into structures of culture and law in the late twentieth century.

1990 THE NAME "WORLD WIDE WEB" IS SELECTED FOR TIM BERNERS-LEE'S HYPERTEXT SYSTEM AT CERN

Tim Berners-Lee and Robert Cailliau choose "World Wide Web" as a name for the hypertext system they are developing to facilitate information storage and retrieval at CERN (Centre Européen pour la Recherche Nucléaire), near Geneva, Switzerland.

Berners-Lee had worked as a computer consultant at CERN in 1980. He became frustrated with the absence of a network to link the massive stores of data at the institution. Tired of struggling with the numerous platforms used to hold and manipulate information on isolated machines, he devised a new program to address the problem. The program, Enquire-Within-Upon-Everything, enabled him to create links among bits of information. But he left CERN soon after and the program was hardly touched by others.

In 1984 CERN established a link to the Internet, and in 1989 it became the largest Internet site in Europe. In 1989 Berners-Lee, now an expert network programmer, returned to CERN.

Berners-Lee immediately wrote a proposal on information management, in which he outlined the disadvantages of traditional information-storage and -retrieval systems and discussed the superiority of hypertext. The proposal called for a hypertext system to provide "a single user-interface

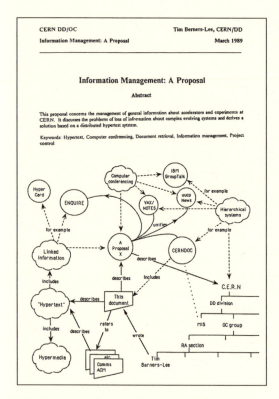

Tim Berners-Lee's proposal to improve information management at CERN: the World Wide Web (Image courtesy of The Computer Museum History Center).

to many large classes of stored information such as reports, notes, databases, computer documentation and online systems help." It received little support from CERN administrators.

Berners-Lee redistributes his proposal in 1990 and this time his superiors are more receptive. They agree to fund development of the proposed system. Berners-Lee and colleague Robert Cailliau reformulate the proposed plan, foreseeing a six-month project with four software engineers and one programmer. Over lunch in the CERN cafeteria, they decide to call the system the "World Wide Web."

Berners-Lee works on a computer from NeXT, Inc. to take advantage of the machine's object-oriented technology. The NeXT software includes a program that allows users to edit pages of information in WYSIWYG ("whizzy-wig") format. WYSIWYG, an acronym for What You See Is What You Get, displays a page on a computer screen exactly as it appears on the printed version.

Berners-Lee and the CERN programmers develop the tools and architecture of a hypertext system that is destined to live up to its worldly name. In 1991 they introduce Hypertext Transfer Protocol (HTTP), Hypertext Markup Language (HTML), and the Universal Resource Locator (URL). The following year the protocol and language are launched onto the Internet (and into the public domain), and programmers around the world begin to use, modify, and improve the system. The World Wide Web is born.

The World
Wide Wonder

For those who have been introduced to the Internet within the last few years, it is difficult to imagine that the Net could have ever been so different from the way it is now—that it was once peopled only by those tech-savvy enough to master the arcane protocols required to navigate it, or that it was once a commerce-free zone. But two things happen in the four years covered by Chapter Six that are of crucial importance to the character of the Internet as we now know it. First, the newly invented World Wide Web comes on the scene. And second, the Internet opens up to commerce.

The chapter begins with universities, research centers, government entities, and nonprofit groups sharing a government-sponsored computer network for research and science-related purposes. It ends with Pizza Hut offering delivery services over the Web and people surfing the Net to check out their friends' home pages. The Wired Era is upon us.

Get Your Motor Running, Head Out on the I-way

The first half of the 1990s saw a significant changing of the political guard. The United States began the decade with George Bush as president and a recession taking hold. As disaffected grunge rock flooded the airwaves, young people faced a bleak job market and declining prospects; Generation Xers were predicted to be the first in U.S. history to end up worse off than their parents. Bush was widely faulted for not pulling the country out of the recession, and his popularity slumped. In 1992, in a presidential contest made much more interesting by the entry of Texas billionaire Ross Perot, Bush lost the presidency to two Baby Boomers: Democratic challenger Bill Clinton and his running mate, Albert Gore.

Much was made of generational issues during the race. As the Clinton/Gore campaign exhorted us, endlessly, to not stop thinking about tomorrow, World War II-veteran Bush became more and more solidly positioned as the Past, with Vietnam-objecting Clinton as his eager foil, the Future. A notable part of the Clinton team's forward-looking strategy, both during the campaign and after the inaugural, was Gore's pet project, the "Information Superhighway."

Gore began using the phrase to describe the Internet in 1990, and the name not only stuck, it spawned countless metaphors—we talked of on-ramps, guard rails, and traffic cops on the I-way. Once in office, Gore continued his role as a major Internet cheerleader, and he was one of the first public officials to invite and answer e-mail from the masses. Indeed, the Clinton administration was the first to grapple with a heavily trafficked, civilian-populated Internet. Regardless of your position on the political spectrum, it's fair to say that the results have been mixed.

Encryption, Privacy, and Smut

A major challenge for the Clinton administration has been—and no doubt will continue to be—the formulation of a sane, safe encryption policy. Encryption can scramble a digital communication so that no one but its intended recipient—the party with a key to its code—can read it. Civil libertarians argue that strong encryption in the hands of private citizens gives them the ability to protect their online privacy. However, law enforcement officials fear that strong encryption in the hands of the criminal element could twist the long arm of the law, or even break it. The Clinton administration has had to choose between appearing soft on crime and appearing hostile to e-commerce and privacy concerns.

In 1993 the administration unveiled its first stab at an encryption policy-the Escrowed Encryption Initiative, a "key-escrow" system in which encrypted messages could be decoded by a third party as well as the intended recipient. The proposal was immediately unpopular with both the business community and privacy advocates. Software companies complained that export controls prevented them from competing against unrestricted encryption sellers in the global marketplace, and privacy advocates insisted that secure communications are a basic right. Many suggested that a system in which the government could access a "backdoor" key was worse than no security at all.

The right to privacy in cyberspace was just one of several issues that, as Internet use increased, became increasingly troublesome. In this vast new forum for expression, there were bound to be First Amendment disputes. What should be done about hate speech, for example, or Web sites that advocate violence? Can people be prosecuted for exchanging objectionable material? In the early 1990s some parents and teachers became concerned about the vast amounts of adult-oriented information that could be obtained over the Internet. These concerns—which were either well-warranted or paranoiac, depending on your perspective—mounted throughout the 1990s and ultimately translated into the 1996 Communications Decency Act, which was struck down by the Supreme Court the following year.

The Web Takes Off, Thanks to Browsers

Tim Berners-Lee completed his software for the World Wide Web in 1991, including (though this is often forgotten) the first GUI browser, called "WorldWideWeb." Between 1991 and 1994 traffic on the original WWW server at CERN, where he had developed it, grew tenfold each year.

In the early days Berners-Lee was repeatedly approached by people wanting to assist him in making a proprietary fortune from his invention. He opted not to, and to this day continues to stand firmly against any corporation achieving a dominant presence on the Web. When the Web architecture was released, Berners-Lee encouraged programmers the world over to write applications for it.

The call was heard from Silicon Valley to Helsinki, but the first widely popular browser was Mosaic, written by Marc Andreessen and Eric Bina of the University of Illinois' National Center for Supercomputing Applications. The popularity of Mosaic was instrumental in opening up the Internet to people who weren't programming-literate.

Andreessen and Bina were not the only people to realize that the Internet was going to have to look a lot friendlier if people were actually going to use it. For example, Gopher, an interface for accessing information on remote computers, had been developed at the University of Minnesota and was made available to the public in 1991. Gopher was popular in the academic community, and it was much easier to use than the protocols that preceded it, but it still didn't have the graphical user interface that the computer-illiterate would need.

Before Mosaic, you practically had to be in a computer science lab to have heard of the Web. Not so after. Mosaic for Unix was distributed free of charge in early 1993; later that year, Mosaic for Windows and the Macintosh were released. Mosaic usership went from zero to one million by the end of 1993. By that time, newspapers were reporting that Internet usership was doubling every eighteen months. Businesspeople began to prick up their ears: was that the sound of a cash register ringing in the distance?

Netscape Proves There's Gold in Them Hills

Andreessen was soon approached by Jim Clark, who had founded the successful Silicon Graphics. Clark wanted to start a company to build a better browser, and he offered $3 million in start-up capital to do it. Andreessen and Clark lured six other Mosaic programmers away from the University of Illinois, and Mosaic Communications was born. After a dispute with the university, the company reemerged as Netscape Communications. In 1994 the company released a beta version of its new browser Navigator, which it hoped would replace Mosaic as the way to get around the Web.

At the time it was not at all clear how creating superior browsing tools and releasing them over the Internet was going to make Netscape any money. The conventional wisdom was that you couldn't make money on the Internet. But this was the era of new business models. Clark was certain that if the company could get upwards of fifty million people using its product, they could make money on it somehow. With Internet usership estimated at twenty-five million in early 1994 and believed to be doubling every year and a half, Clark figured that even though only about a million people were using a browser at the time, the rest of them could potentially use a browser, especially a better one.

As it turned out, Clark was right. By mid-1995, Netscape had killed Mosaic, garnered sixty-five million users, and was licensing its technology to industry. In its first year it reported revenues of $75 million; by its third year revenues topped $500 million. In 1995, in an initial public offering of five million shares, Netscape's stock opened at a stunning $70 (it had been priced at $28). This auspicious debut made Netscape's founders into millionaires; more significantly, it paved the way for other Net-based companies to get the start-up cash they needed. Netscape used the most persuasive form of rhetoric—the bottom line—to prove to the world that there was plenty of money to be made on and around the Internet.

The tricky part, though, was how. Investors began to grasp that a new medium meant that new business models were in order. The meteoric rise of the Web directory Yahoo! is instructive in this respect. Yahoo! was somewhat accidentally founded by two grad students at Stanford, David Filo and Jerry Yang. The two set out to simply exchange URLs of their favorite sites, and they ended up devising a system to categorize the ever-growing list. The site got popular, and soon the two were meeting with investors. But the capital people were confused. While it was great that so many people wanted to use the site, the service was being offered for free. Where does the profit come from? As Yahoo!, Excite, Netscape, and other companies showed in the early 1990s, it comes from unexpected places—from advertising, licensing agreements, and innovative business partnerships.

(Virtual) Business as Usual

In the early 1990s several commercial computer networks existed, but they were wholly separate from the government-sponsored Internet. Members of the commercial networks began to look longingly towards the Internet as a vast marketing opportunity. But they were prevented by something called the Acceptable Use Policy (AUP), part of the National Science Foundation Act, a 1950 law. The AUP laid out what the National Science Foundation's computer networks could and could not do. Internet use was supposed to be restricted to the job-related work of academics, scientists, and bureaucrats. Officially at least, the Internet was a noncommercial zone.

In 1992 Representative Frederick Boucher (D-Virginia) proposed an amendment to the National Science Foundation Act that would make e-commerce possible. Its modest wording said that the NSF could support computer networks "which may be used substantially for purposes in addition to research and education in the sciences and engineering." Commerce was not specifically mentioned, but Boucher argued that the amendment would give the network more flexibility to develop in tandem with the private sector. The bill became law in November 1992, and the doors to Internet commerce were thrown wide.

Until Internet use rose among everyday consumers, many companies felt they had little to gain and much to lose in trying to carry on a virtual business. As online services and the Web grew in popularity, however, more businesses began to see that putting up a billboard along the new superhighway might not be a bad idea. In 1994 the

Internet Shopping Network went online and online banking debuted. Soon, e-commerce came to include not only Web extensions of terra-firma businesses, but companies founded with the express purpose of doing business online, such as CDNow.com.

As well as spawning an entrepreneurial paradise, the spread of the WWW brought with it a whole new distribution medium for "content." With the growth of online services that provided such content, executives in some industries, particularly publishing, began to get nervous. Would people want to read their magazines and newspapers online? Precious few media executives spent the early 1990s feeling complacent about what online content would mean for them. In an echo of Xerox executives' nightmares in the 1970s that the fabled Paperless Office of the Future would put them out of business, those who sold "print products"—magazines, journals, and books—faced the startling possibility that they might one day be relegated to the recycling bin.

What to do? On the one hand, it seemed foolhardy *not* to jump on the bandwagon of a new distribution medium, especially one that was nearly free and could bring in new customers. On the other hand, electronic distribution would surely cut into print circulation bases and profits. And how would copyright be handled?

While these and other questions were being hashed out in the various media industries, the Internet went on growing. Electronic content delivery increased and e-commerce ventures multiplied. A flagship venture in the brave new world of virtual shopping was Amazon.com, purveyors of—what else?—printed books. Life on the Net is nothing if not ironic. True to the curious world of the Internet, Amazon.com's stock has gone through the roof while the company, as of 1998, keeps losing money. Traditionally, investors expect companies to show a profit. But for Internet-based companies, a high revenue stream, lower losses than the previous year, and impressive name recognition are enough to send a stock flying high. In turn, this perceived double standard has led to questions about whether Internet stocks are dangerously overvalued.

A Hyperlinked Horizon

By the end of Chapter Six, the Web had grown substantially. The White House had a home page, as did many businesses and individuals. Tools had been developed that enabled people not only to locate sites on the Web, but to create them. With the release of software that enabled the layperson to set up a Web site, the power to distribute information began to change hands. Previously, one had to know HTML coding to set up a site. Suddenly, anyone could do it.

The Web is a wonder, and it brought the public to the Internet. Across thousands of miles, different cultures, and many languages, anyone with a PC and a connection can go to the same site and locate the same information. In Chapter Six, we see the Web come into its own and propel the Internet into everyday use. We're still not sure where it will take us.

1991 THE COMMERCIAL INTERNET eXCHANGE ASSOCIATION (CIX) IS FORMED

The Commercial Internet eXchange Association (CIX), a nonprofit trade organization, is established to serve as the interconnection point for several existing commercial networks. CIX paves the way for commerce on the Internet.

In 1991 the Internet is running on the National Science Foundation Network (NSFnet) backbone and is providing interconnection among university, research, government, and nonprofit networks. In accordance with 1950's National Science Foundation Act, the NSF's Acceptable Use Policy (AUP) states that commercial traffic is not allowed on the Internet.

Meanwhile, there are several commercial networks operating independently of the Internet. Authorities at a few of these networks decide that it would be beneficial for commercial networks to be able to exchange traffic among themselves. Directors of PSInet, UUnet, and CERFnet create the CIX for this purpose. The CIX interconnection router is located in Santa Clara, California.

The CIX enables commercial networks to exchange commercial traffic with each other. In addition, because the CIX is a nonprofit trade organization, its members are allowed to have full access to the Internet; therefore commercial networks that are members of CIX have access to the Internet. However, the Internet's AUP prevents the commercial networks from being able to send commercial traffic onto the Internet. For a few years there is controversy regarding this restriction. Opponents of the AUP argue that for-profit companies should be able to use the Internet to market products, such as professional journals and research equipment, to universities and other nonprofit institutions. Those who want to keep the AUP intact claim that opening the Internet to commercial traffic would lead to undesirable mass advertising and solicitation.

Gradually, commercial traffic makes its way onto the Internet, because the wording of the AUP lends itself to loose interpretation. In 1992 Rep. Frank Boucher (D-Virginia) proposes an amendment to the National Science Foundation Act, which opens the legal door to commercialization of the Internet. By 1995 commercial network backbones have taken over most of the traffic on the Internet and NSFnet is dissolved. By the late 1990s business and commerce are integral parts of Internet culture.

1991 PRETTY GOOD PRIVACY IS RELEASED ON THE INTERNET

Concerned about imminent anti-encryption legislation, Phil Zimmermann writes public-key encryption software PGP (Pretty Good Privacy) and releases it on the Internet. The action sparks a five-year investigation of Zimmermann and an intense debate about U.S. encryption policy that has yet to be resolved.

In 1991, a bill was pending on the Senate floor which would have forced "trap doors" into encryption software, so that the government could read messages deemed threatening or dangerous. Although that bill was eventually defeated, Zimmermann wrote PGP and posted it on Usenet in June because he felt passionately that strong encryption should be made available before it was made illegal.

The first version of PGP uses a patented algorithm to encrypt the data and render it unreadable to anyone without the proper key. Zimmermann's use of the algorithm, the patent for which was held by Massachusetts Institute of Technology (MIT), plunges him into a legal battle with MIT and with RSA Data Security, who holds an exclusive license on the technology. For several years after PGP's release it is therefore illegal to use it in the United States. The copyright problems are eventually worked out, and in 1994 Zimmermann and MIT release PGP 2.6, the first "legal" version of the software. PGP quickly becomes the world's de facto encryption method for e-mail.

The patent dispute is the least of Zimmermann's legal worries; from 1991 to 1996 he is under investigation by the U.S. Attorney for California, for illegally exporting PGP across U.S. borders. Encryption software has long been classified a munitions by the U.S. government, and exporting encryption source code is a violation of the International Traffic in Arms Regulations (ITAR) agreement. Though Zimmermann maintains he operated within the law and never himself transmitted PGP outside of the United States, federal officials see things differently. They argue that by placing PGP on the Internet, Zimmermann has knowingly made it available to the world, and thus violated ITAR.

After a speaking tour abroad in November 1995, Zimmermann is detained and questioned at length by customs officials at Washington, D.C.'s Dulles airport. According to Zimmermann, he is denied legal counsel during the interrogation, an allegation that sparks outrage among the encryption community. In January 1996 the U.S. Attorney's Office formally closes its investigation into Zimmermann, primarily because there is no evidence that Zimmermann himself ever exported PGP.

In essence, the debate over strong encryption methods such as PGP comes down to privacy versus safety. The National Security Agency and others opposed to PGP argue that the proliferation of unbreakable (or essentially unbreakable) encryption methods runs the risk of weakening law enforcement's ability to catch domestic criminals, as well as the government's ability to protect U.S. interests abroad. Adherents of strong encryption argue that privacy is the cornerstone of freedom, and such risks, if they exist, are part of the price of liberty.

Zimmermann remains committed to PGP, pointing out its importance not only for Americans, but for people internationally: "[PGP] is used to protect witnesses who report human rights abuses in the Balkans, in Burma, in Guatemala, in Tibet." Patrick Ball of the American Association for the Advancement of Science agrees, arguing that "If we are to enable people to monitor violations of internationally recognized human rights, we must be able to communicate anonymously in cyberspace."

1991 LINUS TORVALDS DEVELOPS THE LINUX OPERATING SYSTEM

Linus Torvalds, a twenty-one-year-old student at Helsinki University, begins writing Linux, an operating system based on Unix. What begins as a one-man project in Finland evolves into a global, Internet-based programming phenomenon or, in the eyes of some, a religious reformation.

Linux is an outgrowth of the free (or open-source) software movement initiated by programmer Richard Stallman in 1983. Stallman, a former employee of MIT's Artificial Intelligence Lab, wrote his own Unix-based operating system called GNU, for "Gnu's Not Unix." Based on his strong

Media History

INFOWAR

Unlike the war in Vietnam, which polarized U.S. opinion, the 1991 Gulf War was enormously popular: at times the conflict had a 90 percent approval rating in the United States. Operation Desert Storm, waged in four days with a loss of 148 American lives, was not only the first war with a snappy title, it was also the beginning of a new method of warfare, known as "cyberwar" or more commonly, "infowar"—battle waged primarily against and narrated by communications technologies.

A centerpiece of Desert Storm infowar was when a United States Air Force Stealth bomber aimed a two thousand pound laser-guided weapon at the microwave dishes above Baghdad's international telecommunications building. Iraq's communications were shattered and the country crippled. U.S. television audiences, on the other hand, watched twenty-four-hour CNN coverage complete with Weapon Cam—a computerized view of the "smart bombs" heading through Baghdad's doorways and down ventilator shafts. Journalists frequently referred to Desert Storm as "the world's biggest video game."

The Gulf War inspired the terms infowar and cyberwar, and indeed, no prior battle has been so dependent on digital technology both for its waging and telling. But information has always cut both ways. When U.S. television viewers found themselves in a military-induced news blackout, netizens turned to Internet Relay Chat (IRC), the digital equivalent of worldwide ham radio. Desert Storm is not the only example: in Europe, IRC was the only source of information for hours after the March 17, 1991, bombing of Israel by Iraq. Throughout the fighting, many Israelis stayed online while donning gas masks, giving firsthand updates on IRC's "#report" channel, their stories sometimes anticipating television coverage by days.

Despite U.S. success in the Gulf, those who are most vulnerable in an information war are usually industrialized nations with huge computer networks. The Pentagon rehearses "electronic Pearl Harbor scenarios," preparing for what they might do should an enemy choose to wipe out U.S. financial, transport, and emergency centers by damaging computer systems. The RAND Corporation, former home to Internet pioneers like Paul Baran, has called infowar "the new warfare."

It's important to remember that ever since the Pentagon relinquished military control of the Internet, infowar has been used both as a tool for conflict and a tool with which to critique conflict. Even as Desert Storm wallpapered televisions around the world, not everyone sat entranced. Legend has it that during the most dangerous days of the fighting, hacktivists jammed military satellite signals, intentionally interspersing bomb schedules with messages of reconciliation and peace. To read more about the infowar project by the Ars Electronica Festival of Art, Technology and Society, check out http://www.aec.at/infowar. The Gulf War logs are online at ftp://sunsite.unc.edu/pub/academic/communications/logs/Gulf-War.

conviction that, as the hacker motto goes, "information should be free," Stallman made GNU and the computer code that ran it (called source code) freely available. His "GNU Manifesto" outlined the principles of the free software philosophy and exhorted programmers to contribute their energies to GNU's expansion and improvement. Stallman also outlined his principle of "copyleft." Copylefted software can be distributed freely and altered by anyone: the only requirement is that users not make any changes to the software to make it proprietary—in other words, once the source code is open, it must stay open. No secret formulas are allowed.

Torvalds develops the Linux operating system specifically for use on personal computers (PCs). In writing the software, he borrows elements of the GNU kernel—the central part of the operating system, which interacts directly with the hardware. In homage to Stallman, Torvalds copylefts Linux in 1992 and distributes it on the Internet.

Slowly but surely Linux catches on with the programming community, as legions of inveterate tinkerers set about writing improvements, fixing bugs, and sharing information over the Net. It becomes especially popular with Internet Service Providers (ISPs) and other small businesses, who are attracted both by the low cost and by the ability to tailor the system to their own specific needs.

1991 GOPHER, A NETWORK BROWSER, IS INVENTED AT THE UNIVERSITY OF MINNESOTA

Computer scientists at the University of Minnesota develop Gopher, an Internet tool for finding and viewing information stored on remote computers. Gopher, named after the university's mascot, becomes widely used for searching libraries and other large databases.

Gopher consists of a browser and a data transfer protocol. Noted for its simple, user-friendly interface, the browser employs a system of hierarchical menus. The data transfer protocol allows users to view text files from remote computers. The Gopher program is made available to the public via the Internet and is soon adopted at universities all over the world.

In 1992 the University of Nevada introduces Veronica, an accessory for Gopher. Veronica is a database program that allows users to perform advanced searches of Gopher servers. Descriptively called an "indexing spider," Veronica travels through Gopher servers reading directory and file names and creating an index. It can then check a user's query against its index.

However, by the mid-1990s the World Wide Web (WWW), with its Hypertext Transfer Protocol (HTTP), is favored over Gopher systems to a large degree.

1991 THE WORLD WIDE WEB IS DEVELOPED AT CERN BY TIM BERNERS-LEE

Tim Berners-Lee completes the original software for the World Wide Web (WWW), the hypertext system he had first proposed in 1989. He envisions the WWW as a shared information space—a web of hypertext documents—within which people communicate with each other and with computers.

Berners-Lee had been motivated to design the WWW because he and his colleagues in the high-energy physics community were frustrated by computing incompatibilities. Their vast stores of data were difficult to access and exchange due to differing encoding formats and networking schemes.

Berners-Lee was working at CERN (Centre Européan pour la Recherche Nucléaire; European Laboratory for Particle Physics), in Geneva,

Tim Berners-Lee, inventor of the World Wide Web (AP / Wide World Photos).

Tim Berners-Lee

Ten years ago, only a fraction of the population knew what the Internet was. Then in 1991 the World Wide Web (WWW) burst onto center stage and raised Internet use exponentially. Tim Berners-Lee, the WWW's humble inventor, doesn't see himself as directly responsible for the revolution in communication and information caused by the Web. He says he provided only the blueprint, whereas communities of Internet users assembled the pieces and made the WWW grow with breathtaking speed.

Berners-Lee was born in London, England, with computing in his blood. His parents met when they were both working to develop the Ferranti Mark I, an early computer. As a child Tim played with computer paper tape and built model computers out of cardboard boxes. He also enjoyed mathematics and was pleased to find that it played an important role in applied science.

Berners-Lee studied physics at Queen's College, Oxford University, graduating in 1976. While many of his peers were pursuing graduate studies in physics, he turned instead to electronics and started by building a computer from a M6800 processor and an old television.

For the next eight years Berners-Lee held various posts within England's telecommunications industry and gained experience developing real-time control firmware and writing programming code for graphics and communications software. In 1984 he was granted a fellowship at CERN, a prestigious high-energy physics facility in Switzerland, where he joined efforts to improve real-time data-acquisition systems.

In 1989 Berners-Lee proposed to CERN management that they fund the development of a hypertext data system; he thus began the project which yielded the WWW. Continuing to work at CERN for a few years, he facilitated the design and construction of the Web. But by 1994 he and his supervisors at CERN agreed that a high-energy physics lab was not the best place to oversee a global electronic communications system. So Berners-Lee moved to the United States to join the Laboratory for Computer Science at the Massachusetts Institute of Technology (MIT) as director of a new organization, the W3 Consortium. From this post he continued to coordinate the development of Web tools and standards. In 1998 Berners-Lee was awarded a MacArthur Foundation "Genius Grant" for creation of the Web.

When Berners-Lee first completed the software that runs the Web, several companies approached him about commercializing his creation. After some thought, he turned them down. He chose not to copyright and gain financially from his inventions, and Berners-Lee remains committed to preventing any single corporation from dominating the Web, a situation he thinks would destroy the Web's potential to remain a public, easily accessible means of communicating and gathering and offering information.

While many view the WWW as a get-rich-quick opportunity, to Berners-Lee it represents something else entirely. In the T.V. documentary "Nerds 2.0.1," he says: "The fact that the World Wide Web did work—I find it not just exciting for itself, but exciting for the whole idea that you can have an idea . . . and it can happen. It means that dreamers all over the world should take heart and not stop."

Switzerland, when he developed the WWW. His vision for the system was far broader than many of his authorities at CERN were aware. He hoped that the WWW would be transformed from its origins as an information-retrieval system for physics researchers into a public information and communication device available on all computing platforms.

During 1990 and 1991 Berners-Lee develops the components of the WWW system. He works from several criteria: the system must be flexible and designed with minimal constraint so that it is compatible with numerous languages and operating systems; the system must be capable of recording random links between objects; and the system must be constructed so that entering and correcting information is easily performed. The first version of the WWW includes three basic architectural principles that aim to accommodate these criteria. The first is called Universal Document Identifier (UDI), an address scheme for pointing the system to a particular location within the WWW information space. UDIs are later renamed Universal Resource Locators (URLs). The second element is Hypertext Transfer Protocol (HTTP); it serves as the protocol for accessing data and traversing hypertext links. Hypertext Markup Language (HTML), a documentation code designed to resemble the existing and widely used Standard Generalized Markup Language (SGML), is the third principle.

Berners-Lee unleashes the WWW first within CERN, then throughout the physics-research and hypertext-programming communities, and finally onto the Internet. From 1991 to 1994 use of the original WWW server (info.cern.ch) grows by a factor of ten each year as the world begins to take note of a new information phenomenon.

1991 Members of the Internet Community Are Encouraged to Write Applications for the WWW

Funding for the WWW project at CERN runs out, so Tim Berners-Lee and other project authorities encourage members of the Internet community at large to write applications for the WWW.

The most influential results of this push for outside assistance are a number of browsers, programs that enable people to read and navigate hypertext documents on the WWW. The first browsers include Erwise, Midas, Cello, and Viola-WWW. These pave the way for the more successful Mosaic, which in turn predates the ubiquitous Netscape Navigator and Microsoft Internet Explorer.

Placing control of the WWW's evolution into the hands of programmers across the world yields a unique global experiment in creative innovation.

1991 THE STEALTH PROJECT (LATER THE GREEN PROJECT) IS BORN, AND JAVA BEANS BEGIN ROASTING

Sun Microsystems' "Stealth Project" is born in Aspen, Colorado, to develop innovative devices and software for the consumer electronics market. The most significant product of this collaboration is a computer programming language later called Java, which eventually adds animation, audio, and real-time interactivity to the World Wide Web (WWW).

Sun Microsystems, a computer workstation manufacturer, had been founded in 1982 by Andreas Bechtolsheim, Bill Joy, Vinod Kholsa, and Scott McNealy. Immensely successful originally, by 1990 the company's directors were actively scanning the horizon for glimpses of consumer computing's future. On January 15, 1991, Joy and Bechtolsheim, along with Wayne Rosing, Mike Sheridan, James Gosling, and Patrick Naughton, meet in Aspen, Colorado, and call themselves the Stealth Project team. Their goal is to build a system consisting of a network of consumer electronics devices that can be controlled digitally with a handheld remote control. Their plan of attack: Naughton will be in charge of graphics, Gosling will focus on programming languages, and Sheridan will develop a business plan.

Back in Silicon Valley, California, they set to work. In April they rename their endeavor the Green Project. New members Ed Frank, Craig Forrest, and Chris Warth round out the team by offering hardware, chipware, and software expertise.

Gosling begins to develop a programming language, which he calls "Oak," adhering to several strict criteria. The language has to be operable on any platform (that is, on any central processing unit [CPU], the part of a computer that controls its operation). It has to be capable of exchanging code seamlessly within a network. And it has to be reliable, simple, and compact. Gosling's language is later renamed "Java," because "Oak" is already copyrighted for another language.

As the project gains momentum, a hardware system unfolds in what might be record time. Dubbed "*7" (pronounced "star seven"), it consists of a handheld "personal digital assistant" (PDA) with an extensive string of applications written in what is then still called Oak. The

WHY CAN'T JOHNNY READ: HYPERTEXT AND LITERACY

When he designed the World Wide Web, Tim Berners-Lee envisioned a resource-sharing device specifically for academics. It's especially ironic, then, that some of the most intense criticism of the Web—namely, that it is creating a culture of poorly trained readers—comes from within academia. Although teachers have come to accept the ubiquity of word processing (despite fears it would increase plagiarism) and e-mail (considered inferior to "proper" letter writing), hypertext remains the ugly stepchild of the digital age, associated with attention deficit disorder and a lack of scholarly authority.

Web historians place the beginning of the so-called hypertext holy war with the publication of Jay Bolter's book *The Writing Space* in 1991. Bolter enthused that as the Web proliferated, linked documents would ultimately phase out printed books, and a new age of "hypertext literacy" would ensue. Critics formed on either side of the battle line, most all of them ignoring the possibility that print and hypertext cultures might live comfortably, without displacing one another.

The arguments against hypertext are threefold. First, critics charge that its structure encourages readers to merely skim the surface of a document, bypassing the deeper meanings within a text. Next, because a hypertext can be read in multiple ways, critics worry that there is no right way to read it at all. Finally, some scholars claim hypertext lacks the effect that a sequential printed book has on its readers. As communications scholar Nancy Kaplan puts it, there is a fear that "the text will exhaust the reader, rather than the other way around."

In her essay "Literacy Beyond Books," Kaplan critiques hypertext's critics, arguing that their objections have more to do with old-fashioned ideas about "great books" than they do with contemporary reading practices. To the charge that hypertext discourages deep reading, Kaplan notes that there are all sort of books—scientific, legal, self-help, travel, encyclopedias, cooking—which have never been designated as deep, but rather have been meant to be skimmed and read selectively.

For those who argue that hypertext seduces readers with technology rather than content, Kaplan points out that no book reading ever escaped its own technological trappings of pages and font sizes. Kaplan argues that in fact, hypertext's explicit technological focus actually may work to empower its reader. Because it demands that we choose what we will read and what we will not, Kaplan argues that hypertext may actually create a better, more critical class of readers than those who grew up with books. As she puts it, "Whatever else we might observe about the process, it's certain that there's no automatic pilot for reading a hypertext."

Beyond the Net

Green Project team demonstrates *7 to Sun Microsystems directors on September 3, 1992.

Although *7 leads nowhere, continued attention to programming eventually leads to a refined Java programming language and several Java-based Internet-searching and WWW-development tools. Java is the first "universal" software, meaning that it can run on any operating system—a key criterion for any software used over the Internet.

1992 THE INTERNET SOCIETY IS CHARTERED

In January the Internet Society (ISOC) is established. The ISOC's mission statement asserts that the organization's goal is "to assure the beneficial, open evolution of the global Internet and its related internetworking technologies through leadership in standards, issues, and education."

The ISOC is chartered by numerous members of the Internet Engineering Task Force (IETF), a group that had been formed in the early 1980s by the government's Defense Advanced Research Projects Agency (DARPA). At that time DARPA was still the main body regulating the operation of the Internet. The IETF was an international group of network designers, operators, and researchers devoted to assuring the smooth evolution of the Internet's architecture. One of the IETF's important efforts was the maintenance of Internet standards, and by 1990 IETF members had become concerned that government funding of these efforts would soon dissolve. In early 1991 they discussed plans for the creation of a non-governmental, internationally recognized organization to oversee various activities related to the development of the Internet.

The ISOC is chartered in January 1992. It is funded by members (professional groups and individuals), and its mission is tightly associated with the work of the IETF and the IETF's mother organization, the Internet Architecture Board (formerly the Internet Activities Board). ISOC directors are committed to assuring discrimination-free Internet access, halting censorship of online communication, limiting government control over essential elements of networking architecture, encouraging cooperation between interconnected networks, and guarding against misuse of personal information offered on the Internet.

To realize this vision, the ISOC initiates activities which it hopes will influence the Internet's evolution. These activities include standards development task forces, legal efforts aimed at protecting the Internet from commercial ownership, international conferences, symposiums on Internet security, and multiple educational programs in primary schools and in nonindustrialized countries.

1992 AFTER MUCH HYPE, THE MICHELANGELO VIRUS CAUSES ONLY MINIMAL DAMAGE

In February, computer users around the world are warned of a computer virus that will activate on March 6. Named Michelangelo, the virus is programmed to release its payload within infected computers on the birthday of Renaissance artist Michelangelo Buonarroti.

Although computer engineers had been speaking of system "bugs" ever since programming errors had caused the earliest digital computers to crash, the first *intentional* computer bugs were created in computer science research laboratories in the 1960s. Fred Cohen, who studied computer bugs at the University of Southern California, coined the term "computer virus" in 1983. He defined a virus as a program that can infect another program and replicate itself inside its host. Later computer scientists made the definition more specific, stating that viruses are written to enter a computer without the user's knowledge and that they often damage a host program or an entire system.

During the 1980s several harmful viruses were unleashed on Apple and IBM-compatible computers, and in 1988 the first antivirus software was marketed. But viruses received little media attention until Michelangelo was unveiled.

The Michelangelo virus enters computers via infected diskettes. Once a Michelangelo virus gains entry into a machine's memory, it infects the machine by taking the place of the machine's boot sector (the part of the computer that starts it up). It replicates there undetected and remains dormant until March 6. It also infects other diskettes that are inserted into the disk drive. If the boot sector is activated on March 6, the virus kicks into action, destroying data within the computer's hard disk.

An early warning alerts operators of MS-DOS computers (the Michelangelo virus infects only those machines running on the operating system MS-DOS) to look for and try to eradicate the virus before March 6. The warning also causes a hail of frantic reports in the media predicting a devastating electronic nightmare. The number of possibly infected—and thus potentially doomed—computers is estimated at around five million.

But when the day arrives only about two thousand computers around the world suffer serious damage, because many fewer machines had been infected than predicted and because the forewarning had allowed some machines to be fixed. Rather than a graveyard of scrambled hard disks, the Michelangelo virus leaves in its wake a booming antivirus software industry, as computer users hurry to safeguard their machines against any coming epidemics.

1992 FIRST AUDIO MULTICAST ON THE INTERNET GIVES RISE TO THE MBONE

The Internet Engineering Task Force (IETF) "multicasts" live audio and video, via the Internet, from its meeting site to various locations around the world. These multicasting endeavors grow into the Multicast-Backbone, or MBONE, an experimental network that operates within the Internet.

Television and radio stations had been broadcasting programs over airwaves for decades. The MBONE architecture was conceived to operate in a similar fashion, "multicasting" electronically stored audio and video over the Internet from one transmitter to a few receivers (with the hope that advances in technology would allow transmission to many receivers). In the late 1980s at Xerox PARC Steve Deering developed what would become the MBONE addressing scheme, called IP (Internet protocol)-Multicast. By 1990 the IETF, a group of network designers, operators, and researchers who oversee the evolution of the Internet's architecture, began multicasting research projects.

In 1992 the IETF's projects culminate in the first multicast, which serves as a starting point for the growth of this new technology. Gradually various networks, government agencies, universities, and Internet Service Providers begin to connect to the MBONE and participate in multicasting experiments. Space shuttle missions, conferences, and rock concerts are among the programs that are multicast during the MBONE's first few years.

1993 ESCROWED ENCRYPTION INITIATIVE INTRODUCED BY CLINTON ADMINISTRATION

Pitting the defense of national security against the right to personal privacy, the cryptography debate heats up as the Clinton administration announces a dramatic change in encryption strategy.

Historically, U.S. encryption policy had been the province of the National Security Agency (NSA), which is charged with the protection of diplomatic and military secrets. But in 1987 Congress grew alarmed at the muscle-flexing of the NSA and passed the Computer Security Act (CSA), which gave primary authority in encryption matters to a civilian group, the National Institute of Standards and Technology (NIST).

From its inception the CSA was controversial. Critics charged that federal agencies like the NSA routinely overstepped their assigned boundaries, ignoring warnings to act only in an advisory capacity on encryption matters. For their part, federal agencies argued that in order to effectively pursue terrorists and criminals (who are now themselves using off-the-shelf digital encryption devices to thwart court-approved wiretaps), law enforcement must play a strong role in cryptography decisions.

In 1993, the Clinton administration issues what they believe to be a compromise measure: the Escrowed Encryption Initiative (EEI). Described as "a voluntary program to improve security and privacy of telephone communications while meeting the legitimate needs of law enforcement," the EEI plan recommends that a government-approved voice encryption chip called "Clipper" be placed in secured telephones, and that a digital signature standard called "Capstone" be used for secured computerized data transactions. The encryption method is called a key-escrow system, which is different from private-key systems (in which only the sender and the receiver hold the key) and public-key systems (in which the key is available for anyone to use): in a key-escrow system, encrypted communications can be deciphered by the intended recipient *and* by a third party holding the key. In the EEI plan, responsibilities of this third party are divided between the citizen-run NIST and the Treasury Department.

The scientific community, civil libertarians, and the software industry all oppose the EEI for various reasons. Scientists argue against the use of a classified algorithm (called "Skipjack") to enact the Clipper chip—the government maintains that Skipjack must be classified in order to protect the chip from being cracked by terrorists. Scientists argue that public algorithms are more robust because they can be scrutinized and tested. A classified algorithm like Skipjack, on the other hand, might contain weaknesses undetected by NSA officials. Worse, cynics wonder if it contains "back door access" for government officials deciding to forego a trip to the NIST for civilian permission to crack a private message.

Civil libertarians point out that since very few criminals will "volunteer" to use government-sponsored encryption devices, it is unclear what exactly the EEI will accomplish. Many decry the entire notion of key-escrow encryption: John Perry Barlow, cofounder of the Electronic Frontier Foundation, argues that "trusting the government with your privacy is like having a Peeping Tom install your window blinds." They wonder aloud whether the "voluntary" nature of EEI isn't an interim step on the way to mandatory enforcement of the act, which has the potential to violate the privacy of every American using any digitized equipment. Even international security experts question the wisdom of EEI, citing Clipper's incompatibility with many other encryption devices used abroad.

Meanwhile American software manufacturers, sensing they are about to be edged out of the encryption industry, are infuriated. For decades, encryption devices had been classified as munitions and held to tight export restrictions. U.S. companies watched helplessly as cryptography markets flourished abroad. Expecting there to be little or no international market for encryption devices that contain a key held in escrow by the U.S. government, software companies accuse the Clinton administration of interfering with their right to conduct commerce.

Despite the criticisms, the EEI passes into law in 1994 as a voluntary Federal Information Processing Standard. Observers speculate that it might not be long before it is adopted by organizations like the Internal Revenue Service for online tax filing, ultimately replacing industry-preferred encryption methods. But just three months later, computer scientist Matt Blaze announces that he has done what the NSA claimed couldn't be done: he has "cracked the Clipper Chip." The ensuing bad publicity leads the administration to announce plans to cut back on Skipjack, and "investigate other solutions for high-speed data communications."

1993 MOSAIC, A GRAPHICAL BROWSER FOR THE WORLD WIDE WEB, IS DEVELOPED

Marc Andreessen develops the first versions of Mosaic, a point-and-click browser with a graphical user interface (GUI). Mosaic is released to users free of charge, and its ease of use makes it immensely popular, helping to spark an unprecedented explosion of traffic on the Web.

Andreessen had been working at the University of Illinois' National Center for Supercomputing Applications (NCSA), a government-funded research facility. The NCSA, which received large sums of money and had a loose internal structure, supported the creative investigations of its talented staff of programmers and engineers.

Biography

MARC ANDREESSEN

Marc Andreessen is the inventor of the Mosaic Web browser and cofounder of Netscape Communications Corporation. By the time he was twenty-four years old, his stake in Netscape was worth more than $250 million and he had been written up as a celebrity in the pages of *People* magazine. But such fame baffles Andreessen, who has said of the *People* profile: "Isn't that hilarious?" He has been described by interviewers as mellow and self-conscious, and he doesn't seem interested in hogging either the media spotlight or the credit for his accomplishments. Nor does he seem interested in divulging much personal information—except that he has a pet, a bulldog named Lily.

Andreessen grew up in Wisconsin and studied computer science at the University of Illinois at Urbana-Champaign. He would later say that he might have been happier having chosen something less technical, like history or philosophy. Still, it was his computer interests that landed him a position—while still an undergraduate—doing research in a well-funded and loosely structured laboratory at NCSA. And there he developed the original Mosaic software. He earned his bachelor's degree in 1993, just before relocating to the West Coast to start a corporate career.

A few months later Andreessen cofounded the company that would soon be known as Netscape. He adapted smoothly to operating within a high-profile, consumer-oriented corporation. When reporters have asked him what his basic goals are, invariably his response has been that he is simply interested in helping to make Netscape successful by devising great products that satisfy customers.

By 1998 he was serving as Netscape's vice president of products. He spends a lot of time online, reading computer-industry news, trying to balance attempts to predict future markets with efforts to make the right calls about whatever current issues are on the table.

When pressed to comment on what makes him personally happy, Andreessen says that he takes great pleasure sleeping in—way in—and then greeting the late afternoon with a good cup of coffee.

Inspired by a browser called Midas, Andreessen decided that it would be both fun and practical to design his own graphical browser for the Web (browsers are programs that allow users to seek, retrieve, and read hypertext documents). Andreessen and fellow graduate student Eric Bina led a team of enthusiastic programmers in an effort to create a user-friendly browser with a graphical user interface (GUI). In a matter of months they completed Mosaic for X, which runs on Unix machines.

Mosaic for X is introduced onto the Internet in early 1993, and users are encouraged to download the program via FTP (file transfer protocol). In August 1993 Andreessen's team releases free copies of Mosaic designed for Macintosh and Microsoft Windows operating systems. The adoption of Mosaic is quick and ubiquitous, revealing how eager Internet users are to explore the Web. By September an estimated one percent of Internet traffic is Web traffic—whereas prior to the introduction of Mosaic, the Web had been virtually unknown outside of computer science circles.

Software companies begin approaching Andreessen with offers to commercialize Mosaic. These opportunities appeal to him because funding for research centers such as NCSA has begun to drop and thus self-supported research has become desirable. But as Andreessen's supervisors become aware of the browser's significance and potential for generating commercial revenue, they begin to take charge of Mosaic-related affairs. Andreessen graduates in the fall and decides to head west, to Silicon Valley, California.

With no intentions of continuing to develop his wildly successful invention, Andreessen takes a position at Enterprise Integration Technologies. After only a few months he leaves to cofound the company that will later be called Netscape.

1993 The InterNIC Is Established to Administer Domain Names

The National Science Foundation (NSF) enters into a cooperative agreement with Network Solutions, Incorporated (NSI), a private consulting company in Virginia, to administer domain names on the Internet. With funding from the NSF, NSI creates InterNIC, the organization that will offer directory and database services and register the names.

The collection of addresses of computers connected to the ARPAnet began as a simple database file called "hosts.txt," administered by the Network Information Center (NIC) at the U.S. Department of Defense. As the network expanded, "hosts.txt" became unwieldy and engineers began brainstorming new ways to administer the database. In the 1980s the notion of using more user-friendly domain names as addresses evolved, and in 1984 a document called RFC (Request For Comments) 920 by Jon Postel and Joyce Reynolds established the first top-level domains: .com, .edu, .gov, .mil, and .org. (The domains .net and .int were subsequently added.) RFC 920 also approved the use of two-digit country domain names, such as ".jp" for Japan and ".uk" for United Kingdom. (It is worth noting that the top-level domain ".us" for the United States does exist but is rarely used—probably because of the popularity of the ".com" domain. This bias will spark criticism from the rest of the world, who argue ".com" is being abused by U.S. registrants.)

Beyond the Net

ONLY WORDS

"They say he raped them that night. They say... he forced them to have sex with him, and with each other, and to do horrible, brutal things to their own bodies."

Thus begins Julian Dibell's 1993 *Village Voice* article, "A Rape in Cyberspace," detailing a virtual assault that occurred in the online environment of Xerox PARC's LamdaMoo system. The facts of the crime were never in doubt: a "Mr. Bungle" used MOO object commands in order to harm his victims in a public forum with multiple witnesses. Following the attack, the LamdaMoo community considered a number of punishments, like alerting Bungle's university of his assault (offline, he was a student). In the end, these ideas were rejected. As Dibell puts it, "He had committed a MOO crime, and his punishment, if any, would be meted out via the MOO." It was decided Bungle would be "toaded"—the MOO equivalent of execution.

Bungle's toading turned out to be an imperfect penalty, as he was later "reincarnated" as another character. Nevertheless the case demonstrated how virtual crimes might be dealt with in virtual environments. In 1994, however, a University of Michigan student named Jake Baker mixed his online fantasy life with his offline social life, complicating utopic visions of cyber-justice.

Objectionable as they were to some, the "snuff" stories Baker posted to the Usenet group alt.sex.stories wouldn't have attracted much notice online, except for the fact that Baker gave one of his fictional victims the name of a real female classmate. This caused school officials to escort him off campus and inspired F.B.I. officials to search his computer files. When they located some e-mail about forcibly transporting young (unnamed) women to Canada, the F.B.I. charged Baker with a "threat to kidnap or injure," which carries a five-year federal prison term.

Arguing to prosecute, attorney and anti-pornography activist Catharine Mackinnon maintained that because Baker's words contained no intrinsic value, they were not "protected speech" under the Constitution. The American Civil Liberties Union (ACLU) countered that the issue wasn't the value of Baker's speech, but whether his words posed a bonafide threat. As the ACLU states, "The notion of thought-crimes is not consistent with that of a free society." Ultimately the courts agreed, dismissing Baker's case.

Though the Constitution may protect the virtual nature of speech, it doesn't protect citizens from the social costs of words. Battles over the proper limits on speech—and whether there should be any limits at all—are as old as the First Amendment itself. The "unreal" nature of cyberspace further complicates these discussions, and Baker's case won't be the last. In early 1999, a U.S. Federal court heard a civil case concerning an anti-abortion Web site that, according to the plaintiffs, encourages violence against abortion doctors. Echoing the Baker case, the attorney for the defendants told the jury that "This is a case involving words and only words." The jury disagreed, awarding the plaintiffs more than $100 million in damages.

In 1992 the NSF begins seeking a private firm to administer domain names under the aegis of the U.S. government. NSI, a consulting firm that had been founded by engineers in 1979, wins the contract and creates the InterNIC. Individuals or corporations can apply to the InterNIC and request a second-level domain name (i.e., the "apple" in "apple.com"). The names are given out on a first-come, first-served basis—a practice that will lead to a tangled series of lawsuits in the following years.

In the beginning, domain name registration is free—NSI is paid by the NSF on a cost-plus basis. In 1995 NSI begins charging fees for all domain-name registrants. The announcement raises a howl of protest from users, but it soon becomes an accepted part of life on the Net. Thirty percent of the funds raised are earmarked for an Internet Intelligence Infrastructure Fund, and the other seventy percent are kept by NSI. The InterNIC is the only place where users can register .com, .edu, .gov, .net, and .org addresses (the other domains—.mil and .int—are not available to the general public). The InterNIC quickly becomes a phenomenally lucrative part of NSI; in 1996 *Wired* magazine estimates the InterNIC monopoly's value at one billion dollars.

At the time of the InterNIC's creation, the Internet is a relatively small, essentially U.S.-based phenomenon, of interest primarily to educational institutions and the military. When, as if overnight, the Internet explodes in 1995, the InterNIC is square in the middle of an administrative whirlwind for which it is ill-prepared. And NSI, previously one small consulting company among thousands, wakes to find itself with a monopoly on cyberspace addresses—some of the most lucrative real estate around, but also the most contentious. When NSI's contract with NSF expires in 1998, however, the Net is a very different world from the one into which the InterNIC was born, and the search for a new, nonmonopolistic approach to domain-name registry begins.

1993 THE UNITED NATIONS AND THE WHITE HOUSE GO ONLINE

The United Nations and the White House create World Wide Web sites, offering the public an easily accessible glimpse into international affairs and national politics. The sites are early representations of what is becoming one of the Web's most visited resources, the "home page."

As soon as the point-and-click Web browser Mosaic was introduced in early 1993, home pages of organizations and individuals began to proliferate on the Web. At first the majority of these informational sites remained restricted to computer experts and groups belonging to the academic and corporate computer communities. But as it became clear that the Web was evolving into a widespread phenomenon, others joined the online frontier, posting home pages for anyone with an Internet connection to view.

The posting of home pages by the United Nations and the White House indicates that government officials have embraced the communication-technology revolution. The pages offer historical, educational, and general-interest information about the UN and the White House, as well as up-to-date news about current issues and legislation.

Home pages of corporations also begin to go online, offering a new medium for transmitting information to the public. Home pages of individuals, which increase in popularity in the late 90s, represent an unprecedented home-publishing forum, as well as a new method of personal expression, exhibition, and communication.

1994 Marc Andreessen and Jim Clark Found Mosaic Communications

Marc Andreessen and Jim Clark launch Mosaic Communications, which later changes its name to Netscape Communications. Their goal is to build a company that can become the leading provider of software for linking people and information across computer networks.

In 1993 Andreessen had developed Mosaic, a point-and-click browser for the WWW, and released free versions of the program for Unix, Windows, and Macintosh platforms. Mosaic resulted in enormous public interest in the Web and thus created a market for more advanced Web tools. At the time Andreessen was still working at the University of Illinois' National Center for Supercomputing Applications (NCSA), a government-funded research facility. At the end of that year he had moved to Silicon Valley, California, to take a position at Enterprise Integration Technologies.

Three months into his new job Andreessen is approached by Jim Clark, the founder of Silicon Graphics, a Fortune 500 company that had spearheaded the development of high-end digital graphics. Clark wants to start an Internet software company, and he handpicks Andreessen because of the success of Mosaic. Together they fly to Illinois and gather up as many of the original Mosaic team members as they can entice away from NCSA. Their venture, officially founded in April 1994, is called Mosaic Communications Corporation.

The original mission of Mosaic Communications Corp. is to provide consulting and support to Mosaic users, to operate an Internet information server, and to develop and deploy an improved version of Mosaic. This third goal is realized in October 1994 with the release of free test versions of Netscape Navigator onto the Web. Two months later, final versions of Netscape Navigator are completed.

By August 1995 the company is renamed Netscape Communications Corporation, and it makes a public-share offering, reporting annual revenues of $85 million. The following year revenues top $340 million. Expanding its product pool to encompass tools for Web-site management, electronic commerce, and various aspects of information sharing, Netscape continues to introduce innovative, effective Internet software.

1994 THE NATIONAL COMMUNICATIONS COMPETITION AND INFORMATION INFRASTRUCTURE ACT OF 1994 BECOMES LAW

The National Communications Competition and Information Infrastructure Act, which had been introduced into the United States Congress in 1993 by Representative Edward Markey (D-Massachusetts), passes into law on June 28.

The act alters several elements of national telecommunications systems. Companies providing telecommunications services are now obligated to provide equal access to any person who is willing to pay for service. The act's authors intend that competition among providers will keep service affordable for all citizens. In the months following the passing of this act, the phrase "universal access" begins to appear in the media as a desirable goal for the future of national telecommunications. To some observers, the phrase means that all people should have equal access to communication and information. To others, it means that all people should have an equal opportunity to create the information that is available within the national telecommunications system.

The act also calls on the Federal Communications Commission (FCC) to establish policies and standards for interconnection among public and private telecommunications networks. The FCC is responsible for smoothing any legislative processes associated with the introduction of future telecommunications technologies. Allotting federal funds to education and health, the act ensures that telecommunications services will be offered to public educational institutions, health care institutions, and public libraries.

The act breaks the monopolies held by local telephone companies by allowing any service provider—for example, a long-distance service provider—to offer local telephone service. Removing restrictions on cable-television service, the act also allows local telephone companies to offer video programming so they can compete with local cable companies.

The National Communications Competition and Information Infrastructure Act of 1994 is applauded by the Electronic Frontier Foundation (EFF), a group that works to guarantee the civil rights of computer-network users.

The act is part of a broader movement within the federal government to make the maintenance of information systems a top priority. Putting this aim into practice, the Clinton administration establishes a National Information Infrastructure task force to monitor and help build the technologies involved in an emerging and revolutionary era of global information.

1994 WORLD WIDE WEB CONSORTIUM IS FORMED TO PROMOTE EVOLUTION OF WWW

In October the World Wide Web Consortium (W3C) is formed under the direction of Tim Berners-Lee, the inventor of the World Wide Web (WWW or Web). Its purpose is the promotion of the Web's evolution and the development of standards for interoperability. Its mission: "Realizing the full potential of the Web" as a medium for interaction between humans and computers.

Berners-Lee had invented the WWW, a networked universe of information linked via hypertext, in 1990 at CERN. By 1993 the Web had grown enormously and was catalyzing an information revolution, as more and more people gained access. Funding and resources for maintaining the Web were becoming scarce at CERN, so Berners-Lee moved development to the United States.

The W3C is established with initial financial support from CERN, the European Commission, and DARPA (the U.S. Defense Advanced Research Projects Agency—the agency that had funded the Internet's predecessor, the

ARPAnet). The new consortium is offered a home within the Laboratory for Computer Science at the Massachusetts Institute of Technology (MIT). MIT is well-equipped to handle the setup of W3C, as its staff includes numerous computer engineers experienced in advanced networking.

W3C intends to work with the emerging international WWW community to outline specifications and standards for the Web, with the hope that such standards will ensure the Web's continued evolution as an interoperable unit. The consortium's staff plans to meet this goal by producing sample programming code and reference software that will be freely available to the public. Commercial and academic entities are encouraged to join W3C; member services include a forum for discussing Web-related issues. Membership dues, private contracts, and public research funds support the consortium's efforts.

In April 1995 W3C moves beyond the United States' borders by partnering with France's National Institute for Research in Computer Science and Control (INRIA). And the following year the consortium gains a third host, Keio University in Japan, as both its membership pool and influence grow.

1994 SHOPPING MALLS, BANKS, AND RADIO STATIONS ARRIVE ON THE NET

Internet commerce makes its debut, with entities such as shopping resources, banks, and radio stations announcing their goods and services online. Such events herald the arrival of the global electronic marketplace and raise concerns about Internet security.

In April 1994 the Internet Shopping Network (ISN) goes online, featuring a forty-thousand-product Computer Superstore. Other Internet retailers follow suit: shopping malls put up informational Web sites featuring sales and special events, and department stores and catalogs offer the option of ordering products via the Web.

Banks begin to offer online services, so that customers can conveniently maintain their accounts from their home or office computers. Sending financial information over the Internet or via private networks—for banking or shopping purposes—makes people uncomfortable at first. Online security becomes a hot topic in the news and in the board rooms of corporations that want to appease their customers. Research efforts yield improved encryption techniques and tools that apply at all levels of online transactions.

Radio stations go online, representing one of the first creations of a link between the Internet and other media. Initially, radio station Web sites offer general information and program schedules—which isn't much different than distributing information in a printed format. However, some sites are also featuring online shows, discussion forums, and pictures and graphics to accompany their audio broadcasts—an unprecedented twist to radio programming and an innovative use of Internet bandwidth. By the late 1990s numerous radio stations are even broadcasting online, heralding the beginning of a new era in the radio business.

1994 STANFORD GRADUATE STUDENTS FOUND YAHOO! SEARCH ENGINE

Ph.D. candidates David Filo and Jerry Yang turn a passion for Web surfing into a fast-track career with their Yahoo! search engine. Within a few years Yahoo! becomes not only one of the most popular search engines on the Web, but also one of its most successful businesses.

College buddies Filo and Yang were sharing an office and a thesis advisor at Stanford, where they were both pursuing Ph.D.s in electrical engineering. In early 1994 Filo discovered the Mosaic browser and the World Wide Web. Soon the two are spending more time on the Web than on their degrees—building home pages and links to their favorite sites. Because Filo is interested in seeing Yang's bookmarks and vice versa, they begin passing them back and forth; soon they simply collect the links on one page, called "Jerry's Guide to the World Wide Web."

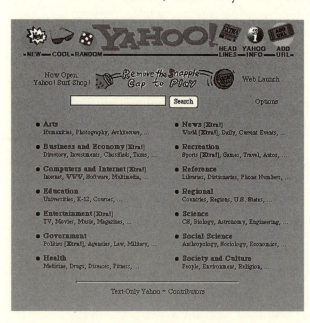

A screen shot of the Yahoo! web site (AP / Wide World Photos).

Netspeak

DIRECTORIES, ENGINES, AND METASEARCHERS

There are many ways to get where you need to go on the WWW. For example, Yahoo! is a leader among **Web directories**—collections of Web sites organized by topic. Web directories also include a search engine (Yahoo!, for example, uses the AltaVista engine) as well as special features like news services, horoscopes, classifieds, and yellow pages. Other Web directories include AOL Netfind, LookSmart (http://www.looksmart.com), the Mining Co. (http://www.miningco.com), Snap (http://www.snap.com), and Webcrawler (http://www.webcrawler.com).

While Web directories use human editors to sift through sites and classify them appropriately, **search engines** use programs called "spiders" to index the Web. Quality basic search engines include Altavista (http://www.altavista.com), Excite (http://www.excite.com), GoTo (http://www.goto.com), Google (http://www.google.com), HotBot (http://www.hotbot.com), Infoseek (http://www.infoseek.com), Lycos (http://www.lycos.com), Northern Light (http://www.northernlight.com), and Planet Search (http://www.planetsearch.com).

To distinguish themselves from the pack, many engines offer special features like free e-mail or personalized splash pages. Northern Light has a collection of some five thousand magazines and journals that can be searched. (Abstracts of the articles are free; complete articles cost between one and four dollars.) Meanwhile, the Excite search engine uses a technique called Intelligent Concept Extraction, which searches for terms that are closely related to the search request; if you search for "children," Excite will also look for "kids." One recent entrant in the search-engine race is GoTo, launched in 1998. Unlike other engines, GoTo has an uncluttered front page that focuses exclusively on searching. Keep in mind, however, that GoTo asks sites to pay for a prominent listing in their index. The sites that GoTo lists first are not necessarily the most relevant—they may have paid to be there.

A recent trend in Web searching are the **metasearchers**, which search numerous engines simultaneously. These include Ask Jeeves (http://www.askjeeves.com), Dogpile (http://www.dogpile.com), Mamma (http://www.mamma.com), MetaCrawler (http://www.metacrawler.com), and MetaFind (http://www.metafind.com). The Ask Jeeves site uses "natural language" searching—users type in a question ("Why is the sky blue?") and get back sites that may answer the query. Dogpile searches not only the Web but also the newswires, Usenet, and FTP databases.

As the list grows and becomes difficult to sort through, they divide it into subject categories, and then subcategories. Filo devises a search engine to complement the hierarchical list. Initially, the database is housed on Yang's workstation, while the search engine resides on Filo's: the workstations are named "akebono" and "konishiki," after beloved sumo wrestlers. What started as a hobby becomes a public service: by that summer the site is logging tens of thousands of visitors a day. Many visitors send e-mails to Filo and Yang, offering suggestions of how the site can be improved.

One aspect that definitely needs work is the name. "Jerry's Guide . . ." had been changed to "Dave and Jerry's Guide . . . ," but the men soon begin seeking something with more panache. They eventually hit on Yahoo! and decide that it stands for "Yet Another Hierarchical Officious Oracle." But in fact, the two subsequently confessed to interviewers, they chose it more because they felt like "yahoos" themselves.

That fall Yahoo!'s popularity continues to swell, Filo's and Yang's Ph.D.s have been all but forgotten, and the time comes to seek venture capital. With help from a business-minded friend named Tim Brady, Filo and Yang begin meeting with potential investors. While investors are intrigued by the amount of attention Yahoo! has garnered in such a short time, they are also confused: what sensible venture capitalist would invest in a service that's given away for free?

After fending off a buyout offer from America Online (AOL), who is looking to fold Yahoo! into its own service, in April 1995 Yahoo! finds its bene-factor in Sequoia, the renowned firm that financed Apple Computer, Atari, and Cisco Systems. Filo and Yang hire a small team, including Brady and fellow Stanford student Srinija Srinivasan, who becomes the first "Ontological Yahoo," or full-time Web categorizer. Perhaps Yahoo!'s real "big break," however, is an invitation from Marc Andreessen to develop a partnership with Netscape: Netscape begins including a link to Yahoo! as part of its Web browser, a practice that continues through most of 1995.

Yahoo! carves out a space for itself on the Web, eclipsing some of its ear-liest competitors like EINet Galaxy, World Wide Web Worm, and the World Wide Web Virtual Library. The human element, combined with the early Netscape endorsement, helps Yahoo! stand out from the many other search engines cropping up in the mid-'90s, including Webcrawler (bought by AOL when Yahoo! turned them down), Lycos, AltaVista, and Excite (which all hit the Net in 1995). After a successful initial public offer-ing on Wall Street in April 1996, Filo and Yang become millionaires—just two short years after the graduate students started trading bookmarks.

1994 Navisoft Releases a WWW Program That Can Browse and Edit at the Same Time

Software company Navisoft (a subsidiary of America Online [AOL]) releases AOLPress, a product for simultaneous Web-page browsing and editing.

AOLPress is one of the first products that allows the creation of Web pages without knowledge of the underlying HTML programming code.

The design of Web pages had previously been restricted to those who had the time and ability to learn HTML, and the authoring and maintenance of Web pages had been time consuming. Numerous steps were required: for instance, to edit an existing page, an author had to open the page using a browser, save the page onto a local disk, start an authoring application, open the saved page, make changes, save the result, view the changes with a browser, open a server connection, use file transfer protocol (FTP) to insert the altered page into the server, and finally access and review the page using a browser.

AOLPress makes the process simpler. To edit a page, an author opens the page in AOLPress (using either a browser or a tool within AOLPress), makes changes, and saves the page directly to a server over the Web. The program allows editing in a WYSIWYG (What You See Is What You Get) environment, which means that the page is presented on the screen for alterations exactly the way it will appear when it is called up by a Web browser.

AOLPress—which is made freely available via download—simplifies the job of Webmasters, people who design and maintain corporate Web sites. It also opens the realm of Web site publishing to nonprogrammers, thus allowing the general public to more easily be active participants in the creation of Web material.

1994 LAURENCE CANTER AND MARTHA SIEGEL LAUNCH A SPAM ATTACK ON USENET

Spam, the online community's name for unsolicited bulk e-mail and mass postings on bulletin board systems (BBSs), comes into its own this year as two Phoenix attorneys launch a massive advertising campaign that pushes the boundary between free speech and abuse of resources.

Named for a Monty Python comedy sketch about a diner that serves "Spam, Spam, Spam, Spam, Spam, Spam, baked beans, Spam, and Spam," virtual spam usually features advertising—get-rich-quick schemes and sexually explicit materials are two of the most common types. Advertising had long been a contentious issue within BBSs on the Internet, as subscribers to online discussion forums tended to frown upon putting lists of newsgroup e-mail addresses to commercial use. There were no laws against spamming, and it was technically difficult for BBSs to identify and filter out unwanted messages.

Proponents of spam as an advertising technique usually defend it on free speech grounds, environmental grounds (spam, unlike junk mail, uses no paper), or on the grounds that it is no different from television or newspaper advertisements. But like unsolicited fax advertisements, spam costs the recipient—in online time and bandwidth, sometimes in hard-drive space, and always in frustration—while it is free or nearly free for the sender.

In 1994 married attorneys Laurence Canter and Martha Siegel launch a "mega-spam" from Internet Direct, their Arizona ISP, posting advertisements to nearly six thousand Usenet groups (out of about nine thousand total) in ninety minutes. The ads offer assistance to non-U.S. citizens in filling out forms for an upcoming green card lottery—for a fee, of course, even though the lottery itself is free. The barrage of complaints from around the world is so intense that Internet Direct's servers crash repeatedly, and Canter and Siegel are booted from the service. The event is picked up by mass media outlets like *The New York Times* and *The Washington Post*, and it catapults both the attorneys, who become known derisively as "the green card lawyers," and the practice of spam itself into Net infamy.

The practice of spamming continues to expand in the second half of the 1990s, as does the anti-spam movement. By the end of 1997 several battles between spammers and ISPs are settled out of court. At about that time, U.S. legislators begin to draft laws to regulate spam, and four different bills are introduced by mid-1998. The bills are similar in their requirement for bulk e-mail messages to wear some kind of tag identifying them as advertising prior to delivery. The states of California, Nevada, and Washington pass laws aimed at reducing spam in early 1998, and in Virginia a law is proposed that would criminalize spamming entirely. For several months it seems that Congress is going to make a similar legislative move, but by the end of the year it is clear that a federal decision is not imminent. In December anti- and pro-spam groups hammer out an agreement that they hope will lead to consensus-based legislation in 1999.

1994   THE FIRST INTERNATIONAL WORLD WIDE WEB CONFERENCE

The First International World Wide Web Conference is held at CERN—the birthplace of the Web—in Geneva, Switzerland, at the end of May. Three hundred and eighty participants arrive from across the globe to celebrate the growth of the WWW and the revolution it has kindled, and to share ideas relating to the evolution of Web technology and culture.

The conference hosts forty-nine formal presentations, eleven workshops, and many informal discussion groups. Topics are varied and numerous: software, the Mosaic browser, hypertext, Web searching, Web security, Web privacy, HTML, virtual libraries, education and the Web, multilingual Web text, and the phenomenon of home pages. Some sessions of the conference are multicast on the MBONE, a live audio and video Internet service that debuted in 1992.

With background music provided by a band called Wolfgang and the Were Wolves, an award ceremony is held at the conference dinner. Marc Andreessen, inventor of Mosaic and cofounder of Netscape, is inducted into the newly formed WWW Hall of Fame, and Best Site award goes to the National Center for Supercomputing Applications (NCSA)—Andreessen's employer at the time that he developed Mosaic.

The Second International World Wide Web Conference is held in October 1994 in Chicago, Illinois. By the end of 1998, seven such conferences have taken place.

1994 THE PRIME MINISTER OF JAPAN, THE U.S. CONGRESS, AND PIZZA HUT GO ONLINE

The Internet's public value continues to broaden and globalize as government entities and international pizza chains join the frenzy to create "home page" Web sites. Pizza Hut, Inc. makes history by being the first company to allow people to order food via the Internet.

The United States Congress adds its own home pages—one for the House of Representatives and one for the Senate—to the White House Web site that had gone online the previous year. These congressional sites feature a selection of information about current events in the legislature, educational material about politics, and outlines of committee progress. They also point to information about individual Senators and Representatives—which provides an unprecedented opportunity for people to inform themselves about their elected officials with the simple click of a mouse. Eventually, the sites offer links to Senators' and

SCIENTOLOGY V. THE NET

The flames on newsgroup alt.religion.scientology (a.r.s.) have always burned brightly. Scott Goehring told *Wired* that he originally formed the newsgroup in 1991, "half as a joke and half because I felt Usenet needed a place to disseminate the truth about this half-assed religion." Of course, not everyone takes such a dim view of the Church of Scientology (COS), an international movement begun by science fiction writer L. Ron Hubbard. Both pro- and anti-COS factions inhabit the a.r.s. newsgroup, and there was a time when scholars pointed to a.r.s. as an example of spirited public debate on the Internet, free from interference of church and state. All that changed in 1994.

According to Scientologists, the trouble began when a.r.s. members started posting "scriptural" information. Scientologists regard their teachings as sharply divided between public writings and the private scriptures, which must be paid for and imparted to believers over many years of training. By leaking this information, the COS argued, people were spreading copyrighted trade secrets protected by law. In the words of Church official Lisa Goodman, "freedom of speech does not mean freedom to steal."

The argument remained academic until just before Christmas 1994, when a large number of messages posted to a.r.s. are anonymously removed due to "violation of copyright." The COS files copyright lawsuits against five a.r.s. posters: Dennis Erlich, Arnaldo Lerma, Grady Ward, Keith Henson, and Zenon Panoussis, a Swede who actually invited the COS to sue him.

When Panoussis is ordered to pay damages, he arranges for the contested documents to be entered into Swedish court records, where they are available to the public. Police raid the homes of Erlich, Lerma, and Henson, and the men are also ordered by the courts to stop posting COS materials. In addition, the FACTnet bulletin board, run by ex-Scientologists, is raided by police and closed.

The COS extends their suits to include ISPs as well as offending posters, which *Wired* writer Wendy Grossman likens to "charging the post office for complicity in mail fraud." When the COS demands that offending Web pages be removed from a Dutch ISP, providers around the Netherlands respond by duplicating the information all over the country. The COS reacts by suing the ISPs as well as Karin Spaink, who helped initiate the campaign. Although a Dutch court rules against the Scientologists and clears the defendants, many targets of the church are not so lucky.

Mike Godwin of the Electronic Frontier Foundation points out that the fear created by the Scientologists "may accomplish what legal theories do not: the effective silencing of many critics of the church." But the battle isn't over yet. As Godwin notes, "the sheer power of the Net as a mass medium, together with its decentralized character, make (information) potentially impossible to stop." To catch up on the most contentious place in cyberspace, begin with the Electronic Frontier Foundation's archive at http://www.eff.org/pub/Censorship/CoS_v_the_Net/.

Beyond the Net

Representatives' e-mail addresses, and citizens can send messages directly to the legislative body without phones or stamps.

Solidifying the international nature of the Internet, the Japanese government establishes a WWW presence. The official residence of the Prime Minister, located in Tokyo, sets up its own Internet server and creates a home page that can be accessed in Japanese and English.

Meanwhile, across the Pacific Ocean, Pizza Hut, Inc. launches a pilot program called PizzaNet, which enables customers in Santa Cruz, California, to order pizza over the Internet. In this venture Pizza Hut partners with Santa Cruz Operation (SCO) Global Access, a provider of Internet business solutions. The program is a little before its time, as too few people are actually on the Internet in 1994 (at least in Santa Cruz) to make online ordering immediately successful. The program fizzles out within several months. However, Pizza Hut's competitors soon follow suit by initiating online ordering programs across the country, and gradually the trend spreads beyond the pizza world to encompass other cuisines.

The rise in online food-ordering services (expanding later to grocery shopping) demonstrates that the WWW has the potential to meld together the advertising capability of television broadcasting and the communication capability of telephone networks.

Living on
Internet Time

Seemingly overnight the Internet went from a fledgling network to a massive commercial infrastructure. This explosive growth took everyone by surprise: administering entities, world governments, and users themselves. We collectively awoke to find that we were all "stakeholders" in the future of the Net. So it's not surprising that conflicts increased during this period, on subjects as diverse as domain names, freedom of speech, privacy, encryption, and commerce. By 1995 one thing is clear: the Internet is not part of the Zeitgeist, it *is* the Zeitgeist.

The supersonic speed of life on the Net has led many to observe that the Internet operates on its own time frame, akin to "dog years," which has come to be known as "Internet time." It seemed like just yesterday that the Net was a playground for hackers and entrepreneurs. Suddenly we all had a lot to lose, and the quip "road kill on the information superhighway" sounded more ominous than funny.

What's in a Name?

A rose by any other name is . . . a lawsuit. When InterNIC was first created in 1993 to register domain names—under an agreement between the U.S. government and a private company, Network Solutions—it was processing a few hundred requests each month. This quickly jumped to a few thousand registrations each month, bringing an understaffed and unprepared agency to its knees. In the interest of expediency, InterNIC implemented a "first-come, first-served" policy on domain names. But instead of solving problems, this hands-off policy created them-when more than one individual, group, or company desired the same domain name, one frequently ended up suing the other. Seeking shelter from the storm, InterNIC implemented a dispute-resolution policy, which automatically ceded disputed domains to the trademark holders. Critics declared the policy to be ill-conceived, and predictably, it led to more disputes and more lawsuits.

To be fair, one must admit that when living on Internet time, attempts to formulate policy are often futile, because today's pragmatism is tomorrow's naivete. Who would have thought, for example, that the top-level domain name for the tiny island nation of Tuvalu would end up as one of the hottest—and most expensive—pieces of real estate in cyberspace? Well, what media executive wouldn't give her right arm for a domain at ".tv"?

With InterNIC's contract running out in 1998, a debate ensued regarding the plans for succession. Given the global nature of the Net, U.S. control of the institutions that governed the Internet was met with increasing resistance from other governments, individuals, international organizations, and even the corporate world. As the 1990s came to a close, a compromise solution appeared to be near, with the formation of the Internet Corporation for Assigned Names and Numbers (ICANN), the new body that replaced, among others, the Internet Assigned Numbers Authority (IANA) for root-server management, domain-name management, and IP-address allocation. Network Solutions, whose control of domain-name registration became a multimillion-dollar business, was forced to begin sharing the wealth with new registrars who would be chosen sometime in 1999, probably through a lottery system. While there were many Internet management issues left unresolved (e.g., the introduction of additional top-level domains), it was widely agreed that ICANN was a step in the right direction—although complaints have been heard from many quarters about ICANN's continued insistence on holding meetings in private.

Whose Rights are They, Anyway?

Our right to know what ICANN was up to was only one of the rights under fire on the Internet during this time. Privacy rights. Civil rights. Free speech rights.

Even due process rights had either been trampled on or trumpeted, depending on whom you asked.

In the "real" world these concerns could be addressed, more or less, by the laws and the courts of each country, to the satisfaction or dismay of the local constituents. But the minute we plugged in to the Net, the issues took on a new dimension. In a spectacular recent case, a radical antiabortion Web site called "The Nuremberg Files" was fined more than $100 million for inciting violence against doctors who perform abortions. Defendants argued that no direct threats were issued, but in the opinion of the federal jury that heard the case, the site's "wanted posters" and its list of doctors—with the names of murdered doctors crossed out and the names of wounded doctors in light gray—was plenty threatening. The case is expected to be appealed and, according to legal experts, will probably end up before the Supreme Court.

Debates about what constituted acceptable online speech were not limited to extreme right-wing Web sites. In 1996 U.S. legislators passed into law the Communications Decency Act (CDA), intending to stem the (supposed) flood of pornographic material over the ether. The U.S. Supreme Court declared the CDA to be an unconstitutional infringement of free speech. Law makers made a second attempt, with 1998's Child Online Protection Act (COPA). As of this writing, it looks like COPA will meet the same fate as the CDA.

While legislators debated the best way to protect the public morality, law enforcement agencies continued to hunt down, arrest, and confiscate the computer equipment of alleged "hackers." The most famous—or infamous—of the arrested hackers remains Kevin Mitnick, whose trial in the second half of 1999 is eagerly anticipated by legal scholars and Internet observers alike.

Is There Life After Microsoft?

Hackers were not the only ones on trial. For the second time in Microsoft's history, the company found itself defending its business practices, having been accused of "predatory" behavior designed to keep the Redmond, Washington, software giant on top. Interestingly, in early February 1999 while the case was still in the courts, Gates remarked at a conference in Copenhagen that in twenty years Coca-Cola will likely still be the world market leader in soft drinks, while Microsoft's leadership position is at best uncertain. His comment was of little solace to the companies that accuse the giant software maker of unfair competition and monopolistic practices.

This latest conflict was very much Internet related. Although Microsoft had been at the technology forefront for more than a decade, it was nearly left behind by the Internet. When Gates finally became convinced that the Internet was central to the future of his business, he issued a now-famous memo, entitled "The Coming Internet Tidal Wave," intended to refocus Microsoft's entire business plan in one stroke. Gates' and Microsoft's new interest in the Internet was announced to the public on December 7, 1995—a day that certainly would live in infamy, for Netscape at least. Gates acknowledged the historic event in his speech, paraphrasing Japanese General Yamamoto's comment that Pearl Harbor had merely awakened a "sleeping giant."

Fully awake and eager to become a leading seller of Internet software as well as traditional software, Microsoft first had to deal with Netscape. Gates announced that Microsoft would offer its Web browser, Internet Explorer, for free. Several versions and two years later, Microsoft and Netscape were neck-and-neck on market share, and the financially troubled Netscape was forced to offer its browser for free as well. At the end of 1998, it was announced that Netscape would be swallowed up by America Online (AOL) in a $4.21 billion deal. While AOL and Netscape were working out their prenuptial agreement, Microsoft reveled in the news, arguing that the deal proved that competition was alive and well in the industry. To more cynical observers, all the deal proved was that Netscape went into battle with the Beast from Redmond and lost.

Making things worse for Microsoft's public relations department, a two-part Microsoft memo was leaked just after Halloween 1998. Nicknamed "the Halloween Memo," it detailed potential Microsoft strategies to combat Linux, a Unix-based operating system gaining popularity among technophiles. Linux is especially popular among Internet Service Providers who use it along with a popular open-source Web server, Apache. The combination of these two top-performing, robust environments—both of which are, by the way, completely free—had apparently given Microsoft pause. To some onlookers, the Halloween Memo was written evidence that Microsoft would do anything to wipe out its competition. So it's not surprising that enemies of Microsoft are also prominent cheerleaders of Linux and Apache, hoping that the combination will stymie Microsoft's advance in the Internet server market. The fierce competition in this area is not going to abate anytime soon.

Go Virtual, Young Man

In the honorable pursuit of market dominance, companies began to take advantage of the Internet in new and creative ways. No longer was a company limited by its location, labor pool, or even labor laws. One router and half a world away was a wealth of cheap, available talent. Anyone with computer skills and an Internet link can, in theory at least, venture into cyberspace find their fortune, just as a hundred years ago anyone with a pick-ax and muscle could—maybe, just maybe—strike it rich in California.

Of course such globalization did not come problem-free: while some were describing the new labor opportunities as the "gold rush" of the information age, others raised difficult questions about international information "sweat shops." Some hailed the dramatic opportunities afforded to the skilled workers of developing countries, while others admonished the lack of labor laws, collective bargaining agreements, employee benefits, and intellectual property rights. The Internet has created an international, cross-cultural workplace. How this will change our world it is too early to tell. But change the world it has, and more is on the way.

By 1998 most major software companies had established offices in India, taking advantage of the large pool of skilled computer programmers and a convenient twelve-hour time-zone difference. A problem discovered during the day in New York could be fixed overnight by a programmer in Bangalore at significantly reduced cost. Other countries of choice included Brazil, Hungary, and Russia—among an ever increasing list. Was it possible that the Internet, rather than the North American Free Trade Agreement, would create Ross Perot's predicted "great sucking sound" of jobs leaving the United States?

Of course, labor issues were just the beginning. The results of this international labor were also immersed in controversy. For example, different countries have different copyright laws and afford different levels of protection on intellectual property. Furthermore, the U.S. government has very strict policies about the type of software that can be exported to other countries because of the different levels of encryption used within them.

This Just In

The U.S. government was not the only one concerned about encryption. Conflict abounded between privacy advocates, data miners (the process of "mining" relevant information about an individual's habits and preferences from many different databases and selling the results to interested parties), and those wishing to protect their intellectual property and copyrights across media and national borders.

Steps towards resolution of some of these issues started with the 1996 World Intellectual Property Organization (WIPO) Digital Copyright Treaty. The WIPO treaty successfully passed two treaties—one on performance and sound recordings, another on copyright. In October 1998 the U.S. Congress passed the Digital Millennium Copyright Act, which was signed into law by the president. This law, containing stronger provisions than the WIPO treaty, sparked heated debates on both a national level, over the place of "fair use" in digital environments, and an international level, with many overseas observers challenging a U.S.-centric approach to an international issue.

The nonsequential nature of "content" on the Net was revolutionizing both the way we absorbed information, and the way we shared it. At the same time, the new medium offered an immediacy and interactivity not found anyplace else. For the first time in the history of the Net we saw news stories breaking concurrently on traditional media and the Internet. The Internet delivered news, even as it made news. For that matter, news organizations started to use the Net for "in-depth" coverage of a story—offering a "sound bite" on television and directing you to their Web site for further details. We experienced live events including concerts, verdicts, weddings, births, and operations, all online.

Like it or not, we are all living on Internet time—and, in cases like guru Timothy Leary, who chronicled his losing bout with prostate cancer on leary.com, we are even dying on it.

1995 Network Solutions Institutes a Domain-Name Dispute Policy

As trademark-infringement suits pile up, the administrators of top-level domain names institute a policy intended to limit disputes. Unfortunately, the policy does little to stop the cascade of domain-related lawsuits; in fact, additional lawsuits spring up in protest of the dispute-resolution policy itself.

When Network Solutions, Inc. (NSI) and the National Science Foundation (NSF) created the InterNIC to administer domain names in 1993, the Internet was still a mystery to corporate America. The InterNIC received roughly three hundred requests for domain names per month in their first year of operation; a year later the number had swelled to 1,300 requests a month, and the exponential growth would continue throughout the 1990s. Understaffed and overworked, InterNIC employees took a pointedly hands-off attitude towards domain-name registry. Unless a name was already taken or was blatantly inappropriate, the InterNIC registered any name to any individual or group, no questions asked.

When Internet use increases dramatically in 1995, the InterNIC finds many of its decisions under unexpected scrutiny. Some questions are political: if the stated policy is to refuse to register "offensive" names, then why, some wonder, is "godhatesfags.com" allowed to exist? Many criticisms are more down-to-earth: why had Sprint been allowed to register MCI.com? In the Sprint case, once alerted to the problem, the InterNIC gives the address to MCI. Much more frequently, domain-name disputes are left to the courts.

NSI is understandably eager to remain above the fray, but that ends in early 1995 when they are named as codefendants in a suit over www.knowledgenet.com. Knowledgenet, an Arizona company bringing suit against a Virginia-based consultant who had previously registered the name, alleges that NSI assisted the infringement of their trademark and is therefore also liable. In order to avert this problem in the future, NSI institutes a policy that in cases of trademark dispute, corporations should send a copy of their trademark to the InterNIC, and the holder of the registered trademark will be given the domain name.

Criticism of the policy is almost immediate: opponents argue that the dispute-resolution policy is at best extremely naive, since trademarks are registered nationally while the Internet is global. Furthermore, trademark law provides for the existence of two companies with the same name, as long as the two companies are not in competition; the Internet is not nearly so flexible. This results in a series of 1996 lawsuits in protest of the dispute policy itself. For example, an Internet Service Provider named Roadrunner Computer Systems gets into a dispute with Warner Brothers over www.roadrunner.com. Warner Brothers produces their U.S. trademark on the name for NSI, and Roadrunner retaliates with their own trademark, registered in Tunisia. NSI sides with Warner Brothers and Roadrunner sues NSI.

Unhappiness with NSI's resolution of trademark disputes fuels growing criticism of NSI. The Department of Justice initiates an investigation into the InterNIC monopoly, but the point quickly becomes moot as time on

Location, Location, Location: The Domain Name Frenzy

Beyond the Net

Corporate America was slow to catch on to the value of the Internet, but when word of the Web finally reached the boardrooms, they made their move. To their chagrin, many companies found that someone else had gotten there first. In the mid-1990s, a gold-rush effect surrounded domain names, and a cottage industry nicknamed "domain speculation" sprung up, in which Net-savvy opportunists deliberately registered names, then turned them over for a fee. As corporate presence on the Web came to be considered *de rigeur*, the lengths to which companies were willing to go to get their names back—including the amount they were willing to pay—hit new highs. For instance, Net lore has it that Microsoft paid $10,000 for the rights to www.slate.com, the site of a Microsoft-funded online magazine.

When negotiations failed, big corporations were more than willing to bring in the lawyers, and the number of domain-name related cases in U.S. courts multiplied rapidly. MTV veejay Adam Curry beat his former employers to the punch with www.mtv.com, and when MTV demanded that Curry release the name, he refused. Curry assumed a Patrick Henry-style pose with the media—he assured *Wired* in 1994 that the case was "the *Roe v. Wade* of the Internet"—but after extensive legal wrangling, MTV ultimately won out.

The trademark policy instituted by NSI helped cut down on the number of corporations going to court over domain names, but it didn't address the larger question of intellectual property. In 1996 the animal rights group PETA (People for the Ethical Treatment of Animals) was dismayed to find that www.peta.org was being used as a parody site, People Eating Tasty Animals. Animal lovers can comfort themselves with the knowledge that two years later, Ringling Brothers had to call out the lawyers to fight for www.ringling-brothers.com, which had been shanghaied by a group protesting the treatment of elephants in the circus. Which group? PETA, of course.

Whether the dismantling of the NSI monopoly in 1998, complete with brand-new top-level domain names like .store, will lead to better resolution of trademark and intellectual property disputes remains to be seen. Some pundits argue that fights over domain names are inevitable. To paraphrase a *Wired* article on the issue, the real world can allow for Samuel Adams law firm and Samuel Adams beer, but the virtual world permits only one www.samadams.com.

the contract between NSI and NSF runs out. When negotiations over new domain-name registration procedures begin in 1997, satisfactory resolution of trademark issues is at the top of the docket.

1995 Hacker Kevin Mitnick Arrested

After eluding authorities for three years, Kevin Mitnick, notorious computer hacker, is tracked down and arrested for having committed various computer crimes. With a criminal record dating back to 1981 and several newsworthy arrests under his belt, Mitnick garners considerable media attention. His arrest and the associated media blitz portray his pursuer, Tsutomu Shimomura, as a cybersleuthing hero. But in other circles, the arrest transforms Mitnick himself into a hero—to some in the online community, Mitnick's case represents the government's suppression of civil rights on the cybertechnology frontier.

In 1989 Mitnick had been found guilty of computer fraud and had served one year in prison, plus time at a rehabilitation center to correct his addiction to illegal computer activity. After his release from jail, he found legitimate computer work, but before long, signs of his old behavior started turning up. For instance, police records of his conviction disappeared from computer systems. By 1992 the police had caught up with Mitnick and gathered enough evidence to arrest him—but he slipped through their fingers and went into hiding. Thus began his fame as a wily outlaw whom the authorities were too incompetent to apprehend.

In 1994 Mitnick allegedly tried to obtain a false driver's license identification, and the Department of Motor Vehicles issued a $1 million warrant for his arrest. The press continued to run stories about Mitnick, gradually giving him legendary status.

In December 1994 the events that will lead to his arrest begin to unfold. First, hundreds of documents are electronically removed from the personal computer files of Tsutomu Shimomura, a computational physicist who researches computer security. Analyzing subsequent break-ins as they occur, Shimomura concludes that the thief is probably Mitnick. In January and February 1995 Shimomura and police detectives follow the hacker's online movements and suspect him of confiscating twenty thousand credit card numbers belonging to Netcom customers (Netcom is an Internet Service Provider).

By tracking Mitnick's activities, Shimomura is able to trace the hacker's calls to Raleigh, North Carolina. Authorities zero in on Mitnick and arrest him on February 15, 1995. Over the next year and a half, Mitnick's case unfolds. On September 30, 1996, he pleads not guilty to charges of wire fraud, software theft, computer vandalism, and interception of wire communications. He is denied bail. In an unprecedented move, the judge in his case mandates that Mitnick is not allowed to use a computer to review evidence or to construct his defense, because of the possibility that he will perform computer wizardry to change documents in his favor.

Meanwhile, groups of computer hackers have banded together into a movement whose slogan is "Free Kevin!" Disapproving of the decisions to deny Mitnick bail and use of a computer, they believe that Mitnick has been treated unjustly and unduly singled out simply to set an example to other would-be computer outlaws. In 1997 and 1998 these groups perform several spectacular acts of online vandalism to draw attention to Mitnick's plight. They hack the Web sites of Yahoo!, UNICEF, and *The New York Times,* replacing regular screens with their opinions on the case and calls for supporters to rally behind Mitnick.

Originally scheduled for fall 1998, Mitnick's trial is postponed until January 1999, and in December, at the request of Mitnick's lawyers, it is pushed back again to April 20, 1999. Hackers, legislators, civil libertarians, and curious observers await the outcome, suspecting that the case will set precedents for computer-related crimes.

1995 HONG KONG SHUTS DOWN INTERNET SERVICE PROVIDERS, SPARKING CRISIS OVER GOVERNMENT INTERVENTION

On March 3, the Commercial Crimes Bureau of the Hong Kong police department raids seven Internet Service Providers (ISPs), claiming that providers are operating without licenses. The ensuing events cause confusion and frustration about government intervention into public and private telecommunications.

In 1993 Hong Kong Internet and Gateway Services (HKIGS) and Hong Kong Supernet, the first two Internet Service Providers (ISPs) to establish themselves in Hong Kong, had begun operation. Hong Kong Supernet attained a license to provide Public Non-Exclusive Telecommunications Service (PNETS), a requirement under Hong Kong law. The PNETS license serves as a means for the government to exact a tariff on telecommunications providers. Other service providers, as they are founded, are not informed that they need a PNETS license.

By January 1995 price wars among Hong Kong ISPs have begun to sizzle. Supernet becomes aware that other providers are offering customers lower per-hour rates, because they do not have licenses and thus are not paying the PNETS tariff. Supernet starts billing itself as the only legal ISP in Hong Kong.

Soon thereafter, the government's Office of Telecommunications Authority (OFTA) writes to all ISPs informing them of the PNETS license law, and a few providers seek legal advice.

On March 3, without warning, officials from the Commercial Crimes Bureau (CCB) raid seven ISPs, confiscating equipment, shutting down operation, and arresting eight people. An estimated five thousand individuals and businesses are left without Internet access. The CCB's search warrants state that the service providers are operating without a PNETS license. However, the following day the CCB changes its public statement, claiming that the raids had represented an attempt to apprehend hackers. The statement is criticized by the computer community, some of whom assert that shutting down ISPs is not an effective way to catch hackers.

On March 6, a press conference is held by Asia Online, and representatives of the raided service providers roundly accuse the government of misguided, reprehensible behavior. This general attitude is widely adopted by the press in and outside of Hong Kong; many reporters call for freedom of information and for an absence of government regulation. Meanwhile, some service providers attain their PNETS licenses, and others shut down rather than pay the tariff. Still others remain confused about how to interpret OFTA's explanation of the law, and legislators begin a revision process to clarify the situation.

Observers note that the CCB's conflicting statements leave the public ignorant of the real motivation for the raids. Some speculate that the raids were, as the second statement claimed, linked to government investigations of hacking. In a possibly related incident, in June 1995 hacker Raymond Chen is found guilty of having broken into secure computer systems at two Hong Kong universities the previous fall.

1995 SUN MICROSYSTEMS INTRODUCES JAVA, A PROGRAMMING LANGUAGE FOR INTERNET COMPUTING

Sun Microsystems in Palo Alto, California, unleashes Java, a programming language that promises to spice up the World Wide Web by adding animation and interactive features. Java, a simple, compact language, is unique in being able to run on any operating system. Its debut is followed by an evolution of Java products and an ongoing debate about just how wonderful they actually are.

Java's origins date to 1991, when Sun Microsystems had initiated an endeavor called the Green Project. Its purpose was the development of products for the consumer electronics market, but little other than Java was salvaged from two years of Green Project toil. Java, originally named Oak, had been written for the most part by Sun employee James Gosling.

In 1992 and 1993 Sun became involved in an industry-wide push to develop interactive television, and the company saw this as a potential application for Oak. But all of Sun's potential projects related to interactive television were squashed, and Oak's champions were left to find another venue for the language.

Meanwhile, in 1993 Marc Andreessen introduced Mosaic, a World Wide Web browser featuring a graphical user interface (windows, graphics, point-and-click abilities), and interest in the World Wide Web rocketed. Sun cofounder Bill Joy was the first person to make a connection between Oak and the Web. He got excited about Oak's prospects and set Gosling to work adapting the language for use on the Web. Patrick Naughton was asked to devise an Oak interpreter, a program for Web browsers that would enable Oak to operate on the desktop of any operating system.

In December 1994 Sun places Oak on the Internet, in a location revealed only to the select members of the computer industry who are invited to test it. The language is renamed Java in January 1995, after a trademark search shows that Oak is a proprietary name. The following month Sun gives a copy of Java to Andreessen (now of Netscape Communications), who tries it out and proceeds to speak highly of it to reporters. Andreessen's praise, which Java manager Kim Polese called "a blessing from the god of the Internet," suggests that Java is going to be a hit and increases Sun's faith in their investment.

Soon Netscape and Sun make a deal for Netscape to license Java and include it on Netscape Navigator, Netscape's Web browser. In August 1995 Sun ships polished versions of Java and its interpreter, HotJava, to Netscape, representing the first sale of Java for commercial use. At the same time, Sun begins distributing free copies of Java and HotJava for noncommercial use on the Web.

Java is platform-independent (among graphics-supporting platforms), which means that it can run on Windows, Macintosh, or any other GUI

Biography

Scott McNealy

If Sun Microsystems CEO Scott McNealy has his way, he will go down in history as David to Microsoft's Goliath—just a regular Joe with a slingshot called Java. The real story, as always, is more complicated.

McNealy's father, an executive with American Motors, raised his son in the ways of the corporate world: long hours and hard work, the battle for market share, and golf. Unlike many Silicon Valley superstars, McNealy was a jock with no real interest in computers. After prep school came Harvard, where he overlapped one year with his future nemesis, Bill Gates, ("At least I graduated," McNealy jokes) and then, after two rejections, Stanford Business School.

In 1981 McNealy took a job as director of operations at Onyx Systems, a maker of microcomputer systems, and got his first taste of computers. Shortly thereafter, Stanford buddy Vinod Kholsa convinced him to join the cofounders of a brand new company, Sun Microsystems, as the vice president of manufacturing and operations. McNealy had to take a class in electronics in order to keep up, but he had found his calling.

Kholsa departed as CEO in 1984 and, although he was not everyone's first choice, McNealy stepped in. Sun took off under McNealy's watch, reaching $1 billion in sales in 1988. By the early 1990s Sun's profits had begun to drop, and McNealy knew a drastic step was in order. He also felt that the real threat to Sun was not other workstation manufacturers but Microsoft, who was gunning for the business computing market with their Windows NT system.

When Sun engineers demonstrated the Java programming language for McNealy in 1995, he thought he might have found his giant killer. Since programs written with Java could run on any machine—a quality programmers call Write Once/Run Everywhere, or WO/RE—then theoretically, software developers would no longer be shackled to Microsoft's Windows operating system. When run over the Internet, WO/RE programs put the network in the foreground and thus (McNealy hoped) diminished the importance of the operating system. This vision is reflected in Sun's slogan, "the network is the computer." Or, as McNealy likes to say, "in a world without fences, who needs Gates?"

McNealy's passion for the success of Sun and the failure of all enemies is combined with an astute business sense; *Business Week* named him one of the nation's top twenty-five managers in 1995. He cultivates the impression that he is "just a regular guy," peppering his speech with "you know" and even delivering the keynote at the 1998 Consumer Electronics Show on rollerblades.

In an economy more and more focused on service industries, McNealy is rather unique in his commitment to manufacturing. "I love the factory," he says. "That's what business is all about. Making stuff. Not this Wall Street stuff, not this consulting stuff . . . . You gotta make something."

(graphical user interface)-based system. It doesn't have to be translated for every platform so a different version doesn't have to be introduced for every platform. Due to built-in coding shortcuts, Java is easier than many languages to program: to create an application in Java, a programmer can "snap together" units ("objects") of already constructed code.

Gradually, Java begins to enliven the Web and to expand its practical uses. Whereas prior to Java, Web pages looked like printed brochure pages, Java allows animation and real-time interactivity. Java-equipped Web sites contain compact Java programs called "applets," which are loaded onto the user's desktop to perform stunts of animation or to calculate, for example, a loan with individualized specifications.

Web site developers learn how to incorporate applets, and Java quickly becomes widespread across the Web. Sun pushes the popular image of Java as a revolutionary element in Internet computing, but some observers hesitate, questioning whether Java will follow through on its apparently immense promise.

1995   Release of the Web Server Apache 1.0

The Apache Group, which consists of Brian Behlendorf, Cliff Skolnick, and numerous other volunteer programmers, releases Apache 1.0—the first official version of the Apache Web server. Significantly, Apache is "free software" or "open source," which allows the user to access the source code of the program for free. Adapted from the first Web server, written by Rob McCool at the National Center for Supercomputing Applications, Apache quickly becomes the most popular Web-server software on the Internet.

Apache development began in 1994 when Behlendorf was tasked with establishing a Web site for HotWired, *Wired* magazine's first online foray, that included a name and password function. This required a Web server—the software that enables a computer to function as a home for a Web site—that could support names and passwords. But McCool's software, which at the time was the most popular one available and in the public domain, could not. So Behlendorf fixed the server himself, writing a "patch"—lines of computer code that can be grafted on to preexisting software—that brought the Web server into line. Behlendorf was not the only one giving McCool's server a facelift. Programmers began sharing patches and advice, and by the spring of 1995 the server had been completely—and collaboratively—rewritten. The programmers called themselves the Apache Group, in honor of their creation: "A Patch-y" server.

In April 1995 the Apache Group releases their Web software over the Internet. Although it is well received, the programmers keep tinkering and on December 1, 1995, the "official" Apache 1.0 is released. Within a year Apache is the most popular Web server on the Net. The source code is freely available and can be changed by anyone; support for Apache software is provided by the entire Apache community via Web pages, newsgroups, and mailing lists. Apache's success seems to have been motivated by a number of factors—in addition to the unbeatable price, many say that Apache is quite simply a superior product. Free software advocates claim that the give and take involved in Apache's evolution—the collaborative development that is a primary feature of all "free software" projects—is the key to Apache's high performance.

At first, the majority of Apache users are Internet Service Providers (ISPs) and small businesses; the notion of "free software" with no formal support is viewed as too risky by big corporations. However, in June 1998, IBM announces that it will distribute Apache software as part of a larger IBM Web package: to soothe corporate anxieties, IBM will provide product support for their users, while also contributing to and benefiting from the Apache development process. The announcement is trumpeted as a major victory for not only the Apache Group but the Free Software Movement generally. As the 1990s draw to a close, free software is rapidly gaining acceptance—due to its price, quality, and perhaps the fact that, whatever else it may be, free software presents an alternative to the ubiquity of Microsoft products.

1995 COMPUSERVE BLOCKS NEWSGROUPS AFTER GERMANY COMPLAINS OF ILLEGAL ONLINE CONTENT

CompuServe Incorporated, an Internet Service Provider (ISP), temporarily blocks access to more than two hundred of its newsgroups in response to threats that the German government plans to bring charges against the company for transmitting illegal material. The event results in a surge of public concern about censorship on the Internet, and it forces governments and administrators to consider the legal status of international cyberspace.

In November 1995 the German federal prosecutor's office begins investigations into the content of CompuServe's newsgroups (online discussion forums where users post text and graphics for other users to view). Government officials find that German CompuServe customers have access to material that is illegal in Germany—child pornography, images of bestiality, neo-Nazi propaganda, and other sexual and political material.

In December investigators raid CompuServe's Central European offices in Munich, Germany, and notify CompuServe's headquarters in Columbus, Ohio, of their actions and concerns. During the last week of December, CompuServe suspends access—for its customers worldwide—to newsgroups that might contain sexually explicit material. According to the company's press release about the action, the German prosecutor's office had threatened CompuServe with criminal prosecution if it did not disallow German access to the newsgroups. Having no way to selectively block access, CompuServe administrators choose to block access globally. The press release also states that German authorities had mandated which specific newsgroups were objectionable.

Caught in a storm of outbursts about free speech and civil rights, CompuServe is criticized for caving in to Germany's demands and for censoring public information. On January 2, 1996, prosecutors in Germany claim that they did not tell CompuServe which newsgroups to ban, and that they did not threaten the company with criminal charges. CompuServe stands by its original statements. The blocked newsgroups are reinstated in February, as CompuServe introduces new parental control software. The company reiterates its position that individual users—not ISPs—are responsible for online content.

By April 1996 German authorities have indicted Felix Somm, the head of CompuServe's Central European operations, for complicity in the dissemination of child pornography, Nazi symbols, and violent computer games. The charges imply that Somm is being held responsible for the illegal (in Germany) content of CompuServe's newsgroups.

In summer 1998 Somm's case comes to trial in Munich. During the trial, prosecutors are convinced that Somm had no way to monitor and regulate CompuServe's online content, and they join the defense in recommending acquittal. Nevertheless, on May 28, the judge hands down a conviction. Somm is given a two-year suspended (probationary) sentence and fined close to U.S. $57,000. Within weeks the prosecutor's office appeals the decision, and as of this writing the case remains unresolved.

Imagining the Net

THE INTERNET'S INTERNET

When most people think of the Internet, they think of computers linked through the infrastructure once sponsored by DARPA. But in the rarefied world of academia, people don't just compute, they supercompute—and they connect through vBNS, the "Internet's Internet."

"During the supercomputing boom of the late 1970s and 1980s there were two ways to do your work," explains Philip Galanter, of New York University's Academic Computing Facility. "Either you computed remotely (via the Internet), or you actually traveled to a supercomputing center. Though most researchers preferred the former, the latter was the only alternative when doing sophisticated visualization."

Galanter is referring to the Internet's never-ending "bandwidth problem"—the fact that while it may work fine for e-mail and Web site surfing, the Internet is just too slow a delivery system for high-level computing needs. In 1995 the National Science Foundation and the telecommunications company MCI spent $50 million to create a solution: vBNS, a high-speed network reserved primarily for supercomputing applications. In 1996 the vBNS could carry approximately fourteen times more traffic than the former NSF Network, the older backbone of academic Net traffic. When it originated vBNS carried information at 622 million bits per second (an average home modem, by comparison, transmits at 28,800 bits per second). By the year 2000 vBNS is expected to operate at 2.4 gigabits per second.

"The vBNS is the critical connection for enabling super-cluster computing and data mining," reports Robert Grossman, director of the Laboratory for Advanced Computing at the University of Illinois at Chicago. Cluster computing is a kind of "nonsuper-computer supercomputing"; by hooking up a series of workstations via vBNS, a system

can be created with the power of a super-computer, at a fraction of the cost. To do "super-cluster computing," two or more clusters in different locations are linked via vBNS. Super-clustering is often used in "data mining"—the systematic search for patterns, associations, and changes in large data sets. Researchers in medical imaging, particle physics, and astrophysics all use data mining techniques to predict outcomes of events such as surgeries, weather systems, and geological phenomena.

Not just anyone gets to use vBNS. Today there are about one hundred U.S. universities connected, plus international connections in Canada, Singapore, Taiwan, Russia, and the Asian Pacific Network Consortium. Though its membership criteria is exclusive—clients must prove the scientific merit of their need for extra bandwidth—in the future there may be an expansion of the client base of the "Internet's Internet." In 1996 President Clinton proposed a "Next Generation Internet" (NGI) program, which pledges $100 million per year for three years to connect more research universities and national laboratories via vBNS. Both the NGI program and the "Internet2" will use vBNS as their initial interconnect backbone. Currently, fifty-three Internet2 university members have received grants to support the acquisition of high-performance network connections to the vBNS.

It's possible that those who once used vBNS may have to migrate to an even more powerful backbone. Certainly, this is the hope of the developers of Abilene, a high-performance network under development by the University Corporation for Advanced Internet Development. Abilene, which has been touted as the newest Internet's Internet, is slated for initial operation by 2000.

The CompuServe episode exposes the inevitable clash of priorities when local standards of morality meet a global network. Germany is not the only country grappling with these issues: in the online debates that ensue, some Netizens express the quandary in more U.S.-centric terms, wondering what to do "when the Constitution is a local ordinance."

1995 Operation Home Front Connects American Soldiers Stationed Abroad with Their Families

A Web site called Operation Home Front goes online, offering an electronic means for American service people stationed abroad to connect with their families and supporters back home.

Prior to the advent of the Web, people serving in the armed forces were relatively isolated from home. Since telephone service was usually prohibitively expensive, they relied on written letters to carry news to and from their stations. The delay of the international postal service often meant waiting weeks for a reply to a letter. When e-mail became possible, service people were not always able to use the new communication system, because remote service locations weren't outfitted with Internet connections.

But by 1995 opportunities on the peacekeeping front to connect to the Internet—and thus the Web—are more widespread, and e-mail becomes a common tool for corresponding quickly with friends and family. Operation Home Front enhances these communication opportunities by creating a global virtual community of Americans associated with the military. The Web site hosts online service clubs for each branch of the military, real-time "talk" sessions with distant family, a message forum featuring numerous online discussions, and a posting place for open letters.

Operation Home Front is sponsored by numerous organizations, including VISA, NBC, CNN, Steelcase Corporation, and various Internet services.

1996 U.S. Communications Decency Act Passes into Law

On February 6, the Communications Decency Act (CDA) is signed by President Clinton, causing a hailstorm of debate. Part of the larger Telecommunications Reform Act, the CDA criminalizes indecent content and the knowing transmission to minors over the Internet of any message "that, in context, depicts or describes, in terms patently offensive as measured by *contemporary community standards, sexual or excretory activities or organs." In addition, the act contains a controversial section imposing $100,000 fines and prison terms for anyone posting obscene or indecent material on the Internet.*

The CDA is first introduced on the Senate floor in 1995 by Senator Jim Exon (D-Nebraska). Almost immediately, the constitutionality of the bill comes under fire from legal scholars. Supporters claim the bill's purpose is to restrict children's access to online pornography, which they believe has become ubiquitous in the late 1990s. Legal scholars counter that the transmission of obscene material is already a felony, and that the CDA's "decency" language is crafted with more than pornography in mind. Noting that portions of comedy routines, talk shows, and even poetry readings had been found "indecent" in the past, critics wonder aloud if the real aim of the CDA is to restrict what some consider "objectionable" speech among adults on the Internet.

Historically, "indecency" as a legal term applied only to broadcast industries regulated by the Federal Communications Commission (FCC), like television and radio. In industries not regulated by the FCC (print and film, for example) the term had no legal meaning. The CDA debate draws attention to the Net's unclear legal status: is it a broadcast medium like radio and television, or is it a forum for published material and speech? According to American Civil Liberties Union (ACLU)'s Lisa Kamm, "things which would be protected, were they published in a newspaper, or said over the telephone, were suddenly illegal acts under [the CDA], simply because they occurred over the Internet."

The Electronic Frontier Foundation (EFF), the ACLU, and other organizations that work to secure constitutional rights immediately challenge the CDA, and their claims are upheld when the Supreme Court declares the CDA unconstitutional in 1997. Meanwhile, a number of Web sites with explicit sexual content (some pornographic, some literary, others with health information) complain of the CDA's "chilling effect." Some sites respond to the threat of fines and prison by requiring age verification procedures to access information, while others remove any potentially questionable content altogether. By 1998 revised versions of the CDA are circulated as bills in Congress.

1996 PROTOTYPE NETWORK COMPUTER EXHIBITED AT ORACLE DEVELOPERS CONFERENCE

On February 26, Larry Ellison, chief executive officer of Oracle Corporation, unveils the first working prototype of a network computer at the Oracle Developers Conference in San Francisco, California. Ellison envisions the network computer (NC) as a low-cost, unembellished computing device tailored for browsing the World Wide Web, performing word processing, and accessing networked data and software.

Ellison wholeheartedly believes that the NC is the technological wave of the near future. Oracle does not plan to build the hardware of the machine but will develop several suites of software to run on it. At the February conference Ellison asserts that he expects the first NCs to be introduced onto the market at the end of the year. The NC is not expected to replace the personal computer, but to offer a $500 alternative in situations where an elaborate workstation is not required.

By late 1996 the first NCs have hit the market: IBM's Network Station and Sun Microsystems' Javastation. Sun markets its product to the corporate office. NCs within an office would be connected to a central server, where

Larry Ellison displays a prototype of the Network Computer at a February 1996 Developers Conference in San Francisco (AP / Wide World Photos).

all significant software and data would be stored; according to Sun, this setup could save a business thirty percent of the cost of equipping workers with PCs. Sun says the NC also offers an opportunity for managers to have more control over their employee's work-time computing capabilities. The Sun NC has no external disk drive and no CD-ROM drive, preventing the introduction of unwanted viruses and the removal of company secrets. Unlike a personal computer it does not allow workers to install recreational software.

Personal computer manufacturers counter that using the NC to regulate workers' activities will create an office ambiance of distrust, and that removing the flexible attributes of the personal computer will stunt workers' creativity.

The NC doesn't create the sensation that Ellison had expected it to, but it doesn't fizzle and die, either. Although actual NC sales are not stellar, the NC philosophy begins to make inroads. Ellison and other NC supporters continue to tout the advantages of NC technology and to predict its success in the future. With the advent of embedded systems, some form of the NC seems sure to make an impact.

1996   THE BROWSER WAR HEATS UP

On August 12, Netscape Corporation sends a letter to the U.S. Department of Justice claiming that Microsoft Corporation is violating antitrust laws. The move marks the beginning of a new stage in an ongoing Web browser war; unofficial complaints and accusations have evolved into fierce legal allegations.

Back in 1990 the U.S. Federal Trade Commission (FTC) had begun investigating software giant Microsoft for possible antitrust activities related to selling application software and operating systems as bundled units. (An application, such as a word processor, is a useful program that is not related to the computer it runs on, whereas an operating system is a program that actually controls the computer.) Microsoft's operating system ran on a majority of computers. Thus, if Microsoft was including its own applications with its operating system, it was effectively preventing other software manufacturers from marketing competing applications. The company remained under scrutiny.

Meanwhile, the World Wide Web goes into full swing following the introduction of Web browsers with point-and-click interfaces, such as Mosaic (1993) and Netscape Navigator (1994). In 1996 Microsoft releases Internet Explorer 3.0, a much improved version of its Web browser, and a competitive battle between Microsoft and Netscape evolves. Most significantly, Microsoft includes Internet Explorer for free with other software packages, a maneuver that puts Netscape, who charges customers for Navigator, in an untenable position. As Netscape cofounder Jim Clark told author Stephen Segaller: "Microsoft came along and in an attempt to put us out of business, gave away the browser totally free . . . . It definitely had an impact on us. As a consequence, we had to give away our browser." For its part, Microsoft denies there was any plan to exterminate Navigator: they simply included Explorer as a part of Windows, in the same way they include Print Manager or any of a number of programs.

Regardless of the intent of Microsoft's actions, their effect is undeniable. In May 1996 Netscape has more than eighty percent of the browser market share and Microsoft has less than ten percent; six months later, Microsoft is gaining with fourty percent and Netscape dropping to near fifty percent. Netscape challenges the statistics, but it is undisputed that Microsoft is catching up.

The war heats up in August 1996 after Netscape sends a letter to the Department of Justice arguing that Microsoft is guilty of antitrust violations and urging an investigation. The letter alleges: that Microsoft offered hundreds of thousands of dollars to Internet Service Providers not to sell Netscape software; that Microsoft withheld technological information from other Web-server software manufacturers to make its own software fare better in reviews; and that Microsoft charged original equipment manufacturers (OEMs) higher licensing fees if the OEMs requested Netscape Navigator with their Microsoft networking software packages. (An OEM is a company that manufactures and sells a product to another company that then incorporates the product into its own saleable item.)

When the letter becomes public two weeks later, reporters flock to OEMs to receive confirmation of Netscape's accusations. Numerous OEMs verify and even embellish the claims—although they ask to remain anonymous because they fear retribution from Microsoft. Microsoft vehemently denies all the allegations and asserts that Netscape's letter represents a malicious public relations campaign aimed at distracting the public from noticing that Microsoft's products are actually superior.

The government's ensuing investigation turns out to be only the beginning of an enormous drama, as Microsoft comes under increasing scrutiny by the Department of Justice during the following years.

1996 USENET CANCELBOT WIPES OUT MORE THAN 25,000 MESSAGES

On September 22 an unauthorized "cancelbot"—a program that issues commands to delete particular newsgroup messages—is unleashed on Usenet, erasing more than 25,000 messages. Although cancelbot hacks have occurred in the past, the event is unprecedented in scale.

Usenet, which is one of the oldest and largest online bulletin board systems (BBSs), features thousands of discussion forums, or newsgroups, worldwide. Newsgroups consist of lengthy threads of messages posted by participants. There are various commands (called "bots") that Usenet system operators and participants can apply to newsgroups; a cancelbot is one such command. Cancelbots were created to deal effectively with people who post hundreds or thousands of empty or rude messages to bog down the system. A cancelbot can be programmed to recognize a particular attribute of a message (for example, whom the message is from). Programmed and issued by a person, the cancelbot runs through Usenet, automatically earmarking the designated messages with a cancellation flag. The messages are then deleted.

Usenet bots have a checkered past. According to April 1996 *Wired* magazine, one of the earliest was written in early 1993 by Richard Depew. Feeling that the ability to post on Usenet anonymously was inspiring irresponsible behavior, Depew programmed a bot called ARMM (Automated Retroactive Minimal Moderation) to scan the network looking for anonymous posts and post a warning to readers. On March 31, 1993, ARMM ran amuck in the group news.admin.policy: ARMM recognized its own warning messages as new anonymous messages, and thus unleashed a waterfall of empty posts that ultimately crashed a number of Usenet mail systems.

The unauthorized cancelbot of September 22, 1996, is written by a subscriber of Cottage Software, an Internet service provider in Tulsa, Oklahoma. Most of the 25,536 newly posted messages that the cancelbot deletes appear to have been chosen randomly, as they cover a wide range of incongruous topics. However, some deleted messages are related to either computers, homosexuality, or pornography, and some of the cancellation tags include racial slurs. With only these clues, observers are left to speculate about the perpetrator's agenda.

Cottage Software turns over information about the cancelbot author to the Federal Bureau of Investigation (FBI), but authorities there are reluctant to pursue an investigation. There are no laws that prohibit creating and running cancelbots through public BBSs. Since cancelbots are useful for shutting down excessive message posters, system operators are reluctant to get rid of them. And since cancelbots are simple for any programmer to construct, Usenet remains susceptible to similar attacks in the future.

1996 INTERNET PHONES GAIN POPULARITY

Equipment that allows computer users to make long-distance telephone calls via the Internet emerges and quickly becomes popular. Internet phone use may contribute to changes in the structure and fee systems of both Internet service and long-distance telephone service.

Several computer corporations introduce the first Internet phones in mid-1996. New telephony software joins the necessary hardware (modem, sound capability, speakers, and microphone) to enable voice transmission over Internet connections. With such "Internet phones" installed, people can sit at their computers and make long-distance phone calls anywhere in the world for no cost other than their fee for Internet access.

Internet phone technology goes through the growing pains typical of a new technological development. The first equipment is limited: voice quality is often poor; connections are possible only between two people running the same software; only audio (no video) is offered; and calls are sometimes disconnected mid-sentence. Despite these inconveniences, the prospect of free long-distance calls attracts thousands of users. In August 1996, Intel Corporation releases test versions of Internet phone software online, and over the following few weeks more than 100,000 people download the software—ten times as many as Intel had anticipated.

Technological improvements arrive quickly. Voice quality improves and standards emerge, allowing calls between computers running distinct software. Soon it is even possible to call a regular telephone from an Internet phone.

As long-distance telephone service providers become aware that people are making calls for free, they demand that Internet Service Providers (ISPs) be regulated in the same manner as they are. Long-distance phone companies are required to pay local phone companies fees which support the maintenance of universally affordable phone service. ISPs do not pay these fees, but if they are made to do so in the future, they will likely pass the costs on to subscribers. At the end of 1998, the U.S. government is considering revising the regulations that govern long-distance phone companies and ISPs.

1996 DIGITAL COPYRIGHT TREATY PASSED BY WORLD INTELLECTUAL PROPERTY ORGANIZATION

On December 20 the World Intellectual Property Organization (WIPO) meets in Geneva to develop international copyright protocols for books, movies, music, and software distributed in cyberspace. The results of the meeting will set global standards for copyright protection in the digital era.

WIPO attendees pass two treaties—one on performance and sound recordings, another on copyright—which then move on to the domestic governments of 170 member-states for ratification. The third treaty, on the protection of digital databases, is postponed.

The results of the meeting (itself an extension of the 1886 Berne Convention on International Copyright) are both positive and negative for American entertainment interests. WIPO pleases Hollywood by recognizing the rights of owners of intellectual property to draw income from transmission of their work via digital networks. However, many WIPO members disagree strongly with U.S. conference delegate Bruce Lehman throughout the proceedings, believing he is more interested in American corporate gain than in global intellectual growth.

Lehman, chair of the Clinton administration's Intellectual Property Working Group, first came to public attention in 1995 with his infamous "White Paper on Intellectual Property." In it, he argued that the ubiquity of digital networks made it necessary for governments to provide even stronger protections for holders of intellectual property than those currently in existence.

With heavy support from Hollywood, Lehman advocates reversing current "fair use" policies (long claimed by educators and writers) by outlawing the forwarding, duplication, or even online reading of digital material without permission from the copyright holder. In a strict interpretation, even having a document in the cache of one's computer would constitute theft (the cache is a temporary memory space; caching documents is a common practice when reading online). Most American legislators find Lehman's notions on copyright too "maximalist," to borrow the phrase of attorney Patricia Samuelson, and Lehman's White Paper is never reported out of Congressional committee.

Lehman remains undaunted and argues for many of the same principles at the WIPO meeting. One particularly troublesome Lehman addition is a draft treaty for intellectual property rights in databases, which would grant copyright protection to publishers of telephone directories or sports statistics—and make the quotation of "substantial portions" of them a crime. The database treaty, which is unpopular with world scientists, consumer advocates, and even the Clinton administration, is quickly tabled by other WIPO members.

In his *Wired* article, "Africa 1, Hollywood 0," John Browning notes that in the end, the WIPO conference will be remembered "not so much for what it did as for what it did not do. It did not give copyright holders many of the new legal powers they asked for—mostly because delegates feared that they would use those powers to force the future into the mold of the past, and so rob the Net of its potential to create change."

1997 America Online's Offer of Unlimited Internet Access Leads to Class-Action Suits

Several class-action suits are filed against America Online, Inc. (AOL), an Internet Service Provider, by dissatisfied customers. AOL settles out of court, offering compensation packages to subscribers. The event illustrates what can happen when the expectations of Internet users meet the limitations of Internet technology.

Following the advent of the World Wide Web and the introduction of point-and-click Web browsers, Internet use had increased exponentially, and numerous new Internet Service Providers (ISPs) had been established. AOL boasted the largest number of customers in the United

States. Starting December 1, 1996, AOL began offering its seven million customers unlimited online time for a flat rate of $19.95 per month. Previous AOL packages had included per-minute rates and rates for limited amounts of online time, and the change represented a scheme to compete with other ISPs (many of whom were offering flat rates for unlimited time). Within weeks AOL's unlimited-time flat rate drew more than a million new customers and caused an increase from 1.6 million hours (October 1996) to 4.3 million hours (January 1997) in AOL's total daily online usage.

AOL's new policy begins causing online traffic jams in early January 1997, hinting that the company's technological resources are not substantial enough to support their promise of unlimited online time. Customers are greeted with unlimited busy signals at peak times and are sometimes unable to access their accounts even after trying for hours. The overloads cause several complete crashes of AOL's service.

Seeking damages for misrepresentation, five AOL subscribers file a class-action suit against the company in a Los Angeles Superior Court in the second week of January. Subscribers in New York follow with another; eventually thirty-seven states join the effort. AOL responds, in a letter to customers, that it is in the process of pouring $350 million into upgrading its network and expanding customer service. The letter explains to customers that the increase in usage was beyond the company's expectations, and it asks for their patience and loyalty.

At the end of January, AOL reaches an agreement with the Attorneys General of the thirty-seven states involved. The settlement states that AOL must not exceed its customer base of eight million (and must not proceed with advertising campaigns) until it can reasonably support more subscribers. It also grants two-month refunds to customers who feel they have not received sufficient value from the service due to busy signals.

A few class-action suits remain after the settlement, and AOL limps through several bouts of legal trouble but lands on its feet. A significant outcome of the crisis is that ISPs and customers are left with the understanding that the technology behind the Internet still has limits. A demand for expanded capabilities clearly exists, and engineers set to work drawing up improvements.

1997 INTERNET2 HOLDS FIRST TWO MEETINGS

The Internet2 (I2) project is established and begins pursuing its goal of leading the next stage of Internet technology development. The project is a collaborative effort among universities, government agencies, and industry participants to create an advanced network infrastructure and a host of cutting-edge applications to meet the emerging needs of research and education.

The first Internet had originated in a similar manner, as the brainchild of an alliance between government, academia, and industry. Until the early 1990s most of the network's capacity had been used for research purposes. But when the World Wide Web arrived and evolved into a widely popular Internet feature, public use of the network increased drastically and began to cause congestion. In 1996 representatives from thirty-four universities began discussing the creation of a faster, more advanced Internet for the research community.

On January 22, 1997, in San Francisco, California, I2 holds its first official general meeting. The project now includes more than one hundred participating universities and has been promised funds in excess of $50 million. At the meeting, the 250 attendees outline I2 goals: the implementation of advanced network designs, synchronous communications systems, digital libraries, virtual laboratories, real-time remote instruction, state-of-the-art modeling and simulation, and immense database processing. I2 aims to have its first sites operating within a year.

Excited to have met the first goal, I2 participants convene in Washington, D.C. in October 1997 to demonstrate I2 in action. In one presentation, a network connection with the University of Illinois at Chicago enables meeting attendees to view, in real time, a remote lecture involving a high-resolution video simulation of the intricate anatomy of the human inner ear. In another, the director of Indiana University's School of Music shows how I2 can retrieve a clear digital recording of Beethoven's Fifth Symphony. For comparison he retrieves the same audio file using the original Internet, and the sound is choppy due to packets being lost in the transmission.

I2 participants foresee that the network technologies they develop will become available within the public and commercial realms after a number of years.

1997 U.S. COMMUNICATIONS DECENCY ACT FOUND UNCONSTITUTIONAL

On June 26, the Supreme Court of the United States holds that the Communications Decency Act of 1996 is unconstitutional because it violates the First Amendment's guarantee of free speech. This precedent-setting decision promises to influence future legal battles surrounding privacy and speech on the Internet.

The Communications Decency Act (CDA) had passed into law in February 1996. Within weeks the Electronic Frontier Foundation (EFF), the American Civil Liberties Union (ACLU), and seventeen other organizations committed to upholding constitutional rights challenged the CDA in a Philadelphia district court. On June 12, 1996, this court found the law unconstitutional. An appeal to the Supreme Court was then filed by the U.S. Department of Justice (the case became known as *Reno v. ACLU*— because Janet Reno was Attorney General at the time).

On March 19, 1997, both sides of the case present arguments before the Supreme Court, and on June 26, 1997, the Court issues its opinion: the CDA violates the First Amendment and must therefore be repealed. Anticensorship constituents of the online community rejoice.

But Congressional supporters of the CDA do not give up, and in October 1998, President Bill Clinton signs into law the Child Online Protection Act (COPA), nicknamed "CDA II." The act makes it illegal to knowingly transmit any material considered "harmful to minors" for commercial purposes. The ACLU and similar groups claim that the COPA's flaws are identical to those of the CDA. The Justice Department itself admits, in an analysis that accompanies the bill to Clinton's desk, that the law has "serious constitutional problems." On November 20, Federal Judge Lowell A. Reed, Jr. issues a temporary restraining order on COPA, preventing it from being enforced until the question of constitutionality can be resolved.

1997 EUGENE KASHPUREFF DIVERTS INTERNET TRAFFIC FROM InterNIC TO AlterNIC

Self-described "domain name radical" Eugene Kashpureff exploits a flaw in the system in order to route Net traffic from InterNIC, the domain name registry run by Network Solutions, Inc. (NSI), to his own site, AlterNIC.

Beyond the Net

DON'T PANIC

"Here's an interesting experiment," challenges Mike Godwin in his book *Cyber Rights*. "Try combining the topics of sex, children, and the Net in a magazine or newspaper story or even in an online discussion. The combination will almost invariably cause ostensibly intelligent people to shut down their higher thinking centers."

Here, Godwin, who is chief counsel for the Electronic Frontier Foundation, answers questions about the social condition he calls "cyberporn panic."

Q: Legally speaking, what precisely is pornography?

In the United States, pornographic material is generally defined as that which presents sexual content, with the intent of being arousing. Not all pornography is illegal, however. To be illegal, pornography must be found to be either "obscene" or "child pornography."

Q: Do you believe that today's Internet consists primarily of pornography?

No. Most of the American public is convinced that some large amount of Net content is pornography, when in fact only a small fraction of that content is pornographic. Certainly the infamous 1995 *Time* magazine article on "cyberporn," which was read into the Congressional Record, has helped perpetuate this misconception.

The chief resource for the *Time* story was a Carnegie Mellon University "study" by Martin Rimm, in which his generalizations about the entire "information superhighway" were actually based on data from sixty-eight adult-oriented computer bulletin board systems (BBSs), most of which were unreachable through the Internet. The Rimm study was so faulty that ultimately *Time* was forced to retract its story, for only the third time in that publication's history. After all, to generalize from commercial porn BBSs to the Net at large is like generalizing from Times Square adult bookstores to the entire publishing industry. Still, the passage of the CDA shows how vulnerable people are to cyberporn panic.

Q. Do we need to pass laws protecting children from exposure to pornography on the Internet?

As a parent, I don't take this question lightly. The fact remains, however, that existing law covers this fairly well. Almost every state has laws making it illegal to expose minors to certain classes of sexually explicit material—even when such material is otherwise legal for nonminors.

Q. But what about child pornography on the Net?

There is not an instance of child pornography trafficking I can think of that wouldn't be adequately prosecutable under current laws. The fact is, exchanging child pornography—defined by the courts as "any material depicting a child engaging in a sexual act or posing in a 'lewd and lascivious' matter"—is already illegal, regardless of whether the material is ruled obscene or not. Online or offline, nobody likes child pornographers, and our existing laws don't need much fine tuning when it comes to punishing their activities.

Although the stunt does not have a significant effect on daily life on the Net, it does expose a potentially fatal loophole in the Domain Name System (DNS), and it splashes the NSI monopoly across the front pages.

Longtime Seattle resident Eugene Kashpureff first became interested in computers as a kid, when he saw one in the James Bond film, *Diamonds Are Forever.* As an adult his first major programming effort was the creation of software for the towing company he was working for at the time. When he discovered the Net in 1995, Kashpureff fell head over heels. After competing against NYNEX to put the yellow pages online, Kashpureff turned his attention to the NSI domain name monopoly.

On April Fools' Day 1996, Kashpureff gets his AlterNIC up and running, offering alternative domains like .xxx and .med. His domain name servers will acknowledge traditional domains like .com as well as the alternative ones. In order to use these alternative domains, users need merely set their computer to query one of Kashpureff's servers, rather than the default ones. Kashpureff would later claim that at AlterNIC's height, up to three percent of Internet traffic had made the switch to AlterNIC servers.

In July 1997, angered by NSI statements that generic top-level domain names belong to InterNIC exclusively, Kashpureff launches an attack from his laptop, otherwise known as kissmyass.com. The hack involves sending out misleading information to domain name servers, causing the servers to misroute Web browsers: those looking for http://www.internic.net end up at Kashpureff's site instead, where they see the message: "By redirecting the domain name www.internic.net, we are protesting the recent InterNIC claim to ownership of ".com", ".org", and ".net," which they are supposed to be running in the public trust."

Kashpureff's action causes no damage to the InterNIC site, and indeed his site includes a link back to InterNIC. Some call it a dumb stunt, but Kashpureff considers it a protest—an act of civil disobedience against an unfair and oppressive monopoly. The misrouting ends after five days.

NSI files suit against Kashpureff on July 21, 1997, based on loss of revenue from the approximate five thousand new registrants NSI services per day. The suit is quickly settled when Kashpureff agrees to pay a small fee and publish an apology on the Internet for his actions. Ironically, even the settlement itself serves to highlight how powerful the NSI monopoly really is. As Peter Wayner writes in *The New York Times* on November 21, 1997,

"Network Solutions probably did not lose the $100 fee paid by each of these 25,000 registrants, because most of them probably found another way to register. They . . . had no choice if they wanted a domain name."

Observers claim that NSI is much more concerned about copycat hacks than they are about punishing Kashpureff—thus they are happy to settle and keep the publicity at as low a level as possible. The same can not be said for the U.S. Attorney General's office, who pursues their criminal investigation; on Halloween 1997 Kashpureff is arrested in Canada, where he and his family had fled earlier that year, and is extradited on fraud charges. Kashpureff is eventually flown to New York City, where he is released on $75,000 bond on Christmas Eve. On March 20, 1998, Kashpureff pleads guilty to one count of computer fraud and is sentenced to two years probation. AlterNIC will go on registering alternative domain names, but without the help of Kashpureff, who (according to his attorneys) plans to lay low, pay off debts, and spend time with his children.

1997   PUSH TECHNOLOGY DEBUTS

"Push" technology—also called Internet broadcasting, content delivery, and Webcasting—is among the most sensationalized Internet developments of 1997. It consists of services that deliver individualized information packets (gathered from the Internet) straight to a computer user's desktop.

Traditionally, users click on links or bookmarks to give instructions to their Web browsers, and the browsers then retrieve the information (this is called a "pull"). With push, the information is provided automatically, usually at regular intervals specified by the user. Push advocates liken it to television and radio: signals are broadcast constantly, and it's up to the user to tune in. The aim of push technology is to sidestep the sometimes time-consuming and frustrating processes associated with surfing the Web: locating desired information, waiting for Web pages to load, and getting disconnected.

A company called PointCast emerges as the largest push-providing venture. PointCast's push system, which is available via download off the Internet for free, collects six hundred sources of news information on the Internet and categorizes the information into fifty channels. When a user subscribes to a channel, updated headlines from the chosen channel are regularly and automatically sent to the user's desktop. PointCast's service displays the information as a screen saver; other push providers employ banners that run across the top of the screen. In both cases, the information includes hypertext links to the complete version of the information so that users can simply click on items of interest and go directly to them.

By the end of 1997 PointCast has 700,000 subscribers, and other push providers claim about 200,000 users. Despite initial public enthusiasm, the buzz surrounding push technology largely fades by the end of 1998. However, the quest for more efficient methods of information retrieval continues.

1997   CELLULAR MODEMS IMPROVED, BUT STILL NOT SELLING IN DROVES

In 1997 vastly improved versions of the handheld cellular modem are introduced, fostering the popular perception that the wireless age of information and communication has arrived. But numerous practical roadblocks mean the devices continue to be largely neglected on retail shelves.

The earliest cellular modems had been introduced in 1995, and gradual advances in cellular technology had made them practical for consumers. By far the most common user of the cellular is the "mobile corporate worker," an employee whose job requires frequent travel either within a large office setting or to and from distant locations. Cellular modems connect to laptop computers, cellular phones, and personal digital assistants (PDAs), allowing mobile users to connect to the Internet or to local area networks (within a single business) without being plugged into the wall.

Despite the promise of great convenience—and numerous advertisements featuring people sending e-mail from scenic beach locations—cellular modems are limited by technological drawbacks. Standards for wireless data transmission are conspicuously absent, cellular modems gulp down excess battery power, few applications for the devices exist, and transmission speed is slow compared to wired connections. Moreover, cellular modems sell for an average of $400, about twice as much as high-end desktop modems. Market analysts assert that these factors will continue to conspire against the cellular modem's wide success until technological advances remedy them.

1998   DEPARTMENT OF JUSTICE FILES SUIT AGAINST MICROSOFT

The legal battle between software giant Microsoft and the United States Department of Justice (DOJ) hits a crescendo as the DOJ's investigation into Microsoft's anticompetitive business practices transforms into a full-fledged criminal suit.

In 1990 the Federal Trade Commission had begun investigating Microsoft for bundling application software with sales of its operating system; two years later the DOJ took charge of the investigation. The DOJ and Microsoft settled out of court in 1994, with Microsoft agreeing not to include software contingencies in its operating system licenses. The settlement went into effect a year later, after several squabbles between judges were resolved.

In 1995 Microsoft announced plans to bundle Microsoft Network software with the Windows 95 operating system, and the DOJ reopened its investigation. In 1996 the battle was boosted, as Netscape Communications Corp., maker of the Web browser Netscape Navigator, filed a complaint with the DOJ claiming Microsoft had been violating the 1994 antibundling settlement. Microsoft denied wrongdoing. The DOJ began requesting official documents from Microsoft and Netscape to use in its investigation.

In 1997 Texas becomes the first state to launch an antitrust investigation of Microsoft, and a few months later Texas files a lawsuit against Microsoft for allegedly interfering with the state's investigation. Massachusetts starts

In March 1998 (l to r) Microsoft CEO Bill Gates, Sun Microsystems president Scott McNealy, and Netscape Communication president Jim Barksdale testify before a Senate Judiciary Committee hearing on anticompetitive issues and technology (AP / Wide World Photos).

a separate investigation of Microsoft. In December, Judge Thomas Jackson of the U.S. District Court issues an order forbidding Microsoft from requiring computer manufacturers to include Internet Explorer (Microsoft's Web browser) with the Windows 95 operating system. Microsoft responds by offering manufacturers a choice between an old version of Windows 95 without Explorer and the new version of Windows 95, of which Explorer is an integrated part. The DOJ is not satisfied with this solution, arguing that Microsoft could separate Explorer from the new version, so that manufacturers who don't want Explorer are not forced to install an outdated version of the operating system.

1998 starts off with a hearing to establish whether Microsoft has complied with Jackson's order, and it is revealed that the DOJ and Microsoft have interpreted the order differently. At the end of January Microsoft agrees to license the new version of Windows 95 without an Explorer icon on the desktop.

In February the Attorneys General of eleven states join the investigation of Microsoft. Numerous Internet Service Providers (ISPs) receive subpoenas as investigators search for evidence that Microsoft is attempting to use its operating system dominance to control the Internet software market. Twenty-seven states file a brief declaring their support for the DOJ's emerging antitrust case against Microsoft.

Giving testimony at a Senate Judiciary Committee hearing on competition in the computer industry, Microsoft chairman Bill Gates argues that his company is no more a monopolist than IBM had been during its dominance of the computer manufacturing industry. Jim Barksdale and Scott McNealy, the heads of Netscape and Sun Microsystems, who are present at the hearing, strongly disagree. After the hearing Microsoft begins to unbundle applications from operating system licenses, although it denies doing so under government pressure.

The DOJ begins to research Microsoft's involvement in the Java market (Java is a language prevalent in World Wide Web programming), its marketing of Windows NT (an operating system), and its partnerships with ISPs. Microsoft alters contracts it had made with ISPs, which had prohibited the ISPs from promoting products made by Microsoft's competitors.

Two official criminal suits are filed against Microsoft in May: one by the DOJ and one by a collaboration among twenty states. The suits, which are soon consolidated into one, focus on Microsoft's alleged anticompetitive practices targeting Netscape. Although a trial date is originally set for September 8, the date is postponed through the end of the year.

In June the DOJ's case is weakened by a federal appeals court ruling which questions whether the prohibition against Microsoft's bundling of Internet Explorer with Windows 95 is legal. The DOJ responds by increasing its investigations into Microsoft's business activities related to technologies such as Java, Intel microchips, and Apple Computer media software, and in October the DOJ announces that it will be calling executives from Apple and Sun Microsystems to testify at the trial. Microsoft, complaining that the government is introducing new elements only weeks before the trial is to begin, requests a delay and is denied.

In October 1998 the world watches the start of what promises to be the most sensational and dramatic court case in the history of the computer industry. Analysts predict that the case may take years to be completely resolved.

1998 Extensible Markup Language (XML) Is Introduced for the World Wide Web

The World Wide Web Consortium (W3C) develops Extensible Markup Language (XML) to enable more versatile documentation and data exchange within the Web. XML promises to lift the constraints of HTML (Hypertext Markup Language), the standard language of Web documents, and consequently lead to a more useful network of information.

Tim Berners-Lee, the inventor of the Web, had specified HTML as the standard language for creating Web documents, because it is well suited for displaying simple documents and for accommodating hypertext links. HTML is an application of a much more complex language called SGML (Standard Generalized Markup Language), which describes the structure and content of electronic documents. SGML is difficult to use and impractical for creating Web documents.

The W3C, a group of computer science professionals led by Berners-Lee who work to maintain the progressive evolution of the Web, formulates the idea for XML in late 1996. The purpose of XML, which is a simplified version of SGML, is to offer more flexibility in Web documentation than HTML allows. The W3C's XML working group develops the specifics of the new language over the following year.

Netspeak

BODYSHOPPING AND SPLIT SHIFTING

In 1998 the Clinton administration appeased software lobbyists by doubling the number of H1B visas currently available to foreign workers in the United States. These six-year "high-tech visas," used mainly by students and foreign computer programmers, have become a mainstay of a Silicon Valley practice known as "bodyshopping."

In the 1970s the term "bodyshopper" was a badge of honor: it described a hotshot computer programmer brought in to solve problems for large software manufacturers. Today, "bodyshop" usually refers to foreign-owned companies that subcontract international computer workers to the American software industry. A. Balachandranan of DSQ Software in Mumbai, India, claims that "there is no room for foul play and exploitation" because market forces dictate a fair wage for computer programmers. Not everyone agrees. In their essay "The Uneven Development of Places: From Bodyshopping to Global Assembly Lines," Ali Mir and Maya Yajnik argue that in reality these "techno-coolies" often earn far less than their American counterparts. They cite a Softpac (Software Professionals' Political Action Committee) study, which found that while American contract programmers at IBM in Texas made $60,000 to $100,000 a year, Indian programmers doing contract work for IBM made only $33,000 a year.

Bodyshopping isn't the only way corporations have globalized. Nearly thirty of the largest U.S. computing corporations have moved some of their operations overseas, as countries like Hungary, India, and Ireland have offered tax incentives to American companies. One spectacular example is the Multimedia Super Corridor in Kuala Lumpur, Malaysia, where the city of Cyberjaya is being constructed in the hopes that once the high-tech infrastructure is built, high-tech dollars will follow.

It's unclear whether LDCs (less developed countries) realize major long-term benefits by hosting foreign software manufacturers. In their essay "Computing in Chile," R.A. Baeza-Yates, et. al. concluded that "except in the dubious domain of providing bodyshopping labor, it is proving very difficult for embryonic software industries in LDCs to be competitive in mature markets." In short, globalization allows LDCs to work for Microsoft, but not necessarily to compete with Microsoft.

Corporations don't need to relocate in order to take advantage of the global digital economy—the Internet has made the long-envisioned "international split shift" a functional reality. In this scenario, one "shift" of workers in the United States completes certain tasks, while a second shift works overseas via telecommunications networks. A software glitch at a U.S. company at 5 PM can be solved by overseas consultants before work begins the following morning. The World Bank has even suggested using labor in Africa to monitor the closed-circuit security systems in American shopping malls.

While it is clear that American businesses benefit from international workers linked via telecommunications, economists have yet to agree on whether practices like bodyshopping and international split shifting help or hinder workers in developing nations. It remains to be seen how much gold these wired workers will find at the end of the digital rainbow.

In all markup languages, text is marked with tags that identify which type of text it is (for example, a heading or a subheading) so that it will be displayed correctly in the document. With XML, authors can define their own tabs. XML tabs can contain information about the content of the text in addition to indicating how it should be displayed. The content information earmarks the text to be recognized by advanced (XML-capable) search engines, enabling more specific search results.

Other applications for XML include the exchange of information between two distinct databases and the switching between different views of the same information without having to download the views separately.

By mid-1998 Microsoft's Internet Explorer and Netscape's Navigator, the two most widely used Web browsers, are adding XML to their products.

1998 GeoCities Settles Charges of Deceptive Online Privacy Practices

GeoCities Inc., a provider of World Wide Web resources, signs a consent order issued by the Federal Trade Commission (FTC), requiring the company to implement several new policies regarding the collection of private information from viewers. The event warns other Web services to clearly disclose how they use private information gathered online.

GeoCities, based in Santa Monica, California, provides an online forum for creating personal Web pages. The company offers various Web sites specifically for children; some sites request the viewer to input personal identifying information such as name, address, and phone number.

Prior to the FTC investigation, GeoCities was not itself collecting this personal information; rather, the information was being gathered directly by third parties hosted on GeoCities' sites (possibly for advertising purposes). GeoCities' viewers were not informed of this practice anywhere on the sites.

In June 1998 the FTC formally accuses GeoCities of violating the Federal Trade Commission Act by misrepresenting the use of collected personal identifying information on its Web sites. In September GeoCities signs an agreement in which the FTC orders it to do the following: clearly post an explanation of the use of personal information at each online location where such information is requested; institute a means of obtaining parental consent before gathering personal information from children under the age of thirteen; provide a way for viewers to remove their personal information from GeoCities sites; and initiate a program by which GeoCities staff and volunteers are educated about online privacy policies.

The FTC announces that the online service industry should learn from GeoCities' experience and establish self-regulation policies by the end of the year. Some industry and professional organizations, such as the Information Industry Association (IIA), urge their members to establish and practice effective online privacy policies. The FTC promises that if the industry can not effectively police itself, privacy issues will be regulated by bodies outside the industry.

1998 ICANN Is Chosen by the U.S. Commerce Department as Successor to InterNIC

After years of internecine battles between governmental, commercial, and private interests, the future of Internet administration is put in the hands of the Internet Corporation for Assigned Names and Numbers (ICANN), an entity created by Net guru Jon Postel. Not everyone is satisfied, however, and issues of accountability and public access linger unresolved.

In 1993 the consulting firm of Network Solutions, Inc. (NSI) won a five-year contract with the U.S. government to create InterNIC, an entity that administers domain names ".com," ".net," and ".org." As Internet usage expanded beyond all expectation, many industry observers questioned both the appropriateness and the ability of having one company single-handedly administer the most popular top-level domain names in the world. When time on the NSI contract began to run out, the Internet community began discussing the future of domain name registration.

What started in late 1996 as a discussion about Internet administration quickly devolved into something of a civil war, as multiple groups with varying agendas began putting forward their own proposals. A U.S. Commerce Department report issued in 1997 opened the floodgates of debate and, occasionally, rancor. In essence, the paper outlined the U.S. Government's desire to privatize domain name administration. It called for the dismantling of the InterNIC system, to be replaced by a new, international policy-making board to oversee the Internet.

President Clinton's senior policy advisor Ira Magaziner was appointed to lead U.S. government discussions on the issue, while Internet pioneer Jon

JONATHAN POSTEL

Contentious as it was, the creation of ICANN was nevertheless a major victory for Jon Postel, who had been an influential behind-the-scenes leader of the Internet for some thirty years.

In 1969 Postel was working on a master's degree in engineering at UCLA when the university was chosen as one of the first four nodes of the ARPAnet. Along with fellow students Vint Cerf and the rest of the Network Working Group, Postel was charged with establishing the first ARPAnet node—linking up the first Interface Message Processor to the UCLA host computer. Postel stayed on at UCLA, finishing his doctorate in computer science in 1974, and he stayed with the Internet, achieving a Maharishi-like status in the eyes of the technically savvy.

As the editor of RFC (Requests for Comment) documents, he guided the creation and refinement of the structure of the Internet. As the Internet Assigned Numbers Authority (IANA), Postel oversaw the administration of Internet protocol (IP) numbers, the numerical addresses that correspond to domain names on the WWW. (Postel's influence was such that although the IANA is, technically speaking, an organization rather than an individual, Postel was routinely referred to as "the IANA" or even "our IANA.") Running IANA isn't a job that gets one on the cover of *Wired*, but it's one of importance and no small power.

The scope of Postel's influence became clear in the late 1990s, when he was thrust into the middle of the extremely public battle for control over the next generation of Web domains. As often happens on the Net, a philosophical debate between concerned parties quickly spiraled into an all-out war, with Postel cast sometimes as Yoda-like savior and sometimes as Darth Vader-esque villain. In early February 1998 Postel was accused of attempting to hijack the Internet when he rerouted at least half of the thirteen root servers (computers that run the Net) to run through his own server at the University of Southern California. According to Postel, the rerouting was a routine test, like many others he performed regularly as the IANA. However, the timing—coinciding as it did with the release of the U.S. government's "Green Paper" on domain names—led observers to suggest that Postel's real intent was to let Uncle Sam know who was boss.

Always more comfortable in front of a screen than inside the fishbowl of media coverage, friends say the path to ICANN took a large toll on Postel. He died on Friday, October 16, 1998, at age 55, from complications resulting from heart surgery. The sense of loss experienced by the Internet community was perhaps best expressed, appropriately enough, in RFC 2648, a eulogy by Vint Cerf entitled "I Remember IANA."

[Postel] had been our rock, the foundation on which our every Web search and e-mail was built, always there to mediate the random dispute, to remind us when our documentation did not do justice to its subject, to make difficult decisions with apparent ease, and to consult when careful consideration was needed . . . . He has left a monumental legacy for all Internauts to contemplate.

Postel spearheaded efforts through his IANA (Internet Assigned Numbers Authority) post to influence the outcome. NSI held their own meetings on the future of domain names, and other groups such as the Boston Working Group, the Commercial Internet Exchange (CIX), Harvard's John F. Kennedy School of Government, the Council of Registrars (CORE), and the World Internet Alliance also strode into the fray.

These wide-ranging discussions gain more focus in January 1998 when the U.S. Commerce Department releases its "Green Paper." The paper lists four main areas of concern—overall stability of the Internet, the introduction of competition into domain name registry, involvement of the private sector, and accountability to Internet users—and makes further recommendations for an international non-profit body to oversee domain names and Internet architecture as a whole. Amidst complaints that this new body might serve only to recreate the monopoly situation rather than eliminate it, negotiations continue throughout 1998.

A formal proposal for the new body, called ICANN, is posted jointly on the Web by IANA and NSI in September 1998, and it is tentatively accepted by the U.S. Commerce Department in October. The ICANN proposal is not without its critics. Objections are voiced from groups such as the Open Root Server Confederation, CORE, and the Electronic Frontier Foundation on a variety of issues: many are concerned that ICANN will have both tremendous power and no accountability; others point out that no civil liberties questions were addressed by the proposal; still others argue that ICANN's board of directors, handpicked by Postel and headed by Esther Dyson, does not represent the full spectrum of Internet users.

Magaziner and the Commerce Department share many of these concerns, and they insist on a number of policy revisions aimed at creating greater openness and accountability. ICANN cooperates with the Commerce Department, but concerns remain that ICANN is simply entrenching the preexisting Internet elite. A November 25 *New York Times* article quotes an online post by Bob Allisat, a Toronto-based domain registrar: "ICANN is currently set up only to serve a handful of unknown insiders . . . . Other than that it leaves the rest of humanity and every other commercial and corporate stakeholder very much out in the cold." When ICANN holds its first public meeting in Cambridge, Massachusetts, in November 1998, the mood is, by all accounts, surprisingly hostile.

To some, ICANN is just another acronym for just another technical committee. Others view ICANN as the beginning of a global government for the Internet, and to them the stakes are extraordinarily high. But despite passionate criticism, infighting, and the sudden death of Jon Postel in October 1998, the creation of a new administrative body for cyberspace inches forward.

1998 STARR REPORT RELEASED ONLINE

In a resounding confirmation of the importance of the Internet as a news source, the House of Representatives makes independent counsel Kenneth Starr's report on the President Clinton/Monica Lewinsky scandal available online on September 11, 1998. The instantaneous nature of the Net means that anyone with a modem can access the full text of the report as easily and nearly as quickly as all the traditional media outlets.

The hand-in-glove relationship between the Internet and the Lewinsky scandal predates Starr's report. Were it not for the persistence of online columnist Matt Drudge, who first began publicizing rumors of presidential involvement with a White House intern in January 1998, it's possible the Starr investigation would have never taken the turn it did. *Salon* online magazine also fueled the fires with its September report of a long-forgotten extramarital affair of Representative Henry Hyde, chairman of the House Judiciary Committee. Nonetheless, the posting of the report is considered by many to be a milestone in the United States's wired history.

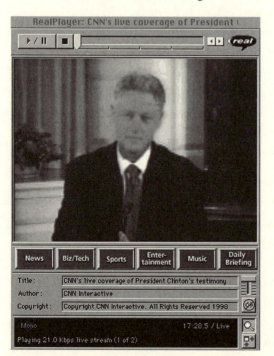

President Clinton's August 17, 1998 testimony in the Kenneth Starr investigation as it was broadcast on the CNN Interactive Web site (AP / Wide World Photos).

Interest in the report is expected to be so intense, and pressure on governmental Web servers so great, that House officials make the report available on four separate government sites as well as on many major media sites. On the big day, Web

Media History

MATT DRUDGE: IT'S NOT THE MEDIUM, IT'S THE MESSAGE

Publishers have always tried to get newspapers into American homes by any means necessary. In "Community or Colony: The Case of Online Newspapers and the Web," Riley et al. recount attempts to use radio technology to broadcast into home fax machines; then to deliver news over phone lines to home television sets. In the 1980s, encouraged by their online readers, CompuServe offered electronic editions of national papers. Each time, the headaches involved in producing news for cyberspace outweighed the benefits.

Enter the World Wide Web, with its cheap technology and low production costs. Some Web news sites (particularly those attached to traditional outlets) consist mainly of "shovelware"—material taken from print journalists. Others, like *Salon* (www.salonmag.com), have no print counterpart, and still others, like *The Drudge Report* (www.drudgereport.com), straddle a line between a one-man-show news outlet and personal Web page.

Drudge, former CBS gift-store employee with no journalistic credentials beyond his Internet mailing list and Web site, doesn't fit anyone's definition of a typical Washington reporter. In a June 1998 speech at the prestigious National Press Club, Drudge painted himself in populist style as the "little man with a big story," and credited the Net with "saving the news business," and ushering in "an era vibrating with the din of small voices. Every citizen can be a reporter, can take on the powers that be." If polls are any indication, he's right: According to Jupiter Communications, 80 percent of Americans online trust online news as much as they trust news from traditional outlets—7 percent view online news as more reliable than other media.

But is this trust well-founded? In his essay, "Preserving Old Ethics in a New Medium," J.D. Lasica argues that the Net poses some never-before experienced problems for news readers, including "reporters lurking invisibly in chat rooms; ad links embedded in editorial copy; the posting of private tragedies in news archives until the end of time; . . . [and] putting the tools of publishing into the hands of Little League coaches and others who aren't trained journalists."

Some say the problem with reporters like Drudge isn't their medium but their shocking lack of journalistic ethics. By his own admission, Drudge is only correct 80 percent of the time—an unacceptably low standard in a traditional newsroom. Defenders counter that there have been plenty of ethical problems at big news outlets—recent incidents, from plagiarism to fakery, have plagued *The New Republic, The Boston Globe,* "60 Minutes," and CNN. Regardless of media, there is not much to stop a report from fabricating material, save her own conscience.

In the end the most reliable news outlets, both online and off, will combine up-to-the-minute stories with an editorial policy where one doesn't publish everything one hears. Snappy headlines won't hurt, either. In a recent interview, *Salon* cofounder David Talbot reminisced that in the early days of print, tabloids knew "how to grab readers in the opening paragraph and hold them, and knew how to cause scandals and controversies." Talbot adds, "I think all of those things are coming back into fashion now in the Internet world."

sites giving access to Starr's report register double and sometimes triple their normal number of hits. Reports indicate that the network itself holds up well, but some Web servers have more visitors than they can handle. ISPs suffer the most problems, as users crowd around their PCs to read the report. No major catastrophes are reported, beyond an early morning train derailment near Atlanta, which negatively affects Internet access in the Southeast when a number of communications lines are cut. Overall, it is a normal—albeit bottlenecked—day on the Net.

Observers point out that the Internet combines news coverage with a sort of "digital water cooler," in which users can not only inform themselves of the issues but also debate them. Some express the hope that Net will lead to a broader-based involvement in the democratic process.

The Internet continues to play an important role in the Lewinsky scandal as more evidence trickles out to the public, including videotape of Clinton's testimony in the Paula Jones case and audio recordings of phone conversations between Monica Lewinsky and Starr informant Linda Tripp. Ironically, these legitimate news stories run afoul of many Internet filters—software implemented by parents and educators to keep sexually explicit content from the eyes of children.

1998   Linux Operating System Becomes a Cause Celebre

Created by Finnish university student Linus Torvalds, Linux is anointed "the next big thing" by industry observers, as corporate investment and anti-Microsoft fervor pushes the Unix-based operating system onto the front page.

Linux is a standard-bearer in the open-source or free software movement. The Linux system and the source code that runs it are available over the Internet for free. For years Linux remained largely the province of hackers, computer scientists, and other Net-savvy users. Mainstream corporate America was largely hesitant to get involved with software that did not come from any specific company and did not offer traditional "product support." But plenty of support was available on the Internet from the hackers who helped build Linux in the first place, and the system was quietly implemented at companies with in-the-know information technology (IT) departments. As Torvalds told *Infoworld* magazine, "corporate IT managers notice someday, 'what is that box in the corner,' and [their employees] tell them that it's the departmental Web server that's been running for a year and a half, and by the way it's running Linux.... So Linux moves onto the unofficially approved list."

1998 is a big year for Linux, as several events catapult it into the technology spotlight. In September both Intel and Netscape make investments in Red Hat, a company that licenses Linux and traditional product support to go along with it. This move, particularly from a major corporation like Intel, goes a long way to make some corporations rethink their previous anti-free software bias. An International Data Corporation study reveals that shipments of the Linux operating system increase 212 percent in 1998: at the end of the year, there are between five and eight million Linux users worldwide.

Another, if slightly perverse, seal of approval comes from Microsoft in November 1998, when the so-called "Halloween Document" is leaked over the Internet. A two-part internal memo written by a Microsoft engineer, the Halloween Document provides a detailed competition analysis of the free software movement in general and Linux in particular, and speculates about various strategies Microsoft might pursue in order to combat the Linux threat. That Linux is perceived as a threat at all comes as a surprise to some—but not to Linux devotees, who have long viewed Microsoft as Enemy #1 of free software. More circumspect industry observers warn that seeing the world through "Linux v. Microsoft"–colored glasses could—much like the hype surrounding Java earlier in the decade—ultimately hinder Linux development.

In what may be the most significant event in Linux's move towards the mainstream, two competing free-software groups release Linux desktop software—both GNOME and the German-based K Desktop Environment Project offer graphical, point-and-click desktops akin to Microsoft's Windows, downloadable from the Internet. Both projects are also developing Linux-based applications, and they are not alone: Netscape Navigator and WordPerfect 8 are also available in Linux-compatible versions. And in the first weeks of 1999 a company called LinuxPPC unveils an operating system for Apple computers. Proponents hope these developments will help popularize Linux among nonexperts.

Driving all this activity is a passionate Linux community, who approach their operating system with something akin to religious devotion. Torvalds emerges as a Silicon Valley celebrity, even likened by *Salon* online magazine to Martin Luther, the sixteenth century religious reformer who insisted on the right of individuals to talk to God without papal intervention. Highlighting the difference between Linux programmers and the rest of the pack, a *Linuxbierwanderung* (Linux Beer Hike)—part conference, part pub crawl through Bavaria—is organized for August 1999.

1998 AMERICA ONLINE ANNOUNCES DEAL TO BUY NETSCAPE

In November America Online (AOL) announces plans to purchase Netscape Communications for $4.21 billion and an additional side deal with Sun Microsystems. Opinions about the impending merger of two Internet giants are, predictably, mixed—but it seems clear that for better or for worse, the landscape of cyberspace will be fundamentally altered.

One online service among many when it was launched in 1989, America Online moved to the front of the pack, first among online services, and then, in the mid-1990s, among ISPs. Despite technical setbacks that led to class-action suits in 1997 and a nagging reputation as a mediocre service for newcomers, AOL established a well-marketed and enormously profitable niche: in 1998 its aol.com portal is one of the four most frequently visited sites on the Internet.

Another of the top four sites is netscape.com, a portal site run by Netscape Communications. After an auspicious beginning in 1994 as the leading provider of Web browsers, Netscape saw its position gradually weakened by fierce competition from Microsoft. In order to stay competitive, in early 1998 Netscape announces that it will give the browser and its source code away for free and it establishes the Mozilla project—a small group of programmers coordinating an Internet-wide effort to improve the browser. Lacking revenue from the browser itself, Netscape repositions itself as a portal, dealing in advertising revenue and "eyeballs," the industry term for the number of users who are drawn to the site. Eyeballs require users, and no one has greater access to users than the ubiquitous AOL—thus the merger.

Although 1998 witnesses severe financial trouble at Netscape, the combined strengths of AOL's marketing abilities with Netscape's superior technology are expected to make a formidable online entity. Meanwhile, Sun Microsystems agrees to license Netscape technology for Sun business customers and to work with AOL to develop low-cost Internet appliances, simple devices for surfing the Net. The companies hope to sell them to

From the Hacker File

SOFTWARE PIRACY: WORTH WALKING THE PLANK?

Thanks to the Information Revolution, "intellectual property" has become the most contested area of law in the 1990s. Perhaps this explains why the computer industry has chosen "piracy"—a word historically designating robbery on the high seas—to describe their latest Internet-inspired anxiety.

Software piracy is the unauthorized duplication of copyrighted computer software; it has existed since there was software (e.g., Bill Gates' "software flap" in 1975). But the Internet has changed the nature of the game. In 1998 an industry-appointed policing group called the Software Publishers' Association (SPA) charged that more than $11 billion per year is lost due to illegal duplication of computer programs. To combat the problem the SPA has pursued offenders and collected $16 million in penalties.

Among the SPA's biggest targets are wares traders. In hacker-speak, "wares" (or "warez") are copies of pirated software passed from one individual to another. There are a number of ways to trade wares, but the most popular include unauthorized software rental, counterfeit software engineering, and downloading programs from the Internet or bulletin boards without publishers' permission.

Wares users commonly dispute the idea that duplicating is stealing. Wares trading doesn't take anything from anyone, they argue, it only makes software more ubiquitous. Critics of the SPA argue that its $11 billion figure is a guess-timate at best, and one based on the (incorrect) assumption that every illegal copy of software would have been purchased in a traditional manner.

One need not agree with either argument in order to see that the ephemeral nature of intellectual property, combined with the virtual arena of the Internet, will defy all traditional notions of ownership.

Perhaps this is why software piracy is not just the province of hackers. In "Yo Ho Ho and a Server of Warez," theorist David Tetzlaff argues that, contrary to the SPA's claims, only a small percentage of the industry's losses come from wares trading, which is generally a hobbyist, nonprofit affair. "Most piracy," Tetzlaff argues, "is more organized and entrepreneurial." He cites the common U.S. corporate practice of duplicating software onto employees' PCs without procuring licenses; as well as the Asian practice of selling unauthorized software copies openly, in supermarket-style stores, for a fraction of their original cost.

Although the SPA has long complained about foreign software piracy (claiming that, for example, more than 90 percent of software in China has been illegally procured), not everyone finds its arguments convincing. "It's long been one of the computer industry's best-kept secrets that not all piracy is bad," rebuts *PC Week* writer Michael Surkan. "I've heard of large (very large) companies uploading applications to pirate bulletin boards in third world countries to help gain market penetration."

Ultimately, the casual attitude adopted by most Americans toward piracy leads Tetzlaff to conclude: "The problem for the software industry is not just that there are a lot of pirates about, but a lot of people who, though they would never pirate a program themselves, don't see this act as any sort of big deal."

consumers who might want to use AOL to reach the Internet, but who have thus far resisted the $1500 PC purchase.

Announcement of the deal inspires an explosion of punditry on the pros and cons for AOL, Netscape, Microsoft, and the Internet as a whole. Insiders point to a perhaps unbridgeable culture gap between the highly corporate environment of Virginia-based AOL and the more freewheeling, California-based Netscape. However, AOL founder Steve Case moves quickly to assure Netscapers that their working environment will not be radically changed, promising that AOL will support the Mozilla project and that Netscape employees will still be allowed to bring their dogs to the office.

Software titan Microsoft actually welcomes the merger, because they view it as proof that they are not an irresistible monopoly, as is being argued in court by the Department of Justice. Microsoft claims that the AOL/Netscape deal demonstrates that there is plenty of competition in the software world and that a free market will take good care of consumers. But, in the words of Nathan Newman of the watchdog group NetAction, using Netscape's failure as an excuse for Microsoft's actions may be akin to "a dictatorial regime that shoots its opponents, then bills the victims' families for the cost of the bullets."

Meanwhile, Ralph Nader's Consumer Project on Technology vows to oppose the deal, arguing that it only serves to further limit consumer options in the online world. Other observers echo that concern, worrying that the Internet will now be divided between two monopolistic conglomerates (Microsoft and AOL). Others claim that the Net is far too broad-based and chaotic for anyone to keep it in a chokehold for long.

Future Trends

It has been a long journey: from Babbage's computer designs to the haze of banner ads and secure transactions; from "Mr. Watson, I need you" to cellular modems; from Hollerith's Tabulating Machine to Torvalds' Linux operating system. We have reached the point in this astonishing story where we stop looking through the window of history and start looking in the mirror.

The chapter that follows considers some of the trends that will have the most profound impact in the future of the Internet: the commercialization of this new medium, capacity issues, government regulation, privacy and encryption concerns, and the brave new world that will result from integrating the Internet with our day-to-day lives. The one common thread among all these issues is the position of the individual "inside" the Net. After all, nothing has made the computer revolution more accessible and more personal than the Internet.

The Need for Speed

It is unclear if instances of information-highway rage have been reported yet, but it is certain that many a computer has been turned off in frustration. The culprit? Bandwidth, or lack thereof. Think of bandwidth as the number of lanes on a highway. The more lanes, the more cars. As it stands now, the information highway is suffering from frequent lane restrictions. So much so that many well-respected industry pundits have proclaimed that all travel on it is doomed. The lust of Web designers for the latest in eye-catching animations and ear-blowing sound leads them to bog down their pages with every bandwidth-hogging applet possible. When the unfortunate 33.6K modem user stops by such a site, she'll wait several minutes before she can even be sure if this is the site she wanted to view in the first place. The combination of increased traffic and Web sites that look like the Las Vegas strip, plus all other competing applications on the Net, can make any user believe that Net traffic is quickly coming to a standstill.

While we wait for cable modems or digital subscriber lines to come to our neighborhoods, the parents of the Internet—academic think tanks, research institutions, and the government—are designing Internet2 (I2). I2 will use the same infrastructure as the existing network but by using advanced networking technologies, it will be many times faster and smarter. This advanced technology will be released to the public gradually, introducing more advanced networking schemes while maintaining the current Internet structure. An example of the "smarts" behind I2 will be its ability to distinguish between a casual e-mail and an urgent medical imaging file.

On the other side of the argument are those who believe that within the problem lies the solution: the very demand for speed will force someone, or many people, to find a way to offer it. Users will insist on greater bandwidth, forcing telephone companies, cable companies, and Internet providers to come up with ways to deliver. And indeed, after years of essentially empty promises, in 1998 cable and telephone companies finally began to expand their high-bandwidth (or "broadband") access, sometimes even at rates average users could afford.

How is the individual user driving the bandwidth issue? With purchasing power. A parallel can be found in cellular telephony. A few years ago a cell phone cost about $500 for the device, several dollars per minute traffic charge, and one could only use it within yelling distance of the transmission tower. Now, companies give them out for free, offering flat rates with CD-quality sound. Some "early adopters" (people who run rather than walk towards new technologies) are even abandoning their traditional service and going all-cellular, all the time. It seems likely that the same evolution will occur in the bandwidth arena. After all, just as the individual is frustrated by the bandwidth drought, so is the corporate world. Industry wants to reach you and be reached by you.

Money Makes the Web Go Around

The corporate world, after all, has a lot to sell. After some initial resistance, as the 1990s draw to a close Madison Avenue let loose its best and brightest straight to your browser screen.

Before this could happen, corporate America had to be convinced that online advertising works. After numerous studies proved beyond a reasonable doubt that online advertising increased brand-name recognition and—in some cases—actually resulted in increased sales, the rush was on. The next task was to find a way to charge for advertising on the Web. The two main methods are "eyeball counts" (the number of times that the ad will appear on a site's pages), and "click-through counts" (the number of users that click on the ad). There are pros and cons to each "objective" measurement, but the bottom line is that if you can claim to the advertiser that your Web site is visited by a large number of people, you're in business. That is, e-business.

If there were any doubts remaining about whether electronic commerce has a future, the 1998 holiday shopping season must have permanently silenced them. An estimated $3 billion changed hands online. This is music to the ears of e-commerce advocates, and will most certainly add to the explosion of e-commerce sites. Others are left with a sinking feeling—picturing empty shopping malls and online fraud horrors. And the government is scrambling to develop new laws, regulations, and taxes to tap the newfound wealth.

There are, of course, very serious implications of e-commerce to both the economy and society. For example, what will it do to the free market landscape? What about antitrust regulation? What will happen when the superstore idea is implemented online? Is the world ready for e-WalMart?

Some observers worry about the presence of megastores in a loosely unregulated environment. If XYZ giant online superstore is accused of monopolistic practices, it can just move its e-commerce server to a friendly island country and continue operations. Perhaps it will be barred from shipping goods to your country—but what if the goods are electronic? For example, many predict that legitimate music and videos will soon be available on the Net for purchase. Instead of buying the latest CD, you download it. Where would you download it from: the "local" friendly online mart for $15 or from the big-bad-island-store for $5?

As they argue over the more abstract e-commerce issues, pundits all agree that there is money to be made on the Net. A lot of money.

But "a lot of money" and "an unregulated, global media" are a volatile mix. The good news is that the Web is a true opportunity for commerce—the bad news is that it's also an opportunity to violate people's privacy in completely new and previously unthinkable ways. For example, as data-mining technologies (the collection and cross-referencing of huge demographic databases) continue to evolve along with increasingly sophisticated data-gathering methods (smarter and smarter cookies), your online personality could be made available for sale to the highest bidder.

There are those who claim that this is not as bad as it sounds. After all, if I am interested in mystery novels, I will want to know when the next one comes out. I certainly will not want to waste my time on information about the next romance novel—so everyone benefits. But, what if I am a member of an online diabetes support group? This could be of great interest to my insurance company. Of course, the government could legislate such data-gathering techniques, but since the Internet is a worldwide medium, one government's prohibition is another government's big chance. And what's to keep a multinational from establishing a Web site in Tunisia and carrying on exactly as they please? Today, nothing.

For the time being, fasten your seat belt and be sure to keep your wallet in an inside pocket. The information highway is not entirely paved yet, and not all toll booths give receipts.

Big Brother and Other Siblings

Few may remember the "party lines" of yesteryear's telephone system. Once upon a time, there weren't enough wires for everyone to have their own telephone number, so houses in these communities had a telephone with a common number. When it rang, everyone picked up. Then, everyone hung up except the person whom the call was directed to. Of course, it is rumored that not everyone always hung up . . . .

The Internet community is on a party line. Each day, innumerable packets of data crisscross the wire grid that's covering the planet. Some of those are for you, some of those are for me. And most of us sort of trusted each other not to eavesdrop. The problem remains: Someone is not hanging up.

Disguised in this simplistic explanation is an issue as big as the Internet itself— encryption. It touches on individual privacy, corporate security, and law enforcement. It is a computer science puzzle, a social science issue, and a criminal justice debate. But, when it is your credit card number that is stolen, it is 100 percent your problem. Meanwhile, many people assume their e-mail to be private. It is unthinkable that it may not be. Normal "snail mail" is private. Telephone conversations are private. Hence, e-mail is private. Surprise! It is not—at least not yet.

It is in this issue that the incredible dichotomy of the individual's role becomes apparent. In e-commerce, you vote with your credit card. In privacy issues, you get to watch while everybody else debates. Scientists debate the best encryption method, governments debate about legal access, and companies implement whichever encryption they feel is right. And beyond downloading your own copy of the undecipherable PGP encryption software, you the individual user cannot do anything about it.

What then, you might wonder, are your representatives doing about it? Quite a number of things, as the Internet was high on the Congressional agenda when they came back to work in 1999. Encryption is sure to top the legislative agenda, as lawmakers make a second attempt at getting the proencryption version of the Security and Freedom through Encryption (SAFE) bill through the House. Other online privacy legislation is expected, as well as antispam regulations and, predictably enough, a lot of debate about cybersmut.

In the name of decency, political expediency, or established law, governments around the world are attempting to control Internet content. In the United States recent attempts to censor content have failed, but legislative efforts continue. Meanwhile free speech advocates vow to fight such attempts to the bitter end. If you think that "decency" legislation will only affect pornographers, think again. Several years ago, for example, in an attempt to stamp out smut on America Online, the word "breast" was censored and the "breast cancer" forums became inaccessible. Since the Internet knows no political or cultural boundaries, these situations have cropped up everywhere. Freedom of expression, free speech, freedom to exchange ideas—all very individual rights—are at risk unless the challenges of regulating content on a worldwide basis are met successfully.

Your Coffee Is Ready, and By the Way, I Took Some Liberties with Your Portfolio

In the future, the Internet won't be limited to the computer in your living room. From Internet-accessible toasters to remote-controlled thermostats and intelligent agents, we've got you covered. Finally, the promise of technology realized. A sudden change of weather? Not a problem—the Internet-ready thermostat has been on top of the situation and your home is warm and cozy awaiting your return. Your car has been programmed with an alternate route, and on your way home a totally personalized version of today's news will be narrated for your listening pleasure. Nirvana? Or technology-induced stupor?

Internet-ready appliances are just one more way that cyberspace is touching our lives. These gadgets are fairly single-minded in purpose—check the weather, figure the best way home, etc. Their proliferation is inevitable and resistance is futile—it is like trying to get a car without some special package added on. Like it or not, your next television will likely have an Internet component. So, it is not a question of "if," it is a question of "when."

On the other hand, the same technology that controls your physical comfort is available for your intellectual pleasure. Through the use of ever-improving intelligent agents, you can create a cyberpersonality that reflects all your wants, preferences, desires, and aversions and send it to "go fetch" everything from the latest music that you might like, to a new restaurant that you should try, to your own version of the news. A personal cyberassistant, there at your beck and call. No need to waste time reading reviews, no need to actually try something that you might not like, and certainly no need for bad news. Even the commercials that you'll be watching will be custom-tailored to your taste.

These descriptions are not from a science fiction novel. These technologies are available—to varying degrees—right now. The debate surrounding their use ranges from whispers to cries about lost individuality. Often forgotten in all the philosophical debate is the fact that users do have the final word. It is ultimately up to each and every individual user to subscribe, use, and support all these technologies. The laws of the marketplace are unforgiving—if a product does not sell, it dies.

Entire industries have sprung up around the corporate desire to predict what individual users will take to their hearts and what they will reject. Their crystal balls are always somewhat cloudy, however, and (we must confess) so is ours. This final chapter details some of the important issues and trends being discussed in legislative chambers, board rooms, chat rooms, and dining rooms. But as these pages are being typeset, we can see the waves of change continue to sweep the Internet. And even as the book rolls off the press . . . someone, somewhere, just had another new and incredible idea . . . .

ADVERTISING GETS PERSONAL

At the end of 1998 Web advertising is a staple of Internet culture and provides many sites with their only source of income. Advertising banners beckon "Click Here!" at the top of most commercial Web pages, inviting consumers to investigate a deal, a product, or maybe just a Web site offering information and resources. Despite the fact that the Internet started out as an entirely noncommercial tool, there has been minimal resistance to the proliferation of Web advertising. Debate is focusing instead on the level of personalization available to Web advertisers: how much demographic information should be collected, and what should be done with it?

Market analysts predict that revenues from Web advertising will continue to grow. That growth is assured, they say, because Web advertising is effective—or at least advertisers believe that it is. And indeed, a study on the effectiveness of online advertising, completed in 1997 by market researcher *Mbinteractive*, presented evidence that online advertising banners successfully create awareness of brand names and lead to the sale of products.

But retailers want Web advertisements to do more than just serve as randomly targeted virtual billboards. They argue that everyone wins if the advertising banners that appear on a viewer's screen have been individually selected to reflect the potential interests of that viewer. The technology to make this happen has begun to be implemented, although not to the extent of its promised potential. One of the major goals of Web advertisers is to create an effective system whereby particular ads are presented to viewers in as personal a fashion as possible.

From the beginning of the Web, it has been possible for sites to gather basic information about their visitors, including how many times a day a site is viewed, which domains visitors come from, and which Web browsers the visitors use. But that doesn't tell anything personal about the visitors. Since that time, two main approaches to giving online ads a personal touch have been instituted. In one approach, the customization occurs anew with every visit, as the site tailors ads to fit the behavior of a particular visitor. For instance, some search-engine sites respond to a user's search request by posting ad banners that reflect (if possible) the words or phrase that the user is searching for. This approach is not exactly personal, because the site doesn't know who the user is.

The second approach actually identifies individual users, and as such, it is the hub of some controversy centering around online privacy. The tool in this approach is called a "cookie." Cookies—small packages of data containing identifying tags—can be created by sites and inserted into a user's browser files. All a cookie does is sit there until the user visits the site again; then the site reads the cookie and recognizes the user by the tags. Cookies offer a way to track a visitor's behavior within a site and to offer advertising that might fit the interests of the individual visitor. Book- and music-seller Amazon.com uses cookies to make "Personal Recommendations" to a previous visitor as soon as he or she arrives at Amazon's site (when the visitor orders a book from Amazon, the order adds content information to the user's cookie).

A cookie can be created without a user providing any information, but some sites create detailed cookies by requesting users to answer questions about themselves, such as age, sex, zip code, profession, and interests. The site is required to include a statement of how it will use the information gathered.

A debate has rolled through the Web community about whether cookies violate people's online privacy, but much of the controversy was resolved when it became clear that many critics' objections were based on misconceptions about cookies. Cookies can only store information that is provided by the user or the site, cookies can't touch other files on the user's hard drive, and cookies can't spread their contents across the Web to other sites. Still, some Web users view cookies as objectionable, and the makers of Web browsers have responded by installing a feature that allow users to choose among three options: to allow cookies, to disallow cookies, or to notify the user before a cookie is created.

Despite the progress toward making online advertising a personal experience, many Web sites concede that the mechanisms they have instituted still fall short of their goals. The reason cited is usually that the amount of data captured from site visitors is so massive that the site doesn't have the time, money, know-how, or tools to do anything useful with it. Perhaps the next step in Web advertising will be to devise more powerful and effective data-mining software.

BANDWIDTH: STRETCHING THE DIGITAL PIPES

Bandwidth is a measure of the rate at which a telecommunication system can transmit information; larger bandwidths can transmit more data in a smaller amount of time. As digital technology advances, engineers are devising applications that require greater and greater bandwidth for transmission via wire or cable. Many observers foresee that there will be a demand for these applications—which include three-dimensional graphics, video, audio, and interactive multimedia—among consumers and in the business world.

Some experts predict that the bandwidth available for Internet transmissions will very quickly stretch to greater capacity in the near future, outstripping the abilities of most personal computers. Others imagine that the applications will be available before transmission lines have been upgraded, that people will demand and use the applications, and that this will lead to a unbearably slow Internet with routine traffic jams and system crashes.

Industry pundit Bob Metcalfe—inventor of the local area network (LAN) protocol, Ethernet—is among the most vocal proponents of the latter scenario. During the mid-1990s, he regularly wrote and spoke about the pokey speed of the Internet and predicted major crashes. To prove his point, he often noted the prominent placement of the "stop" button on Web browsers, because frustrated users frequently need it when the Internet slows to a virtual standstill. Metcalfe expects the situation to worsen as bandwidth-hogging applications become more widely used—or even as the amount of low-bandwidth e-mail continues to increase. It is estimated in the late 1990s that far more e-mail messages are sent every day than the number of letters delivered by postal services. Estimates also indicate that the number of Internet users is increasing by 100 million per year.

One of Metcalfe's proposed solutions is what he has dubbed Pay-As-We-Go Internet™. He and other advocates think that the current system of flat-rate Internet access cannot survive the foreseen glut of high-bandwidth applications. Greater bandwidths, they say, will cost Internet service providers (ISPs) more money, and ISPs will need to pass the costs on to their customers. People who rarely use the Internet but still want access will be unwilling to pay high flat-rate fees. And heavy users, especially heavy users of high-bandwidth applications, will suck profit right out of the ISPs' pockets. Metcalfe firmly believes that Internet users will be willing to support a metered system, whereby they are billed based on how much time and bandwidth they consume (contrary to that belief, many polls indicate people prefer continued flat-rate fees).

In another camp, experts argue that bandwidth costs are going to plummet faster than computer hardware costs. An often mentioned piece of popular wisdom amongst the computer industry is Moore's Law, named in honor of Intel Corp.-cofounder Gordon Moore: computing power will increase at a constant rate, doubling itself every eighteen to twenty-four months. According to some observers, bandwidth is about to do the same dance, but much more rapidly. This will be due to improved cabling technology and increased competition among telecommunications providers. The industry of fiber-optic cables (cables made of thin fibers of glass that carry light signals rather than electrical pulses) is continually advancing, enabling greater bandwidths to be transmitted for less cost. And as the telecommunications giants are decentralized, many small providers are entering into the competition by offering cheaper long-distance telephone service. Some foresee that these cheaper rates will inevitably be applied to all telecommunications services, including Internet access.

But other technologies may not be able to keep up with the readily available increases in bandwidth. The equipment that routes and switches the signals that are downloaded onto a user's personal computer is lethargic compared to the transmission potential of the applications. And despite the recent advances in central processor unit (CPU) speeds, the CPU remains input-output bound. In other words, no matter how fast a CPU is, it still has to wait for the modem to download, for the disk to access, and so on. Significant advances in peripheral architecture are in the wings (usb, firewire, etc.) but it remains to be seen how widely they will be adopted and how fast they will disseminate in the marketplace.

Most experts agree that a bandwidth boom will arrive, driven by technologies like cable modems, which provide high-speed access through cable television lines, and DSL (digital subscriber line) services, which provide the access through standard telephone wires. How long it will take, how much it will cost, and the effects it will have on the shape of computing and multimedia applications remain to be seen.

E-COMMERCE TAKES OFF

For consumers, electronic commerce (e-commerce) is changing the face of the shopping experience. E-commerce is also changing retailers' internal strategies and their competitive practices. Although all the participants seem to come out winners in the short term—customers are finding great

At their Seattle, Washington warehouse, employees of Amazon.com work overtime to fill the thousands of orders that poured into the Web site during the 1998 Christmas shopping season (AP / Wide World Photos).

deals, and online retailers are eliminating the costs of the storefront scenario—opinions about the future effects of e-commerce are varied.

The *Financial Times* reported a 230 percent rise in online shopping for the 1998 Christmas season: there seems little doubt that e-commerce is here to stay. For wired consumers, e-commerce offers a convenient way to make purchases, as long as consumers know exactly what they want to buy. A myriad of goods and services, as well as the ability to instantly investigate the offerings and prices of numerous retailers, are available online. With e-commerce, customers don't have to make a trip to the store only to find that the store nearby is out of stock. And they don't have to worry that their reluctance to visit all the retailers in their area has led them to overlook the best deal.

By the end of 1998 online prices of some products, such as books, videos, music, electronic devices, and computer hardware had reached levels far below prices found in traditional markets. In some cases low prices reflect the ability of retailers to pass on to customers the savings of cutting clerical labor. For other retailers real savings are still a few years off, but the promise of profit has enticed them to go online now at a (hopefully) recoverable loss.

Where is e-commerce heading? Some observers think online buying will place unprecedented power in the hands of the consumer. Armed with a quick way to learn the going price of a particular item at locations all across the country, consumers have a strong platform from which to demand good deals in their local area.

Consumer power may drive prices down, but many experts worry that such low prices may not be sustainable. Some price schemes are so low that it's impossible for small retailers to make a profit, while larger online sellers with well established names have broad customer bases that allow them to maintain low prices. This suggests that big businesses might need to make very little effort to squeeze out the moderate competition.

Indeed, economic studies have warned of the ripe potential for antitrust situations to emerge from e-commerce. The studies simulate and analyze scenarios in which a certain good is sold only through online channels (a scenario some experts think is likely to occur in the future with products that can be acquired via download, such as music and video). The online retailers of a particular good have little other than price over which to compete, since the things that distinguish traditional retailers—location, physical atmosphere, in-person customer service—are absent in the virtual outlet. A price war ensues, and in the end the strongest retailer remains standing while all the others lie in a heap at its feet. Such analyses lead some observers to wonder whether new antitrust laws are going to have to be drawn up to deal with e-commerce.

Most experts agree that most goods will continue to be available both online and in traditional settings, which means that there will be competition between the virtual and traditional commercial sectors. One benefit to consumers of this competition is the likelihood that both sectors will try to maintain stellar customer service. Vying for customers' attention, traditional merchants will emphasize their ability to provide in-person contact. And online retailers will attempt to make up for their inability to service consumers in person by offering the most sensitive customer responses they can muster.

Those who criticize the antisocial nature of the electronic age worry that e-commerce—especially if it eventually dominates commercial transactions—will strengthen a growing trend for people to stay at home, isolated from others. But many sociologists think that e-commerce will never overshadow traditional retailing, because consumers will never lose their desire for the social, hands-on experience of shopping in real stores.

Encryption Debate Continues

As it is challenged in the courts, tinkered with by Congress, and debated on the world stage, encryption legislation continues to galvanize public opinion on the Net. Those who advocate strong encryption herald it as the protector of individual rights in a digital age. Those opposed point out that encryption in the wrong hands is a threat to national security.

Urged on by national security advocates and the success of 1993's Escrowed Encryption Initiative (EEI), the U.S. Congress spent 1997 debating HR 695, the SAFE (Security and Freedom through Encryption) bill. As introduced by Representative Robert Goodlatte (R-Virginia), SAFE was an attempt to liberalize U.S. encryption policy, both in the areas of export restrictions and of key recovery systems. Amazingly, by the time SAFE made it out of committee, its intentions had been completely reversed. For example, SAFE (or, as it became known on the Net, "unSAFE"), made it a crime to use encryption in furtherance of any criminal offense. Though inoffensive enough on its surface, this "crypto-in-a-crime" punishment was likened by the Electronic Frontier Foundation to "making it an extra crime to speak English or to wear shoes during the commission of a crime." Critics argued that the bill's real purpose was buried deeper, in language that would allow law enforcement officers access to encrypted messages without notification to the owners of the information. The battle is far from over: it is expected that Goodlatte and Rep. Zoe Lofgren (D-California) will reintroduce the original version of SAFE to the House in 1999.

During the SAFE debates the Clinton Administration circulated legislation of its own. The Secure Public Networks (SPN) bill would direct the President to negotiate with foreign countries for access to their encryption keys. It would also require third-parties holding decryption keys to surrender them prior to judicial approval and without notice to the encryption user. The SPN bill is still in committee; and is opposed by the Electronic Frontier Foundation and other Internet civil liberties groups.

Meanwhile, civil libertarians, still frustrated with existing encryption restrictions, have been challenging current legislation in court. In *Bernstein v. U.S. Department of State*, a Ph.D. student has sued for the right to post an encryption program he wrote to a Usenet group for discussion. Originally, the student was told he would need an arms dealer license before he could post his encryption algorithm. Though the courts have granted an injunction to the student (forbidding the government from prosecuting him), the government has appealed the case.

While U.S. encryption policies are being tweaked and challenged domestically, they have been fiercely debated abroad. The U.S. government has long lobbied foreign powers to adopt compatible encryption standards. But with the exception of France and Russia, the rest of Europe seems to be leaning away from the criminalization of nonregulation encryption. In 1997 the European Commission issued a report finding key escrow systems to be ineffective and calling for unified Europe-wide laws on encryption. Nevertheless, in December of 1998, the United States Department of Commerce Under-Secretary convinced thirty-three member countries of the Wassenaar Arrangement to impose export restrictions on mass-market cryptography products.

Embedded Systems and the Internet

Onstage at the 1999 Consumer Electronics Show, Cisco Systems CEO John Chambers told the audience that in the future, "Everything will be connected, and I mean literally everything . . . . Not just electronic devices, but everything down to your piano. We'll have as many as four or five Internet devices on our bodies." To prove his point, he demonstrated a Web-controlled fireplace, window blinds, and, as he promised, a piano—all controlled by embedded systems.

Embedded systems are the applications that fuel some of the microprocessors that play a hidden but crucial role in our everyday lives. These are the tiny, quick, and smart microprocessors that live inside printers, answering machines, elevators, cars, cash machines, refrigerators, thermostats, wristwatches, and even toasters. Embedded systems are on the cutting edge of consumer electronics, poised to revolutionize various technologies by making them "smarter." A branch of the embedded-systems industry wants to see some of this newly smart equipment hooked up to the Internet, so that networking capabilities become a ubiquitous feature of modern machines.

Some experts estimate that embedded systems technology, which in 1998 is a $250 million industry, will be worth more than $2 billion within three years. Predictions are based on the commercial promise of smart devices. According to market researchers, consumers love electronic equipment that can do "smart" things like: transmit instructions to other devices wirelessly via infrared signals; be programmed to operate automatically; and connect to super-technologies, such as satellites, to bring remote power into their own hands.

An embedded system consists of two components: a compact, ultrareliable operating system that controls the microprocessor inside a device, and the suite of applications that runs on the operating system. Various corporations are racing to develop embedded systems for Internet-enabled devices, which include network computers (also called Internet appliances or thin clients), Internet phones, and traditional machines embedded with Internet connections—such as printers, various medical devices, and thermostats.

The thermostat in a family home is an example of a theoretical Internet-enabled appliance of the future. The thermostat would be embedded with a smart microprocessor that supports an Internet server connection, a Web browser (and screen) for viewing Web information, software and graphics for programming and displays, and a protocol for communicating with the Internet. Users would be able to program the thermostat to gather information from the Web, such as local weather forecasts, to use in regulating the temperature of the house. In addition, users would be able to contact the thermostat remotely, via the Web, to instruct it to alter its settings.

Internet-enabled appliances might also become a staple of the future version of the home entertainment center, the "digital data center." A multimedia set of living-room devices might include, for example, a digital television that doubles as a personal computer, Web browser, and e-mail host; a stereo that can download tunes off of the Internet; and a video camera that can record the kids' pillow fight, send the video images directly onto the Web, and install them on the family's home page.

Cisco, Wind River Systems, Sun Microsystems, Integrated Systems, Microware Systems, and QNX Software Systems are among the prominent

DISABILITY AND THE NET

A quadriplegic student uses an eye-scanner device to type out an invitation to a party. Over the Internet, her blind friend "reads" it with his ears. He forwards it to another friend, who is deaf; she in turn "types in" a phone call, asking what she can bring to the party.

Today communications accessibility isn't just a nice idea, it's the law: specifically, Section 255 of the 1996 Telecommunications Act. At thirty-seven million strong, disabled people—those functioning with impaired vision, hearing, mobility or cognition—now comprise the largest minority group in the United States. Due to the fact that America's population is growing older (one in two people over age 65 is disabled) this number will certainly rise in the future.

Nevertheless, technical "improvements" in telecommunications often forget the needs of disabled users. When phone companies updated telephone receiver designs in the 1980's, for example, they ignored a significant group of people who had retrofitted older receivers (which leaked magnetic signals) to work with hearing aids. This spurred a decade-long effort to achieve hearing aid compatibility in all telephones.

As it was originally conceptualized, the Net was more accessible to the blind than the telephone was for the deaf. Although it wasn't originally planned, text messaging found its way to the design of the Internet. Why? Because a lead ARPAnet engineer used a "text telephone" system called TTY to communicate with his deaf wife, and he appreciated its value. Text interface can be read out loud for blind computer users through a machine called a text reader.

Currently, however, the drive is on to make Web sites look more and more like television screens, full of big images, movie clips and audio files. Without corresponding key-based navigation for those who can't click a mouse, and text-based descriptions for those who can't see or hear, these "improvements" are a step backward for many. As one blind student puts it, "What's a window for you can be a locked door for me."

To deal with the increasing exclusion of the blind from the Web, the World Wide Web Consortium (W3) takes pains to remind its members that universal design—the practice of making telecommunications products for broadest possible audience—is no mere euphemism. Many inventions that began as tools for a small minority became so useful that they were adopted by the public at large. Vibrating pagers, elevator bells, and voice activation are a few examples of technologies used by populations far broader than their original target groups.

As the Net becomes more of a full-body experience, it's important to remember to design with multiple bodies in mind. At this writing, for example, scientists are experimenting with a virtual reality modeling language (VRML) called "haptic VRML," where space is "felt" with a joystick. Today, the technology is used by blind Netizens seeking a non-visual way to experience virtual space. But like the telephone (a byproduct of research into deafness) and the cassette tape (conceptualized as a "talking book" for the blind) experts predict that haptic VRML will soon be adapted by so-called "able" bodies, particularly industrial engineers in fields like mining, where low-vision conditions prevail.

Beyond the Net

developers of embedded systems. In December 1998 Microsoft held a "soft" or low-publicity launch of AutoPC, a car stereo with a Windows-based operating system, featuring voice recognition, wireless messaging, and a global positioning system (GPS). The several-thousand-dollar price tag is sure to limit AutoPC's popularity for a time—but that price is just as sure to drop in the coming years.

The world envisioned by embedded-systems engineers and executives is one in which the long fingers of the global Internet stretch and reach into every conceivable aspect of the modern person's life. With the fast pace of technological progress, that future may be right around the corner.

Extranets: Good for Business But Bad for the Net?

At the end of 1998 companies worldwide are implementing "extranets," which link businesses to their customers and to other businesses via secure lines across the Internet. Extranets are hailed as revolutionary because they link the information and people involved in business trans-actions in ways and at speeds never before encountered in the corporate world. Although extranets appear to be saving companies time and money, industry experts are concerned about the security issues involved and about how widespread extranet use might damage the public-access element of the Internet.

As the Internet grew to allow commercial traffic through the early 1990s, corporations began to use Internet technology to create internal networks called "intranets." Traffic within an intranet travels along the same telecommunications lines and via the same protocols (TCP/IP) as other Internet traffic, but it passes only among employees of a single company. Intranets have become important features of many businesses, particularly very large businesses and businesses with remotely located subsidiaries.

As the communications opportunities of the Internet became clear to commercial enterprises, they began to build what industry pundit Bob Metcalfe called extranets. Extranets open corporate intranets up to a larger pool of users—not to the whole public, but to parties associated with a company's activities, such as customers and business partners.

The great advantages of extranets is that they close the communication gap among the various participants involved in corporate transactions.

For instance, an automobile manufacturer's extranet might enable its engineers to have direct, electronic access to information provided by dealerships regarding feedback from car buyers. This, say proponents, has the potential to shorten significantly the time it takes a product or improvement to come to market. Or, an extranet might link numerous corporations with similar products and goals, for the purpose of sharing databases filled with consumer information, marketing strategies, and distribution resources.

The traffic on an extranet is often comprised of sensitive or confidential material. Corporations thus have to keep close tabs on who has permission to access the extranet. And since extranets use the same lines and transfer protocols as the rest of the Internet—to which the public has access—security is one of the major issues facing the continued development of extranets.

Extranets require several strong measures of security. Firewalls—virtual gateways that monitor information traveling into and out of an extranet— make sure that only authorized transmissions take place. Encryption and password technologies used within an extranet system must be reliable and thoroughly implemented. In many cases, the security requirements of extranets mean that corporations have to hire a whole new department of information technology employees to operate the network.

This requirement creates concern among some workers, who foresee extranet technology making their jobs obsolete, as executives decide to commit salaries to electronic security departments. Extranets have the potential to do much of the work, for example, of customer service and information management representatives. Indeed, observers have pointed out that some employees might view extranets as serious threats to maintaining human power over information and data. Some authorities are concerned about whether intangible but important elements of business transactions may be lost if networking takes the place of all human contact between sellers and buyers, or even between employees of a single company.

Still other experts imagine that extranets will change the face not only of business, but also of the Internet itself. Existing now as a publicly accessible network of information, the Internet might be partitioned into smaller and smaller subsections as extranets become ubiquitous and as more and more Internet traffic becomes commercial, private, and confidential.

GOVERNMENT REGULATION

As the newest mass medium, the Internet has attracted the regulatory eye of the federal and state governments, and fiery debates continue to rage concerning how large a hand government should play in regulating the Internet. In the late 1990s censorship and taxes were two major ongoing issues associated with government regulation of the Internet.

Censorship

The most contentious issue related to censorship centers around "indecent" online material, such as pornography. In 1997 the Supreme Court of the United States deemed the Communications Decency Act (CDA)— which would have outlawed the transmission of all "indecent" sexually explicit material on the Internet—as unconstitutional, because its wording was too vague and because it would have violated the free-speech rights of adults. Advocates of free speech argue that the best way to protect children is to place responsibility in the hands of parents and school authorities, who can utilize software for blocking objectionable material. Some members of the legislature maintain, however, that the ready accessibility of the Internet—at public libraries, for example—makes it necessary for the government to extend to the online world the laws that protect children from indecent material. Furthermore, they argue, parents should not be obligated to install blocking tools to make sure their children can't view material that is unlawful for them to buy in a store.

Another attempt to regulate online material was temporarily shut down in November 1998. A district court in Philadelphia ordered a restraint on enforcing the Child Online Protection Act (COPA), signed by President Clinton in October. COPA would require Web sites that contain material considered "harmful to minors" to install measures for verifying the legal age of viewers. Opponents of the bill say that it is overly broad and would end up applying not only to pornographic sites but also to a host of others, such as discussions of safe sex, medical information, and sales of books about sexuality. They argue that the bill would violate adults' guarantee of free speech, inhibit adults from taking advantage of online resources, and curb electronic commerce. In February 1999 a federal judge agreed, and as of this writing it looks as though COPA will go the way of the CDA.

Those who support bills like COPA believe that because the Internet represents a new medium, new laws are needed to cover it. But legal scholars have argued that the existing tenets of the First Amendment (free-speech guarantees) are sufficient to apply to the Internet. The courts will ultimately decide, and experts say it could go either way. There are precedents, like the 1997 ruling that the CDA was unconstitutional, that suggest the government's attempts to regulate online content are doomed. On the other hand, precedents have also been set in television-related cases in which courts have decided that new media do require regulation via new laws.

Taxes

As online services and electronic commerce gained momentum during the 1990s, taxation rarely reared its head as a concern among service providers, buyers, sellers, and even most legislators. Only a handful of states instituted online taxes.

In 1998 the federal government began to take notice, and a bill was drafted to prohibit for three years (until investigations could determine the appropriate measures to take) political entities from imposing taxes on Internet services or commercial transactions that take place over the Internet. The bill is called the Internet Tax Freedom Act.

Since citizens in the United States tend to be against taxes in general, there is little opposition to the Internet Tax Freedom Act. It is seen as a blessing for electronic commerce, as people will be likely to purchase a product via the Internet if it is possible to evade sales tax by doing so. But some opponents argue that outlawing all taxation of Internet transactions could create problems in the near future. Considering that Internet access is cheap, fast, and readily available, it seems reasonable to believe that any store could install Internet accounts at registers and perform the actual sale of merchandise—the transfer of money from the consumer to the retailer—on the Internet. Every sale would be exempt from taxation. It is plausible that electronic commerce could replace taxable commerce almost entirely. That would leave a small tax bucket to dig into for public needs.

In October 1998 the Internet Tax Freedom Act was received by Congress with a modification to take care of the potential state-tax problem. The bill now includes an exception that individual states may draft laws to collect taxes on electronic commerce within the state.

As electronic commerce is expected to skyrocket in the future, some experts predict that government regulation via taxation will become an increasingly important issue. At the end of three years, for example, the federal government may have become discontent having no control over taxation of Internet services and transactions. And it is unlikely that states will be willing to give up their control. Consumers, on the other hand, are likely to resist all attempts to exact Internet taxes.

INTELLIGENT AGENTS

Intelligent agents are programs that use "human" characteristics, such as initiative and the ability to draw conclusions, in order to perform tasks independent of their users. Depending on one's perspective, these agents are the beginning of a revolution or the beginning of the end of online privacy.

The algorithms that drive intelligent agents were inspired by research in artificial intelligence (AI). Traditionally, AI studies focused on the programming of high-level reasoning. More recent experiments in AI have focused on "artificial life"—robots that *learn* to perform tasks, rather than being preprogrammed. But unlike robots, intelligent agents reside within computers and networks. They recognize patterns of use and then offer users the ability to automate tasks that they would have done manually. For example, one primitive agent is the e-mail filter: users can instruct the agent that e-mail with a particular subject heading should automatically be placed in a particular folder.

The current media darling of intelligent agents is Firefly Networks, a company cofounded by MIT Media Labs professor Pattie Maes. Users who log on to Bignote, Firefly's music site, are asked to rate a series of musicians or bands on a scale of one to seven. Firefly matches these ratings with those of other users who gave similar answers and then recommends other musical artists based on what the other users also like. As Maes explains, "If you tell the system . . . [what] you like and dislike, and everybody else does the same thing, then the system can identify who your taste-mates are." The technology, called collaborative filtering software, comes in a variety of formats—for example, a site called Boston Eats employs Firefly technology to find users' favorite restaurants and make recommendations based on the preferences of others whose tastes seem to correspond.

The use of intelligent agents on the Internet exploded in the late 1990s, as corporations hoped that the personalization of the online experience would develop brand loyalty. If a user has already invested time in sharing book preferences with Amazon.com, the theory goes, then she is more

PATTIE MAES

Biography

One of *Newsweek*'s "100 People to Watch in 2000," Dr. Pattie Maes was born in Belgium in 1961. She earned a bachelor's degree in computer science at Vrije Universiteit Brussels in 1983, and stayed on to complete her doctorate in the same field four years later. Rodney Brooks, a researcher at MIT Artificial Intelligence Labs, heard Maes speak in 1987 and invited her to join him and AI visionary Marvin Minsky at MIT for a few months. An invitation to visit soon became an invitation to stay, and Maes accepted a professorship that year.

Brooks and Minsky were developing the notion of artificial life, a then revolutionary concept in AI. Small robots, called "animats," were developed to learn basic tasks through trial and error. One of Maes's first projects at the lab, for example, involved "teaching" a six-legged animat to walk.

Frustrated by the physical limitations of robot-making, in 1990 Maes moved to the MIT Media Lab to explore the notion of "intelligence augmentation"—using computers to extend human intelligence, rather than recreating human intelligence in computers. It wasn't necessary, Maes realized, for computers to be independently intelligent, if software could be programmed to learn from users.

Maes soon became a leader in the burgeoning field of intelligent agents. One of her agents, called Maxims, was a sophisticated e-mail trafficker. It could not only prioritize messages but also contact other Maxims agents on the network and seek "advice" on what to do with a particular message. Maxims and software like it are called "collaborative agents" because they not only learn but work with other agents and proactively gather information.

Maes cofounded Agents, Inc. (later renamed Firefly Network), a company dedicated to developing and marketing agents. Firefly was anointed the "next big thing" by the U.S. media, and Maes found herself in the middle of a publicity onslaught, even branded "download diva" by *People* magazine. As the unofficial spokesperson of software agents, Maes is often called upon to defend the technology from those who see in agents a new form of online surveillance.

Maes rejects the notion that proactive agents are a tool of Big Brother. "Why shouldn't my Web browser track what pages I look at and at least make some suggestions for other stuff I may want to check out?" she asked Jaron Lanier in their 1996 debate. "Even if only 25 percent of those suggestions turn out to be good ones, it is a very useful thing to have."

This commitment utility—to extending the abilities and improving the lives of technology users—is Maes' primary motivator. She envisions a "knowledge marketplace" in which someone seeking information on a topic could be almost instantaneously connected to an expert, all through the use of intelligent agents. But best of all would be an agent that could keep track of the milk in her refrigerator. "I have a two-year-old who drinks a lot of milk," she explains, "so it's one of the concerns I have to deal with."

likely to shop at Amazon again. Intelligent agents are an advertiser's dream, as the data gathered can be used to instantaneously tailor online ads to the perceived tastes of the user. As Salman Malik, a vice president at Firefly, told *The New York Times* in 1996, "We can find women living in urban areas who are between the ages of X and X and who like Martha Stewart."

Proponents of intelligent agents contend that we have only seen the beginning of what the technology can do. Agents are being programmed to buy and sell stocks automatically, to scan online chat groups and make recommendations, to search the Web for the best deal on a car. One agent in development at MIT Media Labs, called Yenta, would perform matchmaking services. In the September 1995 issue of *Scientific American*, Maes claimed that "agents will bring about a social revolution: almost anyone will have access to the kind of support staff that today is the mark of a few privileged people."

Intelligent agents "learn" about users by monitoring their activities, and for many observers, therein lies the rub. Scholar Sherri Turkle remarks, "It's not the advertising per se that bothers people, it's the idea that there is an agent tracking you, and keeping a record . . . . There's this digital alter ego of you that you didn't want and didn't create." Maes herself has been accused of naivete for presuming that these digital alter egos will never be used for nefarious purposes. Furthermore, because agents depend on previous online experiences in order to make further recommendations, some observers point to a discomforting circularity: in the words of Internet analyst John Robb, "All of a sudden, your history is your future."

In a 1996 online debate between Maes and virtual-reality pioneer Jaron Lanier, Lanier expressed uneasiness with the anthropomorphizing of software agents, arguing that "a hierarchy of servants doesn't make you more powerful, just more insular." He also worried that users could cede their choices to what is, ultimately, nothing but an algorithm: "Imagine living your life so that a moron could understand your tastes."

This discomfort with agent technology—foisted on an online population already concerned with privacy—may explain the fact that although software agent start-up companies proliferated in the late 1990s, none of them have so far proven to be major money-makers. However, the 1998 purchase of Firefly Network by Microsoft would seem to indicate that agents are not going away any time soon.

INTERNET2, THE NETWORK OF TOMORROW

The world of computer networking evolves quickly. While the public's embrace of the Internet is only half a decade old, a new generation of Internet computing has already begun to unfold. This new generation, complete with rapidly advancing technologies that promise to challenge even modern distinctions between science fiction and reality, is being led by a project called Internet2 (I2). The project is a collaboration among universities, government agencies, and corporations to create a high-speed Internet and to implement advanced networking applications for research and education.

The main motivation for devising a new network infrastructure is the great volume of Internet traffic which now clogs lines and slows transmission. Like the planned I2, the first Internet was designed largely to facilitate and bolster research efforts. But now that networked research resources are bogged down by having to share the Net with copious amounts of e-mail, academicians and others want a high-speed passing lane for their research activities.

Conceived in 1996 I2 was well on its way by the end of 1998. I2 constitutes an unusual situation in the Internet community, in the sense that there is little controversy surrounding it. No one (at least no one vocal) doubts that the project will survive and deliver on its promise of, for instance, a network that transmits 100 times faster than the current Internet. However, there does appear to be one popular misconception about I2, that its physical architecture will consist of brand new wiring. In fact, I2 is planned to operate within networks that already exist among universities and other federally funded organizations—the old networks will just be upgraded.

There are numerous advanced applications planned for I2, including some that are already being tested or implemented. Networked virtual-reality programs might allow several researchers sitting in different locations to meet online, see and hear each other, pass documents back and forth, and all the while maintain the collaborative feeling of actually being in the same room together. Massive online audio, video, and print libraries may bring any work of music, art, or literature to a student's fingertips in sharp definition—including works that are hard to find or out of production. And advanced networked modeling applications are expected to revolutionize cooperative efforts among scientists at remote institutions.

Some organizations consider data mining, a process whereby enormous databases in remote locations are combined and analyzed, to be one of the most promising potential I2 applications. Studies of cross-population medical phenomena, for example, could benefit from the efficiency of using I2 to gather disparate chunks of data together into a single unit.

A few critical voices have been heard to complain about the government's involvement in I2. The original Internet, although created through government funding and initiative, has developed a firm commercial foundation. Some observers note that it may spell trouble to bring federal involvement back into what has become a commercial enterprise. I2 and its applications are intended to enter the public commercial sector after a few years. Critics claim that developers of I2 technology might have proprietary rights over something that the government helped them create, which makes it seem like the government, by funding I2, is assisting the developers in gaining a competitive advantage.

But others argue that Internet2, and probably other future Internet developments, are crucial endeavors for the progress of networking technology—technology that is intended to be for the benefit of everyone.

MICROSOFT'S FUTURE

In October 1998 the software giant Microsoft Corporation went on trial, accused by the United States Department of Justice of using its domination of the operating-system market to wield anticompetitive schemes aimed at crushing its competition. The trial promises to be among the most significant events in the short history of the digital era, perhaps setting legal precedents for all businesses involved in the expanding computer industry. As millions of observers follow reports of the proceedings, predictions of the outcome change with every new turn of events.

Some industry pundits are confident that the Department of Justice (DOJ) will win and that the trial spells the beginning of the end for Microsoft. At one extreme, the corporation might be divested, splitting into several small, independently operated companies. Or a light sentence might mean a stiff fine (probably representing pocket change for a company that earns more than $27 million a day), a rap on the knuckles, and a watchful government eye forever kept on its activities. Even the latter scenario, argue some, would mean that Microsoft would no longer be the monopolist it has allegedly been—or at least not as much of a bully.

This school of thought posits that, regardless of the trial's outcome, the Beast from Redmond—as the Redmond, Washington-based company is satirically named—will never be the same. In an online column in October 1998, Robert Cringely argued that simply as a matter of self-defense, Microsoft executives will have to take the position that the repeated threats they made to competitors were empty—that their words are being taken out of context and that they wouldn't have followed through on the threats. Following such an admission, Cringely surmises, any future Microsoft threats really will be hollow, and the company will lose its power to intimidate.

Two events that took place outside of the Microsoft-DOJ trial in November 1998 led to a fresh spray of prophesies about Microsoft's future. In a separate trial, Sun Microsystems won a preliminary injunction against Microsoft in an ongoing suit over Sun's Java technology. Microsoft had licensed Java for its Windows 98 and NT operating systems, and in the process of implementation, Microsoft programmers made alterations to Java—either to improve it (says Microsoft) or to destroy its cross-platform compatibility (says Sun). The pretrial ruling gave Microsoft ninety days to modify its Windows 98 operating system (to be compatible with Sun's version of Java) or to pull all of its Java-adorned products from the market.

Bill Gates addresses the COMDEX computer and electronics show on February 3, 1998 (AP / Wide World Photos).

Not surprisingly, industry-watchers with a bone to pick with Microsoft rejoiced in the pretrial verdict. But some pundits warned it could be a

Pyrrhic victory for Sun, as it may encourage Microsoft to launch an anti-Java campaign at a time when insiders are already beginning to have doubts about Java's superiority.

Others argued that Sun's victory will bolster the DOJ's case, because the ruling is a vindication of Sun's argument that Microsoft had tried to undermine Java's quality and usefulness—yet another anticompetitive scheme. Indeed, James Gosling, the creator of Java, was called by the DOJ to testify in the antitrust case on exactly this point: on October 19 he likened Microsoft's adaptation of Java to "adding to the English language words and phrases that cannot be understood by anyone else."

Meanwhile, on November 24, 1998, America Online (AOL) and Netscape announced plans for a merger. AOL, the reigning provider of Internet services, agreed to buy Netscape, the makers of the reigning Web browser (Netscape Navigator), for $4.1 billion worth of stock. A third player in the merger negotiations was none other than Sun Microsystems, who is expected to add Netscape technology to its products and pay royalties to AOL. The new AOL-Netscape entity could represent a force as mighty as Microsoft itself; it certainly spells trouble for MSN, Microsoft's perpetually struggling online service.

Typically, opinions about the merger and its relationship to the DOJ case were many and varied. Some observers claimed the deal might add fuel to the DOJ's argument, because it demonstrates that even the former giant Netscape was unable to survive Microsoft's stomping feet. Other pundits—and indeed, Microsoft itself—trumpeted the merger as a boost to Microsoft's defense. Microsoft has continually protested that its aggressive strategies are justified because there are plenty of formidable competitors in the computer arena. An AOL-Netscape combination could easily represent such a competitor.

NC OR NOT NC?

During the late 1990s several forward lookers within the computer industry touted the coming age of the "network computer" or "Internet appliance," a device whose main purpose is to access the Internet. The technology has been realized in a handful of such machines, but so far the hype seems to have been larger than the market. At the end of 1998, opinion was split. Perhaps, say some, the Internet-appliance era will arrive, but possibly wearing a different costume than expected. According to others, network computers (NCs) still don't stand a chance against PCs.

In 1996 the chairman of Oracle Corporation, Larry Ellison, was the most outspoken and enthusiastic champion of the NC. His faith in the idea may have been one of the most significant forces driving the development of the first NCs late in the year. Although NCs have not done nearly as well as Ellison and his supporters had hoped, sales are beginning to pick up, and more companies are expressing interest in both producing and purchasing them.

Network computers vary in their capabilities, but most are alike in being marketed as unembellished, simple computers for browsing the World Wide Web. Some allow word processing and other basic applications. The idea is to offer home users who want e-mail and Web access a device that doesn't cost as much and isn't as hard to use as the typical personal computer. Manufacturers of NCs gear their product toward the business setting as well as the home. At businesses, a network of Internet appliances sitting on employees' desks can be hooked up to a central server that provides all the necessary software. Employees can obtain information from the Internet and perform their work duties, but they can't take home company secrets on a diskette. An added benefit for the company is that NCs—supposedly, although it's too early to judge—require less maintenance and technical support than PCs.

NCs are supposed to cost less than personal computers, but manufacturers haven't been able (or, perhaps, willing) to create a satisfactory device that markets for less than $500. Modest PCs retail for not much more than that. If the NC is to make any headway, argue some industry experts, it is going to have to be sold for a lot less than a PC since it offers many fewer capabilities.

High cost is not the only roadblock believed to be inhibiting sales of NCs. Critics claim they are just too slow. And once PC users have become accustomed to a certain rate of computing, they are not going to sit still for a sluggish Internet appliance.

Ellison's vision is still bright. He imagines a networked world in which most computer users have a simple computing appliance—perhaps similar to today's NCs, or perhaps much more powerful—that is linked to a vast network. Users would be able to download any application or program from central servers and remote mainframes, similar to the way they

Beyond the Net

THE DIGITAL THIRD WORLD

Many enthusiasts of the digital revolution are surprised to hear that more than 98 percent of the globe remains unwired. And telecommunications poverty doesn't discriminate; it hits the world's wealthiest nations along with its poorest. In his essay, "Forsaken Geographies," Olu Oguibe argues that there is now a "digital third world" running through deprived neighborhoods from California to Chad. Digital poverty areas are marked by low tele-density—the number of telephones per hundred people. The Panos Organization reports that in low-income countries such as Afghanistan and Somalia, there is only one telephone for every 500 people. In the poorest nations, like Chad and Cambodia, there is one for every 1,000.

Because it will soon be a crucial means to democratic representation as well as economic opportunity, there is a move afoot in the United States to declare access to the Internet a "basic human right." Provision of universal Net access need not be incompatible with profit-making, advocates say. The Telecommunications Act of 1996, for instance, balanced its massive phone company deregulation policies with programs like the "e-rate" (government subsidies for secondary schools and libraries to get wired) as well as the Telecommunications Development Fund, which "promotes delivery of telecommunications services to underserved rural and urban areas."

Internationally, the obstacles to universal telecommunications require far more than local government assistance. For this reason, *telecenteres*—"public Net pay phones"—have been advocated as an alternative means to access cyberspace. In a number of developing nations, wireless radio (by far the most common communications device) is being linked with satellite technologies to give Net access. Phone shops—cellular network phone booths, moved around the countryside—are being used throughout Africa to enable people to make calls and send e-mail.

Daunting problems remain to be solved in the future. Globally, the rural poor (comprising nearly half the world population) have been overlooked in development initiatives. There is also a fear of donated equipment going unused because of lack of service or lack of education. Finally, debate rages on about the relative importance of the Net in poor areas. As Panos puts it, "While some health workers praise the satellite system that has brought them e-mail connections and cheap access to health information, others complain that Internet connections will not pay for aspirin or syringes."

Net advocates counter that telecommunications is no longer something that can be delayed until other needs are met. Since more computers than television sets were sold worldwide in 1996 and the fastest increase in computer sales is happening in some of the poorest countries, they argue that the issue is not whether to go online, but how to fight online poverty. After all, while three-fourths of the world's population still has yet to make a call, it's entirely possible that children of the future may send e-mail before they talk on the phone.

now download documents from the Internet. Critics of Ellison's idea think that computer users regard their personal computers and their software as personal belongings, and that they will be unwilling to give up those belongings and adopt a situation of less power and less ownership.

One market study made public at the end of 1998 predicted that NCs might get an unforeseen boost from the year-2000 computer problem. As the millennium approaches, or after it arrives, many businesses are likely to encounter glitches associated with older computers that were not designed to deal with the year 2000. One way to deal with some of these problems is to replace all personal computers, which could be tremendously expensive. Opting for installing NCs, even though they are only somewhat cheaper, might make all the difference.

Portals—Victims of Their Own Success?

In the summer of 1998 business news about the World Wide Web was crawling with discussions of portals, the single Web sites—such as Yahoo!, Netcenter, and Excite—that offer users an efficient and convenient jumping-off point for diving into the online world. The success of a few portals at enticing a large pool of users, and thus a wad of advertising revenue, generated a frenzy of portal start-ups in 1998. In contemplating the future of portals, experts are envisioning a range of scenarios, from portals as a passing fad, to portals (but probably only a couple of them) as a staple and lucrative Web niche.

A portal is a Web site that purports to provide everything a user needs to navigate the Web in a valuable and productive way. It not only includes a search engine, a program that surfs the Web looking for documents that contain keywords, but also a diverse set of links to other resources. These resources might include current news articles, deals on airfare, stock quotes, horoscopes, and categorized information about sports, health, education, travel, etc.—and these channels connect users to more specific Web destinations, which generally contain links to still more sites. Portals also provide interactive content, such as e-mail services, Web-wide games, map services, links to electronic-shopping pages, chat groups, and online bulletin board systems.

Many Web authorities consider America Online (AOL) to have been the original portal, because it was the first outfit to offer an array of Internet services and resources, such as e-mail, newsgroups, interactive chat, and links to various informational directories. Another extremely successful portal is managed by Yahoo!, which began in 1994 as a Web index and search engine run by two Stanford University students. In June 1998 Yahoo!'s Web site was receiving nearly one hundred million user visits each month. Other prominent portals include Excite, Lycos, Infoseek, and Snap.

Many portals were originally designed to provide Web users a way to search for information on the Web. They were exactly what the name they've been given implies: portals, or grand doorways, to the larger Web. As portals evolved, however, their purpose seemed to shift toward keeping users at the site, rather than spinning them off toward other points on the Web. This change in philosophy is reflected in the term "destination site," which is slowly replacing the term "portal." These sites want to be not only the page that users start from every time they fire up their Internet connection, but also a page where users spend significant time—checking the weather, chatting, reading the news. The more visitors a portal can entice, the more it can charge corporations to advertise on its Web site. And for many portals, advertising is the sole source of income.

But some observers are noting that the very changes portals have gone through to make their sites more attractive—adding accessories and services above and beyond the Web search engine—might actually spell their downfall, or even wipe out the portal phenomenon altogether.

In order to generate revenue, many portals have partnered with corporations such that viewers are preferentially directed toward the corporations' wares or services. Some consumer analysts predict that Web users will start to reject portals that conspicuously try to steer users to particular merchants. Proponents of this view argue that users regard a portal as a service to help them locate what they're looking for on the Web—and users do not want to be manipulated or restricted, or to have their desires presumed by portal-site authors.

Other industry pundits foresee that users will have less and less use for portals as they discover the option of creating a personalized start page. Several portals now allow viewers to create a custom page, although the individual elements that can be placed on the page have to be chosen from among the portal's offerings. It is also possible, although it requires a certain degree of programming literacy, for Web surfers to create their own start page from scratch, working independently of commercial portals.

A report issued in 1998 by market analyst Forrester Research stated that the top nine portals attract nearly 60 percent of Web advertising, while they actually receive only 15 percent of Web traffic. According to the report's authors, such situations generally end in a shakedown, as advertisers recognize the incongruity and distribute their advertising more carefully. The authors predicted that over the next few years, two or three businesses—probably including current leaders Yahoo! and AOL—will become the only prominent portals. And they may be very profitable; the amount of advertising funds flowing to portals by 2003 has been estimated at $2.4 billion. The top portals, claim the report's authors, will be trailed by a few moderately successful ones, and the remaining portals will fade away and disappear. Indeed, despite the "portal mania" reported in 1998's news, Yahoo! and AOL were the only ones showing a net profit (as of the end of the year). Observers have suggested that the success of these two has been due to their name recognition—and experts say that means they will likely retain their lead, as competition for advertising dollars stiffens and less familiar portals fail to attract viewers.

In actuality, most commercial portals offer nearly identical information, links, services, and resources. Virtual bystanders have pointed out that if portals were to adopt personality and attitude, thus offering a unique online experience, they might be able to attract a specific subset of the Web audience. This might be one way a multitude of portals could remain standing. If portals come in different styles, there will be reasons for users to choose one over another, and perhaps more than a few will remain afloat. For example, in early 1999 new sites were launched by entertainment conglomerates Disney and Warner Brothers, each offering proprietary, Disney-flavored or Warner Bros.-flavored content.

VIRTUAL COMMUNITIES

The short history of groups of people communicating via computers is richly documented, from the earliest grassroots attempts in the 1970s to the thousands of systems that were operating by the late 1990s. As a result of online communication, the lives of millions of people are different in the 1990s than they would have been if history had veered away from the development of computer networks. Few observers would be likely to argue otherwise. However, questions about the future of virtual communities remain: how will these communities affect offline society? And just what path will the evolution of virtual communities take? While many participants declare their firm faith in the potential of the online world, others—from within and from afar—are skeptical at best.

Imagining the Net

WHY REINVENT THE WHEEL?

As we hurtle toward virtual communities of the future, it's important to learn from the experiences of Netizens of the past and present. Between them, Cindy Tittle Moore and Paul Wallich, co-moderators of the Usenet group soc.feminism, have more than thirty years of experience building community over the Internet. Here, they share some of their thoughts.

Q: Describe the history of community at soc.feminism.

CTM: I helped form soc.feminism in late 1989. At the time, there was considerable debate over the subject matter of the group, who would be allowed to post, and who would moderate. The group tries to provide a pro-feminist (but not women-only) space on Usenet.

PW: Around 1990, I returned to the Net from a hiatus and found that some acquaintances had been driven out of soc.men and soc.women (which had been viable forums a few years earlier) by people whose views of gender roles would have been thought outdated in the 1950s. That's when I started hanging out at soc.feminism.

Q: Why is soc.feminism a moderated group?

CTM: Sometimes there are certain topics where there is just too much heat for a free wheeling discussion. It's hard for those actually interested to have an ongoing discussion without being interrupted with hostility. Moderation can smooth all that out.

PW: I believe that moderation is becoming increasingly important for working Usenet groups, especially given the continuing presence of spam programs.

Q: How has the Net community changed?

CTM: When the Internet expanded so rapidly in '94 and '95, a lot of what made Usenet interesting was destroyed. Prior to this, if you can believe it, we did not have spam. We did not have the gigabytes of newsgroup discussion moving through. You were likely to know the regulars on your newsgroup. That's gone now. Too many people and too many spammers—just plain noise. I can't even begin to describe what it used to be like in the 80's and early 90's. Mailing lists capture some of that flavor—I think they have much more to offer these days.

Q: What advice would you give to people who are new to an online space?

CTM: Read for a while before posting. And I don't mean read a few articles then jump in. Read for a week or so.

PW: You don't walk into a cocktail party without being introduced and insist that everybody drop what they're doing and listen to *you*. Unless, of course, you're really really interesting, and with ten million people already online the odds just aren't that good.

CTM: Ignore flame wars—concentrate on what you're really interested in and ignore the chaff. And I would say to women—climb aboard! It's really not a male wasteland out here. Just don't give out your phone number.

One current debate about virtual communities revolves around the question of what their social and cultural benefits are likely to be. Many people with faith in the promise of online communication believe that virtual communities offer unprecedented opportunities that will benefit society.

Global online bulletin board systems (BBSs), such as Usenet, are eye-opening forums where people can be exposed to the opinions and experiences of others who come from diverse cultures. In a similar vein, online communities give rise to friendships between people who will never have a chance to meet in person. American Online, in particular, has been successful in creating hobby-based networks of people over its computer network. Virtual communities also provide a means for people who would otherwise remain isolated—due to illness, shyness, or time-consuming obligations—to develop connections with other human beings.

According to some advocates, the most dramatic potential of virtual communities would be their role as a new political entity. Being online, connected to thousands of other people, provides a chance to build mass political consciousness around important issues. It gives every person a ready opportunity to voice an opinion to masses of other people—whereas traditionally, in late twentieth-century Western society, the only people able to do this are those with enough money to have access to the broadcast end of mass media. Champions of virtual community think that it could cause a reawakening of democracy, wherein people actually take an active part in the governance of their society.

These optimistic views have their critics. How many more people in the United States vote, they ask, since the inception of virtual communities? Indeed, in many parts of the country, voters turned out in record lows in the 1990s. For every Jesse "the Body" Ventura, whose successful 1998 gubernatorial campaign depended on the Internet, there are dozens of legislators who do not read their e-mail. Critics wonder how a digital democracy will be possible, especially if the gap between the wired and the nonwired continues to increase. Indeed, if only a certain privileged sector of society has access to the Internet, one will have to question exactly what kind of "communities" could or should be created.

Others foresee disadvantageous outcomes arising from the virtual community revolution. Taking television as an example, they point out the possibility that online communication might end up being infused with advertising. And advertising, since it is intended to make people think this or that, wouldn't foster the atmosphere of free thinking and open communication that occupants of electronic discussions want in their communities. Even more at odds with participants' desires would be government censorship of online communication—Internet censorship is a real threat and many experts believe that virtual communities should be working more actively to prevent it.

Furthermore, as more and more commercial "virtual communities" (GeoCities, Xoom, FortuneCity, and Angelfire, to name a few) offer free Web pages and e-mail but little in the way of communal interaction, the term itself is becoming suspect. Skeptics charge that these companies, which in 1998 multiplied rapidly and claimed millions of members, are far more interested in advertising revenue than community. As virtual community veteran Howard Rheingold told *Salon*, "Putting up message boards and chat rooms is a step towards community, but online community does not automatically happen just by throwing the tools at people. It requires thought." The creation of a community also requires time and effort—it's clear that many GeoCities and Xoom members signed up for the free Web space, rather than to make new friends. It remains to be seen whether commercial sites will be able to capture and keep an audience that wants to invest in the idea of an online community, and whether advertising-driven environments will be able to facilitate that evolution.

Some critics worry that the digital age is breaking human communities apart, rather than bringing people together in any effective way. Could the success of online communities lead to fewer and fewer people interacting in person? Most pundits agree that while computer-mediated communities may bring pleasure to the individuals who take part, it will take more than AOL accounts to impact society as a whole. Perhaps it will require online citizens to take what they learn from their digital communities, about themselves and about social interactions, and use those lessons to effect change in other realms.

Appendix:
Internet Statistics

Contents

WORLDWIDE PERSONAL COMPUTER DISTRIBUTION AND INTERNET ACCESS

Country	Personal Computers (per 1,000 people) 1996	Internet users (per 10,000 people) as of 7/1997	Country	Personal Computers (per 1,000 people) 1996	Internet users (per 10,000 people) as of 7/1997
Albania	na	0.32	El Salvador	na	0.34
Algeria	3.4	0.01	Eritrea	na	0.00
Angola	na	0.02	Estonia	6.7	45.35
Argentina	24.6	5.32	Ethiopia	na	0.00
Armenia	na	0.88	Finland	182.1	653.61
Australia	311.3	382.44	France	150.7	49.86
Austria	148.0	108.25	Gabon	6.3	0.00
Azerbaijan	na	0.11	Gambia	na	0.00
Bangladesh	na	0.00	Georgia	na	0.55
Belarus	na	0.44	Germany	232.2	106.68
Belgium	167.3	84.64	Ghana	1.2	0.15
Benin	na	0.02	Greece	33.4	18.76
Bolivia	na	0.69	Guatemala	2.8	0.79
Bosnia and Herzegovina	na	0.13	Guinea	0.3	0.00
Botswana	6.7	1.58	Guinea-Bissau	na	0.09
Brazil	18.4	4.20	Haiti	na	0.00
Bulgaria	295.2	6.65	Honduras	na	0.94
Burkina Faso	na	0.04	Hong Kong, China	150.5	74.84
Burundi	na	0.01	Hungary	44.1	33.29
Cambodia	na	0.01	India	1.5	0.05
Cameroon	na	0.05	Indonesia	4.8	0.54
Canada	192.5	228.50	Iran, Islamic Rep. of	32.7	0.00
Central African Rep.	na	0.02	Iraq	na	0.00
Chad	na	0.00	Ireland	145.3	90.89
Chile	45.1	13.12	Israel	117.6	104.79
China	3.0	0.21	Italy	92.3	36.91
Colombia	23.3	1.81	Jamaica	4.6	1.36
Congo, Dem. Rep. of	na	0.00	Japan	128.3	75.80
Congo, Rep. of	na	0.02	Jordan	7.2	0.38
Costa Rica	na	12.14	Kazakhstan	na	0.70
Côte d'Ivoire	1.4	0.17	Kenya	1.6	0.16
Croatia	20.9	14.08	Korea, Dem. People's Rep. of	na	0.00
Cuba	na	0.06			
Czech Rep.	53.2	47.66	Korea, Rep. Of	131.7	28.77
Denmark	304.1	259.73	Kuwait	74.1	21.72
Dominican Rep.	na	0.03	Kyrgyzstan	na	0.23
Ecuador	3.9	0.90	Lao People's Dem. Rep.	1.1	0.00
Egypt	5.8	0.31	Latvia	7.9	21.03

WORLDWIDE PERSONAL COMPUTER DISTRIBUTION AND INTERNET ACCESS (CONT.)

Country	Personal Computers (per 1,000 people) 1996	Internet users (per 10,000 people) as of 7/1997	Country	Personal Computers (per 1,000 people) 1996	Internet users (per 10,000 people) as of 7/1997
Lebanon	24.3	2.72	Saudi Arabia	37.2	0.15
Lesotho	na	0.08	Senegal	7.2	0.31
Libya	na	0.01	Sierra Leone	na	0.00
Lithuania	6.5	7.46	Singapore	216.8	196.30
Macedonia, Former Yugoslav. Rep.	na	2.15	Slovakia	186.1	20.47
			Slovenia	47.8	85.66
Madagascar	na	0.03	South Africa	37.7	30.67
Malawi	na	0.00	Spain	94.2	31.00
Malaysia	42.8	19.30	Sri Lanka	3.3	0.33
Mali	na	0.03	Sudan	0.7	0.00
Mauritania	5.3	0.00	Sweden	214.9	321.48
Mauritius	31.9	1.84	Switzerland	408.5	207.98
Mexico	29.0	3.72	Syria	1.4	0.00
Moldova, Rep. Of	2.6	0.39	Tajikistan	na	0.00
Mongolia	na	0.07	Tanzania	na	0.02
Morocco	1.7	0.32	Thailand	16.7	2.11
Mozambique	0.8	0.02	Togo	na	0.01
Myanmar (Burma)	na	0.00	Trinidad and Tobago	19.2	3.24
Namibia	12.7	2.16	Tunisia	6.7	0.02
Nepal	na	0.07	Turkey	13.8	3.60
Netherlands	232.0	219.01	Turkmenistan	na	0.00
New Zealand	266.1	424.34	Uganda	0.5	0.01
Nicaragua	na	1.60	Ukraine	5.6	2.09
Niger	na	0.04	United Arab Emirates	65.5	7.66
Nigeria	4.1	0.00	United Kingdom	192.6	149.06
Norway	273.0	474.63	United States	362.4	442.11
Oman	10.9	0.00	Uruguay	22.0	3.18
Pakistan	1.2	0.07	Uzbekistan	na	0.06
Panama	na	1.44	Venezuela	21.1	2.06
Papua New Guinea	na	0.18	Vietnam	3.3	0.00
Paraguay	na	0.47	Yemen	na	0.00
Peru	5.9	2.63	Yugoslavia (Serbia and Montenegro)	na	2.72
Philippines	9.3	0.59			
Poland	26.2	11.22	Zambia	na	0.27
Portugal	60.5	18.26	Zimbabwe	6.7	0.24
Puerto Rico	na	0.30			
Romania	5.3	2.66			
Russian Federation	23.7	5.51			
Rwanda	na	0.01			

na = not available

Source: *World Development Indicators 1998,*
Washington, D.C.: International Bank for Reconstruction
and Development/The World Bank, 1998.

Percent of U.S. Schools with Internet Access

	1994	1995	1996	1997	Percent of schools in 1996 having or expecting to have access to the Internet by the year 2000
Total (Combined Schools)	35	50	65	78	95
Instructional level:					
Elementary	30	46	61	75	94
Secondary	49	65	77	89	98
Size of enrollment:					
Less than 300	30	39	57	75	93
300 to 999	35	52	66	78	96
1,000 or more	58	69	80	89	97
Percent minority enrollment:					
Less than 6 percent	(na)	52	65	84	95
6 to 20 percent	(na)	58	72	87	97
21 to 49 percent	(na)	54	65	73	98
50 percent or more	(na)	40	56	63	91
Percent of students eligible for free or reduced-price lunch:					
Less than 11 percent	(na)	62	78	88	97
11 to 30 percent	(na)	59	72	83	98
31 to 70 percent	(na)	47	58	78	93
71 percent or more	(na)	31	53	63	93

na = not available.
Source: U.S. National Center for Education Statistics, "Internet Access in Public Schools," *Issue Brief*, February 1998.

Computer and Math Scientists in the Labor Force, by Occupation, Sex, and Highest Degree: 1993

Field of occupation	Total		Bachelor's		Master's		Doctorate		Other	
	Men	Women	Men	Women	Men	Women	Men	Women	Men	Women
Total science and engineering	2,493,000	720,000	1,421,000	358,000	677,000	244,000	364,000	108,000	31,000	10,000
Computer/ mathematical sciences	667,000	296,000	423,000	204,000	193,000	81,000	46,000	10,000	4,000	–
Computer sciences	592,000	255,000	405,000	192,000	165,000	59,000	19,000	3,000	3,000	–
Mathematical science	30,000	18,000	11,000	8,000	11,000	8,000	7,000	3,000	–	–
Computer/ mathematics teachers	45,000	23,000	7,000	5,000	17,000	14,000	21,000	4,000	–	–

Key: – = fewer than 500 estimated
Notes: Teachers include only postsecondary teachers. Because of rounding, details may not add to totals.
Source: National Science Foundation/SRS. 1993 National Survey of College Graduates.

NUMBER OF HOSTS IN THE DOMAIN NAME SYSTEM
As of January 1999

Date	Hosts	Sources and Notes	Date	Hosts	Sources and Notes
08/81	213	host table	07/92	992,000	
05/82	235		10/92	1,136,000	
08/83	562		01/93	1,313,000	
10/84	1,024		04/93	1,486,000	
10/85	1,961		07/93	1,776,000	
02/86	2,308		10/93	2,056,000	
11/86	5,089		01/94	2,217,000	
12/87	28,174	old domain survey	07/94	3,212,000	
07/88	33,000		10/94	3,864,000	
10/88	56,000		01/95	4,852,000	5,846,000 (adjusted)[1]
01/89	80,000		07/95	6,642,000	8,200,000 (adjusted)
07/89	130,000		01/96	9,472,000	14,352,000 (adjusted)
10/89	159,000		07/96	12,881,000	16,729,000 (adjusted)
10/90	313,000		01/97	16,146,000	21,819,000 (adjusted)
01/91	376,000		07/97	19,540,000	26,053,000 (adjusted)
07/91	535,000		01/98	29,670,000	new domain survey
10/91	617,000		07/98	36,739,000	
01/92	727,000		01/99	43,230,000	
04/92	890,000				

Source: Network Wizards (http://www.nw.com)

GROWTH OF THE WORLD WIDE WEB

Month	Total Number of Web sites	Percentage of sites in the ".com" domain	Hosts per Web server
6/93	130	1.5	13,000
12/93	623	4.6	3,475
6/94	2,738	13.5	1,095
12/94	10,022	18.3	451
6/95	23,500	31.3	270
1/96	100,000	50.0	94
6/96	230,000 (est)	68.0	41
1/97	650,000 (est)	62.6	na

Source: Matthew Gray of the Massachusetts Institute of Technology.

[1] The rapid expansion of the number of hosts necessitated changes in the way this survey was conducted. Data was adjusted starting in January 1995 to account for under-representation, and the survey method was entirely revised in 1998. For more information on the survey methodology, consult Network Wizards (http://www.nw.com).

TOP-LEVEL DOMAIN NAMES BY HOST COUNTRY
As of January 1999

Domain	Hosts	Type	Domain	Hosts	Type
com	10301570	Commercial	tr	27861	Turkey
net	7054863	Networks	th	25459	Thailand
edu	4464216	Educational	unknown	23610	Unknown
mil	1359153	US Military	cl	22889	Chile
jp	1352200	Japan	is	20678	Iceland
us	1302204	United States	su	20024	Soviet Union
uk	1190663	United Kingdom	cn	19313	China
de	1154340	Germany	ee	18948	Estonia
ca	1027571	Canada	si	18084	Slovenia
au	750327	Australia	uy	16345	Uruguay
org	644971	Organizations	sk	14154	Slovakia (Slovak Republic)
gov	612725	Government	ro	13697	Romania
nl	514660	Netherlands	ae	13519	United Arab Emirates
fi	513527	Finland	ua	13271	Ukraine
fr	431045	France	co	11864	Colombia
se	380634	Sweden	id	10691	Indonesia
it	320725	Italy	in	10436	India
no	312441	Norway	lt	8746	Lithuania
es	243436	Spain	lv	8115	Latvia
ch	205593	Switzerland	ph	7602	Philippines
dk	190293	Denmark	ve	6825	Venezuela
nz	177753	New Zealand	lu	6145	Luxembourg
kr	174800	Korea, Republic Of	bg	6141	Bulgaria
br	163890	Brazil	hr	6117	Croatia (local name: Hrvatska)
be	153760	Belgium	kw	5597	Kuwait
za	140577	South Africa	yu	5270	Yugoslavia
at	132202	Austria	do	4917	Dominican Republic
ru	130422	Russian Federation	pe	3763	Peru
tw	103661	Taiwan, Province Of China	cy	3286	Cyprus
pl	98798	Poland	cr	2844	Costa Rica
il	87642	Israel	eg	2043	Egypt
mx	83949	Mexico	bm	1993	Bermuda
hu	73987	Hungary	pk	1923	Pakistan
hk	72232	Hong Kong	nu	1608	Niue
cz	65672	Czech Republic	tt	1531	Trinidad and Tobago
sg	59469	Singapore	to	1446	Tonga
ar	57532	Argentina	lb	1400	Lebanon
arpa	47910	Mistakes	kz	1397	Kazakhstan
pt	45113	Portugal	ec	1227	Ecuador
ie	44840	Ireland	gt	1046	Guatemala
my	40758	Malaysia	py	855	Paraguay
gr	40061	Greece	int	853	International Organizations

Top-Level Domain Names by Host Country (cont.)

As of January 1999

Domain	Hosts	Type	Domain	Hosts	Type
zw	836	Zimbabwe	gi	191	Gibraltar
mt	785	Malta	sn	189	Senegal
pa	766	Panama	ai	189	Anguilla
bn	740	Brunei Darussalam	kg	182	Kyrgyzstan
ni	692	Nicaragua	sm	154	San Marino
ke	692	Kenya	mc	154	Monaco
om	666	Oman	mo	143	Macau
na	665	Namibia	nc	141	New Caledonia
sv	647	El Salvador	tz	137	Tanzania
by	636	Belarus	tc	129	Turks and Caicos Islands
ge	632	Georgia	fj	127	Fiji
lk	580	Sri Lanka	pr	123	Puerto Rico
bw	578	Botswana	np	123	Nepal
fo	560	Faroe Islands	gf	121	French Guiana
gl	515	Greenland	gp	115	Guadeloupe
vi	514	Virgin Islands (U.S.)	hn	106	Honduras
bo	506	Bolivia	fm	95	Micronesia, Federated States of
ma	478	Morocco	bf	93	Burkina Faso
ad	477	Andorra	ng	91	Nigeria
am	466	Armenia	gu	89	Guam
mk	407	Macedonia, FYRM	cu	85	Cuba
li	402	Liechtenstein	tg	83	Togo
sz	397	Swaziland	mz	83	Mozambique
mu	370	Mauritius	gb	81	United Kingdom
md	370	Moldova	dm	79	Dominica
jo	360	Jordan	et	76	Ethiopia
ky	359	Cayman Islands	al	76	Albania
ba	348	Bosnia And Herzegovina	mv	70	Maldives
bh	337	Bahrain	st	64	Sao Tome and Principe
tm	296	Turkmenistan	pg	62	Papua New Guinea
pf	273	French Polynesia	kh	58	Cambodia
ci	265	Côte d'Ivoire	gy	58	Guyana
ir	262	Iran	tn	57	Tunisia
bz	262	Belize	tj	57	Tajikistan
cc	259	Cocos (Keeling) Islands	io	56	British Indian Ocean Territory
jm	253	Jamaica	nf	55	Norfolk Island
bs	247	Bahamas	vu	47	Vanuatu
gh	241	Ghana	bb	45	Barbados
zm	236	Zambia	sa	42	Saudi Arabia
az	231	Azerbaijan	ug	41	Uganda
uz	198	Uzbekistan	ck	33	Cook Islands
ag	196	Antigua And Barbuda	vn	25	Vietnam

Top-Level Domain Names by Host Country (cont.)
As of January 1999

Domain	Hosts	Type	Domain	Hosts	Type
sb	24	Solomon Islands	ga	1	Gabon
lc	24	Saint Lucia	fk	1	Falkland Islands (Malvinas)
qa	23	Qatar	cv	1	Cape Verde
mr	22	Mauritania	cg	1	Congo (Republic)
im	21	Isle of Man	af	1	Afghanistan
dz	19	Algeria	zr	0	Zaire
mg	18	Madagascar	yt	0	Mayotte
as	18	American Samoa	ws	0	Samoa
mq	17	Martinique	wf	0	Wallis And Futuna Islands
mn	17	Mongolia	vc	0	Saint Vincent and the Grenadines
ls	17	Lesotho	um	0	United States Minor Outlying Islands
ye	14	Yemen	tv	0	Tuvalu
je	14	Jersey	tk	0	Tokelau
vg	13	Virgin Islands (British)	td	0	Chad
gw	13	Guinea-Bissau	sy	0	Syrian Arab Republic
gg	13	Guernsey	sr	0	Suriname
bj	13	Benin	so	0	Somalia
cx	11	Christmas Island	sl	0	Sierra Leone
va	9	Vatican City State	sj	0	Svalbard and Jan Mayen Islands
km	9	Comoros	sd	0	Sudan
mp	8	Northern Mariana Islands	rw	0	Rwanda
cd	8	Congo (Democratic Republic)	pn	0	Pitcairn
tf	7	French Southern Territories	pm	0	St. Pierre and Miquelon
sc	7	Seychelles	nr	0	Nauru
ms	7	Montserrat	mw	0	Malawi
an	6	Netherlands Antilles	mm	0	Myanmar
ne	5	Niger	la	0	Lao People's Democratic Republic
cm	5	Cameroon	ki	0	Kiribati
ac	5	Ascension Island	iq	0	Iraq
mh	2	Marshall Islands	ht	0	Haiti
bt	2	Bhutan	gq	0	Equatorial Guinea
ao	2	Angola	gn	0	Guinea
tp	1	East Timor	gm	0	Gambia
sh	1	St. Helena	gd	0	Grenada
re	1	Reunion	er	0	Eritrea
pw	1	Palau	dj	0	Djibouti
ml	1	Mali	cf	0	Central African Republic
ly	1	Libyan Arab Jamahiriya	bv	0	Bouvet Island
lr	1	Liberia	bi	0	Burundi
kn	1	Saint Kitts and Nevis	aw	0	Aruba
hm	1	Heard And Mc Donald Islands	aq	0	Antarctica
gs	1	South Georgia and the South Sandwich Islands			

Source: Internet Domain Survey by Network Wizards (http://www.nw.com/).

Top 100 Second-Level Domain Names By Host Country

Hosts	Name	Hosts	Name	Hosts	Name
1667245	aol.com	125426	edu.tw	68876	grid.net
1238252	uu.net	121271	ad.jp	66316	cw.net
848820	ans.net	118915	umich.edu	65758	sch.uk
708159	ac.uk	117624	bc.ca	65595	epa.gov
637202	af.mil	113641	hp.com	65533	nextel.com
585233	co.uk	112558	nasa.gov	65522	casecorp.com
505645	ne.jp	102023	il.us	65038	radian.com
485316	bbn.com	99856	rr.com	64933	jdrp.com
424038	or.jp	97654	mindspring.com	64858	novo.dk
403169	att.net	94679	bellsouth.net	64733	umn.edu
387390	ac.jp	93367	pacbell.com	64450	darpa.mil
357571	home.com	91416	mediaone.net	64237	auspex.com
349525	army.mil	90268	cisco.com	64232	hal.com
334187	psi.net	90190	t-online.de	63886	megsinet.net
328000	edu.au	89311	wcom.net	63750	icl.fi
318197	navy.mil	88681	autonet.net	63741	net.com
296346	dialsprint.net	88246	slb.com	63681	tellabs.com
275416	ca.us	85798	erols.com	63252	vlsi.com
271547	ibm.net	85636	berkeley.edu	63215	bcbsm.com
213767	co.jp	82890	co.kr	63093	ixos.de
210921	hinet.net	80777	co.us	62948	uswest.net
193754	cdc.com	80476	intel.com	62647	acuson.com
190602	splitrock.net	80024	ut.us	62178	bellatlantic.net
187914	dec.com	78767	co.za	61778	ub.com
185019	com.au	78306	ac.kr	61355	ecitele.com
171321	net.au	78290	pacbell.net	61191	co.nz
157989	mn.us	77814	shaw.ca	61101	boeing.com
152699	or.us	77680	gsa.gov	60850	mediaone.com
147202	kivex.com	74795	concentric.net	59050	medtronic.com
141509	tx.us	74182	gov.au	58629	mit.edu
140801	net.tw	73518	3com.com	58539	ac.at
136440	com.br	71866	symantec.com	58048	egginc.com
135608	netcom.com	69910	baynetworks.com	57458	eni.net
		68886	on.ca		

Further Reading

This source list is organized into nine sections. Broad references relating to more than one chapter are listed first, followed by specific sources for entries in each of the eight chapters. Research for the book was completed in January 1999; Internet addresses are accurate as of that point. When a source is available in both online and traditional formats, both formats are given.

GENERAL

Bowen, Jonathan. "The Virtual Museum of Computing." http://www.comlab.ox.ac.uk/archive/other/museums/computing.html

Campbell-Kelly, Martin and William Aspray. *Computer: A History of the Information Machine.* New York: Basic Books, 1996.

Cardwell, Donald. *The Norton History of Technology.* New York: W. W. Norton & Company, 1995.

The Computer Society. "Timeline of Computing History." *Computer.* 1996. http://www.computer.org/computer/timeline/

Condon, Chris. "NetHistory: An Informal History of BITNET and the Internet." http://www.geocities.com/SiliconValley/2260/

Cringely, Robert X. *Accidental Empires: How the Boys of Silicon Valley Make Their Millions, Battle Foreign Competition and Still Can't Get a Date.* Menlo Park, Calif.: Addison-Wesley, 1992.

———. "I, Cringely." http://www.pbs.org/cringely/index.html

———. *Nerds 2.0.1: A Brief History of the Internet.* 25 November 1998. PBS. Television Broadcast.

———. *Triumph of the Nerds.* New York: Ambrose Video, 1996. Videorecording.

Dery, Mark. *Escape Velocity: Cyberculture at the End of the Century.* New York: Grove Press, 1996.

———. *Flame Wars: The Discourse of Cyberculture.* Durham, N.C.: Duke University Press, 1994.

Diffie, Whitfield and Susan Landau. *Privacy on the Line: The Politics of Wiretapping and Encryption.* Boston: MIT Press, 1998.

Downing, Douglas, Melody Mauldin Covington, and Michael Covington. *Dictionary of Computer and Internet Terms,* 5th ed. Hauppauge, New York: Barron's Educational Series, 1996.

Dunham, William. *The Mathematical Universe: An Alphabetical Journey Through the Great Proofs, Problems, and Personalities.* New York: John Wiley & Sons, 1994.

Gaffin, Adam. "EFF's Guide to the Internet, Version 3.20." 11 December 1996. http://www.eff.org/pub/Net_info/EFF_Net_Guide/netguide.eff

Gardner, Robert and Dennis Shortelle. *From Talking Drums to the Internet.* Santa Barbara, Calif.: ABC-CLIO, 1997.

Graf, Rudolf F. *Modern Dictionary of Electronics.* Boston: Newnes, 1997.

Gromov, Gregory R. "History of Internet and WWW: The Roads and Crossroads of Internet History." *Internet Valley.* http://www.hooked.net/netvalley/intvalold.html

Hafner, Katie and Matthew Lyon. *Where Wizards Stay Up Late: The Origins of the Internet.* New York: Touchstone, 1996.

Internet Society. "All About the Internet." 11 Nov 1998. http://www.isoc.org/internet-history/

Kline, Morris. *Mathematical Thought from Ancient to Modern Times.* New York: Oxford University Press, 1972.

Krol, Ed and Mike Loukides, eds. *The Whole Internet User's Guide & Catalog.* 2nd ed. Sebastopol, Calif.: O'Reilly & Associates, 1994.

Leiner, Barry M., Vinton G. Cerf, David D. Clark, et al. "A Brief History of the Internet." 20 Feb 1998. http://www.isoc.org/internet-history/brief.html

Levy, Stephen. *Hackers: Heroes of the Computer Revolution.* New York: Dell Publishing, 1984.

Newton, David E. *Encyclopedia of Cryptology.* Santa Barbara, Calif.: ABC-CLIO, 1997.

Palfreman, Jon and Doron Swade. *The Dream Machine: Exploring the Computer Age.* London: BBC Books, 1991.

Polsson, Ken. "Chronology of Events in the History of Microcomputers." 23 October 1998. http://www3.islandnet.com/~kpolsson/comphist.htm

Raymond, Eric S., ed. "The New Hacker's Dictionary 4.0.0." 25 July 1996. http://www.tuxedo.org/~esr/jargon/jargon_toc.html

Reid, Robert H. *Architects of the Web: 1000 Days That Built the Future of Business.* New York: John Wiley & Sons, 1997.

Rheingold, Harold. *Virtual Communities.* New York: HarperPerennial, 1993. http://www.rheingold.com/vc/book/3.html

Richie, David. *The Computer Pioneers.* New York: Simon & Schuster, 1986.

Slater, Robert. *Portraits in Silicon.* Cambridge, Mass: MIT Press, 1987.

Smithsonian Institution. "Computer History." http://www.si.edu/resource/tours/comphist/computer.htm

Spencer, Donald. *Great Men and Women of Computing.* Ormond Beach, Fla.: Camelot Publishing, 1996.

Sterling, Bruce. "INTERNET, aka A Brief History of the Internet." 1993. http://www.eff.org/pub/Privacy/Security/Hacking_cracking_phreaking/Net_culture_and_hacking/internet_sterling.history

Stoll, Cliff. *The Cuckoo's Egg.* New York: Pocket Books, 1989.

Turkle, Sherri. *Life on the Screen: Identity in the Age of the Internet.* New York: Simon & Schuster, 1997.

CHAPTER 1

AT&T Labs. "Claude Shannon: Information Theory." *Inside AT&T Labs.* 1997. http://www.att.com/attlabs/archive/shannon.html

Austrian, Geoffrey. *Herman Hollerith: Forgotten Giant of Information Processing.* New York: Columbia University Press, 1984.

Bourbaki, Nicolas. *Elements of the History of Mathematics.* Trans. John Meldrum. Berlin; New York: Springer-Verlag, 1994.

Brand, Robert R. "Internet Info for Real People: Hoaxes on the Net." January 1998. http://www-060.connix.com/bweb/iinfo30.htm

Bronson, Po. "The Long Now: Time Travel with Danny Hillis." *Wired* 6.05. May 1998. http://www.wired.com/wired/6.05/hillis.html

Bukatman, Scott. *Terminal Identity: The Virtual Subject in Postmodern Science Fiction.* Durham, N.C.: Duke University Press, 1993.

Burton, David M. *The History of Mathematics: An Introduction.* New York: McGraw-Hill, 1997.

Bush, Vannevar. "As We May Think." *The Atlantic Monthly* 176; (July 1945): 101-108. http://www.theatlantic.com/unbound/flashbks/computer/bushf.htm

Coe, Lewis. *The Telegraph: A History of Morse's Invention and Its Predecessors in the United States.* Jefferson, N.C.: McFarland & Company, 1993.

Coopman, Ted M. "Pirates to Micro Broadcasters: The Rise of the Micro Radio Movement." 1998. http://www.cruzio.com/~rogue/TCoopman.html

Cortada, James W. *The Computer in the United States: From Laboratory to Market, 1930 to 1960.* Armonk, N.Y.: M.E. Sharpe, 1993.

Data Fellows, Inc. "Anti-Virus HOAX Warnings Page." 1998. http://www.europe.datafellows.com/news/hoax.htm

Department of English, Urbana, Illinois. "Cybercinema—An Interactive Site Devoted to the History of Computers and Artificial Intelligence in Film." 1998. http://128.174.194.59/cybercinema/

The Edison-Ford Winter Estates. "Thomas Edison Biography." 1998. http://edison-ford-estate.com/ed_bio.htm

George Washington University. *A Retrospective Technology Assessment: Submarine Telegraphy.* San Francisco: San Francisco Press, 1979.

Goldstine, Herman. *The Computer from Pascal to von Neumann.* Princeton, N.J.: Princeton University Press, 1972.

Greengard, Samuel. "Head Start: Neuroscientist Theodore Berger Is Working Real Hard to be the First Person to Implant Microchips Between Your Ears." *Wired* 5.02. February 1997. http://www.wired.com/wired/5.02/esberger.html

Gurney, Kevin. "An Introduction to Neural Networks: The Early Years." 1998. http://www.shef.ac.uk/psychology/gurney/notes/l10/subsection3_2_1.html

Hailperin, T. *Boole's Logic and Probability Theory.* New York: Elsevier Science, 1976.

Heims, Steve. *John von Neumann and Norbert Wiener.* Cambridge, Mass.: MIT Press, 1980.

Hodges, Andrew. "Alan Turing Homepage." 24 October 1998. http://www.turing.org.uk/turing/

———. *Alan Turing: The Enigma.* London: Vintage Books, 1992.

Katz, Victor J. *A History of Mathematics: An Introduction.* New York: HarperCollins, 1993.

Kloss, William. *Samuel F. B. Morse.* Washington, D.C.: Smithsonian Institution, 1988.

Lee, J. A. N. *Computer Pioneers.* Los Alamitos, Calif.: IEEE Computer Society Press, 1995.

Lewis, Clarence Irving and Cooper Harold Langford. "History of Symbolic Logic." In *The World of Mathematics.* Ed. by James R. Newman. New York: Simon & Schuster, 1956.

Mackay, James A. *Sounds Out of Silence: A Life of Alexander Graham Bell.* Philadelphia, Penn.: Mainstream, 1997.

Macrae, Norman. *John von Neumann.* New York: Pantheon Books, 1992.

Martin, Richard. "Present at the Creation: An Oral History of the Dawn of the Internet." *PreText Magazine.* March 1998. http://www.pretext.com/mar98/features/story1.htm

Melosi, Martin V. *Thomas A. Edison and the Modernization of America.* Glenview, Ill.: Scott, Foresman/Little, Brown Higher Education, 1990.

Napper, Dr. R. B. E. "Computer 50: The University of Manchester Celebrates the Birth of the Modern Computer." http://www.computer50.org/

Pasachoff, Naomi. *Alexander Graham Bell: Making Connections.* New York: Oxford University Press, 1996.

Riordan, Michael. *Crystal Fire: The Birth of the Information Age.* New York: W. W. Norton & Company, 1997.

Rosenberger, Rob. "Computer Virus Myths Home Page." 1998. http://kumite.com/myths/home.htm

Sarle, Warren S. "Neural Network FAQ, part 1 of 7: Introduction." 1998. ftp://ftp.sas.com/pub/neural/FAQ.html

Sobchack, Vivian C. *The Limits of Infinity: The American Science Fiction Film, 1950-75.* Stamford, Conn.: A.S. Barnes & Company, 1980.

———. *Screening Space: The American Science Fiction Film.* Piscataway, N.J.: Rutgers University Press, 1987.

Springer, Claudia. *Electronic Eros: Bodies and Desire in the Postindustrial Age.* Austin: University of Texas Press, 1996.

Stein, Dorothy. *Ada: A Life and a Legacy.* Cambridge, Mass.: MIT Press, 1985.

T.A.P., The Ada Project. "Past Notable Women of Computing." 1998. http://www.cs.yale.edu/homes/tap/past-women-cs.html

von Neumann, John. *The Computer and the Brain.* New Haven, Conn.: Yale University Press, 1958.

Weiner, Neil. "Early Internet Business: Stories from Early Radio." *Background Briefing.* 14 April 1996. http://www.backgroundbriefing.com/radio.html

Winegrad, Dilys and Akera Atsushi. "ENIAC's 50th Anniversary: The Birth of the Information Age—A Short History of the Second American Revolution." *University of Pennsylvania Almanac* 42, no. 18. (January 1996). http://www.upenn.edu/almanac/v42/n18/eniac.html

CHAPTER 2

Baran, Paul. "On Distributed Communication Networks." In *Rand Memoranda*, vols. 1-11. Santa Monica, Calif.: Rand Corporation, August 1964. http://www.rand.org/publications/RM/baran.list.html

Beam, Alex. "A Building with Soul." *The Boston Globe.* 29 June 1988. Reprinted in *MIT Tech Talk,*. 41, no. 9 (30 October 1996). http://w3.mit.edu/newsoffice/tt/1996/oct30/42944/42938.html

Bradford, Clint. "JFK Assassination Research Materials Home Page." 1998. http://www.pe.net/~atd/

Brand, Stewart. "Spacewar: Fanatic Life and Symbolic Death Among the Computer Bums." *Rolling Stone.* 7 December 1972. http://www.baumgart.com/rolling-stone/spacewar.html

———. "Foreword." *Millennium Whole Earth Catalog.* http://www.well.net/mwec/frontmatter/foreword.html

Cerf, Vinton and Robert Kahn. "A Protocol for Packet Network Interconnection." *IEEE Trans. Comm. Tech.* COM-22, no. 5 (May 1974): 627-647.

DePalma, Anthony. "Canadians Mix Their History." *The Arizona Republic.* Front Section, 5 July 1998.

Digital Ages Online. "History of Gaming: From Spacewar To Pong 1962-1972." *DAO's Complete Guide to Videogame History.* http://www.digital-ages.com/dao/news/editorials/history.htm

Edwards, Paul N. "'We Defend Every Place: Building the Cold War World." *The Closed World: Computers and the Politics of Discourse in Cold War America.* Cambridge, Mass.: MIT Press, 1996. http://www.stanford.edu/group/STS/cw.ch1.shtml

Eisenhower, Dwight D. "Military Industrial Complex Speech." *The Cumulated Indexes to the Public Papers of the Presidents of the United States, Dwight D. Eisenhower, 1953-1961,* 1035-1040. http://ah3.cal.msu.edu/~hst306/documents/indust.html

Greenberger, Martin. "The Computers of Tomorrow." *The Atlantic Monthly* 213, no. 5 (May 1964): 63-67. http://www.theatlantic.com/atlantic/atlweb/flashbks/computer/greenbf.htm

Herz, J. C. *Joystick Nation.* New York: Little, Brown, 1997.

IHTFP Hack Gallery. "Interesting Hacks to Fascinate People: The MIT Gallery of Hacks." 11 November 1998. http://hacks.mit.edu/Hacks/

Koistinen, Paul A. C. *The Military-Industrial Complex: An Historical Perspective.* Westport, Conn.: Greenwood Publishing, 1980.

Licklider, J. C. R. "The Man-Computer Symbiosis." *IRE Transactions on Human Factors in Electronics.* HFE-1 (March 1960): 4-11. http://memex.org/licklider.pdf

Licklider, J. C. R., Robert Taylor, and E. Herbert. "The Computer as a Communication Device." *International Science and Technology* (April 1968). http://memex.org/licklider.pdf

Marchand, Philip. *Marshall McLuhan: The Medium and the Messenger.* Revised edition. Cambridge, Mass: MIT Press, 1998.

McLuhan, Marshall. *The Gutenberg Galaxy: The Making of Typographic Man.* Toronto: University of Toronto Press, 1962.

———. *The Medium is the Massage: An Inventory of Effects.* San Francisco: Wired Books, 1996.

———. *Understanding Media: The Extensions of Man.* Reprint. Cambridge, Mass: MIT Press, 1984.

McLuhan, Marshall and Quentin Fiore. *War and Peace in the Global Village: An Inventory of Some of the Current Spastic Situations That Could Be Eliminated by More Feedforward.* New York: McGraw-Hill, 1968.

Murray, Charles J. *The Supermen: The Story of Seymour Cray and the Technical Wizards Behind the Supercomputer.* New York: John Wiley & Sons, 1997.

National Archives and Records Administration. Assassination Records Review Board. "Hearing on the Status and Disposition of the 'Zapruder Film.'" Washington, D.C. 2 April 1997. Transcript. http://www.pe.net/~atd/arrb-001.htm

Nyce James M. and Paul Kahn, eds. *From Memex to Hypertext: Vannevar Bush and the Mind's Machine.* San Diego, Calif.: Academic Press, 1991.

Rapaport, Richard. "The Playground of Big Science." *Wired* 3.10. October 1995. http://www.wired.com/wired/archive/3.10/sandia_pr.html

Raymond, Eric. *Eric Raymond's FAQ Collection: Hacker History and Culture.* 1998. http://www.tuxedo.org/~esr/faqs/

———. "How To Become a Hacker."1998. http://www.tuxedo.org/~esr/faqs/hacker-howto.html

———. "A Brief History of Hackerdom." 1998. http://www.tuxedo.org/~esr/faqs/hacker-hist.html

Request for Comments (RFC) Editor. "RFC Editor Homepage." 1998. http://www.rfc-editor.org/index.html

SABRE Group. "The SABRE System Story." 19 November 1998. http://www.sabre.com/corpinfo/history.htm#The SABRE Story

Simon, Art. *Dangerous Knowledge: The JFK Assassination in Art and Film.* Philadelphia: Temple University Press, 1996

Sobchack, Vivian. "Reading Mondo 2000. " In *Flame Wars.* Ed. Mark Dery. Durham, N.C.: Duke University Press, 1994.

Sterling, Bruce. "War Is Virtual Hell." *Wired* 1.01. March/April 1993. http://www.wired.com/wired/archive/1.01/virthell_pr.html

Video McLuhan Inc. "Marshall McLuhan Video Archive Home Page." 1998. http://www.videomcluhan.com/

Walker, Martin. *The Cold War: A History.* New York: Henry Holt, 1995.

Whole Earth Review Gopher Site. http://gopher.well.com:70/1/WER

Wolf, Gary. "The Curse of Xanadu." *Wired* 3.06. June 1995. http://www.wired.com/wired/archive/3.06/xanadu_pr.html

———. "The Wisdom of Saint Marshall, the Holy Fool." *Wired* 4.01. January 1996. http://www.wired.com/wired/archive/4.01/saint.marshal_pr.html

CHAPTER 3

Barry, Rey. "The Origin of Computer Bulletin Boards." *Freeware Hall of Fame*. 29 April 1998. http://www.freewarehof.org/ward.html

Boulware, Jack. "Mondo 1995: Up and Down with the Next Millennium's First Magazine." *SF Weekly*. 1995. http://www.suck.com/daily/95/11/07/mondo1995.html

Campbell, Todd. "The First Email Message." *Pretext Magazine*. March 1998. http://www.pretext.com/mar98/features/story2.htm

Christensen, Ward and Randy Seuss. "Hobbyist Computerized Bulletin Boards." *Byte*. November 1978.

Davies, Simon. "The Ever-Widening Gaze of Big Brother." *The Daily Telegraph*. 10 September 1998.

Discovery Online. "Hackers' Hall of Fame." 1998. http://www.discovery.com/area/technology/hackers/elderdays.html

Doyle, Roger. "By the Numbers: Privacy in the Workplace." *Scientific American*. January 1999. http://www.sciam.com/1999/0199issue/0199numbers.html

Eney, Dick, et al. "Egoboo." *Fancyclopedia II*. 1998. http://www.sff.net/people/Diccon/ECHO.HTM

EPIC. "The Privacy Page." 1998. http://www.privacy.org/

Florida Association for Nucleation and Conventions (F.A.N.A.C.). *Fan History Archives*. 1998. http://fanac.org/index.html

Free Software Foundation. "GNU's Not Unix!—The GNU Project and the Free Software Foundation (FSF)." 1998. http://gnu.via.ecp.fr/

Gates, Bill. *The Road Ahead*. New York: Viking Penguin, 1996.

Grennell, Dean. "Filler #52.3." http://fanac.org/fanzines/Abstract/Abstract9-42.html

Hanson, Rob. "Then: A History of UK Fandom 1930-1980. " Unpublished manuscript. 1994. http://www.dcs.gla.ac.uk/SF-Archives/Then/

———. "Who's Who in SF Fandom: The FAQ." 1998. http://www.fiawol.demon.co.uk/who/

Hilf, Bill. "Media Lullabies: The Reinvention of the World Wide Web." *First Monday* 3, no. 4 (6 April 1998). http://www.firstmonday.dk/issues/issue3_4/hilf/index.html

Ichbiah, David and Susan L. Knepper. *The Making of Microsoft*. Rocklin, Calif.: Prima, 1991.

Jaffe, Saul. "SF-Lovers Home Page." 1997. http://sflovers.rutgers.edu/

Kirchner, Jake. "Al Gore's High-Tech Hopes." *PC Magazine*. 1 December 1998. http://search.zdnet.com/pcmag/insites/kirchner/jk981112.htm

Leonard, Andrew. "The Free Software Story." *Salon*. 11 December 1998. http://www.salonmagazine.com/21st/feature/1998/12/11list.html

———. "Let My Software Go! An Interview With Eric Raymond." *Salon*. 4 April 1998. http://www.salonmagazine.com/21st/feature/1998/04/cov_14feature.html

———. "The Saint of Free Software." *Salon*. 31 August 1998. http://www.salonmagazine.com/21st/feature/1998/08/cov_31feature.html

———. "The Stallman Saga, Redux." *Salon*. 11 September 1998. http://www.salonmagazine.com/21st/feature/1998/09/11feature.html

Long, Vince. "The BBS: A History and Commentary." *Montana Council for Computers and Technology in Education Newsletter*. December 1996. http://208.150.195.31/mcce/dec96.htm#bbs

Manes, Stephen and Paul Andrews. *Gates*. New York: Doubleday, 1993.

Metcalfe, Robert. "Bob's Personal Web Site." http://www.idg.net/metcalfe/

———. "From the Ether: Bob's Columns." *InfoWorld*. http://www.infoworld.com/cgi-bin/displayNew.pl?/metcalfe/bmlist.htm

———. "Packet Communication." *Computer Classics Revisited Series*. Ed. Peter H. Salus. San Jose, Calif.: Peer to Peer Communications, 1996.

Meyer, Gordon R. "The Social Organization of Computer Underground." Master's thesis, Northern Illinois University, 1989. http://ftp.eff.org/pub/Privacy/Newin/New_nist/hacker.txt

National Cable Television Association. "The Cable Industry at a Glance—History." 1998. http://www.ncta.com/glance-body.html

Omega Foundation. "An Appraisal of the Technologies of Political Control." Report for the European Parliament. September 1998. http://www-douzzer.ai.mit.edu:8080/conspiracy/paulwolf/eu_stoa_2.htm

Phrack Archives. 1998. http://www.phrack.com/Archives/

Project Xanadu. "Xanadu Australia Homepage." 14 February 1998. http://www.xanadu.com.au/

Raymond, Eric S. "The Cathedral and the Bazaar." 12 November 1998. http://www.tuxedo.org/~esr/writings/cathedral-bazaar/

Rosteck, Tanja S. "Computer Hackers: Rebels with a Cause." http://securityserver.com/cgi-local/ssis.pl/docs/hacker1.htm

Sanders, Craig. "Xanadu." *Desktop Magazine*. August 1994. http://www.xanadu.com.au/xanadu/desktop.html

Smith, Ralph Lee. *The Wired Nation—Cable TV: The Electronic Communications Highway*. New York: Harper & Row, 1972.

Stranahan, Paul. "Cable TV: Advanced Technology." *The Jones Telecommunications and Multimedia Digital Century Encyclopedia*. 1998. http://www.digitalcentury.com/encyclo/update/catvtech.html

Surman, Mark. "Wired Words: Utopia, Revolution and the History of Electronic Highways." http://commons.web.net/wiredwords/default.html

Vest, Jason. "Listening In: The U.S.-led ECHELON Spy Network Is Eavesdropping on the Whole World." *The Village Voice*. 12 - 18 August 1998. http://www.villagevoice.com/features/9833/vest.shtml

Wallace, James and Jim Erickson. *Hard Drive*. New York: John Wiley & Sons, 1992.

Whirlwind Software. "The TAP/Y.I.P.L. Archives." 1998. http://a3a18294.sympatico.bconnected.net/ItchyCFiles/Tap/Index.htm

CHAPTER 4

Ansk, Daniel. "Finding Folks of Like Mind on the Web." *The Los Angeles Times.* 17 June 1996.

Barbrook, Richard and Andy Cameron. "The California Ideology." Hypermedia Research Centre. University of Westminster, London, England. http://ma.hrc.wmin.ac.uk/ma.theory.4.2.1.db

Brown, Janelle. "A Kinder, Gentler USENET." *Salon.* 15 September 1998. http://www.salonmagazine.com/21st/feature/1998/09/15feature.html

Carlton, Jim. *Apple: The Inside Story of Intrigue, Egomania, and Business Blunders.* Revised edition. New York: HarperCollins, 1998.

Gibson, William. *Neuromancer.* New York: Berkley Publishing Group, 1984.

Gore, Andrew. "The Vision Thing: Defying Gravity . . . Again: The iMac Is the Most Concrete Proof Yet That Apple Is Actually Thinking Different." *MacWorld.* July 1998. http://macworld.zdnet.com/pages/july.98/Column.4357.html

Harraway, Donna. "A Cyborg Manifesto: Science, Technology, and Socialist-Feminism in the Late Twentieth Century." In *Simians, Cyborgs and Women: The Reinvention of Nature.* New York: Routledge, 1991. http://www.stanford.edu/dept/HPS/Haraway/CyborgManifesto.html

Hauben, Michael and Rhonda Hauben. *Netizens: On the History and Impact of USENET and the Internet.* Los Alamitos, Calif.: IEEE Computer Society Press, 1997. http://www.columbia.edu/~hauben/netbook/

Herz, J. C. *Joystick Nation.* New York: Little, Brown, 1997.

"iMP3.com, Play for Pay: A Service of TEN.COM." Total Entertainment Network Homepage. 1998. http://www.ten.com

Jacobs, Karrie, "Utopia Redux." *Word.* http://www.word.com/machine/jacobs/

Kunzru, Hari. "You Are Cyborg." *Wired* 5.02. February 1997. http://www.wired.com/wired/archive/5.02/ffharaway_pr.html

Leckenby, John D., et al. "Using Reach/Frequency for Web Media Planning." *Journal of Advertising Research.* 11 October 1997. http://uts.cc.utexas.edu/~admedium/Ivory/JAR_paper_PCMeter_Final.htm

Levy, Steven. *Insanely Great: The Life and Times of the Macintosh, the Computer that Changed Everything.* New York: Viking Penguin, 1994.

Linzmayer, Owen W. *The Mac Bathroom Reader.* Alameda, Calif.: Sybex, 1994.

Nelson, Theodor H. *Computer Lib: Dream Machines.* Redmond, Wash.: Microsoft Press, 1987.

———. *Literary Machines 93.1.* Watertown, Mass.: Eastgate Systems, 1992.

Pfaffenberger, Bryan. "'If I Want it, It's OK': Usenet and the (Outer) Limits of Free Speech." *Information Society* 12, no. 4. (October-December 1996).

Short, Robert. "BBS! I Was Calling Granny!" *Computer Bits.* March 1998. http://iago.computerbits.com/archive/19980300/bbsintro.htm

Stone, Allucquere Rosanne. "Agency and Proximity: Comunites/ComuniTrees." In *The War of Desire and Technology at the Close of the Mechanical Age.* Cambridge, Mass.: MIT Press, 1995.

Sutherland, Ewan. "Minitel—The Resistible Rise of French Videotex." *International Journal for Information Resource Management* 1 no. 4 (1990). http://www.lamp.ac.uk/~ewan/minitel/

Tedeschi, Bob. "Study Finds Ad Banners Make an Impression." *The New York Times.* 7 October 1998. http://www.nytimes.com/library/tech/98/10/cyber/articles/07advertising.html

Webchat Broadcasting System. "Emoticom Page." 1997. http://wbs.net/wbs3/flypaper/wbs/chat_book.html

Wolf, Gary. "The Curse of Xanadu." *Wired* 3.06. June 1995. http://www.wired.com/wired/archive/3.06/xanadu_pr.html

CHAPTER 5

America Online. "Profile." http://www.aol.com/corp/profile/

Ankomah, Baffour. "This Man Is Hot." *New African.* July/August 1996. http://www.emeagwali.com/europe/england/new-african.html

Avnet Industries. "The History of Microprocessors." 1998. http://www.avnet.com/annrpt96/micrhist.htm

Barlow, John Perry. "Crime and Puzzlement." *The Computer Professionals for Social Responsibility Newsletter* 8, no. 4. http://www.cpsr.org/publications/newsletters/1990s/Fall1990.txt

———. "A Not Terribly Brief History of the Electronic Frontier Foundation." 8 November 1990. http://www.eff.org/pub/EFF/history.eff

Echo Communications. "Echo's Home Page." 1998. http://www.echonyc.com

Emeagwali, Philip. "Philip Emeagwali's Web Site." http://www.emeagwali.com/

Farmer, F. Randall, Chip Morningstar, and Douglas Crockford. "From Habitat to Global Cyberspace." http://www.communities.com/paper/hab2cybr.html

Hafner, Katie. "The Epic Saga of the WELL." *Wired* 5.05. May 1997. http://www.wired.com/wired/archive/5.05/ff_well_pr.html

Hafner, Katie and John Markoff. *Cyberpunk: Outlaws and Hackers on the Computer Frontier.* New York: Simon & Schuster Trade, 1995.

Horn, Stacy. *Cyberville: Clicks, Culture, and the Creation of an Online Town.* New York: Warner Books, 1998.

Intel Corporation. "Intel Museum Home Page." 1998. http://developer.intel.com/intel/museum/25anniv/

Kapor, Mitchell. "Mitchel Kapor Homepage." http://www.kei.com/homepages/mkapor/

Littman, Jonathan. *The Fugitive Game: Online With Kevin Mitnick.* New York: Little, Brown, 1996.

Magid, Larry. "We've Gotta Have It: Intel's Marketing Genius." *Computer Currents Magazine* (Bay Area edition). 20 January 1998. http://currents.net/magazine/national/1602/uout1602.html

Morningstar, Chip and F. Randall Farmer. "The Lessons of Lucasfilm's Habitat." In *Cyberspace: First Steps.* Ed. Michael Benedikt. Cambridge, Mass.: MIT Press, 1991.

Poulsen, Kevin. "Grassroots Hacktivism." ZDTV. 16 September 1998. http://www.zdnet.com/zdtv/cybercrime/chaostheory/story/0,3700,2137656,00.html

Slatalla, Michele with Joshua Quittner. *Masters of Deception: The Gang That Ruled Cyberspace.* New York: HarperPerennial, 1996.

Stallings, Ben. "A Critical Study of Three Free-Net Community Networks." 10 November 1996. http://ofcn.org/whois/ben/Free-Nets/

Sterling, Bruce. *Hacker Crackdown.* New York: Bantam, 1992. http://www.lysator.liu.se/etexts/hacker/

Townsend, David. "Black History Page: Philip Emeagwali." http://www.cam.org/~pbt/feb22.html

Tsutomu Shimomura with John Markoff. *Takedown: The Pursuit and Capture of Kevin Mitnick, America's Most Wanted Computer Outlaw—By the Man Who Did It.* New York: Hyperion, 1996.

Ubois, Jeff. "Prime Time: Interview with Steve Case." *InternetWorld* 8, no. 12 (December 1997). http://www.internetworld.com/print/monthly/1997/12/interv.html

Williams, Brandt. "Real Genius: Dr. Philip Emeagwali Rewrites Book on Supercomputer Technology." *Insight News.* Minneapolis, Minn. 11 May 1996. http://www.emeagwali.com/Insight_News_1996.html

CHAPTER 6

Akst, Daniel. "Postcard from Cyberspace: Religious Fracas Debunks Myth of Anarchy on Net." *The Los Angeles Times.* 25 January 1995. http://www2.thecia.net/users/rnewman/scientology/media/latimes-akst-1.25.95

American Civil Liberties Union. "Summary of Argument in ACLU amicus brief Criminal No. 95-80106 United States Of America, Plaintiff v. Jake Baker and Arthur Gonda, Defendants." http://www.aclu.org/court/baker.html

Berners-Lee, Tim. "Information Management: A Proposal." March 1989. http://www.w3.org/History/1989/proposal.html

———. "Tim Berners-Lee's Home Page." http://www.w3.org/People/Berners-Lee/Overview.html

Bolter, Jay David. *The Writing Space: The Computer, Hypertext, and the History of Writing.* Hillsdale, N.J.: Lawrence Erlbaum Associates, 1991.

Cailliau, Robert. "A Little History of the World Wide Web." 3 October 1995. http://www.w3.org/History.html

Campbell, K.K. "A Net.Conspiracy So Immense . . . : Chatting with Martha Siegel of the Internet's Infamous Canter & Siegel." Electronic Frontier Foundation Archive. 1 October 1994. http://www.eff.org/pub/Legal/Cases/Canter_Siegel/c-and-s_summary.article

Carlin, John. "A Farewell to Arms." *Wired* 5.05. May 1997. http://www.wired.com/wired/archive/5.05/netizen_pr.html

CERN. "Welcome to CERN." 19 August 1998. http://www.cern.ch/Public/

Chang, Nora. "Tiananmen: The Gate of Heavenly Peace." Long Bow Group. http://www.nmis.org/gate/

Clark, Tim. "Berners-Lee: Consider the People." *CNET News.* 11 April 1997. http://www.news.com/News/Item/0,4,9618,00.html

Coddington, Michael, et al. "Transcript of Debate on March 10, 1995, at the University of Michigan, Regarding the Jake Baker Case." *The Michigan Telecommunications and Technology Law Review Archives.* http://www.umich.edu/~mttlr/archives/bakerconf/

Commercial Internet Exchange. "CIX Information." http://www.cix.org/CIXInfo/cix-info.html

Dewitt, Philip Elmer. "Snuff Porn on the Net." *Time.* 20 February 1995. http://cgi.pathfinder.com/time/magazine/archive/1995/950220/950220.technology.html

Dibbell, Julian. "A Rape in Cyberspace; Or How an Evil Clown, a Haitian Trickster Spirit, Two Wizards, and a Cast of Dozens Turned a Database into a Society." Originally published in *The Village Voice,* 21 December 1993. Reprinted in *Flame Wars: The Discourse of Cyberculture.* Ed. Mark Dery. Durham, N.C.: Duke University Press. http://gopher.well.sf.ca.us:70/0/Publications/authors/dibbell/Rape_In_Cyberspace

Dominguez, Ricardo. "Digital Zapatismo." 1998. http://www.thing.net/~rdom/ecd/DigZap.html

Electronic Frontier Foundation. "EFF Legal Cases—Church of Scientology Archive." 21 May 1997. http://www.eff.org/pub/Censorship/CoS_v_the_Net/

———. "EFF Legal Cases—PGP & Phil Zimmermann Archive." 12 January 1997. http://www.eff.org/pub/Legal/Cases/PGP_Zimmermann/

Fallows, James. "The Java Theory." *The Atlantic Monthly* 277, no. 3 (March 1996): 113-117. http://www.theatlantic.com/issues/96mar/java/java.htm

Fearer, Mark. "Scientology's Secrets: The Internet Is a Battleground in a Clash Between the Church of Scientology and Its Adversaries." *Internet World* 6, no. 12 (1995). http://www.internetworld.com/print/monthly/1995/12/scientol.html

Fisher, Marc. "Church in Cyberspace: Its Sacred Writ Is on the Net, Its Lawyers Are on the Case." *The Washington Post.* 19 August 1995. http://www.cs.cmu.edu/~dst/Fishman/OT_Fight/washpost-fisher.html

Flaming, Todd. "The Rules of Cyberspace: Informal Law in a New Jurisdiction." *Illinois Bar Journal.* April 1997. http://www.sw.com/rulescyb.htm

Garfinkel, Simson. *PGP: Pretty Good Privacy.* Cambridge, Mass.: O'Reilly and Associates, 1995.

Godwin, Mike. *Cyber Rights: Defending Free Speech in the Digital Age.* New York: Times Books, 1998.

———. "Law of the Net: Church and Statutes." *Internet World* 7, no. 4 (1996). http://www.internetworld.com/print/monthly/1996/04/law.html

Grossman, Wendy M. "alt.scientology.war." *Wired* 3.12. December 1995. http://www.wired.com/wired/archive/3.12/alt.scientology.war_pr.html

———. *Net.wars.* New York: New York University Press, 1997.

Gulak, Laura J. *Persuasion and Privacy in Cyberspace: The Online Protests over Lotus Marketplace and the Clipper Chip.* New Haven, Conn.: Yale University Press, 1997.

Gulf War IRC Directory. 1997. ftp://sunsite.unc.edu/pub/academic/communications/logs/Gulf-War

Information Infrastructure Task Force. "List of All Documents." http://www.iitf.nist.gov/alldocs.html#Old

Johnson, Stephen. *Interface Culture: How the New Technology Transforms the Way We Create and Communicate.* San Francisco: HarperEdge, 1997.

Kalb, Marvin, et. al. "Turmoil at Tiananmen: A Study of U.S. Press Coverage of the Beijing Spring of 1989." The Joan Shorenstein Barone Center on the Press, Politics and Public Policy, John F. Kennedy School of Government, Harvard University. June 1992. http://www.nmis.org/gate/themes/Tatintro.html#anchor415747

Kaplan, Nancy. "Literacy Beyond Books." In *World Wide Web: Myth Metaphor Magic.* Eds. Thomas Swiss and Andrew Herman. New York: Routledge, 1999.

Kline, David. "A Global Village the Net Is Not." *Hotwired.* 22 April 1996. http://www.hotwired.com/market/96/17/index1a.html

Levy, Steven. "Cypher Wars: Pretty Good Privacy Gets Pretty Legal." *Wired* 2.11. November 1994. http://www.wired.com/wired/archive/2.11/cypher.wars_pr.html

———. "Crypto Rebels." *Wired* 1.02. May/June 1993. http://www.wired.com/wired/archive/1.02/crypto.rebels_pr.html

Lohr, Steve. "His Goal: Keeping the Web Worldwide." *The New York Times.* 18 December 1995. http://www.w3.org/People/Berners-Lee/951217-NYT/

Mackinnon, Richard. "The Social Construction of Rape in Virtual Reality. " In *Network and Netplay: Virtual Groups on the Internet.* Eds. Sudweeks, M. McLaughlin and S. Rafaeli. Cambridge, Mass.: MIT Press, 1998. http://www.actlab.utexas.edu/~spartan/texts/rape.html

Miller, Adam S. "The Jake Baker Scandal: A Perversion of Logic." *Trincoll Journal.* 6 April 1995. http://www.trincoll.edu/~tj/tj4.6.95/articles/baker.html

Netscape. "A Company on Internet Time." http://www.netscape.com/company/about/index.html

Oikarinen, Jarkko. "IRC History." IRC3 Web page. 1998. http://www.the-project.org/history.html

Quittner, Joshua, et al. *Speeding the Net: The Inside Story of Netscape and How It Challenged Microsoft.* New York: Atlantic Monthly Press, 1998.

Reid, Robert H. "Jerry Yang: Finding Needles in the Internet's Haystack." *Architects of the Web.* http://www.architectsoftheweb.com/jw/yang1.html

The Scientology Home Page. http://www.scientology.org/

Steele, Shari. "Is Free Speech Too Expensive?" *BBS Magazine.* April 1995. http://www2.thecia.net/users/rnewman/scientology/media/steele-bbs-4.95

Sproule, Warren. "Virtual Battlefields: Informatics, 'Irreality,' and the Sociology of War." *Undercurrent: An Online Journal for the Analysis of the Present.* Spring 1996. http://darkwing.uoregon.edu/~ucurrent/uc4/4-sproule.html

Stallman, Richard. "GNU Manifesto." 1993. http://www.gnu.org/gnu/manifesto.html

Stark, Thom. "The Marc Andreessen Interview Page." 1995. http://www.dnai.com/~thomst/marca.html

Stellin, Susan. "ClNet Spotlight: Marc Andreessen." *ClNet.* http://www.cnet.com/Content/Features/Quick/Andreessen/index.html.

Sun Microsystems, Inc. "Sun Corporate Information: History." http://www.sun.com/corporateoverview/who/html_history.html

SunWorld Online. "Java: The Inside Story." http://www.sunworld.com/swol-07-1995/swol-07-java.html

Swan, P. J."Jake Baker Information Page." http://ai.eecs.umich.edu/people/pjswan/Baker/Jake_Baker.html

Torvalds, Linus. "Meet Linus Torvalds." *ComputerWorld.* 1998. http://www.computerworld.com/home/features.nsf/all/980817linus

Virilio, Paul. "Cyberwar, God and Television: Interview with Paul Virilio." *CTHEORY.* 1 December 1994. http://www.ctheory.com/a-cyberwar_god.html

"The Web Maestro: An Interview with Tim Berners-Lee." *Technology Review.* July 1996. http://www.techreview.com/articles/july96/bernerslee.html

World Wide Web Consortium. "About the World Wide Web Consortium." http://www.w3.org/Consortium/

Wray, Stefan. "Electronic Civil Disobedience and the World Wide Web of Hacktivism." Unpublished notes for a presentation at the World Wide Web and Contemporary Cultural Theory conference at Drake University, Des Moines, Iowa, November 6-7, 1998.

———. *The Electronic Disturbance Theater and Electronic Civil Disobedience.* June 17, 1998. http://www.thing.net/~rdom/ecd/EDTECD.html

———. "On Electronic Civil Disobedience." Paper presented to the 1998 Socialist Scholars Conference, March 20-22. New York, N.Y. http://www.thing.net/~rdom/ecd/oecd.html

Yahoo! Inc. "Yahoo!—Company History." http://www.yahoo.com/info/misc/history.html

Zimmermann, Philip R. Declaration in *Daniel J. Bernstein vs. United States Department of State.* http://www.eff.org/pub/Privacy/ITAR_export/Bernstein_case/Legal/960726_filing/Text/zimmermann_decl.txt

———. *The Official PGP User's Guide.* Cambridge, Mass: MIT Press, 1995.

CHAPTER 7

Arvidson, Cheryl. "Is Online Journalism 'Different'? A Wide Divergence Of Views." *Freedom Forum Web Site.* 1998. http://www.freedomforum.org/technology/1998/1/9conffinal.asp

Baeza-Yates, R. A., D. A. Fuller, J. A. Pino, and S. E. Goodman. "Computing in Chile: The Jaguar of the Pacific Rim?" *Communications of the ACM* (September 1995): 23-28. Revised and updated for 1998 at http://dichato.dcc.uchile.cl/~rbaeza/cv/unido.html

Bank, David. "The Java Saga." *Wired* 3.12. December 1995. http://www.wired.com/wired/archive/3.12/java.saga_pr.html

"Budget Compromise on High Tech, Low Tech Braceros." *Immigration News Briefs, Weekly News Update on the Americas* 1, no. 7 (November 1998).

Carney, David, "Summary: H1-B Visa Bills." *Tech Law Journal.* 1998. http://techlawjournal.com/congress/s1723h1b/Default.htm

Cerf, Vinton. "RFC 2468: I Remember IANA." 17 October 1998. ftp://ftp.isi.edu/in-notes/rfc2468.txt

Clausing, Jeri. "Clinton Aide Stands Behind Net Founder Who Altered Network." *The New York Times.* 5 February 1998. http://search.nytimes.com/search/daily/bin/fastweb?getdoc+site+site+14993+5+wAAA+postel

Cooperative Association for Internet Data Analysis (CAIDA) Home Page. 1998. http://www.caida.org/

Cringely, Robert X. "Microsoft and Me: How Microsoft Has Already Been Crippled by the Department of Justice." *I, Cringely.* 22 October 1998. http://www.pbs.org/cringely/pulpit/pulpit19981022.html

Diamond, David. "Whose Internet Is it, Anyway?" *Wired* 6.04. April 1998. http://www.wired.com/wired/archive/6.04/kashpureff_pr.html

Electronic Frontier Foundation. "COPA ("CDA II") Legal Challenge Page." 4 January 1999. http://www.eff.org/pub/Legal/Cases/ACLU_v_Reno_II/#toc.

———. "EFF, ACLU, et al. v. Dept. of Justice (ACLU v. Reno) Archive." 26 June 1997. http://www.eff.org/pub/Legal/Cases/EFF_ACLU_v_DoJ/

Gates, Dominick. "Culture Clash in the Root Zone: Should Jon Postel be the Master of Your Domain?" *PreText Magazine.* March 1998. http://www.pretext.com/mar98/features/story4.htm

Glave, James. "Net Mourns Passing of Giant." *Wired News.* 18 October 1998. http://www.wired.com/news/news/culture/story/15682.html

"GNOME FAQ 1.0." http://www.mindspring.com/~tlewis/gnome/faq/FAQ.html

Graham, Stephen and Simon Marvin. *Telecommunications and the City.* New York: Routledge, 1996.

Greenberg, Ilan. "Do-It-Yourself Supercomputers." *Wired News.* 3 July 1998. http://www.wired.com/news/print_version/technology/story/13440.html?wnpg=all

Hafner, Katie. "A Net Builder Who Loved Invention, Not Profit." *The New York Times.* 22 October 1998.

"Has Online Reporting Tainted Journalism?" Editorial, *Online Journalism Review.* 18 May 1998. http://olj.usc.edu/sections/editorial/98_stories/commentaries_cowan_05189

"Interview with Mr. A. Balachandran." Winjobs and India Online. 1998. http://www.winjobs.com/intrview/archive/bala.htm

"Issue of the Week, Ethics and the Media: Influence of Electronic Media." *Policy.com.* 6 July 1998. http://policy.com/issuewk/98/0706/070698e.html

The K Desktop Environment Project. "KDE Frequently Asked Questions." 13 December 1998. http://www.kde.org/faq/kdefaq.html

Kawamoto, Dawn. "Privacy Order for GeoCities." *CNET News.* 12 June 1998. http://www.news.com/News/Item/0,4,23130,00.html?st.cn.nws.rl.ne

Lasica, J. D. "Breakthrough on the Web: Salon's Savvy Blend of Old and New Media Strengths Has Made It an Online Journalism Pacesetter." *American Journalism Review.* June 1998. http://ajr.newslink.org/ajrsalonb98.html

———. "Preserving Old Ethics in a New Medium. " *American Journalism Review.* December 1997. http://ajr.newslink.org/ajrjd24.html

Layne, Ken. "Amateur Hour at the National Press Club." *Online Journalism Review.* 8 June 1998. http://olj.usc.edu/indexf.htm?/sections/departments/98_stories/citizen_060898.htm

———. "The Fiction of Cyber Journalism." *Online Journalism Review.* 19 May 1998. http://olj.usc.edu/sections/departments/98_stories/citizen_051998.htm

Ledbetter, James. "Drudge Match." *The Village Voice,* Press Clips. 28 January-3 February 1998. http://www.villagevoice.com/columns/9805/ledbetter.shtml

Leonard, Andrew. "Apache's Free Software Warriors." *Salon.* 20 November 1997. http://www.salonmagazine.com/21st/feature/1997/11/cov_20feature.html

———. "The Little Operating System That Could." *Salon.* 26 June 1998. http://www.salonmagazine.com/21st/feature/1998/06/cov_26feature.html

Luening, Erich. "W3C Makes XML a Standard." *CNET News.* 10 February 1998. http://www.news.com/News/Item/0,4,19008,00.html?st.ne.bp..bphed

Macavinta, Courtney. "World Rushes to Net for Starr Report." *CNET News.* 11 September 1998. http://www.news.com/News/Item/0,4,26265,00.html?st.cn.gp.rl.ne

"Management of Internet Names and Addresses." National Telecommunications & Information Administration. http://www.ntia.doc.gov/ntiahome/domainname/domainhome.htm

Maney, Richard. "H1-B Visas." *Richard Maney & Associates United States Immigration Visa Guide*. 1998. http://www.richard-maney.com/visa-guide.htm#temporary

Mann, Charles C. "Programs to the People." *Technology Review*. January/February 1999. http://www.techreview.com/articles/jan99/mann.htm

Martinez, Michael. "Hacker Case May Set Legal Precedents." *ABCNEWS.com*. 2 April 1998. http://abcnews.go.com/sections/tech/DailyNews/complaw0401.html

MCIWorldCom. "MCI and NSF's Very High Speed Backbone Network Service Home Page." 1998. http://www.vbns.net/

———. "vBNS Press Kit." 1998. http://www.vbns.net/press.html

"Microsoft Explored." PBS Online Newshour. 13 January 1998. http://www.pbs.org/newshour/bb/cyberspace/jan-june98/microsoft_1-13.html

Mir, Ali and Maya Yajnike. "The Uneven Development of Places: From Bodyshopping to Global Assembly Lines." *Samar Journal*. 1998. http://www.solinet.org/THIRDWORLD/maya1.htm

"The National Computational Science Alliance (NCSA) Home Page." University of Illinois. 1998. http://access.ncsa.uiuc.edu/

Next Generation Internet (NGI) Initiative Home Page. 1998. http://www.ngi.gov/

"NLANR Applications Support-vBNS History." National Laboratory for Applied Network Research. 1998. http://dast.nlanr.net/History.html

Oakes, Chris. "Point, Click, Supercompute." *Wired News*. 5 November 1998. http://www.wired.com/news/print_version/technology/story/13440.html?wnpg=all

Operation Home Front. http://www.worldshop.com/HomeFront

Patel, Hitesh. "Understanding Indian Software Industry." *Indiaworld*. 1998. http://indiaworld.com/understanding_indian_software_in.htm

Postel, Jonathan. "Proposal for the Internet Corporation for Assigned Names and Numbers (ICANN)." National Telecommunications & Information Administration. 2 October 1998. http://www.ntia.doc.gov/ntiahome/domainname/proposals/icann/icann.html

Ramo, Joshua Cooper. "How AOL Lost the Battles but Won the War." *Time* 150, no. 12. 22 September 1997. http://cgi.pathfinder.com/time/magazine/1997/dom/970922/business.how_aol_lost_.html

Raouf, Neda. "Editorial or Advertorial: What's the Difference?" *Journalism Review*. 15 May 1998. http://www.ojr.org/sections/features/98_stories/stories_advertorial.htm

Raymond, Eric S. "The Halloween Documents." http://www.opensource.org/halloween.html

"Remembering Jon Postel." Internet Assigned Numbers Authority. 20 October 1998. http://www.iana.org/postel/iana-pr102098.html

Riley, Patricia and Colleen M. Keough. "Community or Colony: The Case of Online Newspapers and the Web." *Journal of Computer Mediated Communications* 4, no. 1 (September 1998). http://www.ascusc.org/jcmc/vol4/issue1/keough.html

Samuelson, Pamela and John Browning. "Confab Clips Copyright Cartel." *Wired* 5.03. March 1997. http://www.wired.com/wired/archive/5.03/netizen_pr.html

Sandberg, Jared. "Hacker Introduces the Sound of Silence to Noisy Internet—'Cancelbot' Computer Program Erases 25,000 Messages on Bulletin Board System." *The Wall Street Journal*. 27 September 1996.

Schlender, Brent. "Javaman: The Adventures of Scott McNealy." *Fortune*. 13 October 1997. http://www.pathfinder.com/fortune/1997/971013/jav.html

Scoville, Thomas. "Martin Luther, Meet Linus Torvalds." *Salon*. 12 November 1998. http://www.salonmagazine.com/21st/feature/1998/11/12feature.html

"SPA Anti-Piracy Home Page." Software Publisher's Association. 1998. http://www.spa.org/piracy/homepage.htm

Stephenson, Wen. "Out of Context." *The Atlantic Monthly Online*. 11 June 1997. http://www.theatlantic.com/atlantic/unbound/media/ws970611.htm

Surkan, Michael. "Piracy on the Digital Seas." *PC Week Online*. 12 June 1998. http://search.zdnet.com/pcweek/opinion/0608/08worth.html

Taft, Darryl. "Scott McNealy." *CMP.net* http://www.crn.com/sections/special/comdex97/764_25top1.asp

Tetzlaff, David. "Yo-ho-ho and a Server of Warez: Internet Software Piracy and the New Global Information Economy." Talk delivered at the World Wide Web and Contemporary Cultural Theory Conference, Drake University. Des Moines, Iowa. 7 November 1998. http://www.drake.edu/swiss/webconference/tetzlaff.html

Ubois, Jeff. "Prime Time: Interview with Steve Case." *InternetWorld* 8, no 12(1997). http://www.internetworld.com/print/monthly/1997/12/interv.html

United States Department of Commerce. "Management of Internet Names and Addresses (White Paper 6/5/98)." National Telecommunications & Information Administration. http://www.ntia.doc.gov/ntiahome/domainname/6_5_98dns.htm

United States Department of Justice, Antitrust Division. "United States v. Microsoft (Trial)." Antitrust Case Filings: Antitrust Division. http://www.usdoj.gov/atr/cases/ms_index.htm

Verzola, Roberto. "Towards a Political Economy of Information." November 1995. http://www.solinet.org/THIRDWORLD/obet1.htm

Vizard, Michael. "Open Source Guru." *InfoWorld Electric*. 8 June 1998. http://www.infoworld.com/cgi-bin/displayStory.pl?/interviews/980608torvalds.htm

Weise, Elizabeth. "Scientology Church Gets Mired in Guerrilla Conflict on the 'Net." *Houston Chronicle*. 28 July 1996: 44.

CHAPTER 8

"Access to Telecommunications Equipment and Customer Premises Equipment by Individuals with Disabilities." Final Report of the Telecommunications Access Advisory Committee (TAAC). January 1997. http://www.access-board.gov/pubs/taacrpt.htm

Anderson, Heidi. "The Rise of the Extranet." *PC Today & Processor Online.* http://www.pctoday.com/editorial/goingonline/970235a.html

Bergman, Eric and Earl Johnson. "Towards Accessible Human-Computer Interaction." In *Advances in Human-Computer Interaction,* Volume 5. ed. Jakob Nielsen. Norwood, N.J.: Ablex Publishing Corporation 1995. http://www.sun.com/tech/access/updt.HCI.advance.html

Brewer, Judy and Daniel Dardailler. "Web Accessibility Initiative (WAI) Home Page." World Wide Web Consortium. 1999. http://www.w3.org/WAI/

Brummel, Susan. "People with Disabilities and NII: Breaking Down Barriers, Building Choice." Excerpted from "The Information Infrastructure: Reaching Society's Goals-Report of the Information Infrastructure Task Force Committee on Applications and Technology." U.S. Department of Commerce, Technology Administration, National Institute of Standards and Technology. 7 September 1994. http://www.yuri.org/webable/disabled.html

Brown, Janelle. "There Goes the Neighborhood." *Salon.* 19 January 1999. http://www.salonmagazine.com/21st/feature/1999/01/cov_feature.html

Campbell, Leslie M. and Cynthia D. Waddell. "Electronic Curbcuts: How to Build an Accessible Web Site. CAPED Communique, California Association on Postsecondary Education and Disability. 24 June 1997. http:// www.prodworks.com/ilf/w5bcw.htm

CIO Online. "Enter the Extranet." 15 May 1997. http://www.cio.com/archive/051597_et.html

CNNfn. "Microsoft, DOJ Timeline: Highlights of the Legal Battle Between Microsoft and Justice Department." 12 May 1998. http://cnnfn.com/digitaljam/9805/12/chrono/#TOP

Cringely, Robert X. "For Tomorrow We Comply: Why Microsoft's Competitors Should Be Merry, If Only for a Moment." *I, Cringely.* 20 November 1998. http://www.pbs.org/cringely/pulpit/pulpit19981119.html

———. "Where Is Eleanor Roosevelt When We Need Her?: Why the Linux World Is Upset and Shouldn't Be." *I, Cringely.* 5 November 1998. http://www.pbs.org/cringely/pulpit/pulpit19981105.html

Diamond, David. "Lord of the Toasters." *Wired* 6.09. September 1998. http://www.wired.com/wired/archive/6.09/wind_pr.html

Doheny-Farina, Stephen. *The Wired Neighborhood.* New Haven, Conn.: Yale University Press, 1996.

Flynn, Laurie J. "Agents Track the Once and Future Consumer." *The New York Times.* 12 June 1996.

Gilder, George. "The Bandwidth Tidal Wave." http://www.seas.upenn.edu/~gaj1/bandgg.html

Goslee, Susan, et al. "Losing Ground Bit by Bit: Low-Income Communities in the Information Age." The Benton Foundation. 1998. http://www.benton.org/Library/Low-Income/intro.html

Gotcher, Renée and Laura Kujubu. "The Network Comes Home." *InfoWorld Electric 20th Anniversary.* 1998. http://www.infoworld.com/pageone/news/features/anniversary/98ann.home.shtml

Hodges, Mark. "Is Web Business Good Business?" *Technology Review.* August/September 1997. http://www.techreview.com/articles/as97/hodges.html

Harrison, Colin and Alper Caglayan. *Agent Sourcebook: A Complete Guide to Desktop, Internet, and Intranet Agents.* New York: John Wiley & Sons, 1997.

Hoeller, Christian. "On Digital Third Worlds: An Interview of Olu Oguibe." Original interview published in German in *Springer: Heftefuer Gegenwartskuns.* September 1996. http://arts.usf.edu/~ooguibe/springer.htm

Holloway, Maugerite. "Pattie." *Wired* 5.12. December 1997. http://www.wired.com/wired/archive/5.12/maes_pr.html

Lanier, Jaron and Pattie Maes. "Intelligent Agents/Stupid Humans?" *Hotwired.* July 1996. http://www.hotwired.com/braintennis/96/29/index0a.html

Lipton, Beth. "Portal Strategy: Destination Hollywood." *CNET News.* 13 January 1999. http://www.news.com/News/Item/0,4,30886,00.html?st.ne.lh..ni

Lyons, Daniel. "The Buzz About Firefly." *The New York Times.* 29 June 1997.

Maes, Pattie. "Intelligent Software." *Scientific American.* September 1995. http://pattie.www.media.mit.edu/people/pattie/SciAm-95.html

Metcalfe, Robert. "Here We Go Again: It's Time to Make Predictions for the Brand New Year." *InfoWorld Electric.* 6 January 1997. http://www.infoworld.com/cgi-bin/displayNew.pl?/metcalfe/bm010697.htm

———. "Is the Internet-traffic Bubble About to Burst?" *InfoWorld Electric.* 15 June 1998. http://www.infoworld.com/cgi-bin/displayNew.pl?/metcalfe/980615bm.htm

———. "Pay-As-We-Go Internet Puts Your Money Where Your Consumption Is." InfoWorld Electric. 21 September 1998. http://www.infoworld.com/cgi-bin/displayNew.pl?/metcalfe/980921bm.htm

Milewski, Allan E. and Stephen H. Lewis. "Delegating to Software Agents." *Inside AT&T Labs.* http://www.att.com/attlabs/archive/agnt_sum.html

Millward Brown Interactive, Inc. "Internet Advertising Bureau Online Advertising Effectiveness Study." 1998. http://www.mbinteractive.com/site/iab/study.html

National Telecommunications And Information Administration. "The Digital Divide: A Survey of Information 'Haves' and 'Have Nots' in 1997." http://www.ntia.doc.gov/ntiahome/net2/falling.html

Negroponte, Nicholas. "Bandwidth Revisited." *Wired* 6.06. June 1998. http://www.wired.com/wired/archive/6.06/negroponte.html

Oguibe, Olu. "Forsaken Geographies: Cyberspace and the New World 'Other.'" Paper delivered at the Fifth International Cyberspace Conference, Madrid, Spain, June 1996. http://arts.usf.edu/~ooguibe/madrid.htm

Pruett, Duncan and James Deane. "The Internet and Poverty: Panos Briefing No. 28." Panos Communications and Social Change Programme. April 1998. http://www.oneworld.org/panos/briefing/interpov.htm

Rosenberg, Scott. "Bandwidth in Our Time." *Salon.* 14 January 1999. http://www.salonmagazine.com/21st/rose/1999/01/14straight.html

———. "Windows on the Wane?" *Salon.* 19 November 1998. http://www.salonmagazine.com/21st/rose/1998/11/19straight.html

Schön, Donald A., Bish Sanyal, and William J. Mitchell, eds. *High Technology and Low-Income Communities: Prospects for the Positive Use of Advanced Information Technology.* Cambridge, Mass.: MIT Press, 1999. http://web.mit.edu/sap/www/high-low/

Stepanek, Marcia. "Internet: The Sequel." *Salon.* http://www.salonmagazine.com/news/news970127.html

Tittle-Moore, Cindy. "Soc.Feminism Frequently Asked Questions." 1998. http://www.faqs.org/faqs/feminism/resources/

Tittle-Moore, Cindy. "Soc. Feminism Information." 1998. ftp://rtfm.mit.edu/pub/usenet/news.answers/feminism/info

University Corporation for Advanced Internet Development. The Internet2 Project. http://www.internet2.edu

Vanderheiden, Gregg C., et al. "Design of HTML Pages to Increase their Accessibility to Users with Disabilities." http://www.trace.wisc.edu/text/guidelns/htmlgide/htmlgide.txt

———. "Making Screen Readers Work More Effectively on the Web." http://www.trace.wisc.edu/docs/screen_readers/screen.htm

———. "Thirty Something (Million): Should They Be Exceptions?" Trace Research and Development Center, Waisman Center and Department of Industrial Engineering, University of Wisconsin-Madison. http://www.trace.wisc.edu/docs/30_some/30_some.htm

Waddell, Cynthia D. "Applying the ADA to the Internet: A Web Accessibility Standard." Speech presented at the request of the American Bar Association for their National Conference—In Pursuit . . . A Blueprint for Disability Law and Policy. 17 June 1998. http://www.rit.edu/~easi/law/weblaw1.htm

Walsh, Jeff and Emily Fitzloff. "Web Sites Cater to Connections." *InfoWorld Electric* 20/21, no. 52/1 (28 December 1998 / 4 January 1999). http://www.infoworld.com/cgi-bin/display Archive.pl?/98/52/i01-52.39.htm

Wexler, Joanne. "Roadwork Ahead." *InfoWorld Electric 20th Anniversary.*1998. http://www.infoworld.com/pageone/news/features/anniversary/98ann.roadwork.shtml

Glossary

Artificial intelligence: The simulation of human intelligence by computers.

Bandwidth: The width of the "pipe" that transmits data over a network. The higher the bandwidth, the more quickly data can be transmitted.

Binary: Numerical system using base 2 (as opposed to decimal, which uses base 10). The binary system has only two digits, 0 and 1 (as opposed to the decimal system that has digits 0 through 9). Because computers are digital (dual state), the binary system becomes the natural way to represent both the data and the instructions.

Bit: Short for binary digit. A bit can only be a 0 or a 1. Eight bits equal one byte.

Bot: Slang for "robot" that has been extended to computer programs that perform specific tasks. For example, "cancelbots" delete messages on the Usenet system.

Browser: Software that enables the user to view and navigate the World Wide Web.

Bulletin board: A computer system where users log on and view messages left by other users, and "post" their own messages. Functions in a similar manner to a public bulletin board in real life.

Byte: A measurement of computer memory space. One byte equals 8 bits.

Chat room: An online environment where users can interact with each other in "real time" by typing messages and transmitting them over a network.

Compiler: A program that translates a high-level (i.e., more natural for humans to use) computer programming language (source code) into device-specific machine (computer) language (object code).

Cookie: A small file left on computers by Web pages (sites). Typical cookie use is to identify users and, sometimes, to gather information about their surfing habits.

Cracker: Slang for a person who breaks into computer networks with ill intent. Compare to "Hacker."

Cyberspace: The theoretical space created by a network; for example, online chats happen "in cyberspace." Coined by author William Gibson in Neuromancer.

Digital: A system operating in discrete states (e.g. abacus). In a binary digital system the states are two, e.g. modern electronic computers.

Domain name: The name assigned to a unique Internet protocol (IP) address (e.g., HistoryOfTheInternet.com is assigned 209.239.59.120). A domain name server is used to translate (or resolve) the domain name to the corresponding IP address.

Encryption: The process of converting information into secret code; only those with the right key can translate it.

Ethernet: A computer network communications protocol (i.e., method), invented by Robert Metcalfe.

Gopher: A menu-style program for accessing data on the Internet.

Graphical user interface: Also known as "GUI," pronounced "gooey." A system that allows users to communicate instructions to their computers through windows, icons, and mouse clicks-rather than the text-only system of early computers.

Hacker: Slang for a person with a high degree of computer skill who writes programs and/or breaks into networks. In the media, "hacker" is often synonymous with "criminal," but among computer users "hacker" is a complimentary description.

Hardware: Computer equipment. As opposed to software, the programs that make the hardware run.

Host Computer: The computer that provides services to other computers connected to it.

Hypertext: A format for documents in which users can follow information nonsequentially through links.

Integrated circuit: A silicon chip comprised of numerous mini-transistors.

Interpreter: A computer program that not only translates a high-level language (see "Compiler") but also executes the resulting program. Typical interpreted computer languages include Basic and Java. Typical compiled languages include C, ADA, FORTRAN, COBOL, etc.

IP Number: Numerical address of a particular Web site or computer. Frequently associated with a domain name. For example, instructing a browser to seek out the domain HistoryOfTheInternet.com will cause a computer to look up the corresponding IP address (using a domain name server). These actions will direct the browser to 209.239.59.120, which is the IP number of the host for the Internet History site.

Java: The latest attempt in "portable" programming languages. The idea is that programs written in Java can run on different computers without any device-specific modifications. (See "Write Once/Run Everywhere").

Killer app: Short for "killer application," a particular application or functionality that makes the entire system worthwhile. For example, the spreadsheet is sometimes considered the first killer ap of the personal computer.

Local area network: A computer network confined to a limited number of computers, such as all the computers at a particular place of business.

Mainframe: Typically thought of as a large-capacity, powerful computers designed to accommodate many users and tasks at one time. Although early mainframes took up whole floors of buildings, their size and power today reflects the state-of-the-art in hardware and technology.

Market share: One company's portion of the audience for a particular product.

Microprocessor: The circuit in a personal or microcomputer that contains the CPU, or central processing unit, where instructions are decoded.

Modem: Short for MOdulator/DEModulator. A device that translates the computer's digital signals so they can be transmitted over analog media (e.g., telephone lines).

Name server: A computer whose function is to translate domain names into their numeric counterparts; when surfing the Internet, a personal computer would query a name server to locate a particular site.

Netizen: Slang for citizen of the Internet.

Newsgroup: A bulletin board focused on a particular topic. Usenet is a system hosting thousands of different newsgroups.

Nodes: A specific computer, router, or location along a network. The original ARPAnet structure, for example, had four nodes.

Object-oriented programming: A programming methodology incorporating the use of collections of programs and data encapsulated (or represented) as objects. For example, a programmer developing a financial application may use a "spreadsheet object" as part of the new application.

Operating system: The program that controls the central functions of a computer, allowing other applications to run. Examples include UNIX and Windows.

Packet switching: A networking methodology under which data travels in small, independent pieces (packets) through the network. A packet-switched network is more reliable since packets can travel many different routes to reach their destination.

Parallel processing: A computational method that utilizes more than one processor to run one or more programs. Not to be confused with multitasking which is the ability of a system to time-slice its processor usage among competing tasks.

Phreaking: Hacking as applied to telephone systems.

Protocol: A standardized method of information transmission, such as the Internet protocol.

Real time: In general terms, "real time" refers to computer/user interactions that happen instantaneously: instant messaging over the Internet, for example, occurs in real time. In more technical terms, a real-time system is a computer system that processes information so quickly that it seems to be instantaneous, although it often is not.

Router: A device that acts as a traffic coordinator among networks or devices. Frequently a router will link and direct traffic to disparate networks.

Semiconductor: A type of solid-state device that exhibits electrical conductivity and resistivity within a well defined range. Examples of semiconducting material include silicon and germanium.

Software: Computer programs. Compare to "Hardware."

Spam: Junk e-mail or posts, usually appearing in great, unwanted quantities for advertising purposes.

Supercomputer: A term used to describe the fastest, most powerful computer of a particular era. Typically, supercomputers are used for scientific applications that manipulate hundreds or thousands of variables at one time. A typical example of supercomputer application is weather modeling.

Sysop: Short for system operator, the person who runs a computer system or network.

Time-sharing system: A method for numerous users at different terminals to share the use of one computer. From the days before personal computers.

Unix: An operating system developed in the 1970s; immensely popular among programmers because of its flexibility, but difficult for the uninitiated to use.

Venture capital: Money provided by outside investors to assist in the creation or expansion of small businesses.

Virus: A piece of computer code designed to infect computers and replicate itself by using other programs or data, either for no meaningful reason (a prank) or with malicious intent.

Wide area network (WAN): Collections of computers or local area networks that are connected over large physical distances.

Write Once/Run Everywhere: The holy grail of computer programmers: a Write Once/Run Everywhere (WO/RE) program will work on any type of computer system. Java holds out the promise of WO/RE capability.

Acronyms

ANSI	American National Standards Institute
AOL	America Online
ARPA	Advanced Research Projects Agency
ASCII	American Standard Code for Information Interchange
AUP	Acceptable Use Policy
BASIC	Beginner's All-Purpose Symbolic Instruction Code
BBN	Bolt, Beranek and Newman
BBS	Bulletin Board System
BITnet	Because It's Time/There Network
CDA	Communications Decency Act
CDC	Control Data Corporation
CEO	Chief Executive Officer
CERN	Centre Européen pour la Recherche Nucléaire (European Laboratory for Particle Physics)
CIX	Commercial Internet eXchange Association
CORE	Council of Registrars
CREN	Corporation for Research and Educational Networking
CPU	Central Processing Unit
CUNY	City University of New York
DARPA	Defense Advanced Research Projects Agency
DCA	Defense Communications Agency
DNS	Domain Name System
DSL	Digital Subscriber Line
EDVAC	Electronic Discrete Variable Automatic Computer
EFF	Electronic Frontier Foundation
EGP	External Gateway Protocol
ENIAC	Electronic Numerical Integrator and Computer
FCC	Federal Communications Commission
FTC	Federal Trade Commission
FTP	File Transfer Protocol
GUI	Graphical User Interface
HES	Hypertext Editing System
HTML	Hypertext Markup Language
HTTP	Hypertext Transfer Protocol
I2	Internet2
IAB	Internet Activities Board
IBM	International Business Machines
ICANN	Internet Corporation for Assigned Names and Numbers
ICCC	International Conference on Computer Communications

IETF	Internet Engineering Task Force
IMP	Interface Message Processor
INWG	International Network Working Group
IP	Internet Protocol
IPTO	Information Processing Techniques Office
ISOC	Internet Society
ISP	Internet Service Provider
LAN	Local Area Network
MBONE	Multicast Backbone
MIT	Massachusetts Institute of Technology
MITS	Model Instrumentation Telemetry Systems
MS-DOS	Microsoft Disk Operating System
MUD	Multiuser Dungeon, Domain, or Dimension
NC	Network Computer
NCSA	National Center for Supercomputing Applications
NPTN	National Public Telecomputing Network
NSF	National Science Foundation
NSI	Network Solutions, Inc.
OEM	Original Equipment Manufacturer
OOP	Object-Oriented Programming
OS	Operating System
PARC	Palo Alto Research Center
PC	Personal Computer
PDP	Programmed Data Processor
PGP	Pretty Good Privacy
RFC	Request for Comments
RSA	Rivest, Shamir, and Adleman
SABRE	Semi-Automatic Business Research Environment
SAFE	Safety and Freedom Through Encryption
SAGE	Semi-Automatic Ground Environment
SF	Science Fiction
SGML	Standard Generalized Markup Language
SoPAC	Society for Public Access to Computing
TCP	Transmission Control Protocol
TMRC	Tech Model Railroad Club
UNIVAC	UNIversal Automatic Computer
URL	Universal Resource Locator
UUCP	Unix-to-Unix Copy Protocol
W3C	World Wide Web Consortium
WELL	Whole Earth 'Lectronic Link
WO/RE	Write Once/Run Everywhere
WWW	World Wide Web
XOC	Xanadu Operating Company

Contributors

Christos J. P. Moschovitis, founder and chairman of the Moschovitis Group, is an authority in the Information Technology field. Before founding the Moschovitis Group in 1989, he was vice president for M.I.S. at the O'Connor Group, a commercial real estate management and development firm, and Director of Academic Computing at Pratt Institute. Christos lectures on Information Technology issues at universities and professional organizations, and he has also served as an instructor of computer science at the Stratford School in Rochester, New York. He has a Bachelor of Science degree in physics and computer science, and has completed graduate work in organizational theory and education.

Hilary Poole is a writer and editor specializing in high technology and the fine arts. She served as managing editor for *Sexuality and Cyberspace: Performing the Digital Body*, the 1996 issue of the journal *Women and Performance*. Hilary also served on the journal's Editorial Board for three years, and was a frequent editor and contributor. She is a graduate of Brown University.

Tami Schulyer is a science writer and editor, focusing on technology and the life sciences. For two years, she served as Associate Editor for *Today's Science On File*, a monthly science-news digest for high school students, reporting on the latest developments in science, technology, medicine and the environment. Currently, Tami is a technical editor in the computer science field, and she is also a contributing writer to *Lives and Legacies: Science* (Oryx Press, 1999). Tami has a degree in Biology from University of California at Santa Cruz.

Theresa M. Senft is a host at Echo Communications, a bulletin board system that has been called "The Algonquin Roundtable of Cyberspace." She has appeared as a speaker at the AT&T Communications Forum (George Washington University, Washington, D.C.); the Virtual Culture Seminar (Whitney Museum of Art, New York City) and the Mythologies of Territory Conference (St. Petersburg, Russia). In 1996 she edited *Sexuality and Cyberspace: Performing the Digital Body*, an issue of the journal *Women and Performance*; articles from the journal, which is available on the Web, are currently assigned reading in more than 20 universities. Theresa authored the "Baud Behavior" column on Prodigy Internet (1997-1998), and has been featured in *The Village Voice* and in *Ends of Performance*, an anthology published by NYU Press. She is a doctoral candidate in Performance Studies at New York University.

Index

Note: Page numbers in *italics* indicate illustrations.

A

ABC. *See* Atanasoff-Berry Computer
Abilene (high-performance network), 205
Abramson, Norman, 69, 71
academic centers
   ARPAnet hosts, 38, 60, 102, 126
   BITnet, 99, 105, 107
   Gopher browser, 153-54, 161
   information sharing, 67, 95
   "Intergalactic Computer Network," 37, 48-49
   Internet2, 205, 216, 238, 260-61
   LANs, 66
   NSFnet, 134
   PLATO Notes, 76, 77
   Usenet, 99, 102-3
   vBNS network, 205
   World Wide Web critics, 166
   See also education; scientific research; *specific institutions*
Acceptable Use Policy, 155, 157, 158
Acid Phreak (pseudonym), 123, 144, 145
ACLU. *See* American Civil Liberties Union
acronyms, 103
addresses, electronic
   ICANN formation, 190
   IP numbers, 91, 99, 190, 228
   MBONE system, 169, 185
   name server, 110, 112, 118
   personal name/@ symbol, 73, 74
   See also Domain Name System
Adleman, Leonard, 91, 92
Advanced Dungeons and Dragons Players Handbook (Gygax), 100
Advanced Research Projects Agency. *See* ARPA
ADVENT, 101
Adventure, 85
advertising
   banners, 117, 239-40, 243-44
   of Macintosh computer, 100, 116, 117
   personalized, 243-44, 259
   portals and, 267-68

spam, 183-84
   as virtual community threat, 270, 271
aerospace companies, 40
Afghanistan, 265
Africa, 138, 265
"Africa 1, Hollywood 0" (Browning), 214
African Americans, 138
AFRICA ONE, 138
Agents, Inc. *See* Firefly Networks
AI. *See* artificial intelligence
Aiken, Howard, 8, 21-22, *21*, 26, 27
airline reservation system, 36, 49-52
algebra, 9-10
algorithms, 17, 158, 170, 250, 257
Allen, Paul, 67, 84, 86, 87, 88
Allisat, Bob, 229
ALOHAnet, 65, 66, 69, 71, 78, 80
Altair 8800, 67, 82-84, *83*, 85, 87, 88, 89, 132
AltaVista, 181, 182
AlterNic, 217, 219-20
amateur radio operators. *See* hams
Amazing Stories (magazine), 85
Amazon.com, 156, 244, *247*, 257, 259
American Airlines, 36, 49, 50-52
American Association for the Advancement of Science, 159
American Civil Liberties Union, 174, 207, 217
American National Standards Institute, 47
American Standard Codes for Information Interchange. *See* ASCII
America Online, 126, 133, 182
   birth of, 142-43
   class-action suit against, 214-15, 234
   Navisoft subsidiary, 182-83
   Netscape merger, 143, 192, 234, 236, 263
   as prominent portal, 266, 268
   search engine, 182
   virtual communities, 270
Amnesty International, 81
amplifier, 19, 28
analog, 36, 42
Analytical Engine, 3, 7-8

"AND" (as logical operator), 9, 10
Andreessen, Marc, 171-73
   biography, 172
   Java endorsement by, 200
   Mosaic browser, 153, 171-72
   Netscape cofounding, 154-55, 173, 176-77
   Netscape-Yahoo! link, 182
   WWW Hall of Fame induction, 185
androids, 32
Angelfire, 271
animal rights group, 196
animation, 165, 199, 202
animats, 258
antiabortion Web site, 174, 191
antitrust
   e-commerce potential for, 248
   Microsoft suit, 86, 125, 209, 210-11, 222-23, 236, 261-62, 263
   telephone, 178
anti-Vietnam War protests, 38, 64, 75
antivirus software, 3, 168
AOL. *See* America Online
aol.com, 234
AOL Netfind directory, 181
AOLPress, 182-83
Apache 1.0, 192, 202-3
Apache Group, 202-3
Apollo space program, 45, 56
Apple Computer, 95, 97, 98, 114-18, 143, 182, 224
   classroom use, 113
   first GUI-based personal computer, 114, *115*, 116
   harmful viruses, 168
   Jobs' departure from, 122, 130-31, 148
   LinuxPPC operating system, 233
   Macintosh debut, 100, 116, 117
   See also Macintosh personal computer
Apple II personal computer, 114
applets, 202
appliances, Internet-enabled, 242, 251
armed forces. *See* military
ARMM (Automated Retroactive Minimal Moderation), 211

ARPA (Advanced Research Projects Agency), 34-35, 37, 39, 52, 54, 145
   DARPA as manager, 82
   DCA as manager, 88
   IPTO office, 48, 54, 56, 69, 74
   long-distance computer connection. *See* ARPAnet
   organization and operation, 43-44, 48, 49
   time-sharing system, 53, 72
ARPAnet, 1, 5, 63, 65, 66, 69, 80, 102, 105
   academic counterculture influence on, 38, 60
   creation of, 34-35, 39, 40, 52, 54, 56, 62
   decommissioning of, 127, 145
   e-mail program, 73-74
   expansion of, 125-26
   External Gateway Protocol, 109
   first nonmilitary mailing list, 85
   first plan unveiled, 58-59
   growth of sites, 80, 98, 102
   host computers. *See* IMPs
   hosts.txt file, 173
   initial sites, 61-62, 115, 228
   Internet Configuration Control Board, 98
   Internet evolution from, 49, 103, 104, 110, 134, 216 (*see also* Internet)
   internetwork message transmission, 90-91, 104
   message program, 68
   MUD game, 101
   original outline, *62*
   packet switching, 45, 47
   public awareness of, 68, 87-88
   public debut of, 74, 76
   Spacewar game, 46
   TCP/IP protocol, 109-10
   TELEnet as civilian twin, 80
   text telephone system, 252
Ars Electronica Festival of Art, Technology and Society, 160
a.r.s. newsgroup, 186
artificial intelligence, 15, 23, 257, 258
artificial life, 257, 258
artificial satellites. *See* satellites